THE HISTORY OF THE 1/4TH BATTALION, DUKE OF WELLINGTON'S (WEST RIDING) REGIMENT.
1914—1919.

1914.

1918.

THE CLOTH HALL, YPRES.

THE HISTORY

OF

THE 1/4TH BATTALION
DUKE OF WELLINGTON'S
(WEST RIDING)
REGIMENT,
1914 — 1919.

BY

CAPT. P. G. BALES, M.C.

(Formerly Adjutant of the Battalion.)

PUBLISHED BY
HALIFAX:
EDWARD MORTIMER, LTD., REGENT STREET.
LONDON:
EDWARD MORTIMER, LTD., 34, PATERNOSTER ROW, E.C. 4.
1920.

TO
ALL RANKS
OF
THE 1/4TH BATTALION
WHO FELL IN ACTION.

PREFACE.

FOR more than two years I was responsible for keeping the War Diary of the 1/4th Battalion, and it was this duty which first suggested to me the idea of writing a History of the Battalion in the Great War. Soon after the armistice was signed I submitted the idea to the Commanding Officer, who expressed his strong approval and promised to assist in every possible way. The present book is the result.

The " History " is based mainly on the official documents in the Battalion's possession. These have, on the whole, been well preserved, particularly since the beginning of 1916. They have been supplemented by the personal recollections of many officers and other ranks. Proofs of each chapter have been submitted to at least two senior officers, who were serving with the Battalion during the period covered therein, and many alterations have been made as results of their criticisms and suggestions.

My sincere thanks are due to Brig.-General R. E. Sugden, C.M.G., D.S.O., T.D.; Lieut.-Col. H. S. Atkinson, T.D.; Lieut.-Col. J. Walker, D.S.O.; Major W. C. Fenton, M.C.; and Capt. E. N. Marshall, M.C., for reading part, or the whole, of the proofs; for many valuable criticisms and suggestions; and for much information. I desire also to acknowledge my obligations to Major E. P. Chambers for much help with the earlier period; to Sergt. E. Jones, particularly for his assistance with the Itinerary; and to the many officers and other ranks, too numerous to name, who have willingly placed their knowledge at my disposal. Most important of all has been the help rendered by Lieut.-Col. A. L. Mowat, D.S.O., M.C. Nothing has been too much trouble for him. He has read through the whole of the proofs, and the book owes much to his kindly criticism. He has relieved me of the whole of the business side of the production. It is not too much to say that, without his constant help and encouragement, this book would never have been published.

The book has been written primarily for the men who served with the Battalion. If they experience as much pleasure in the reading, as I have in the writing, of it, its publication is more than justified.

P. G. BALES.

POSTSCRIPT.—Since this book went to press " The West Riding Territorials in the Great War," by Major L. Magnus, has been published. Apart from three or four minor corrections, such as a date and the number of a Division, I have seen no reason to alter anything set down here.

P.G.B.

CONTENTS.

CHAPTER		PAGE
I.	Mobilisation and Training	1
II.	Fleurbaix	12
III.	Ypres, 1915: July to October; October 16th; The Wet Months; December 19th	29
IV.	January to June, 1916	59
V.	The Battle of the Somme: Thiepval Wood; September 3rd; Leipsig Redoubt	69
VI.	With the Third Army: Hannescamps; Fonquevillers; Halloy; Berles; Riviere	101
VII.	With the First Army: Ferme du Bois Sector; Cordonnerie Sector; St. Elie Sector	124
VIII.	The Coast: St. Pol and Ghyvelde; Lombartzyde Sector; Coast Defence and Training; En Route for Ypres	145
IX.	The Belle Vue Spur: October 4th-8th; October 9th; Rest and Reorganisation	160
X.	Winter on the Passchendaele Ridge: Molenaarelsthoek and Keerselaarhoek; Work and Training; Reutel Sector	176
XI.	The Spring Offensive: Erquinghem and Le Veau; Nieppe; Bailleul; St. Jans Cappel; Poperinghe; Kemmel	203
XII.	The Last of Ypres: May, 1918; Zillebeke Sector; Zillebeke Raid; Quiet Days in the Ypres Sector	237
XIII.	The Last Stage: Movements and Training; October 11th and After; Reorganisation; November 1st-2nd	254
XIV.	Demobilisation: Auby and Douai; The Return of the Cadre	276

APPENDIX

I.	Itinerary of the Battalion	287
II.	Nominal Roll of Officers	295
III.	Nominal Roll of Warrant Officers and Company Quarter Master Sergeants	304
IV.	Summary of Casualties	307
V.	List of Honours and Awards	308
VI.	The Battalion Canteen	312

LIST OF ILLUSTRATIONS.

The Cloth Hall, Ypres : 1914 ; 1918 ... ... Frontispiece	
	Facing Page
Lieut.-Col. H. S. Atkinson, T.D.	8
Major E. P. Chambers ; Lieut.-Col. H. A. S. Stanton, D.S.O. ; Capt. H. N. Waller	20
Capt. M. P. Andrews ; Capt. E. E. Sykes, M.C. ; Capt. W. F. Denning ; Capt. T. D. Pratt	32
Lieut.-Col. C. J. Pickering, C.M.G., D.S.O. ; Lieut.-Col. G. K. Sullivan, O.B.E., M.C.	44
Brig.-General E. G. St. Aubyn, D.S.O.	64
Capt. W. N. Everitt, M.C. ; Capt. C. Hirst ; Lieut. J. T. Riley ; Capt. S. S. Greaves, D.S.O., M.C., R.A.M.C.	74
Lieut.-Col. J. Walker, D.S.O.	88
Brig.-General R. E. Sugden, C.M.G., D.S.O., T.D.	112
Capt. A. E. Mander ; Capt. J. G. Mowat, M.C. ; Capt. E. N. Marshall, M.C. ; Capt. N. Geldard, D.S.O., M.C. ...	128
The Lombartzyde Sector : Aeroplane Map	148
R.S.M. F. P. Stirzaker, M.C. ; R.S.M. W. Lee, M.C. ; C.S.M. W. Medley, M.C., M.M. ; Sergt. A. Loosemore, V.C., D.C.M.	164
The Ypres Salient : Winter, 1917-1918	184
Major W. C. Fenton, M.C. ; Capt. N. T. Farrar, M.C. ; Capt. A. Kirk, M.C. ; Capt. P. G. Bales, M.C.	196
Private A. Poulter, V.C.	208
Bailleul Church : After the Bombardment	218
Capt. H. H. Aykroyd, M.C. ; Capt. W. N. Broomhead, T.D. ; Capt. W. Grantham ; Capt. S. Balme	240
Lieut.-Col. A. L. Mowat, D.S.O., M.C.	256
Wellington Cemetery, near Roeux	270
The Cadre at Halifax : June 18th, 1919	284

LIST OF MAPS.

YPRES, 1915	facing page	58
THIEPVAL WOOD, 1916	,, ,,	80
SEPTEMBER 3RD, 1916	,, ,,	96
RAID NEAR FICHEUX, FEBRUARY, 1917	page	117
ST. ELIE RIGHT SUB-SECTOR, 1917	facing page	144
LOMBARTZYDE SECTOR, 1917	,, ,,	156
BELLE VUE SPUR, OCTOBER 9TH, 1917	,, ,,	172
RAID NEAR REUTEL, MARCH, 1918	page	195
ERQUINGHEM AND NIEPPE, APRIL, 1918	facing page	214
BAILLEUL, APRIL, 1918	,, ,,	220
KEMMEL, APRIL, 1918	,, ,,	234
RAID NEAR ZILLEBEKE, JUNE, 1918	,, ,,	246
OCTOBER 11TH, 1918	,, ,,	264
CAMBRAI AND VALENCIENNES	,, ,,	274
FLANDERS	at end of book	
FIFTH AND THIRD ARMY AREAS, 1916-1917	,, ,,	

CHAPTER I.

MOBILISATION AND TRAINING.

At the outbreak of war with Germany, early in August, 1914, the West Riding Territorial Division consisted of the following battalions:—

   1st. West Riding Infantry Brigade : 5th, 6th, 7th and 8th Battalions West Yorkshire Regiment.
   2nd. West Riding Infantry Brigade : 4th, 5th, 6th and 7th Battalions Duke of Wellington's (W.R.) Regiment.
   3rd. West Riding Infantry Brigade : 4th and 5th Battalions King's Own Yorkshire Light Infantry ; 4th and 5th Battalions York and Lancaster Regiment.

Major-General T. S. Baldock, C.B., was in command of the Division, and Brigadier-General E. F. Brereton, D.S.O., of the 2nd West Riding Infantry Brigade. No change of battalions took place in any of the Infantry Brigades until the reorganisation of the British Expeditionary Force at the beginning of 1918, when each was reduced to three battalions ; and even then no fresh battalion was added to the Division.

The 4th Battalion Duke of Wellington's (W.R.) Regt. was under the command of Lieut.-Colonel H. S. Atkinson, T.D., of Cleckheaton, and Major E. P. Chambers, of Brighouse, was second in command. Capt. H. A. S. Stanton, of the Royal Scots Regt., was Adjutant. Though the regular army had recently been reorganised on a four-company basis, a similar change had not yet been made in the Territorial Force, so that the Battalion consisted of eight companies as follows :—

A Company (Halifax) commanded by Capt. V. A. Milligan.

MOBILISATION AND TRAINING

B Company (Halifax)	,,	Capt. D. B. Winter.
C Company (Halifax)	,,	Capt. D. V. Fleming.
D Company (Brighouse)	,,	Capt. R. E. Sugden.
E Company (Cleckheaton)	,,	Capt. J. Walker.
F Company (Halifax)	,,	Lieut. E. P. Learoyd.
G Company (Elland)	,,	Capt. R. H. Goldthorp.
H Company (Sowerby Bridge)	,,	Capt. W. A. Laxton.

All the four companies from the out-lying districts were well up to strength, but the Halifax companies were weak.

On July 26th, the Battalion went to camp at Marske-by-the-Sea for its annual period of training. The time was one of intense anxiety and excitement. On July 28th, Austria-Hungary declared war on Serbia. Three days later general mobilisation was ordered by Russia, which produced an immediate ultimatum from Berlin. The next day mobilisation was ordered in both France and Germany; the latter, as is now well known, had been mobilising and concentrating secretly on its French and Belgian frontiers for some days. On August 2nd, the German armies entered Luxembourg, and violated French territory without any declaration of war. Two days later Britain sent its ultimatum to Germany and as, on the same day, German troops entered Belgian territory, war broke out between the two countries at midnight, August 4/5th. Such was the atmosphere in which the Battalion carried out its training at Marske.

The camp should have lasted a fortnight, but it broke up at the end of a week. The Special Service Section of 100 other ranks, under the command of Capt. R. E. Sugden, with Lieut. H. N. Waller as his second in command, was the first to leave. Orders for it to proceed at once to Grimsby arrived during the church parade on Sunday, August 2nd, and it left the same day. It was employed guarding the Admiralty Wireless Station at Waltham, and the water and electricity works. On August 3rd, the men of the Battalion returned to their homes, where they waited in hourly expectation of orders to mobilise. These came on the evening of the following day, and the same night the Battalion was concentrated at Halifax, the men sleeping in the Secondary Schools in Prescott Street. The Battalion was about 650 strong. Scarcely a man had failed to report.

MOBILISATION AND TRAINING

About 1-30 p.m. on August 5th, the Battalion* marched down Horton Street to the Railway Station, and there took train for Hull, its allotted station. There was no public send-off. War had come so suddenly that people seemed hardly to realise what was happening. On arrival most of the men were billeted in a big concert hall in the town, the remainder occupying a Working Boys' Club in one of the poorer quarters, and buildings near the docks. At Hull the men were variously employed. Guards were provided on the docks and at the Naval Signal Station. Working parties were sent out to dig trenches at Sutton, part of the new system of coast defences which was being prepared. Perhaps the most congenial duty was the rounding up of a number of Germans in the district; these were searched—some of them were found to be in possession of revolvers—and were then marched off to S.S. "Borodino," one of the new Wilson liners, on board of which they were confined. The guard on the vessel was found by the Battalion and this was considered to be a good job.

During these first days of war the ration question was extremely difficult. The carefully planned pre-war scheme had broken down the very first day. The Battalion had no transport, and neither the Quarter Master nor the transport personnel had accompanied it to Hull. Taxis had to be requisitioned to take the place of transport vehicles; food had to be obtained as and where it could be found. Great credit was due to R.Q.M.S. F. J. Cooke and his staff for the way in which they pulled the Battalion through the difficulty. At this time the men were armed with the C.L.L.E. rifle and were fairly well equipped; difficulties of equipment only became serious when drafts began

---

*The following Officers mobilised with the Battalion on August 4th:—
Lieut.-Col. H. S. Atkinson, T.D. (C.O.).
Major E. P. Chambers (Second in Command).
Capt. H. A. S. Stanton (Adjutant).
Capt. A. T. Griffiths, R.A.M.C. (Medical Officer).
Lieut. T. Fielding (Quartermaster).
Captains W. A. Laxton, D. V. Fleming, J. Walker, V. A. Milligan, D. B. Winter, R. H. Goldthorp, C. E. Kirby.†
Lieutenants E. P. Learoyd, E. E. Sykes,† A. H. Helliwell, A. L. Mowat, A. H. Richardson, D. A. Sutcliffe, M. P. Andrews, W. F. Denning.†
Second-Lieutenants J. T. Riley, C. Hirst, S. Balme.
Capt. R. E. Sugden and Lieut. H. N. Waller had gone away with the Special Service Section two days previously.
†From the T.F. Reserve.

to arrive. About 100 National Reservists joined the Battalion at Hull.

On August 11th, the Battalion was relieved by a Special Reserve Battalion of Lancashire Fusiliers and moved by water to Immingham, where it was stationed at the docks. Here it had its first experience of war conditions. There were no proper billets. The officers all slept on the floor of a granary, a part of the same building doing duty as a Battalion Mess. The men were even worse off, having nothing better than a number of sheds with concrete floors. At Immingham the Special Service Section and the transport personnel rejoined. There, too, the whole of the 2nd West Riding Infantry Brigade, except one battalion, was concentrated. A further draft of National Reservists also joined.

Only two days were spent at Immingham, and then the Battalion marched to Great Coates, where it remained for nearly five weeks. This was the beginning of the long period of intensive training which preceded its departure overseas. The men were billeted in barns, granaries and stables, thus getting an early taste of what was to become their normal mode of life for long periods in France. Training consisted mostly of route marches, and battalion and company schemes. Great attention was paid to musketry. Newly-gazetted officers began to arrive, and further drafts of men brought the Battalion up to full strength before it left Great Coates, though a good many National Reservists were rejected at the medical examination. The weather was perfect. Days of glorious sunshine followed one another with monotonous regularity.

On September 15th, the Battalion went under canvas in Riby Park, where training continued for another month. At first there had been few volunteers for service overseas. Little information was available as to the conditions of service, and few men had yet realised the greatness of the crisis. But when the situation was properly understood they responded to the call well. The Battalion became definitely a foreign service unit. All officers and other ranks who had not volunteered for general service left it, and joined the 2/4th Battalion Duke of Wellington's Regt., which was being formed at Halifax. About the middle of October, the whole Battalion moved to the neighbourhood of Marsden, in the Colne Valley, to fire the General Musketry Course. Several ranges were used by different companies, but the shooting was much interfered with by the atrocious weather which was experienced there. Here most of the men were inoculated, and leave was plentiful.

On November 5th, Battalion H.Q. moved by train to Doncaster, at which place the whole of the 2nd West Riding Infantry Brigade was concentrated during the next few days. There it remained throughout the winter and only left when the time came for it to move to France.

It was not until the middle of January, 1915, that the Battalion was reorganised on a four-company basis, in accordance with the system adopted shortly before the war by the Regular Army. The original companies were then amalgamated as follows :—

A and D Companies joined to form No. 1 (afterwards A) Coy.
E and G   ,,   ,,   No. 2 (,,   B) ,,
B and C   ,,   ,,   No. 3 (,,   C) ,,
F and H   ,,   ,,   No. 4 (,,   D) ,, *

Companies were billeted in schools in the town. On the whole these billets were made pretty comfortable, for the men were fast learning how to look after themselves.† Officers occupied rooms in various hotels and private houses, but had a Battalion Mess, first at an hotel, but later in a house which was rented in Regent Terrace.

All available time was occupied in training and organisation. With the exception of a few small guards, the Battalion had no garrison duties to find. During the earlier part of its stay at Doncaster most of the training took the form of field days. Training areas were allotted near the town, and these were frequently changed in order to give variety. Many fierce " battles " were

*Company Commanders and Seconds in Command were as follows :—
　A Company : Major R. E. Sugden ; Capt. M. P. Andrews.
　B Company : Capt. J. Walker ; Capt. H. N. Waller.
　C Company : Capt. D. B. Winter ; Capt. E. E. Sykes.
　D Company : Capt. R. H. Goldthorp ; Capt. A. L. Mowat.

†The following were the billets occupied in Doncaster :—
　Battn. H.Q. and Q.M. Stores : Oxford Place Schools.
　A Company :　　　　　　　Hexthorpe Schools.
　B Company :　　　　　　　Wheatley Road and St. James' Schools.
　C and D Companies :　　　Hyde Park Schools.
　Transport :　　　　　　　Turf Hotel Stables and Wood Street Hotel.

MOBILISATION AND TRAINING

fought both by day and night. Usually the Battalion worked out its own schemes, but occasionally there were Brigade and Divisional days, when the officers and men learned something of the co-operation of the different arms. The training was very strenuous and involved a great deal of route marching. The Battalion would parade about 7-0 a.m. and march out, often a distance of seven or eight miles, to the training area. A scheme would then be worked out, and after it was over the Battalion would be marched back. Considerable distances were thus often covered in a day, and the men got into splendid condition. After the Battalion had been reorganised into four companies, the system of training was considerably changed for a time, as a completely new drill had to be learned. So an ordinary day's training became much as follows. After about half-an-hour's physical training, the Battalion marched down to the Race Course where the morning was spent at the new drill; an hour's bayonet fighting in the afternoon completed the work for the day. Much attention was also paid to musketry. This was carried outunder the supervision of Major R. E. Sugden, who lived at Battalion H.Q. for that purpose, and thus was not able to see much of his Company. Ranges at Cantley and Scunthorpe were used. A little trench digging was done near Armthorpe but, as it was still hoped that the war would soon become one of movement again, this form of training was not taken very seriously. On one occasion the Battalion was inspected on the Race Course by the G.O.C., Northern Command; but otherwise, little attention was paid to ceremonial drill. Lectures on various military subjects were given by the officers and, in order to give variety to the men and lighten the work of the lecturers, senior officers went round the different companies giving the same lectures to each.

Alarms were not infrequent but, only once, was there any real reason for them. That occasion was the day when a few fast German cruisers slipped across the North Sea, and bombarded Scarborough for a short time. That morning the Battalion had marched out about eight miles to do a scheme. It had just arrived when urgent orders to return at once were received. Without any rest the men fell in and marched straight back to Doncaster without a halt. It was very hot for the time of year, and the march was no mean performance. For the rest of that day all troops were confined to billets ; but they were not called upon to do anything further and everything was normal the next day.

The time spent at Doncaster was very pleasant. The townsfolk were very kind to all the men, many of whom made good friends. Long after they had gone overseas several men were still corresponding with Doncaster people, and most of the survivors have warm recollections of the hospitality extended to them. Christmas was celebrated right royally. Few were able to get home, but everything possible was done to make the season an enjoyable one. Dinners were served at the principal hotels* of the town and, thanks to the generosity of the Doncaster Tradesmen's Association, about half the Battalion was entertained in the Corn Exchange on Christmas Day and Boxing Day.

But in spite of everything there was much discontent in the Battalion, though one can hardly grumble at the cause of it. The men longed to be at the " Front." Most of them had expected to go overseas very soon and, as the weeks dragged into months, some began to wonder whether they ever would get there. This long delay was due mainly to shortage of equipment. Practically everything was going to the New Armies, which were in training, and there was little left over for the Territorial Force. Furthermore, there was the ever-present fear of invasion, and it was not deemed safe to send the Territorials overseas until new troops were sufficiently trained to defend the country in case of need. But few of the men understood these things. One man actually deserted in order to enlist in another regiment, because he thought the Battalion was not going out. Another wrote direct to the Secretary of State for War to ask the reason for the delay and, of course, was well " told off " for his pains. Rumours were plentiful, but, as nothing came of them, they only served to increase the feeling of disappointment.

*The hotels used were :—
Nos. 1 and 7 Companies : Red Lion Hotel.
No. 2 Company : Salutation Hotel.
No. 3 Company : Thatched House Hotel.
Nos. 4 and 8 Companies : Burns Hotel.
Nos. 5 and 6 Companies : Danum Hotel.
Battalion H.Q. Details : Good Woman Hotel.
Transport : Wood Street Hotel.

At length, one day early in April, definite news was received. A tactical tour for the officers and senior N.C.O's of the Battalion had been arranged, under the personal supervision of the Brigadier. When the latter arrived he brought the news that the Battalion was to move in a few days. Immediately there was a light-hearted feeling about that party such as there had seldom been before.

The days which followed were full of excitement and activity. There was an enormous amount of work to be done, and very little time to do it. During the last few days there was little rest for officers and N.C.O's. Up to that time it had been extremely difficult to obtain articles of kit and equipment. Owing to the enormous demands of the army already in France, and the fact that the productive power of the British factories was scarcely a hundredth part of what it became towards the end of the war, there was very little material available for distribution to troops at home. But, now that the Battalion was under orders for the Front, all kinds of stores were thrust upon it. The miscellaneous collection of spring carts and vans, which had done duty as transport vehicles, were replaced by the proper limbered wagons; transport animals and harness arrived quicker than they could be dealt with. Men were constantly being paraded to receive some article of kit or equipment; one time it would be new winter underclothing, another time new boots. These articles are particularly worthy of notice. Why a Battalion should be fitted out with winter underclothing early in April is a question which probably only the War Office officials of the period could satisfactorily answer. While as to the boots, it was not long before many a man was yearning for his comfortable old pair. Right up to the end fresh stores were arriving and being issued. Indeed, about midnight of the Battalion's last night in England—reveille was to be at 4-0 a.m.—A Company was hauled out of bed by two enthusiastic subalterns to exchange its old web pouches for new; the men of the company, it should be added, hardly showed themselves so enthusiastic as their officers about the change, particularly when they discovered in the morning that nearly all the pouches received were for the left side. But, in spite of all, things somehow got done.

Lieut.-Col. H. S. ATKINSON, T.D.

MOBILISATION AND TRAINING

On April 12th, the transport men, with their animals and loaded vehicles, entrained for Southampton. They were to move by a different route from the rest of the Battalion. Major R. E. Sugden and Lieut. C. Hirst, the Battalion Transport Officer, were in charge of the party. Considering the men's lack of experience, the embarkation went very smoothly. On board elaborate drill in case of torpedo attack was practised, but the voyage proved uneventful. They disembarked at Havre and proceeded by train to Hesdigneul, where they rejoined the Battalion on April 15th.

April 14th, the fateful day, arrived. Reveille was at 4-0 a.m., and, after breakfast, preparations were soon complete and the Battalion paraded ready to move off. The following is the complete list of officers, warrant officers, and quartermaster sergeants who were to accompany the Battalion overseas:—

Battalion H.Q.

Lieut.-Col. H. S. Atkinson, T.D. (C.O.).
Major E. P. Chambers (Second in Command).
Capt. H. A. S. Stanton (Adjutant).
Hon. Lieut. T. Fielding (Q.M.).
Lieut. E. Lee (Machine Gun Officer).
Lieut. S. Balme (Signalling Officer).
Lieut. C. Hirst (Transport Officer).
Capt. A. T. Griffiths, R.A.M.C. (Medical Officer).
R.S.M. J. McCormack.
R.Q.M.S. F. J. Cooke.

A Company.

Major R. E. Sugden; Capt. M. P. Andrews; Lieut. G. W. I. Learoyd; Lieut. E. N. Marshall; Sec.-Lieut. E. Taylor; Sec.-Lieut. G. P. McGuire.
C.S.M. E. Bottomley.
C.Q.M.S. C. Southern.

B Company.

Capt. J. Walker; Capt. H. N. Waller; Lieut. J. T. Riley; Lieut. B. A. Bell; Sec.-Lieut. J. G. Mowat; Sec.-Lieut. H. H. Aykroyd.
C.S.M. A. Parkin.
C.Q.M.S. D. McKeand.

C Company.

Capt. D. B. Winter; Capt. E. E. Sykes; Sec.-Lieut. W. C. Fenton; Sec.-Lieut. F. Walker.
C.S.M. E. Lumb.
C.Q.M.S. W. Lee.

D Company.

Capt. A. L. Mowat; Capt. W. F. Denning; Lieut. W. B. Yates; Sec.-Lieut. T. D. Pratt; Sec.-Lieut. W. L. Anderton.
C.S.M. C. C. MacKay.
C.Q.M.S. G. Jackson.

The 2/4th Battalion Duke of Wellington's Regt. had come into Doncaster a few days before and was encamped on the Race Course. Officers and men turned out now to give their friends and townsmen a rousing send-off. Their Band played the Battalion to the Railway Station, while their men lined the streets. The townspeople also turned out in considerable numbers to say farewell to their recently-made friends. A platoon of A Company constituted the loading party, under the command of Lieut. E. N. Marshall, who records that among the miscellaneous stores which he helped to load upon the train was one coil of barbed wire. Even in those early days he considered it unnecessary.

Two trains were provided for the journey. The first, under the command of Lieut.-Col. H. S. Atkinson, T.D., carried A and B Companies. It was due to depart at 12-0 noon. When all were entrained and everything seemed ready, the driver, being a civilian, thought it was time to start and began to move off. But, of course, that was all wrong. The train was stopped, the " Advance " was blown on the bugle, and then off they went. The other train, under the command of Major E. P. Chambers, and carrying C and D Companies, started more quietly and with less formality from a siding further down the line.

The journey was uneventful and slow. The trains circled round London, and the first arrived at Folkestone Quay about 8-45 p.m. The men immediately embarked on S.S. " Invicta," which the Battalion had all to itself, and were soon at sea. The night was quiet and the crossing calm. Soon after 10-0 p.m. the vessel arrived at Boulogne, and the Battalion had its first sight of the "promised land." At last it was really on active service, and was to take its place side by side with the men who had made history at Mons, the Marne, Ypres, and a score of other battles.

CHAPTER II.

FLEURBAIX.

THE Battalion was in France. On arrival at Boulogne it disembarked at once and marched to St. Martin's Camp, which was on a hill a mile or two outside the town. This camp had only recently been started and the arrangements were far from ideal. A few tents for the officers, and bivouacs for the men, were the only accommodation. No one had had a proper meal since he left Doncaster, but no food was provided at the camp until the following morning. One blanket per man—sewn up to form a sort of cloak, with a hole in the top for the owner to put his head through if he felt so inclined—was the only covering provided. Tired and hungry the Battalion turned in, but not to sleep. It was a cold and frosty night. After their comfortable billets at Doncaster the men were not in good training for such rigorous conditions, and the memory of that night still lives in the minds of some of the "old-timers" of the Battalion. By a very early hour nearly everyone was out on the road, stamping up and down in an attempt to get warm. Breakfast time was very welcome.

After breakfast, rations for the day were drawn and iron rations issued, and then the Battalion started on one of the hardest marches it ever had to make. A late change in the orders had caused a delay of more than two hours so that, when the men at length moved off, the march was much more strenuous than it would otherwise have been. It was a very hot day, with a blazing sun. Most of the men were tired before they started. They had had a long railway journey and a sea crossing the previous day, and few had been able to get any sleep during the night. Clad in their thick winter underclothing, and with packs much heavier than they had been used to in training, they were none too suitably equipped for a long tramp. But, worst of all, were the new boots with which everyone had been supplied before leaving Doncaster; these had not yet become fitted to the feet, and before long many men were suffering severely. Men who had never fallen out on a march before were compelled to do so then, and there were soon many stragglers on the road, gamely trying to struggle along. It was a very jaded battalion which at length arrived at the little wayside station of Hesdigneul.

The train, with transport vehicles, animals and personnel on board, was already waiting in the station. Some tea was obtained from a little wooden canteen near by and then the Battalion entrained, most of the stragglers having come up by that time. Here the men were first introduced to what would be called a cattle truck in England, but which in France bears the mystic legend "Hommes 40, Chevaux 8"—the type of compartment which was to be their customary means of conveyance on the somewhat rare occasions when they travelled by rail. Many were the speculations as to the Battalion's destination, but no information could be obtained from the railway officials. Wild rumours circulated, the most popular being that a great battle was in progress and the Battalion was being hurried up as a reinforcement. But, as usual, rumour proved false. After a journey, uninteresting but for the fact that it was the first most of the men had ever made on the Continent, the train arrived at Merville about 6-0 p.m., and orders to detrain were issued.

There followed another march, worse in some respects than the first. Certainly it was not so hot, but the rest on the train had allowed muscles to stiffen and sore feet to develop. Only their tremendous keenness, and the novelty of active service, kept many of the men going. One N.C.O. at least arrived at his destination carrying his boots, having tramped the last part of the way in his stockinged feet. It was long after dark before the Battalion reached Estaires where it took over its first billets in France. These were on the edge of the town, on the Neuf Berquin Road. They had previously been occupied by Indian troops and were, almost without exception, filthy. Battalion H.Q. was in the Chateau, but those who had looked for a fine, castellated mansion were grievously disappointed. It was some time before the place could be found, and when it was discovered, it turned out to be a large, but quite uninteresting, building up a side street. According to rumour, it had been occupied by all sorts of undesirables, from Germans to typhoid patients ; at any rate it was very dirty, and much work was necessary before it could be put into a habitable condition. For a day or two all officers messed at a large estaminet by the Hotel de Ville, but then the system of company messes was started and continued throughout the Battalion's period of active service.

All now knew that they were near the Front. Ruined houses along the road had borne silent testimony to the presence of war. In Estaires the sound of the guns could be clearly heard, and there the first aeroplane fight which anyone had seen was witnessed. The Division was now in the IV. Corps of the First Army. A few days after landing it received its new title of the 49th Division ; the 2nd West Riding Infantry Brigade became the 147th Infantry Brigade.

About a week was spent at Estaires and, during that time, practically all the officers and many other ranks visited the front line trenches for short periods of instruction. The first party, which comprised about half the officers and a large number of N.C.O's, went up on April 19th for twenty-four hours. Old London omnibuses carried them to beyond Bac St. Maur, and then they walked up to the section of the line which they were soon to take over the defence of—No. 3 Section of the Fleurbaix Sector. Here they came under the tutelage of the 2nd Battalion West Yorkshire Regiment. On the return of this party, the remainder of the officers and more N.C.O's had their turn. Then the Battalion began to send up whole platoons, each under its own platoon commander, for twenty-four hours. It was during one of these tours of instruction that the Battalion suffered its first casualties. At that time movement to and from the front line, in the Fleurbaix Sector, was almost entirely across the open, communication trenches being practically non-existent. When coming out after their tour of instruction on April 23rd, one man was killed and two were wounded by stray bullets.

Meanwhile the Battalion was resting. Little work was done

at Estaires. Platoon commanders' inspections and occasional short route marches were all the military training that was attempted. The men were given a chance to settle down in their new life. A surprise visit from Lieut.-General Sir H. Rawlinson, G.O.C. IV. Corps, was the one exciting event.

On April 22nd, the Battalion marched to billets at Doulieu. This move caused some discomfort to the platoons which were then undergoing instruction in the line, as they had considerable difficulty in finding the Battalion when they returned. Guides had been left behind for them, but these apparently got tired of waiting and departed. At Doulieu the Battalion was visited by General Sir Douglas Haig, at that time commanding the First Army, who surprised a luckless, though well-meaning, subaltern in the very act of issuing rum to his platoon at unauthorised hours.

Two days later the Battalion moved to the neighbourhood of La Croix Lescornez, where it was in Brigade Reserve to the front line. The following day, an order to provide 400 men for work under the Royal Engineers was an indication of much of the future life of the Battalion. The same day the whole of A Company went into the line, being distributed along the front held by the 3rd Battalion Worcestershire Regt., which had relieved the 2nd Battalion West Yorkshire Regt.

On April 26th, the Battalion relieved the 3rd Battalion Worcestershire Regt. in No. 3 Section of the Fleurbaix Sector.

. . . .

One relief is much like another, and all who know the Western Front can picture the scene in the billet of No. — Platoon of — Company on the morning of April 26th, 1915.

A dirty yard, with the usual midden in the middle, is surrounded by buildings on all sides. Nearest to the road is the great barn, which has been the platoon's home for the last few days. It is not an ideal billet. The floor is of trampled earth, with a little straw here and there; a timber frame-work, filled in with clay and straw, forms the walls; the roof is tiled. Many holes in the walls let in light and air and allow the wind to whistle round the barn; many tiles are missing from the roof and, at night, a sleepless man can lie gazing at the stars, or feel the rain falling on his face, according to the weather. Walls, four to five feet high, subdivide the barn into several compartments.

On the opposite side of the yard lies the house—all ground floor. Its kitchen is well known to the platoon, for the people have been good to the men. Many of them have sat round that strange closed stove, which will burn anything, and have drunk coffee, while they aired their French with their hosts. Stables, pig-sties, and other farm buildings form the other sides of the yard.

"Blankets, rolled in bundles of ten and labelled," have been dumped ready to be collected by the transport. Equipment has been made up and packed, and is lying about the yard. Rifles lean against the walls. The barn has been left "scrupulously clean" and passed as satisfactory. For the moment there is nothing special to do. The men stand about the yard in groups, smoking and talking. Some are drinking coffee in the kitchen. Private X is carrying on a lively conversation with "Mademoiselle."

"Fall in!" Men leisurely don their equipment, pick up their rifles, and obey. Private Y is the last as usual, and is rebuked by his section commander. N.C.O's glance at their men and report "All Correct" to the platoon sergeant. "Platoon—'Shun!" The men come up to the position of readiness, described in the Drill Book. "Right—Dress!" They dress. "Platoon, by Sections—Number! Form—Fours! Form—Two-deep! Stand at—Ease! Stand—Easy!" The platoon is ready to move.

"Platoon—'Shun!" The officer has arrived. "Platoon present and correct, sir!" A rapid inspection, a word of criticism here and there, and the men again stand easy.

"Platoon—'Shun! Slope—Arms! Move to the right in Fours, Form—Fours! Right! Quick—March! Right—Wheel!" The platoon moves out of the yard. "March Easy!" Rifle slings are loosened and the rifles slung; pipes and cigarettes appear; the pace settles down to a steady hundred to the minute. With a cheery greeting to "Madame" and an affectionate farewell to "Mademoiselle," they pass the estaminet. The roads are wet and muddy, and boots soon lose their parade polish. Now the platoon is leaving the village. ' A little ahead are the cross-roads, which mark the Battalion starting point. The subaltern consults his watch. Good! He is exactly on time.

"Platoon, March to Attention!" Pipes and cigarettes disappear; slings are tightened; rifles are brought to the slope. "Left—Left—Left, Right, Left!" The pace smartens up to the regulation hundred and twenty to the minute. "Eyes—Right!" They are passing the cross-roads where the C.O., with his Adjutant, is standing.

"Eyes—Front! March Easy!" Again rifles are slung and matches struck. The pace soon settles down to the old hundred to the minute. The road is muddier than ever now. Few vehicles, except the infantry transport, use it beyond the village; and so it is seldom repaired. The country grows more desolate; on all sides are ruined buildings, shattered trees, and the countless signs of war. But jest and song help to enliven the way, for the men are fresh after their few days' rest.

At "ten minutes to the hour" the platoon falls out on the right of the road. Equipment is taken off. The grass is wet, but some sit down; in later days, in spite of all orders to the contrary, they will sit on their "tin hats." It seems hardly a minute before they are called on to don their equipment and fall in again.

At length a communication trench is reached. The men are quieter now. Over to the right an occasional shell is bursting. The crack of a rifle is heard now and then. The trench is muddy, and, here and there, water is over the duckboards. Private Z slips, and expresses his opinion of the sandbag-ful of charcoal, which he is carrying, in unmistakeable terms.

The trench seems endless, but, at last, the front line is reached. Other men, covered with mud and wearing equipment, are waiting there. The relief goes smoothly. Sentries are changed, duties are handed over, the latest intelligence about "Fritz" or "Jerry" is imparted. "Quiet tour. Not a casualty in our company. He doesn't fire if you lie doggo."

With every sign of satisfaction the relieved troops withdraw.

B

Men who are not on sentry seek their shelters and grouse at the condition they have been left in. The platoon commander inspects his line, swears that the people he has relieved have done no work during the whole tour, and goes off to air his grievances at Company H.Q. The Company Commander wires "Hundred gallons of rum urgently needed," "Love to Alice," or some such message, which has been agreed upon to signify "Relief complete."

The tour has begun.

. . . .

For the first time, the Battalion was responsible for the defence of a sector of the line, with no one between it and the enemy. There it was to remain for about two months, inter-relieving every few days with the 6th Battalion Duke of Wellington's Regt., and spending its rest periods in and near the village of Fleurbaix.

No. 3 Section was about a thousand yards in breadth. There was a continuous front line but, apart from a few strong points with all-round defence, there were no fortifications in rear of it. Those were the days when artillery was scanty and shells few; when Lewis guns were unheard of and the only machine guns available were the two Maxims owned by each battalion. Hence it was to the rifle that everyone looked for the defence of the line, and, in order to secure the maximum of fire effect, as many men as possible were permanently stationed in the front line. At that time there were practically no men extra-regimentally employed, and the personnel of the Transport and the Q.M. Stores was cut down to a minimum. No "trench strength" for this first tour has been preserved, but the Battalion must have been at least 900 other ranks strong. Thirteen out of the sixteen platoons were stationed in the front line, so that, making due allowance for the men attached to Battalion H.Q., there must have been nearly 700 men in that 1,000 yards of trench—in other words, well over a man to every yard of fire bay. It can easily be imagined how crowded the line was. At stand to men stood shoulder to shoulder on every fire step.

During the Battalion's first tour in this Section, A Company was on the right, D Company in the centre, and B Company on the left. C Company lent one platoon to strengthen the garrison of the front line, the remainder occupying Dead Dog Farm and another strong point in the neighbourhood. In subsequent tours these positions were inter-changed in order to give each company its turn in battalion reserve. The main feature of the sector was the Convent Wall, which lay almost at right angles to the front line, near the junction of B and D Companies. There were no communication trenches up to the line. Reliefs were carried out straight up the Rue des Bassiéres and then along the side of the Convent Wall. From the front line the ground sloped gently up to the crest of the Aubers Ridge. No Man's Land was covered with thick grass and rank weeds, and was intersected by many derelict trenches.

The country was so low-lying, and water lay so near the surface, that digging was practically impossible. Hence the defences consisted almost entirely of breast-works, built of sandbags. The line was of the usual stereotyped kind—six yard fire bays alternating with four yard traverses. Shelters were built into the parados. They were very flimsy structures, affording protection against nothing but bullets and the weather. It is doubtful whether there was a shelter on the whole sector which would have stopped a " whizz-bang." Such was the line in which the Battalion served its apprenticeship.

From the G.O.C. to the latest-joined private, every man in the 49th Division was new to trench warfare, and so had everything to learn. Training in England had mostly taken the form of open warfare, and practically no one in the Infantry had had any instruction in field engineering, or in looking after his own comfort. So necessity became the main teacher, and perhaps a better one could not have been found. At first rations were carried up by the reserve company, but later it was found possible to bring pack animals right up to the Convent Wall; a light cart,—one of the many unauthorised vehicles owned by the transport at one time or another on active service—was fitted with axle and wheels, salved from a derelict motor car which was found lying in a ditch, and was used for carrying ammunition and R.E. material. All rations were sent up uncooked, and for a day or two they were issued in that form to each man. But the waste and futility of individuals cooking for themselves was so apparent that the system was quickly given up and section messes were instituted, one man in each being detailed as cook. The main source of water was the Convent pump, but the reserve company sometimes sent men down to the nearest inhabited houses to replenish, and it is rumoured that beer occasionally came back instead of water.

About the time the Battalion reached France the enemy first made use of poison gas in his second great attack on the Ypres Salient. This caused great anxiety among the allied armies and measures were at once taken to protect the men against it. The Battalion received its first issue of respirators a few days after it arrived in the neighbourhood of Fleurbaix. They were clumsy affairs—a piece of cotton waste, saturated with a solution of hypo, and wrapped in black gauze. When in use the cotton waste covered the mouth and nose and was gripped in the teeth, the respirator being held in position by tying the gauze at the back of the head. Old ammunition boxes, filled with hypo solution, were installed in the front line, and the respirators were often worn at stand to for practice. One awful wet night the Divisional Commander visited the trenches to see the working of the respirators. Most men were carrying them in their great coat pockets instead of their haversacks, and when he ordered them to be put on there was great confusion. The rain poured down; in the darkness men dropped their respirators in the mud and the crepe became thoroughly soaked. Altogether the practice was not a success. These first respirators were very uncomfortable to wear, difficult to keep in position, and practically useless against anything more dangerous than a weak concentration of chlorine. Before long the P. helmet superseded them but, though rather more effective, it was quite as uncomfortable. Having no outlet valve, it was difficult to breath through, and made the wearer terribly hot. Its single mica window was very fragile and the least crack in it rendered the whole helmet useless. As helmets had to be inspected at least three times a day at that time, the wastage was very great.

Major E. P. CHAMBERS.

Lieut.-Col. H. A. S. STANTON, D.S.O

Capt. H. N. WALLER.

From the very beginning great stress was laid on two things—the continual wearing of equipment and sentry duties. These were legacies from the experienced troops with whom the Battalion had undergone its brief course of instruction. Periods in the line were very strenuous. Theoretically, 25 per cent. of the men were on duty by day and 50 per cent. by night. But, owing to the accumulation of odd duties and the provision of working parties, no man got much rest. At Fleurbaix the Battalion laid the foundation of its reputation as a working battalion which it held throughout the war. Breast-works, if they are to be kept in good condition, require even more constant attention than trenches. Few of the men possessed any of the necessary technical knowledge, and visits from the Royal Engineers were rare; but all men were willing and, though some of the earlier efforts were very crude, the work quickly improved. Professional bricklayers were in great demand for sand-bagging, and C.S.M. E. Bottomley in particular was looked upon as a great theoretical authority on this subject in his own company. Not only was the upkeep of the trenches taken seriously in hand, but entirely new work was planned and executed. The route to the front line, by the side of the Convent Wall, was made safer, first by the erection of canvas screens to hide movement, and later by the construction of sandbag walls at the more dangerous points. But the most enduring monument of the Battalion in the Fleurbaix Sector was Dead Dog Alley—a regular communication trench which was taped out, and nearly completed, before the Battalion left the district.

The Fleurbaix Sector was a very quiet part of the line. In its inexperience, the Battalion never properly appreciated this fact until it learned real "liveliness" at Ypres. The early War Diaries are full of references to heavy shelling; in reality, the enemy artillery did little. Once a shell dropped right into the Battalion H.Q. Officers' Mess, but, luckily, two "shorts" had given the occupants timely warning, and they had withdrawn to a safer spot. A few salvoes were fired on different parts of the sector daily, the neighbourhood of the pump receiving most attention; but there is only one recorded instance of the front line being hit. This was fortunate for, so crowded was the line, that well-directed shell fire would have wrought fearful havoc.

Unlike their artillery, the German machine gunners and riflemen were extremely active. The Rue des Bassiéres and the Convent Wall were always dangerous spots, while at night the enemy traversed the front line parapet with great accuracy. His snipers were very wide-awake and excellent shots; they had all the advantages of superior observation and high command, and some of them were certainly equipped with telescopic sights. It was almost as much as a man's life was worth for him to show his head above the parapet for a few seconds in the daytime. Nearly all the casualties in the Fleurbaix Sector were from bullet wounds.

As has already been said, the British positions were held at this time almost entirely by rifle fire. Few heavy guns were in use then and, though there were a fair number of field guns, no really effective barrage could be put down owing to the scarcity of ammunition. A very few rounds daily were all that the artillery could fire. Some of their ammunition was of poor quality. " Prematures " were not uncommon and caused much worry to Battalion H.Q. One day a 4.7 shell lodged in the breast-work just outside the Orderly Room, but did not explode.

The two old Maxims which the Battalion had brought out with it were disposed to the best advantage, but, both in attack and defence, the main reliance had to be placed on the rifle. And the amount of rifle fire on that front was colossal. This was particularly the case at night. Often, somewhere far away and for no apparent reason, a perfect storm of firing would open; company after company would take it up, and so it would travel quickly along the line until, literally along thousands of yards of front, every man would be working his bolt as rapidly as possible. Sometimes this would go on for many minutes, and then it would gradually die down. The good old custom of " Five rounds rapid " at stand to was always encouraged in the Battalion. Occasionally rapid fire, to harass enemy transport or carrying parties, would be opened on some back area. In the daytime the use of the rifle was restricted to sniping, but in this the enemy had most of the advantage owing to his higher command and his greater experience in constructing positions. Yet every man in the Battalion was immensely keen to "bag a Bosch." Often one man would hurl the most insulting remarks across No Man's Land, or even show himself above the parapet, in the hope that some very simple-minded German would appear, and thus present a target to another Britisher who was anxiously waiting his chance in a neighbouring bay. But no successes have been recorded. The enemy was much too cute and usually retaliated only in kind. Hand-grenades too were just coming to the fore. When they were relieved the 3rd Worcesters had left two men in the line to instruct the Battalion in the manufacture of "jam-tin" and "hair-brush" bombs. About this time the Brigade Grenadier Company was formed, one platoon from each battalion being sent for instruction in bombing. Sec.-Lieut. W. L. Anderton became the Battalion's first Bombing Officer. But bombing was not taken very seriously until some months later.

The Battalion was handicapped a good deal by the C.L.L.E. rifle, with which it was armed. This weapon was much inferior to the short rifle of the Regulars. It usually jammed before ten rounds "rapid" had been fired, and was thus a source of much anxiety. Also, it could not be used for firing rifle grenades as these were constructed to clip on to the short rifle. As time went on short rifles were gradually obtained, but the C.L.L.E. did not wholly disappear until 1916.

Patrolling had not yet become the highly organised feature of trench warfare which it was to be later in the war. In spite of the excellent facilities offered by No Man's Land, very little was attempted by the Battalion in those early days. B Company tried a few patrols with no very definite result, Sec.-Lieut. J. G. Mowat being the first officer of the Battalion to go out. Late in May, Lieut. B. A. Bell was seriously wounded by an enemy machine gun when out on patrol, and was brought in by Private W. Brown, who afterwards received the Distinguished Conduct Medal for his gallantry on that occasion. There was a good deal of unauthorised coming and going in No Man's Land, where the chance of securing souvenirs was an attraction to many.

Usually, six days were spent in the line and six in Brigade

Reserve. During the rest periods one company was stationed at Croix Blanche Farm and, for tactical purposes, came under the orders of the battalion in the line. The rest of the Battalion, with the exception of a few small garrisons in scattered redoubts, was billeted in farm buildings near Fleurbaix. At first practically no training was attempted, though later a little was begun. Time was mainly taken up with interior economy and inspections. At night large working parties were found, mainly for digging assembly trenches in connection with the operations which were planning for May 9th; later on in the period work was concentrated on Dead Dog Alley. The men wrote shoals of letters, rather to the disgust of the officers whose duty it was to censor them. Many of these epistles were conspicuous more for vivid imagination than for strict adherence to truth. A little cricket was played, bathing in the ponds of the neighbourhood was indulged in, and several company concerts were held. A few officers and N.C.O's were able to visit Armentiéres, then a very pleasant town, in spite of its nearness to the front line. The enemy caused very little trouble; five shells daily into Fleurbaix was his standard " hate."

Few events of importance marked this period of the Battalion's apprenticeship. Its first tour in the line only lasted three days, and it was relieved on April 29th by the 6th Battalion Duke of Wellington's Regt. C Company was stationed at Croix Blanche and, shortly before midnight on April 30th, it was suddenly alarmed and ordered up to support the battalion in the line. The company fell in with the greatest alacrity, some without caps or jackets, but all with rifles and equipment. Down the road they went at the double, No. 9 Platoon leading. Occasional enemy shells were falling in the fields and a British battery of 4.7's was firing vigorously. Some way down the Rue des Bassiéres machine gun bullets began to sweep the road, and the men were ordered to get into the ditch. At this point Sec.-Lieut. W. C. Fenton was hit in the knee and had to be carried to the Aid Post; he was thus the first officer in the Battalion to be wounded. The company remained in the ditch for some time and then received orders to return to billets. It had been nothing but a false alarm.

Meanwhile, the big attack on the Aubers Ridge was preparing. This operation was based on the experience gained in the recent fighting about Neuve Chapelle, and it was commonly believed in the Battalion that the 49th Division had been sent out from England in April specially to take part. Another rumour current about this time was that the G.O.C's of the 49th and 50th Divisions had tossed up to decide which of them should go to Ypres, and which to Fleurbaix. It is not recorded who won. Originally the attack had been fixed for April 22nd. But when the enemy made his gas attack on the Ypres Salient, some of the troops, who had been detailed for the battle, had to be sent north to relieve the Canadians. So the battle was put off until May 9th. No attack was planned on the sector held by the 147th Infantry Brigade, but as the 8th Division was going over on its immediate right it was very probable that the 49th Division would become involved. Actually, the part taken by the Battalion was a very minor one; but the event is of importance as being the first occasion on which the men were engaged in operations on a large scale.

In the normal course of events the Battalion should have relieved the 6th Battalion in the front line on May 8th. But these orders were cancelled and, instead, the men found themselves in reserve for the attack. Their role was as follows :—

1. With the exception of A Company, which was placed under the orders of the O.C. No. 3 Section, the Battalion was to assemble in slits in the ground, near Croix Blanche, on the evening of May 8th.
2. If the attack of the Kensingtons on the extreme left proved successful, the Battalion was to dig a trench across No Man's Land to connect up the old British front line with the old German front line.
3. Later, if Fromelles were captured, a company was to be sent forward to hold a line to the north-east of that village.

On the evening of May 8th the Battalion marched up to its assembly positions. Every man was in full marching order and carried an extra bandolier of ammunition and the usual miscellaneous assortment of sandbags, extra rations, etc. On arrival, all set to work to improve their accommodation.

Battalion H.Q. occupied Croix Blanche Farm, from which building a good view of part of the battle area was obtained the following day. At 5-30 a.m. on May 9th, the British Artillery opened fire, and, to the inexperienced soldiers of the Battalion, the bombardment appeared to be terrific. " The bombardment was a fine sight and (it was) difficult to realise that anyone could be alive after it in that particular zone," says the Battalion's War Diary. Actually, it was very thin, but none of the men had any conception at that time of what massed artillery can do. The German reply was slight, and was entirely confined to counter-battery work on that part of the front. In their ignorance, some put this down to the enemy's scarcity of ammunition. This mistaken idea that the enemy was short of shells was not uncommon then. For a long time nothing was learned of the progress of the attack. At length wounded began to arrive, and rumours to spread. Some of these latter were only too true. The attack had failed. It is unnecessary to tell the details of that day as the Battalion never became engaged. It is sufficient to say that British infantry, who lacked nothing in gallantry but had little artillery support, were ineffective in the face of countless German machine guns.

The Battalion remained at its battle stations all day, without receiving any orders. Very few shells fell near its positions and its only casualty was caused by a premature from one of the British guns. There was little for the men to do. Some of them spent their time making tea, which they served out to the wounded who were dribbling down the road in large numbers. Few prisoners were seen. The British artillery continued firing most of the time, but the attack was really at an end, on that part of the front, quite early in the day.

In the evening orders came to carry out the relief which had been postponed the previous night. This proved by far the most uncomfortable part of the day's proceedings. Though everything was quiet both at Croix Blanche and in the front line trenches, the route between was being fairly heavily shelled, and was swept by machine gun fire. It was the Battalion's first experience of heavy fire in the open and it was not enjoyed, particularly when a hitch in the operation caused a somewhat prolonged halt, and three companies were strung out along the road without any cover. But luckily, and much to the surprise of everyone, the relief was carried out without a single casualty to the Battalion. This was the first and only time that a relief was carried out by night in the Fleurbaix Sector.

Though the battle continued, on and off, for many days further to the south, the Battalion was not again seriously affected by it. Occasionally it received rather more than the usual attention from the enemy's artillery, particularly on May 10th, when a large hole was blown in C Company's parapet. It was then that Capt. E. E. Sykes had his first chance of showing that absolute fearlessness and supreme contempt for danger which later became a by-word in the Battalion. In full view of the extremely accurate enemy snipers, who shot two of the men who were helping him, he built up a rough barricade which served until darkness allowed the breech to be properly repaired.

Towards the end of May the Battalion played a small part in a minor operation on the 148th Infantry Brigade Sector. There a new front line trench was in course of construction in No Man's Land by the 4th Battalion King's Own Yorkshire Light Infantry. They worked on it by night, and withdrew by day. One night, on arriving to occupy it, they found the Germans in possession. To assist in ejecting them, Lieut E. Lee, with part of the Battalion Machine Gun Section, was sent up. They did not go into action, for the men of the 148th Infantry Brigade were able to regain the trench without assistance, but a few casualties were suffered by the party from enemy fire.

On May 24th, the Battalion suffered a serious loss. Lieut.-Col. H. S. Atkinson, T.D., who had trained the Battalion in England and brought it out to France, was invalided home. It was a great misfortune and none felt it more than he. His health had been bad for three years, following on a serious operation, but he had stuck very gamely to his work in England, and hoped to be able to see the war through with the Battalion. Had he undergone a proper army medical examination, he would never have been allowed to leave England; but by keeping out of the way of the doctors he had succeeded in getting to

France. Major E. P. Chambers assumed command of the Battalion, with the rank of Lieut.-Colonel.

By the beginning of June, the Battalion had pretty well settled down in its new life. Perhaps the men did not look quite so smart as in Doncaster days, but they had become far more efficient soldiers. Trench routine was no longer a hidden mystery, and enemy bullets had ceased to be novelties. The Battalion had had to pay for its education. Much discomfort was suffered before the men learned to fend for themselves; much work had proved useless owing to the inexperience of the workers. The toll of life had not been heavy, but the graves near Croix Blanche still bear their testimony to the early work of the Battalion in France.

Early in June the Battalion suffered its third officer casualty. Capt. A. L. Mowat, of D Company, was shot in the head while assisting in the construction of a sandbag shelter.

The night before the anniversary of the battle of Waterloo great preparations were made to annoy the enemy. When the sun rose the following morning, it shone on a parapet gay with the flags of Britain, France, Belgium, Russia and Italy. But the result was most disappointing; the Germans did not show the least signs of annoyance. Perhaps they remembered their own part in that battle exactly a century before. So a stuffed dummy was placed on the parapet, and that certainly did tempt their marksmen, who riddled it with bullets. But they ceased fire when the dummy was decorated with an iron cross.

On the night of June 25/26th, the Battalion said good-bye to Fleurbaix and moved to Doulieu. Thence it marched, by easy stages, halting a day or two here and there, to a wood near St. Jans ter Biezen, which was reached about 1-0 a.m. on July 1st.

The Battalion's period of apprenticeship was over, and it was about to learn what real war was in the very worst part of the British line—the Ypres Salient.

CHAPTER III.

YPRES, 1915.

(a) July to October.

THE Battalion was now in the VI. Corps of the Second Army. Several days were spent in the wood near St. Jans ter Biezen and the men never had any cover there, but, fortunately, it was early July and the nights were not cold. No one was allowed outside the wood in daylight except on duty. Some training was carried out, particularly bombing, instruction in which was pushed on as fast as possible; occasionally short route marches were made in the failing light and cool of the evening. But more time was occupied in the inspection of gas helmets than in anything else. Three inspections of these were held daily, by the platoon commander, company commander, and battalion commander respectively; it can easily be imagined how long a time it took the Commanding Officer personally to inspect the helmets of a strong battalion. On July 2nd, the Battalion was inspected by General Sir H. Plumer, who had formerly been G.O.C. Northern Command, and was now commanding the Second Army. The 49th was the first Territorial Division to be detailed for a long spell in the Ypres Salient, and this probably increased General Plumer's interest in it, in addition to the fact that much of its training in England had been carried out under his supervision. Whether there is any truth in the rumour or not, it was always an article of faith in the Battalion that Plumer had a "soft spot in his heart" for the 49th Division. The next day it was again reviewed, this time by Lieut.-General Sir J. Keir, G.O.C. VI. Corps.

The Ypres Salient bore a very evil reputation—not without cause. Reconnaissance of the forward area began soon after the Battalion's arrival at St. Jans ter Biezen, and it was at once obvious that Ypres was a very different proposition from Fleurbaix. The earliest experience of A Company is worth quoting as an indication of what was to be expected. One day Capt. M. P. Andrews, at that time commanding A Company, spent a day in the line with the 2nd Battalion Royal Dublin Fusiliers. There he made the acquaintance of three officers of the company which he was soon to relieve. Thirty-six hours later one of his subalterns visited the same company, only to find that, during the short intervening period, all the three had become casualties—one was dead, a second had been lost on patrol, while the third had been evacuated wounded. This was indeed a rude awakening after the quiet life at Fleurbaix.

At scarcely any period of the war could the neighbourhood of Ypres be called quiet. In the autumn of 1915 the British held only a small bridge-head to the east of the Ypres-Commines Canal. Frequent attempts were made to extend this, and the enemy was just as anxious to drive the British out of the salient altogether. When the Battalion arrived in the area things had barely settled down after the Second Battle of Ypres, in which the enemy had won for himself all the commanding ridges, except Mont Kemmel. Since then minor operations had kept the front lively. One of these took place near Boesinghe only two days before the 49th Division took over the line, and the 148th Infantry Brigade in particular came in for a good share of the "liveliness" which followed it.

On July 7th, the Battalion moved to Canada Wood, near Elverdinghe, where one night was spent. The next evening it relieved the 2nd Battalion Royal Dublin Fusiliers in the Lancashire Farm Sector. In spite of the narrowness of many of the trenches, the relief passed off very quickly. As the Battalion filed in the Dublins filed out, only too glad to hand over their charge to someone else.

The 49th Division now held the extreme left sector of the British line. Its left rested on the Ypres-Commines Canal near Boesinghe, abutting on the French, whose line however was west of the canal. The 6th Division was on the right. The dominating feature of the sector was the Pilkem Ridge; this was entirely in the hands of the enemy, who thus possessed every advantage of high command and superior observation. This sector the 49th Division was destined to hold until the end of December—six months of continuous trench duty in the very worst part of the British line. Reliefs were so arranged that two brigades held the line while the third was back in rest. Thus the Battalion found itself in several different sub-sectors during its stay in the Ypres Salient. On every sector the defence scheme was simplicity itself—the front line was to be held at all costs ; not an inch of ground was to be lost.

During the first tour in the Lancashire Farm Sector A and D Companies held the front line, B Company was in support, and C Company in reserve. One of the main features of the sub-sector, and indeed of the whole divisional front, was the confusing network of old and disused trenches. Many of these had been hastily dug in the heat of battle and afterwards abandoned when they were found to be badly sited. Some, however, were gradually being incorporated in the regular system. The original notes on the sector, which were handed over by the Commanding Officer of the Dublins, have been preserved ; their outstanding feature is the continual reference to " work to be done." He was right. Never did the Battalion find itself harder worked than during the next few months.

The tour was a very anxious one. Away on the left the 148th Infantry Brigade was having a very rough time of it, the enemy making frequent counter-attacks to recover the ground which he had lost a few days before. Not knowing when the enemy's attention might be turned further south, the Battalion had to be very much on the alert. No one slept at night, and two officers per company were always on duty during the day. The men in the front line trenches were fully occupied with sentry duties and working parties, and it was deemed inadvisable for any of them to go away from their positions. Thus, all carrying fell on the reserve company, which had a very hard time of it. Trolley lines were not yet in use, and all rations and R.E. material had to be carried right up to the line from the Canal Bank—a distance of well over a mile. But all ranks worked magnificently.

"This is a very noisy place after Fleurbaix" is the War Diary's comment on the day the line was taken over. It was! Though nothing extraordinary for the Ypres Salient, the enemy artillery activity was a great increase on anything the Battalion had experienced before. Lacrimatory shells were much in evidence and these were, at that time, rather an unknown quantity. The front line, at one spot, was only about seventy yards from the enemy, but this did not procure for it any immunity from shelling. There, too, the Battalion received its first introduction to trench mortars, and it had nothing effective to retaliate with. Machine gun and rifle fire were also severe. As at Fleurbaix, there were many very accurate snipers among the enemy, and these were always on the look-out for targets. So, from one cause or another, the Battalion suffered a number of casualties before its five days' tour was over. The most important of these were Lieut. E. Lee and C.S.M. A. Parkin of B Company. The former was shot through the head while instructing some of his men of the Machine Gun Section how to repair a weak spot in the parapet. He was the first officer of the Battalion to be killed, and his loss was very deeply felt by all who knew what a fine, keen and enthusiastic fellow he was. C.S.M. Parkin had an arm blown off by an enemy shell.

On July 13th, the Battalion was relieved by the 5th Battalion Duke of Wellington's Regiment, and went into Brigade Reserve on the Canal Bank. During the relief part of the area was heavily bombarded with lacrimatory shells. This considerably interfered with the operation, for the teaching at the time was that men should always remain as still as possible when any form of gas was about. Such action was certainly advisable when no better protection than the P. helmet was available, for it was so stuffy that any movement became a torture to the wearer. However, it proved an effective protection against the lacrimatory shells of the period. About this time Major-General T. S. Baldock, C.B., was wounded by shrapnel at Divisional H.Q. Major-General E. M. Perceval, C.B., succeeded to the command of the 49th Division.

During its stay in the Ypres Salient, the Battalion occupied more than one position on the banks of the Ypres-Commines

Capt. M. P. ANDREWS.
(Killed).

Capt. E. E. SYKES, M.C.
(Killed).

Capt. W. F. DENNING.

Capt. T. D. PRATT.

Canal. All were much alike. Officers and men were accommodated in shelters built into the sunken banks. Things were not always any too quiet. The enemy knew perfectly well that considerable numbers of troops lived there, and naturally selected the canal as one of his barrage lines. As a result, strict orders against loitering near certain points were issued, much to the disappointment of some enthusiastic fishermen in the Battalion. The outstanding feature of this, and all other periods of Brigade Reserve—indeed, of every day of the latter months of 1915—was WORK. During the day men ate and slept. At night there was no rest for officer or man. Many were employed on the construction of communication trenches, sometimes only just in rear of the front line. Great efforts were made to get the trench railways into going order and, when this work was completed, the resting battalions had to do a great deal of truck-pushing along them. One of the main difficulties to be contended with was water. Even in July there was a good deal of rain; it had rained while the Battalion was relieving the Dublins—surely an indication of what the future held. Water lay so near the surface that much digging was useless, and all work had to be built up and revetted. Looked at in the light of later experience, it seems a pity that no drainage scheme was instituted at the very beginning. It was obvious that, as soon as the autumn rains began, the trenches must become waterlogged. Yet nothing was done. Perhaps the higher authorities still hoped that an advance would be made ere the wet weather came. Working parties were not free from danger. There was little artillery fire at night, but machine guns were very active, and rifle batteries frequently played on obvious places like the trench tramways. Slowly, but steadily, the Battalion's total of casualties mounted up. Yet, in spite of all, the men worked magnificently. They possessed almost boundless enthusiasm, and were now reaping the benefit of their training near Fleurbaix. Without exception, officers who served with them during this early period show the greatest enthusiasm when they speak of the splendid spirit of the Battalion. The private soldier, of course, had the hardest time of all; but his officers were little better off. In order to obtain continuity of work a Brigade

Field Officer of the week was appointed from one of the battalions in reserve, his duty being to supervise all work. The job was no sinecure. He was as hard-worked as any honest, though grousing, private. And some people called these spells in Brigade Reserve " rest " periods !

After five days on the Canal Bank, the Battalion did a second tour in the Lancashire Farm Sector. Fears that the enemy was about to make an attack on the French postponed the relief for a few hours, but eventually it passed off smoothly. The only event of any interest during this tour was a gas alarm practice. Shell cases and klaxon horns had been plentifully distributed about the line, and one day a highly successful, full-dress rehearsal was held by all companies. It evidently puzzled the enemy, for he put down a protective barrage along the canal. It also puzzled Battalion H.Q., which no one had thought of warning, and numerous terse, though hardly polite, " chits " circulated in consequence. It is worth while to note here that the highly-organised system of reports, which in later days was a perpetual worry to luckless company commanders and adjutants, had not yet developed. If a company commander wanted to send out a patrol he simply sent one ; he never dreamed of informing Battalion H.Q., much less of asking its permission or submitting a report after the event.

On July 24th, the Battalion moved back to the woods near Oosthoek for its first spell in Divisional Reserve. This can hardly be called a " rest " period, except that baths and clean clothing were available. A little training was attempted, but it was seriously interfered with by the large working parties which had to be found. Some of these were employed in the forward area, moving up and returning daily by motor bus. Others were set to work to convert Trois Tours into a defended locality. The men worked well, but perhaps without quite their earlier enthusiasm. The novelty of active service had worn off. They never properly understood the necessity for all their work. Labour companies and coloured units were then unknown ; everything fell upon the hard-worked infantrymen. The following official communication, circulated by 49th Division " G " to Brigades about this time, shows a certain appreciation of the situation on the part of the higher authorities :—

> " If all the troops with all the tools
> Should dig for half a year,
> Do you suppose," our Captain asked,
> " That then we should be clear ? "
> " I doubt it," said the Adjutant,
> Knowing the Brigadier.

It is not often that the General Staff stoops to such frivolity in the transaction of business. But let no mistake be made. The hard conditions under which the men lived were not the fault of dear old General Brereton.

The Battalion returned to the Lancashire Farm Sector on July 30th. Apart from considerable activity on the part of enemy trench mortars, and a good deal of sniping, the tour which followed was an uneventful one. A little patrolling was done, but nothing more important than a dead Frenchman and a few rats was discovered. Further over to the right, however, there was considerable activity. It was during this tour that the Hooge mine went up, and the 14th Division was attacked with flammenwerfer.

To regain the ground thus lost to the enemy, the 6th Division was brought up. They attacked early on the morning of August 9th and carried all their objectives, but suffered heavy casualties in doing so. The 49th Division co-operated in this attack, though only in a passive way. Gaps were cleared in the wire, dummy bridges were laid over the canal, and artillery fired at intervals on the enemy front line, in an endeavour to distract the attention of the Germans from the real objective. The Battalion took no part in these activities, being in reserve on the Canal Bank at the time ; but it suffered some casualties from the enemy barrage. Later in the day, Battalion H.Q. and B and C Companies were ordered up at short notice to relieve a corresponding portion of the 7th Battalion Duke of Wellington's Regt. who were suffering from a sudden outbreak of ptomaine poisoning, which was so severe that about a hundred of them were sent to hospital. Two days later the other two companies of the 7th Battalion were also relieved.

The sector now occupied by the Battalion was called the

Glimpse Cottage Sector, and was held with three companies in the front line and one in support. Two months later it was to be the scene of the Battalion's first serious encounter with the enemy, and so a detailed description of it is held over until then. But the tour in August was also a very active one, and during it the Battalion suffered two serious losses. The first was R.S.M. J. McCormack, who was killed on August 12th. The second was even more serious, and is especially worthy of attention as a conspicuous example of gallantry and self-sacrifice.

Late in the afternoon of August 14th, a dugout in A Company's line was blown in and a number of men were buried amid the wreckage. Capt. M. P. Andrews immediately hurried to the spot and, under heavy artillery and rifle fire, succeeded in extricating the men. Three were found to be dead and three wounded, one so seriously that, unless he could receive proper attention at once, there was little hope of his recovery. The trenches were too narrow for the wounded man to be carried along them on a stretcher. There was nothing for it but to carry him across the open. Capt. Andrews did not hesitate. Getting out on the top himself, he assisted to raise the wounded man, and then set out across the open with the stretcher party. He paid for his devotion with his life. The ground was swept by bullets and, before the party could reach the shelter of a communication trench, he was hit in the head and died almost at once. So perished one of the most gallant gentlemen and conscientious officers who ever served with the Battalion. Word of what had happened was despatched at once to Battalion H.Q., while the stretcher-bearers, true to their duty, remained in the open, trying in vain to stop the flow of blood. Lieut. B. Hughes, R.A.M.C., then Medical Officer to the Battalion, at once hurried up the line. But he was too late. Capt. Andrews was already dead. The event cast a gloom, not only over A Company, but over the whole Battalion.

About this time the Battalion transport was having a very rough passage, and they too soon recognised the difference between Ypres and Fleurbaix. Almost nightly, heavy shelling of the roads used by the ration convoys caused much inconvenience and some loss. On August 14th, in particular, two horses were hit and, for a time, the column was much disorganised. Cpl. E. Ashworth was in charge and, by his own gallantry and coolness under fire, he restored order and confidence, and was able to deliver his charge. For this he was afterwards awarded the Distinguished Conduct Medal.

When next the Battalion went into Brigade Reserve it occupied a number of farms north-east of Brielen. Though not so safe as the shelters on the Canal Bank, these farms were more comfortable, and they did not suffer so much from enemy artillery fire. Work continued as before, a new feature being the erection of "elephant" frames in the Battalion's new billets.

The next two tours in the front line were spent on the extreme left sector—a part of the line which the Battalion was to know only too well in later days, and to which the minds of most "old timers" turn when Ypres in 1915 is mentioned. It bore an ominous reputation. The trenches lay at the north of the Ypres bridge-head, where it flattened out to join the canal. On the extreme left a tiny sap ran out to a point only fifteen yards from the nearest enemy post. Nowhere was No Man's Land more than sixty yards across. There was very little shelling of the front line by either side; the trenches were much too near together for this to be carried on without serious danger of injuring one's own men; but the enemy used many trench mortars, some of which were of the real "minnie" type. There was also an enormous amount of bombing on both sides, for grenades could easily be lobbed from one front line to the other in several places. The trenches were very confusing—a result of the July attack which had taken place just before the 49th Division moved into the line near Ypres—and so narrow that in places a stout man could easily stick fast. Everywhere they were dominated by the enemy's positions.

The French were on the Battalion's left, but their line was on the west side of the canal and thus they were comparatively secure from sudden attack. They proved themselves very helpful and sympathetic neighbours. When they saw that the Battalion was having a bad time from enemy trench mortars they were always only too ready to help. They did not wait to be asked;

they simply cleared all their men, save a skeleton garrison, into deep dugouts or the British support line, and then opened fire on the enemy with every type of infernal engine they had available. It always amused them to see the enemy turn his wrath from the British and start pounding their deserted lines. They were, at this time, much better supplied with trench mortars than the British, not to speak of their 75's.

After two tours in this sector the Battalion went back for its second spell in Divisional Reserve. Casualties had been a good deal heavier than the Battalion had experienced previously, but the men had stuck to their work splendidly, and many instances of gallantry and devotion to duty brighten the otherwise sordid picture. The little sap on the extreme left was the main centre of activity and there trench-mortaring and bombing were almost continuous. It was constantly being damaged, and as frequently repaired; on one occasion a heavy trench mortar dropped right into it, causing six casualties. How near it was to the Germans is shown by the fact that, on August 26th, they were able to throw the following message from their lines into it:—

"Dear Tommy,—Brest Litovsk fallen to-day. Rippelin, Lieut."

An hour or two after the arrival of this message loud cheering was heard in the enemy lines, presumably rejoicing at the news. During this tour Sec.-Lieut. W. L. Anderton was shot through the head and died almost immediately.

On August 26th, the Battalion moved back to the woods near Coppernollehoek for twelve days' rest. A little more training was done this time, but large working parties were still the order of the day. Endeavours were made to smarten up the men; among other things the cleaning of buttons was instituted for the first time since the Battalion had left England. A somewhat novel duty was the rounding up of spies in the neighbourhood of Proven; this was entrusted to Capt. E. E. Sykes, with a party of forty-five other ranks. He was away for thirty-six hours, but no record has been preserved of what success, if any, he had. While near Coppernollehoek the Battalion was again inspected by General Plumer, who was accompanied by the Earl of Scarborough and Brigadier-General Mends. Probably the G.O.C., Second Army, noticed a change in the men whom he had reviewed about two months before ; they were no longer light-hearted and cheery novices, but fully-blooded and hard-bitten veterans. A short time in the Ypres Salient had worked wonders. A sad loss to the Battalion about this time was Sergt. D. H. Fenton, who was accidentally killed by a bomb on the very day his commission was announced.

When the Battalion again returned to the line it took over the Turco Farm Sector, on the extreme right, abutting on the 6th Division. This was the best and quietest sector on the divisional front. In places No Man's Land was several hundreds of yards across. Of course there was plenty of work to be done, but the trenches were, on the whole, good. After a quiet tour the Battalion came out to a new position on the Canal Bank. Here there was little shelling and the opportunity was seized to hold some swimming sports ; D Company won the inter-company team race. During this period in Brigade Reserve, Lieut.-Colonel E. J. Pickering, formerly Brigade Major of the 148th Infantry Brigade, arrived to take command of the Battalion.

On September 21st, the Battalion returned to the Turco Farm Sector. The tour which followed is chiefly noteworthy for the events of September 25th—the day on which the battle of Loos began. No very serious operation was planned for the Ypres front, but a demonstration was arranged in the hope of distracting the enemy's attention and drawing his reserves northwards. The 6th Division was to attack on the right and capture Bellewaarde Farm and Lake. At the same time the British artillery was to cut gaps in the German wire opposite the 4th Battalion, while a smoke screen was to be put up on both its flanks. It was hoped that this demonstration would cause the enemy to evacuate his front line, in which case the Battalion was to advance and seize the unoccupied trenches. At 4-30 a.m. the bombardment and smoke screen began. The enemy retaliation was quick and heavy. Shells rained down on the front line and the communication trenches ; machine gun and rifle fire swept the ground. It was soon obvious that the Germans had no intention of evacuating any part of their trenches, and so no advance was attempted on the front of the 49th Division. By 7-30 a.m. the artillery fire on both sides had practically ceased. So far as the Battalion was concerned, the only results of the day were a number of casualties and much damage to the lines from the enemy bombardment.

The last days of September were spent at Elverdinghe, where Battalion H.Q. occupied the Chateau and officers and men were accommodated in tents in the grounds. Early in October a move was made to a camp by the Poperinghe-Woesten Road, where another period, very similar to the previous ones, was spent in Divisional Reserve. The Battalion had now been about three months in the Ypres Salient. During that time, in addition to the normal wastage through sickness, 120 casualties had been incurred in action. But far worse was in store. Before, however, entering on an account of the events of October 16th, and of the terrible wet months which culminated in the gas attack of December 19th, there are one or two points which deserve fuller treatment than they have yet received.

The high proficiency of the enemy in sniping has already been mentioned on more than one occasion. Gradually the Battalion came to realise that the most effective way of dealing with this form of annoyance was to adopt similar tactics. Luckily, the very man was to hand—Sergt. A. McNulty. A combination of all the qualities needed by a first-class sniper is rarely to be found in one individual; but this N.C.O. possessed them all to an exceptional degree. A magnificent rifle shot and a first-class observer, he had the patience of a Job, and was also an exceptionally good instructor. Before long there was little that he did not know about marksmanship, telescopic sights, the building of snipers' posts, and observation. He constructed his own posts and waited in them patiently, hour after hour, for suitable targets. How many Germans he had to his credit, no one ever knew; it is more than doubtful whether he knew himself. But certain it is that the enemy had good reason to curse that Winchester of his, and he did much to counteract the hostile sniping which was menacing the Battalion so much. For a time he was taken away to be an instructor at the newly-formed Divisional Technical School, where his energies were not restricted to sniping. Among other things, he was one of the very few men who mastered the intricacies of that awful invention—the West Spring Gun. The Battalion had much to thank Sergt. McNulty for and, later in the war, when he went to America as an instructor—how the Americans ever understood his accent was beyond the Battalion—he was greatly missed.

Another feature of the period was the appearance of trench mortars. Almost from the very beginning of trench warfare the Germans had made use of these weapons and, so effective did they prove, that the British soon tried to imitate them. Their first attempts were very crude. The earliest trench mortars to appear in the line had, apparently, been dragged from the obscurity of some museum, and, needless to say, were not to be compared with the "minnie." The two-inch trench mortar followed, firing its weird, round cannon-ball—affectionately known as a "plum-pudding"—on the end of a rod. Stokes guns were unknown at that early period.

(b) October 16th.

On October 14th, the Battalion relieved the 1/5th Battalion West Yorkshire Regiment in the Glimpse Cottage Sector, C Company going in on the right, A Company in the centre, and D Company on the left; B Company was in support. The main feature of the sector was a sharp salient in the enemy line, opposite the centre company front. From this salient an old communication trench—a relic of the days when both front lines had been part of the same system—crossed No Man's Land to the British line. Both sides had established bombing blocks in this trench, and the locality was the main centre of activity on the front. Owing to folds in the ground, it was impossible to cover the sap-head by rifle fire; but machine guns fired into the dead ground and some two-inch trench mortars, in emplacements near by, helped to protect it. The sap-head itself was held by a squad of battalion bombers. It often received attention from enemy trench mortars.

The story goes that, a few days before the Battalion took over the sector, the enemy had started shelling the sap-head and the adjacent front line, and most of the garrison had withdrawn into the supervision trench, which ran about thirty yards in rear. Only a weak party had been left in the sap. The bombardment had been followed by a small daylight raid to secure a noticeboard which had been hung out to announce some allied success. Whether there was any truth in the story cannot now be said.

The first two days of the tour were comparatively quiet. About 1-30 p.m. on October 16th, the enemy opened an intense artillery and trench mortar bombardment on the greater part of the Battalion area. It was soon apparent that something unusual was happening. Trench mortars were raining down near the sap-head, 5.9's were whistling overhead and bursting in the supervision trench, shrapnel and high explosive were falling on practically the whole area, as far back as Battalion H.Q. Stand to was ordered at once. Two platoons of B Company were moved up into close support, and were employed carrying up bombs and ammunition. The garrison of the sap, on which point it was obvious that much of the enemy's attention was directed, was reinforced. The men crouched down under their parapets—strict orders had been issued that there was to be no firing until the word was given—and waited for the enemy's next move.

The situation was not a pleasant one. It is true that the majority of the shells were bursting behind the front line, but there were sufficient " shorts " to make things very uncomfortable. The wire was torn to shreds, parapets were breached, and many casualties were suffered, particularly by the two flank companies. It was the first time that the Battalion had had to stand a really heavy bombardment in the front line, and they came through it splendidly. For three hours they waited, while the shells crashed around them, longing for the moment when the enemy would appear and they would have the chance to " get a bit of their own back." About 4-30 p.m. their opportunity came. A party of Germans, clad in fatigue dress, emerged from the trenches opposite and began calmly to cut a passage through their own wire, near the sap-head. This was too much for A Company. Perhaps it would have been better had fire been withheld a little longer, until an actual attack came. But no one thought of that at the time. Tired of his long inactivity under heavy shelling, every man was at once on the fire step working his bolt for all he was worth. Shells were still bursting all around, but none paid attention to them. There was the enemy in the open; nothing else mattered. And the wire-cutting part of the operation came to an abrupt conclusion.

By this time, the sap-head had been blown in by a well-directed shell. But the garrison, with whom the indefatigable company commander, Major R. E. Sugden, spent most of his time that day, simply extricated themselves from the debris and set to work to construct a fresh bombing block. Shortly after, the enemy made his next move. A party of Germans, about twenty in number, wearing bombing aprons filled with stick grenades, crawled up in the folds of the ground and began to bomb the sap-head. A brisk encounter ensued. Most of the German grenades fell short and the British proved that they could easily out-throw the enemy. With the assistance of a Maxim gun the attack was driven off with comparative ease, as were two further attacks of a similar character. About the time that the third was made, another party of the enemy was seen moving along a hedge row in the direction of the British line. Fortunately this move was detected early by the crew of a machine gun, which soon drove them to cover. All this time the bombardment continued.

About 6-0 p.m. the enemy apparently saw that success was impossible, and gradually the shelling died down. The Battalion was then able to review the situation and to count its casualties. These latter were heavy enough. Sec.-Lieut. E. Taylor, C.S.M. V. S. Tolley and twelve other ranks were killed, or died shortly after of wounds; Lieut. E. N. Marshall, Sec.-Lieut. F. A. Innes and twenty-two other ranks were wounded. Much damage had been done to the sap-head and to other parts of the line. The night which followed passed quietly, but there was much work to be done. To assist in this the 5th Battalion Duke of Wellington's Regt. sent up a large working party, and also provided a number of stretcher-bearers to remove the wounded and the dead.

Compared with many later events in the history of the Battalion, this episode is of very minor importance. But, at the time, its importance loomed large in the eyes of all. It was the Battalion's first real fight. After several months of passive warfare, the men had at length come face to face with the enemy in active operations. Nothing is harder than to maintain one's morale when inactive under a heavy bombardment. But this the men had succeeded in doing. Three hours of intense shelling had only served to make them the more eager when their chance came. All ranks came through the ordeal with the greatest credit, and the hearty congratulations which were received from Brigade and Division were thoroughly deserved. For their gallant services on this occasion Sec.-Lieut. F. A. Innes—it was his first trench tour as he had only recently joined the Battalion—received the Military Cross, and Lance-Cpl. T. H. Clarke and Cpl. C. Landale were both awarded Distinguished Conduct Medals. Lance-Cpl. Clarke had been the N.C.O. in charge of the bombers in the sap-head, and had behaved with the greatest gallantry throughout the day. Cpl. C. Landale had worked untiringly on the telephone wires during the bombardment, and it was mainly due to him that communication between the front line and Battalion H.Q. was scarcely ever interrupted.

The object of the enemy in making this attack was never understood. Perhaps he expected the intensity of his bombardment would induce the Battalion to vacate its front line, and he would be able to occupy it with comparative ease. If the story of his daylight raid, a few days before, had any truth in it, he knew that the front line had been practically evacuated on that occasion, and may have expected similar tactics again. Certainly his heaviest shelling fell on the supervision trench. But, whatever his object, he found the Battalion alert and only too ready to meet him.

The next few days were very fully occupied in repairing the damage done by the enemy's shells. So well was this work carried out that, at the end of the tour, the Battalion was able to hand over the line in as good a condition as it had been before October 16th. On the night of October 19/20th Lieut.-Col. E. J. Pickering was wounded. He had gone up with Major

Lieut.-Col. G. K. SULLIVAN, O.B.E., M.C.

Lieut.-Col. C. J. PICKERING, C.M.G., D.S.O.

To Face Page 44.

OCTOBER 16TH

Sugden to inspect the wire, which had been put out by D Company. The enemy was only about 150 yards away at that point and evidently saw the party. They opened fire and the Commanding Officer was severely wounded in the right arm. He had only been with the Battalion about a month, but during that time he had done a lot to smarten it and he left a lasting impression on all ranks who served under him.

On October 21st, after a heavy trench-mortaring which destroyed several dugouts, the Battalion was relieved by the 1/4th Battalion King's Own Yorkshire Light Infantry, and went back to the Canal Bank.

(c) The Wet Months.

Towards the end of October His Majesty the King visited Abeele, and there reviewed representatives of all the Divisions of the VI. Corps. To this review the Battalion sent a contingent* of twenty-five other ranks, under the command of Lieut. E. N. Marshall. Needless to say they were a carefully picked body of men, and it is worthy of note that the detachment from the 49th Division was specially commended by His Majesty for its smart turn-out that day.

At the end of the month the weather completely broke up and heavy rain became normal. The Battalion was in comparative comfort on the Canal Bank, but ominous reports soon began to come in from the units holding the line. Bad as these reports were, they were mild compared with the actual conditions under which the men were to exist for the next two months. On October 30th the Battalion relieved the 7th Battalion Duke

---

*The names of the men who made up this party, representing as they did the pick of the "original" Battalion, are worth recording. They were:—
Lieut. E. N. Marshall.
A Company: C.S.M. Walsh, Sergts. Stirzaker and Green, Cpl. Harrison, Lance-Cpl. Payne, Pte. Pamment.
B Company: C.S.M. Lee, Lance-Cpl. Brown, Ptes. Brown, Helliwell, Whiteley and Harkness.
C Company: C.S.M. Greenwood, Sergts. Flather, Robertshaw and Moran, Cpls. Hoyle and Barraclough.
D Company: C.S.M. Sherwood, Lance-Cpls. Asquith and Walsh, Ptes. Sykes, Bentley and Braithwaite.
Transport: Sergt. Crossley.

of Wellington's Regt. in the extreme left sector ; and then began for it such a period of hardship and misery as it has never since been called upon to endure for so long a time.

In one way the telling of this part of the Battalion's history is comparatively easy. During the earlier part of its stay in the Ypres Salient it had seldom done more than two tours in the same sector. But from the end of October, until it was finally relieved in December, the Battalion held no sector of the line except the extreme left ; and, in every way, that sector was the worst on the divisional front. Its proximity to the opposing trenches, and the commanding position occupied by the Germans, have already been described. The trenches lay very little above the water level of the Ypres-Commines Canal and, as soon as the rains began, they naturally received much of the drainage from the Pilkem Ridge. They were badly sited and badly constructed. Consisting mainly of sandbag breastworks, they were the worst possible type to inhabit in wet weather. They had been considered the worst on the front during the fine weather ; words cannot adequately describe what they became early in November.

When the Battalion took over the sector on October 30th the trenches were already in an appalling condition. The front line was in places more than two feet deep in semi-liquid mud, and parts of it were entirely isolated from neighbouring posts, except by cross-country routes ; stretches of the communication trenches were waist deep in water. And this was the result of only about two days of steady rain ! For the next two months the conditions gradually became worse and worse ; occasional short frosts gave a little temporary relief, but the thaws which followed them only made the trenches more awful than before. Thoroughly undermined by water, the revetments bulged and caved in, literally before the eyes of the men. In a few days, hundreds of yards of trenches had become nothing but cavities filled with mud and water. The shelters of the sector had never been protection against anything but bullets and the weather. They ceased to be even that now. Water from the trenches overflowed into them and flooded the floors, their supports were undermined, and one by one they collapsed, often causing casualties to the men who occupied them, until scarcely a habitable one remained near the front line. The enemy made full use of his higher position. Pumping the water out of his own line, he allowed it to flow across No Man's Land into the British line. Often the water was so deep in the trenches that thigh-boots became useless. Had there been a well-planned system of drainage, something might have been done. But it was only the coming of the rain that opened the eyes of the authorities to the condition of the sector, and the drainage scheme which was then started was never far enough advanced to be of much use while the 49th Division was there. What was to be done with the water ? Most of it had to stop where it was. Occasionally it was possible to divert a little of it elsewhere—in some cases, it is feared, into other people's lines. Only in one small trench on the extreme left could it be turned back into the enemy lines, and, in order to effect that desirable operation, the whole had to flow right along the British front line first.

The utter collapse, and consequent evacuation, of long stretches of the line considerably altered the method of holding it. Many of the posts were completely cut off from one another, except by movement across the open. Such movement was extremely hazardous by day, for the enemy snipers and machine gunners were only too ready to take advantage of the many opportunities which the new state of affairs gave them. With parapets sliding in and trenches filling, it was soon impossible for a man to move about in daylight without exposing himself. By night there was an additional danger. It required a man, with a very good sense of direction, to move over that area of water-logged and derelict trenches without losing his way. The case of Pte. T. Atkinson—the first prisoner the enemy secured from the Battalion—was a good illustration of this. In company with another man, he had successfully delivered rations to an isolated front line post, but, on the way back, the two disagreed about the direction of their own lines and separated, each going his own way. The other man rejoined his platoon in safety ; Pte. Atkinson, apparently, walked straight across No Man's Land into the arms of the enemy.

The greatest hardships were suffered by men who were wounded in the front line. If a man had the misfortune to be hit early in the day he could seldom be got away until after dark; often in great pain, and always under the most miserable conditions, he would have to wait for many hours before he could receive proper attention. Even when dusk came his lot was a most unenviable one. The journey to the Canal Bank often took two or three hours, and there was a good chance that he might be hit again before he arrived at the Aid Post, for machine gun fire swept the ground intermittently all night.

One important result of the new conditions was a great increase in patrolling. Now that large portions of the line were entirely deserted and posts were isolated from one another, this was very necessary, for at night the enemy could enter the trenches unseen almost as easily as the British could leave them. Most of this patrolling was purely defensive, but occasionally useful reconnaissances were made, one of which will be described in detail later. There was little opportunity for the men to show an offensive spirit. A little bombing was indulged in, but soon the general policy became one of "live and let live." Had the enemy attempted an infantry advance the defence must have placed its main reliance on the bayonet; in that waste of mud rifles could not be kept properly clean, and few would have fired more than two or three rounds rapid.

Each company held a section of the front line, with two platoons in front and two in support. Usually these platoons inter-relieved every forty-eight hours, but towards the end of the time reliefs were sometimes carried out every twenty-four hours. The Battalion spent four days in the line and four in brigade reserve; these latter periods were sometimes passed on the Canal Bank and sometimes in the farm houses further back. While in brigade reserve every available man was kept hard at work in the forward area either on the new drainage scheme, or trying to clear some of the mud and water from the communication trenches. Only twice during the wet weather did the 147th Infantry Brigade have a spell in divisional reserve, and even then there was not much comfort. The prevailing bad weather had its effect on the back area camps and they were soon deep in mud. Much work was done to improve them. Early

THE WET MONTHS

in November a number of wattle and mud huts were put up in place of some of the tents; some wooden huts were also in course of erection. When the Battalion came back to the same camp at the end of the month they found things more comfortable, for the work had been continued and accommodation improved. But, at the best, it was a poor form of rest for men who had just spent sixteen days in the forward area, and were looking forward to another spell of the same kind.

Everything possible was done for the men's comfort, but, at first, the available supplies of suitable stores were quite inadequate. Until the wet weather began, no one seems to have dreamed of the conditions which would prevail during the winter. At the beginning of November thigh-boots were almost non-existent, though, later, sufficient were available to equip every man. However, the communication trenches were so bad that frequently men lost their boots on the way up to the line. It was no uncommon thing for a man to stick so fast in the mud that he had to be dragged out by his companions, often leaving his boots behind. He would then have to complete his journey in his socks; sometimes he might find a spare pair of boots when he arrived in the front line. Dry socks were always available for men in support, but they could seldom be supplied to men in the front line. Foot grease was provided and periodical foot-rubbing ordered; but how could the men obey the order? Seldom could a man in the line find a dry spot to sit down on while he removed his boots. The result was soon apparent in the enormous number of trench feet which developed; during November, 1915, no less than 146 other ranks were sent to hospital for this cause alone. Sheep-skin coats were provided and proved a great boon. There was plenty of rum—more than during any subsequent winter. Every effort was made to provide hot food and drink, but the difficulties of getting it to the companies before it was cold were almost insuperable. Any attempt to light a fire was bound to draw the attention of the hostile artillery or trench mortars, and so only "Tommy's Cookers" could be used.

Such were the conditions under which the Battalion held the line in the November and December of 1915. For utter misery they have only been equalled once—on the Passchendaele Ridge in December, 1917—and then for a much shorter period. A man had a ghastly prospect in front of him when his turn came to form part of a front line garrison for forty-eight hours. For all that time he would be thoroughly soaked and terribly cold; his boots would be full of water, he would stand in water and mud; physical pain, mental weariness and bodily fatigue would be his constant burden. The chances were that he would not complete his tour of duty—that before his time was up he would succumb to the enemy snipers, or be on his way to hospital, a physical wreck. One example is sufficient to show what appalling casualties were suffered during this period. About the beginning of December, an officer of the Battalion took up twenty-four other ranks for a forty-eight hour tour of duty in the front line. At the end of that time he brought out with him one signaller and three other ranks. Every other man had become a casualty.

But what of the spirit of the men of the Battalion during this time ? How did they bear their hardships ? Many writers have paid tribute to the gallantry of British troops in battle, but few have written of the heroism of those who held the line under such conditions as the 4th Battalion did in the autumn of 1915. The soldier in battle has excitement, and a good deal of exhilaration, to help him through; but the Yorkshiremen who faced the enemy near Boesinghe in 1915 had neither of these. Theirs was heroism of a far higher order—the heroism which, with no excitement to buoy them up, can make men coolly and quietly face horror and death in their worst forms. Such men as Kipling must have been thinking of when he wrote,

"If you can force your heart and nerve and sinew
  To serve your turn long after they are gone,
And so hold on when there is nothing in you
  Except the will which says to them 'Hold on'."

They were MEN, were those of the 4th Battalion, who held the line in 1915. Men of the quiet, tight-lipped and dogged type, who talked little, though occasional flashes of humour brighten even this ghastly picture, but simply obeyed orders without question and held on. Perhaps their feelings can best be expressed by quoting the remark of one of them, when on short leave from that hell. " Well, sir, we either have to laugh or cry, and we prefer to laugh."

Few specific events of this period need be recorded. On November 9th Lieut.-Col. G. K. Sullivan, formerly Adjutant of the 1/5th Batt. King's Own Yorkshire Light Infantry, assumed command of the Battalion. His stay was a very brief one. Eleven days after his arrival he was wounded by a shell splinter on the Canal Bank. As Major E. P. Chambers had been sent to hospital with a sprained ankle the previous day, Major R. E. Sugden assumed command of the Battalion until the arrival of Lieut.-Col. E. G. St. Aubyn. The latter had been second in command of a battalion of the King's Royal Rifle Corps in the 14th Division. Though always in weak health, he retained command of the Battalion for nearly a year. He was a very quiet, but exceptionally competent, Commanding Officer, who earned the respect of all, and the most sincere affection of those who knew him best.

On the night of December 11/12th, Sec.-Lieut. W. N. Everitt, with Sergt. Kitchen, carried out an extremely daring and highly successful patrol. The glow of a light had been noticed at a particular point in the enemy line, and they made straight towards it. No Man's Land was not more than sixty yards across but it was no mean obstacle, owing to its water-logged condition. The enemy wire was very thick and difficult to negotiate but, after much trouble, the two found themselves at the foot of the enemy parapet. Leaving his companion at the bottom, Everitt carefully crawled up the parapet and looked into the enemy trench. He found it to be deeper, better revetted and much drier than the British trenches were. Slowly he moved along the parapet, examining the trench at different points. At length he reached the place where the glow had been observed and suddenly found himself looking into the corner of a bay, almost exactly at the point where an enemy sentry was standing. As he looked the German raised his rifle, and Everitt slid gently down the parapet. He had not been observed, but the chance shot of the sentry passed only just over his head. He had now seen all he could. The light was explained ; it came from a brazier which evidently warmed a shelter hollowed out of the traverse near which the sentry was posted. Two or three Germans were warming themselves round it. There was nothing more the patrol could do. With a thick wire obstacle behind and only one man to support him, it would have been suicidal for Everitt to attempt anything against the enemy post. Besides, his orders were to make a reconnaissance, and the information he had gained would be useless if he did not return to report it. So, regretfully, he turned his back on the enemy, and succeeded in reaching his own line without being discovered. This patrol caused a good deal of stir in the Brigade, for no previous patrol had got so far. It had obtained very valuable information about the condition of the enemy trenches, and had proved that the Germans were very much on the alert. All agreed that the Military Cross, which Sec.-Lieut. W. N. Everitt afterwards received for his work that night, was thoroughly well earned.

On December 12th Major R. E. Sugden was severely wounded in the arm by a bullet. The bridges over the Canal were always dangerous spots. Not only were they well marked by the enemy artillery, but machine guns, posted further to the north, could fire straight down the Canal in enfilade. It was while he was crossing one of these bridges that Major Sugden was hit. He had served continuously with the Battalion since it had been mobilised and his loss was greatly felt.

(d) December 19th.

The enemy first made use of poison gas in the spring of 1915, about the time the Battalion landed in France. On that occasion he employed pure chlorine, but in so weak a concentration that the results were not nearly so disastrous as they might have been. After this first trial—it was probably more an experiment than anything else—he made no use of gas on a large scale for several months. This was fortunate, for it gave allied scientists time to study the whole problem and to devise means of protection, not only against chlorine, but against other harmful gases also. It is true that anti-gas measures were far from perfect at the end of 1915. But the allied armies were better prepared for that form of attack than they would have been had they had no preliminary warning. In particular, the possibility of the enemy using phosgene had been guarded against by the introduction of the P.H. helmet. This was a considerable advance; its two stout glass eye-pieces were a great improvement on the single mica window of the P. helmet, and the outlet valve made it much less stuffy and more comfortable to wear.

There is no doubt that, about the beginning of December, some rumour that the enemy was soon to try a second gas attack on the Ypres Salient had filtered through to the British. One of the reasons for the patrol of Sec.-Lieut. W. N. Everitt, already described, was to discover whether any gas cylinders were in position in the enemy lines. New P.H. helmets had been issued to all the men in the Battalion, but, as the available supply only admitted of one per man, a P. helmet was still carried as a reserve. Much gas helmet drill had been done, and all ranks were warned to be specially on the alert.

On December 17th, the Battalion relieved the 6th Battalion Duke of Wellington's Regt. in the extreme left sector. All knew that this was to be their last tour in the line for the time being and that, on relief, they were to go back for a long period of rest. At night patrols were very active on the Battalion front, on the look-out for indications of the presence of gas cylinders. They reported much hammering in the enemy lines and, on the night of December 18/19th, a great deal of coughing. A raid was contemplated, but that never came off. Much work was in progress, for attempts were being made to put the trenches into better condition for the relieving unit. Working parties from the 6th Division, which was then in Corps Reserve, came up nightly to assist; and the Battalion was also engaged in putting out a great deal of wire on its front.

A special artillery "shoot" had been arranged for the early morning of December 18th. This, it was hoped, would not only damage the enemy trenches, but would also destroy any gas cylinders which were in position for an offensive. As the opposing trenches were so near together, the enemy front line could not be bombarded without grave risk to the British themselves.

Hence, it was arranged that the Battalion should evacuate its front line at 5-0 a.m. and not re-occupy it until the next night. This was done, but the bombardment did not come off as the morning was too misty for satisfactory observation. So similar arrangements were made for the next day.

The night of December 18/19th was comparatively quiet. It was bright and clear, with a gentle breeze blowing from the north-east—in every way ideal weather for an enemy gas discharge. About 5-0 a.m. on the morning of December 19th all front line platoons, except those of A Company, began to withdraw according to plan. Many had actually reached their positions for the day when, at 5-30 a.m., flares suddenly shot up all along the enemy lines. Whether they were red or green is a matter for dispute among those who saw them; but the point is not important. They were evidently a signal for the attack to begin. Immediately, what is described by survivors as a "sizzing" noise was heard, a greenish-white cloud appeared over the enemy parapet and began to drift towards the British lines, and a terrific bombardment with artillery and trench mortars was opened on the Canal, the British communication trenches and reserve positions. Within a few minutes every bridge, except one, was shattered, great damage had been done to the trenches, and every telephone line was broken. And over all drifted that deadly cloud.

Many men were caught in their shelters and gassed before they could be alarmed. Others were caught on their way back from the line and suffered terribly. A Company just managed to get the one word " gas " over the 'phone before the line to Battalion H.Q. broke. But soon gongs and horns were crashing out their warning, while men frenziedly adjusted their helmets, seized their arms, and rushed to their battle positions. There was hurry and confusion almost everywhere, but panic nowhere. Indeed, that day there was not a single case of straggling in the 49th Division.

Fortunately, the British artillerymen were thoroughly on the alert. They were standing to their guns ready for the pre-arranged shoot and, probably for the first time in their experience, they had more shells than they could fire. They saw the S.O.S., they heard the alarms, and soon they themselves were surrounded by the gas. With helmets on they worked their guns as they had never had the chance of working them before. The storm of projectiles which descended on the German lines must have taught the enemy that his age of artillery predominance was near its end. Warning had been sent to the 6th Battalion Duke of Wellington's Regiment, which was in Brigade Reserve, and before long it appeared, moving up across the open. The enemy saw it too and put down a barrage in its way. But the men came forward splendidly and were soon manning their battle stations on the west bank of the canal.

Meanwhile, the Battalion was bearing the full force both of the gas and of the enemy bombardment. The men who had been warned in time were unharmed by the gas, for the P.H. helmet proved a very effective protection. But many men had been gassed before they could do anything, and among them the sights were ghastly. They lay in agony on the ground, sickly greenish-white in colour ; they foamed at the mouth and gasped for breath ; some even tore open their own throats in the paroxysms of their pain. None who saw these sights can ever forget them, and none will ever forgive the enemy who first made use of such fiendish means of destruction. Among them moved Capt. S. S. Greaves, the Battalion Medical Officer ; none worked more devotedly that day than he, and many a man owed his life to him.

Several distinct discharges of gas were made. They seemed to come about once every twenty minutes. Probably the enemy hoped that some men, thinking all was over, would have removed their helmets. About 7-0 a.m. the attack ended, but the air was not clear enough for helmets to be removed with safety until half-an-hour later. Indeed, in some parts of the trenches, the gas lay about the whole day and all through the next night. Intermittent enemy shelling continued all day and the British fire did not slacken for hours. After their terrible ordeal of the early morning all the men were very " jumpy," and false alarms were frequent. But no more attacks came on the front of the 49th Division, though a fresh discharge was made against the French further north, about 9-0 a.m.

Some account must now be given of A Company, which was

holding the extreme left of the Battalion sector. Two platoons were in the front line—in F34 and F35 respectively, as the trenches were commonly called—one platoon near Company H.Q., and a fourth in dugouts on the west side of the canal. Sec.-Lieut. W. N. Everitt was in command in F34 and Sergt. A. Stirzaker in F35, each isolated from the other and from Company H.Q. except by highly dangerous routes across the open. Like the other front line troops they were to have withdrawn in the early morning, but, as they had not so far to go, they had not moved off so soon. Hence, they were still in their positions when the gas discharge started, and helmets were adjusted so promptly that not a man was gassed. It was obvious at once that their duty was to remain in and defend the front line, and this each of the commanders decided to do. Everitt succeeded in getting a message over the 'phone to Company H.Q. just before the line was broken; he then stood to with his men and opened rapid fire until their rifles were red hot. Sergt. Stirzaker kept his men carefully in hand and allowed no firing; his numbers were very small and he feared that, by opening fire, he would only be giving away this fact to the enemy. Everitt's message and the gas arrived at Company H.Q. almost simultaneously, and many of the support platoon were gassed before any warning could be given. Lieut. E. N. Marshall immediately collected every available man and set off with them to reinforce the garrison of the front line. Half he sent across to F34, but most of these became casualties before they reached the comparative safety of that position; the remainder he led himself up to F35. Then followed a weary period of waiting. Harassed by enemy fire and surrounded by gas, in almost complete ignorance of the situation but expecting an enemy attack at any moment, they hung on.

It was long before they had any news from outside. At length Lieut. Marshall decided to send a messenger to Battalion H.Q. The way lay across ground which was swept by machine gun fire; only one bridge was left over the canal and that was being heavily shelled. It required no mean courage to volunteer for such a mission. Just then Pte. W. Bancroft crawled into F35 with a report from Sec.-Lieut. W. N. Everitt. This man knew well the dangers of the journey for he had been with Sec.-Lieut. W. E. Hinton, when the latter had been wounded on that very ground only a few days before. Yet, as soon as he heard what was wanted, he offered to take the message. He reached Battalion H.Q. unhurt, delivered his message, and supplemented it with a very clear report of his own. He then returned to Lieut. Marshall with a cheery message from the Commanding Officer, and afterwards crawled back to his post in F34. Few Distinguished Conduct Medals have been better earned than the one he received for his gallantry on this occasion.

The day came to an end at length and, with the darkness, came relief. The 6th Battalion Duke of Wellington's Regt. had volunteered to take over A Company's front, so that the latter might spend a night in comparative peace near Battalion H.Q. The relieving troops were not equipped for a tour in such a line; they had come up that morning in fighting order, and they had no thigh boots. Nevertheless, they carried out the relief. The following night the rest of the Battalion was relieved, and the whole moved back to near Elverdinghe.

On December 19th the enemy made practically no attempt to follow up his gas discharge and bombardment by an infantry attack. Small patrols were reported at one or two points further to the south, but no German infantry was seen on the Battalion front. Probably, the heavy barrage put down by the British artillery, and the resolute front shown by the few men of A Company deterred the enemy from making an attack. The gas he used that day was a mixture of chlorine and phosgene— far more deadly than the plain chlorine of his earlier attack.

The casualties suffered by the Battalion on December 19th were very heavy, particularly when it is remembered how low its fighting strength was at the time. The majority were due to gas, but the bombardment also claimed many victims. Sec.-Lieuts. J. A. Hartley and F. W. O. Fleming, R.S.M. C. C. MacKay and thirty-seven other ranks were killed, or died within the next few days. Lieut. E. N. Marshall, C.S.M. E. Walsh and about forty other ranks were wounded, or suffering severely from gas poisoning. It was a fitting climax to the ghastly months which had preceded it.

The cool courage and the steadiness of the 49th Division on December 19th were fully appreciated by all who knew what the men had had to endure. Congratulations from the higher authorities soon began to flow in. "The coolness of the troops saved the Army from a disaster," wrote the G.O.C. VI. Corps. A few days later he expressed himself again, in no uncertain terms, in a private letter to the Divisional Commander :—

"My dear Perceval,

Although I have already expressed to you and to your Brigade Commanders the admiration I feel for the gallant stand made by those under their command against the recent German gas attack, I should like to place on record how very highly I value the services rendered by all ranks. I do not think that the importance of their success can be over-estimated. It has re-established a complete confidence in our power of defence which had been severely shaken by the German gas success gained in the Spring, a confidence which however had never deserted the 6th Corps.

Yours very sincerely,

J. L. Keir."

The Battalion may justly claim a considerable share of this praise.

And so the Battalion's first stay in the Ypres Salient came to an end. It had arrived at the beginning of July, inexperienced and practically unknown. It left towards the end of December with a magnificent reputation. But it had paid the price. There, in the vicinity of Ypres, the original Battalion, which had mobilised, trained, and gone out to fight, was disbanded. Its men were scattered in a dozen cemeteries and scores of hospitals.

CHAPTER IV.

JANUARY TO JUNE, 1916.

The earlier half of 1916 is the least eventful period of the Battalion's history. The months in the Ypres Salient had reduced its strength to a very low figure, and reinforcements arrived very slowly, until just before the Battle of the Somme. From January to June there is not one dramatic incident to record. With the exception of one tour in the trenches near Authuille, the Battalion never went into the line. Instead, it was employed mainly on various forms of pioneer work which, though very useful in themselves, are of little interest now.

When the Battalion was finally withdrawn from the Ypres front on December 20th, 1915, it moved back to Elverdinghe Chateau for a few days. There Christmas was spent. Everything possible was done to make the occasion a successful one. Plenty of money was forthcoming and supplies were obtained from Poperinghe—then a much better place for shopping than in later years. Tables, with calico for table-cloths, were set up in the canteen hut, and dinner was served in three sittings. Everything went off splendidly. Plates and glass had been borrowed in Poperinghe, and these were much appreciated by the men, few of whom had had a meal for many months, except from a mess tin.

While at Elverdinghe the Battalion was in Brigade Reserve. On December 27th it was relieved and moved by short marches through Poperinghe, where a night was spent in houses in and around the Square, to Houtkerque, arriving there on New Year's Day. The men were billeted in farms about a mile out of the town and were fairly comfortably housed. Practically no training was attempted. It was realised that the men needed rest more than anything else, and so they were given little to do during their fortnight's stay at Houtkerque.

On January 15th the Battalion marched to Wormhoudt. A band, equipped mainly with Italian horns, had recently been formed; this helped to enliven the march, particularly when the Brigadier's horse took fright at the unusual sight and noise, and bolted. Near the entrance to the town General Sir H. Plumer was waiting to see the Battalion march past.

Most of the men were lodged in farms just outside Wormhoudt. They had a royal time. They thronged the estaminets. They enjoyed the Divisional Band, which played in the Square. Officers' messes vied with one another in the elaborate dinners they gave. All did their best to make up for the hard time they had had at Ypres. As at Houtkerque, very little training was done. Officers' classes in Lewis gun and bombing, under Sec.-Lieuts. W. N. Everitt, M.C. and H. H. Aykroyd respectively, were a feature. The latter, it is rumoured, often developed into throwing contests between the instructor and his pupils. On January 23rd some Battalion sports were held, the most interesting item on the programme being a mule race for officers. This race was of the usual type, neither saddle nor stirrups being allowed. Within a few yards of the starting point most of the mules were riderless, Sec.-Lieut. A. E. Mander in particular taking a beautiful dive over his mule's head and landing on his own. The race was won by Sec.-Lieut. J. G. Mowat, with Sec.-Lieut. E. C. Mee second; practically no one else finished.

About this time the 147th Infantry Brigade Machine Gun Company was formed. Until then machine guns had been battalion weapons. In future they were to be the arm of a separate unit. To form the Company certain officers and other ranks were taken from each battalion of the Brigade. Lieut. G. W. I. Learoyd, Sec.-Lieut. F. Chisnall, six N.C.O's and twenty privates were sent by the Battalion. To replace the machine guns which were thus taken away, each battalion received four Lewis guns. It was the first time any of these weapons had been issued but, in course of time, the number was gradually increased until, by the summer of 1918, the Battalion was in possession of no less than 36.

Just before the Battalion left Wormhoudt the G.O.C. Second Army presented medal ribbons to a number of officers and other ranks of the 49th Division, and he took the opportunity to say good-bye to the men who were about to leave his army. His farewell speech shows clearly how much the work of the 49th Division was appreciated in the Second Army, and is worth quoting in full :—

"General Perceval, Officers, Non-commissioned Officers and Men who are representatives of the 49th Division.

This is a very pleasant ceremony to me, and I hope to you, with which to finish for the time being my connection, and that of the Second Army, with this Division.

I have had the pleasure on two occasions lately—one some weeks ago when you came out of the Line, and one the other day when I gave ribbons representing decorations to Officers, N.C.O's and Men of the Division after the recent Gas Attack— and on those two occasions I expressed briefly, but I hope quite distinctly, my appreciation of the way in which the 49th Division has carried out the duties entrusted to them during the last few months ; but now that it is settled for the time being the 49th Division is to leave the Second Army, and go to another area, while I have nothing to add as regards appreciation of the work you have done, I should like to say to you how sorry I am that you are leaving the Second Army. At the same time I fully realise that when a Division or any other Unit has undergone a long, arduous and strenuous time in a particular part of the Line, as the 49th has done, it is very desirable that they should have a change of scene, if the military situation admits of it, and that is the sole reason why you are quitting the Second Army. I cannot expect you to share my regret ; no one so far as I know has felt any deep regret at quitting the Ypres Salient ; but, while you will not regret your change of scene, when you look back on the time you have spent here, notwithstanding the arduous time that you have gone through, notwithstanding the losses of your comrades—which we all deplore—you will, I hope, have some pleasant recollections to take away with you of the time you have spent up here, and at any rate you will, I know, have some pleasant memories to carry away with you of your comrades of the Second Army. We, I can assure you, will follow your doings with the deepest interest; we are quite confident that no matter where you go you will not only sustain but add to the reputation that you have already won, and we shall always feel a kind of reflected glory when we hear of the gallant deeds which I am quite sure that you are going to accomplish both individually and as a Unit.

On behalf of the Second Army, I say good-bye to you, and I wish you all—Officers, N.C.O's and Men—the very best of luck. Good-bye."

On February 2nd the Battalion left Wormhoudt and the Second Army, and moved to the Somme Area. Transport and personnel entrained at Esquelbecq in the morning and, after the usual tedious journey, arrived late at night at Longueav, near Amiens. There one company was left behind, to assist in unloading the transport, while the rest of the Battalion set off on a long and weary march to Ailly, where motor buses were waiting to convey it to billets at Camps en Amienois. The men were very tired when they arrived about 3-0 a.m. After a few days they moved by stages to Warloy Baillon.

About a fortnight was spent at Warloy. The rolling downs and open country of the Somme district were a very welcome change from the flat clay of Flanders. The men were billeted in barns which were moderately comfortable, but the weather was very bad, snow falling frequently. A little time was devoted to training, but more to organisation and interior economy. Occasionally working parties had to be found. These were employed digging shallow trenches for buried cables, to the west of Martinsart Wood, and had a march of one and a half hours each way to their work.

The Commanding Officer started an officers' riding school. All officers attended, and every available hack was turned out. Several officers were thrown, much to the amusement of the transport sergeant, who laughed uproariously. One inexperienced horseman was heard gravely to explain that his "horse had pushed him in the face with its paw."

On February 28th the Battalion relieved the 1/4th Battalion King's Own Yorkshire Light Infantry, in the right sector of the Authuille trenches. This sector is of some interest as being the most southerly one ever held by the Battalion. At that time the British line, which lay practically north and south from Thiepval Wood to near Authuille, made a right-angled turn due east of the latter place, in order to enclose Authuille Wood. The re-entrant thus formed was occupied, on the enemy side, by the famous Leipsig Redoubt, the southern defence of Thiepval village. The sector held by the Battalion was about six hundred yards in length; it lay along the north side of Authuille Wood, facing the Leipsig Redoubt, with its left on Campbell Avenue. This part of the line had been taken over from the French not very long before.

The sector was in an appalling condition. The communication trenches were full of water, which often reached to the top of one's thigh boots; they were not gridded and the hard lumps of chalk, which littered the bottom, were very painful to men wearing gum-boots. Everywhere, the line was very wet; some parts of D Company's front were quite impassable, and were left unoccupied. Pumps had to be kept going night and day. The trenches were not revetted and were falling in badly, so that all work had to be concentrated on the front line. The awful weather that prevailed during the tour did not improve the conditions. Snow fell frequently.

The enemy was fairly active. He was credited with a desire to straighten out his line by cutting off the north-east corner of Authuille Wood. Perhaps the similar designs of the British, on the Leipsig Redoubt, suggested the idea. The front line was not much annoyed by shelling, though on one occasion it was pretty heavily " whizz-banged "; the hostile artillery fired mostly on the north-east corner of the wood and the vicinity of Battalion H.Q. Medium trench mortars were much in evidence, particularly during the afternoons; but luckily, nearly all of them fell a few yards behind the front line. There was no sniping— the conditions were too miserable—and the machine guns were not very active. The Battalion did not adopt a very offensive attitude. A fair amount of patrolling was done, and the enemy was found to be rather active in No Man's Land too; but no actual encounters are recorded. This was the first time that Lewis guns had been taken into the line, but they were not much used.

JANUARY TO JUNE, 1916

With its Ypres experience behind it, the Battalion naturally did all that was possible for the comfort of the troops. There were, unfortunately, several cases of trench feet, for the means of prevention had not yet been reduced to the science which they became later in the war. The method of cooking in the line was a great advance on anything that had been in existence before. Each company had its own trench kitchen; to it rations were sent up in bulk, and hot meals were served regularly, being carried up to the front line by orderly men.

The tour came to an end on March 4th. It had been most uncomfortable, but very few casualties had been suffered; the only one of importance was Sec.-Lieut. F. H. Kelsall wounded. The condition of the communication trenches was so bad that some companies went out over the open. D Company lost its way in Authuille Wood and got nearly to Albert before anyone discovered it was on the wrong road. One night was spent in Bouzincourt and a second in Authuille village, in Brigade Reserve. At the latter place the billets were awful, and the men had to rig up their ground sheets to prevent the water pouring in through the roofs. On March 6th the whole Battalion moved back to Mailly-Maillet.

With the move to Mailly-Maillet began a period of nearly four months, during which the Battalion never went into the line. Instead, it was employed on various forms of work, and had comparatively few opportunities for training. It is the longest period it ever spent out of action, while hostilities lasted. The billets at Mailly-Maillet were not at all bad. The village had been very little shelled, though, while the Battalion was there, enemy planes dropped some bombs on the outskirts. Practically all the men were in houses; the rooms were often quite bare but there were always fires. Training was impossible. Only very small drafts were arriving and so the strength of the Battalion was still very low. Practically every available man was required for the large working parties which had to be provided.

These working parties were in connection with mining operations to the north-west of Beaumont Hamel, and were very strenuous. The Battalion shared the duty with the 5th Battalion

Brig.-Genl. E. G. St. AUBYN, D.S.O.

JANUARY TO JUNE, 1916

Duke of Wellington's Regt., each having twenty-four hours on and twenty-four hours off. During the twenty-four hours of duty, three shifts, each consisting of two officers and one hundred other ranks, had to be found. Each shift was supposed to do eight hours' continuous work, but it was not allowed to stop until the next shift was ready to take its place ; so late arrivals became very unpopular. To take a typical shift, say one which was due at the mines at 8-0 a.m. The party paraded at 6-15 a.m. and marched to Auchonvillers. From that point it had to carry timber, sandbags and other R.E. material, required in the mines, up a long communication trench. Arriving at the mine at 8-0 a.m., the men had to work continuously until 4-0 p.m. The work was very hard. The men were formed into a chain from the mine face, along a tunnel, and then up the steps of the shaft. Their work consisted of throwing or passing the sandbags of " spoil " from the mine face up to the open, where a further party disposed of them. It can be imagined how monotonous the work was, and how tired the men were at the end of a shift. Then they had another one and a half hours of marching back to billets.

This work was not entirely free from danger. The enemy was known to be counter-mining and, at any time, he might explode his mine. Every now and then all work would be stopped, and there would be absolute silence while experts listened for sounds of the enemy working. Fortunately, there was no untoward incident while the Battalion was engaged on the work. But once some casualties were suffered, though from a very different cause. The trenches, in which the mining was being carried on, were held by a battalion of the Royal Irish Rifles. One night, the enemy put down a heavy artillery and trench mortar barrage, and raided the line. The working party had to cease work and stand to. It did not come into action, but one man was killed and three wounded by the barrage.

All were glad to leave Mailly-Maillet and the mines. On March 29th the Battalion marched to Harponville, and the next day to Naours. This second day's march was a very long one, but the day was splendid, and a hard frost had put the road in good condition. When the Battalion was met by the Divisional

Band near Naours, everyone freshened up, and the last stage of the march was a great success. All who were there look back on their stay at Naours with pleasure. The billets were good, the surrounding country delightful, and beautiful spring weather continued almost throughout. The "Tykes"—the recently-formed Divisional Concert Party—were there the whole time. On April 14th, the first anniversary of the Battalion's landing in France, they gave a special performance to the "old originals." Of these, there were about 340 still serving at that time. There was plenty of sport, particularly football. Above all, there were no working parties. A good deal of training was done, special attention being paid to instruction in the Lewis gun, and to company and other close order drill. There was practice in the assembly, the attack, and consolidation, over taped-out trenches; for already preparations for the Somme Battle were in progress. But all training was carried out during the morning; the afternoons were entirely devoted to sport. Altogether, the Battalion had a "real good time" at Naours, in spite of the Medical Officer, who insisted on inoculating everyone.

On April 23rd the Battalion moved by motor bus to Hedauville, and then followed two months of working parties in the area held by the 36th Division. All this work was in preparation for the attack which was soon to be launched, in conjunction with the French. The Battalion's first job was the digging of assembly trenches in Aveluy Wood. Daily the men were taken up by motor bus as far as Bouzincourt, and marched from thence to their work. It was all task work and the tasks were very heavy. The ground was full of roots, which greatly hindered digging, and, a foot or two below the surface, much flint was encountered. But very good work was done in spite of these difficulties. There Capt. C. Jones, C.F., first became prominent. He had not been long with the Brigade, but he soon became very popular with the men, taking a shovel himself and digging with the best of them, in all weathers.

The life in the woods was really quite enjoyable, in spite of occasional spells of rain. Hedauville Wood was full of nightingales, and many men sat out at night to listen to their song.

JANUARY TO JUNE, 1916

Beetles also abounded and were not so much appreciated; often it was necessary to get up at night to catch enormous flying specimens of these insects.

Strange to say, the enemy artillery made little attempt to harass troops in the area. The Germans must have had a good idea of the attack which was impending. They had good ground observation and plenty of aeroplanes. Martinsart village was crowded with troops and, in the evenings, there were sometimes thousands in its streets. Yet it was never shelled.

It is unnecessary to go into full details about this period. Most of the work was much of the same type. Digging was done both in Aveluy and Martinsart Woods; the Battalion was billeted first in one and then in the other, in order to be near its work. Once it had to carry up gas cylinders for an operation of the 32nd Division. Perhaps this job was the indirect cause of a gas alarm which occurred two nights later. At any rate, someone thought he heard a Strombos horn, and there was great confusion for a time as few could find their gas helmets.

About the middle of June the Battalion started work in Thiepval Wood, digging assembly trenches off Elgin Avenue. There it was sometimes annoyed by shelling, and a few casualties were suffered. On June 24th the work came to an end and the Battalion moved back, taking with it the thanks and congratulations of the G.O.C., 36th Division, under whom it had been working.

The time had almost come when the Battalion was again to take its place in the line. For six months it had done little but pioneer work, with occasional periods of training, and one trench tour. During all that time its fighting, or perhaps it would be better to say " working," strength had been very low, for the wastage in the Ypres Salient had never been made good. Now that it was destined for battle, reinforcements were imperative. On June 24th a draft of 52 other ranks arrived; five days later a further draft, 258 other ranks strong, joined. Many of these were experienced soldiers, who had served earlier in the war with other regiments; among them was a fair sprinkling of old Regulars, who had landed at St. Nazaire with the 6th Division, during the Battle of the Marne. They were fine material, but it was a pity they had not been sent earlier. Not only would they have been of the greatest use in the pioneer work of the last two months, but officers and N.C.O's would not have had to lead into battle so large a proportion of men of whose very names they were ignorant. To incorporate such numbers of reinforcements, in the short time available, meant' much hard work. Thus, the two days which preceded that fateful—and fatal—July 1st were very strenuous ones for the Battalion.

CHAPTER V.

THE BATTLE OF THE SOMME.

(a) July and August, 1916.

THE first half of the year 1916 was a period of comparative quiet for the British Expeditionary Force. During those six months it attempted no serious offensive, and the Germans were far too fully occupied in the neighbourhood of Verdun to be able to expend much energy elsewhere. The terrific attack on their eastern stronghold caused the French much anxiety, and it undoubtedly influenced their strategy. Nevertheless, it did not prevent them making their preparations for the great offensive, which had been planned for the summer, in conjunction with the British. This attack was to take place on a wide front, where the allied lines joined in the Somme district; and the battle which resulted takes its name from that river.

The only part of the Somme battlefield which is of interest in a history of the Fourth Battalion is the neighbourhood of the village of Thiepval and the wood of the same name. From Albert the River Ancre flows in a northerly direction to about St. Pierre Divion, where it turns nearly east towards Miraumont. Its banks rise steeply on both sides; its width is considerable; and the extensive marshes and shallow lagoons, which fringe so much of its course, render it a formidable obstacle. It is surprising that the enemy ever allowed the French to establish themselves on the eastern bank in 1914. By the summer of 1916, many military bridges had been built across the river and its marshes; but the allied bridge-head, though wide, was shallow, particularly at the northern end. Everywhere it was dominated by the Germans, who occupied all the commanding positions on the line of hills. To the north they held the village of Beaumont Hamel, from which they could overlook the whole course of the river, as far south as Albert. Their line crossed the Ancre near St. Pierre Divion and then ran approximately south, including the village of Thiepval, to La Boiselle. Few stronger defensive systems, than that around Thiepval, have ever been constructed on the western front. To the north the village was defended by the mighty Schwaben Redoubt, to the south by the equally formidable Leipsig Redoubt and that network of fortifications, well-styled the "Wonderwork." Everywhere the line was well supplied with deep dugouts, which were comparatively easy to construct in the chalky soil of the district. The Germans thus had many advantages over the British. Their commanding positions gave them better opportunities for observation, and their machine guns could sweep every inch of ground in No Man's Land. The shallowness of the bridge-head cramped the British, and hampered their assembly for the attack, while it gave unrivalled opportunities to the enemy artillery.

Nevertheless, it was with the highest hopes that the allied armies looked forward to "Z" day. Months of preparation had been necessary for this offensive, and some account has already been given of the "spade work" done by the Battalion in that connection. Towards the end of June, much time was spent in reconnaissance. Before the battle began all the officers, and most of the N.C.O's in the Battalion, knew every dump, aid post, ammunition store and source of water supply between the Ancre and Authuille Wood.

The concentration of artillery on the British front was colossal, and the reserves of ammunition seemed almost inexhaustible. A week before the end of the month the guns opened fire, and, from that time, the Germans can have had no doubt of what was coming, and which of their positions were threatened. Day and night, for seven days, the rain of shells poured down on the enemy line without ceasing. A good view of much of the shelled area could be obtained from Senlis Mill, and many officers of the Battalion visited the observation post there, to watch the bombardment. All came away with the same opinion—that nothing could live in the German lines. Their hopes of an early and decisive victory were very high. They had yet to learn the strength of the enemy's deep dugouts.

JULY AND AUGUST, 1916

The opening of the infantry attack was fixed for the morning of July 1st. The 49th Division formed part of the X. Corps, whose left rested on the River Ancre and right near Authuille Wood. The Corps objectives, including as they did the villages of Grandcourt and Thiepval, and all their outworks, were second to none in difficulty on the British front. The attack there was entrusted to the 32nd Division on the right, and the 36th (Ulster) Division on the left. The 49th Division was held in Corps reserve; it was to assemble in previously-selected positions and there await orders. The Battalion's assembly position was in Aveluy Wood, where it was to occupy some of the very trenches it had dug about two months before. Just before the battle, Lieut.-Col. E. G. St. Aubyn was summoned to Corps H.Q. There he remained until nearly the end of July, being held in reserve to take command of a brigade should any Brigadier become a casualty during the battle. The command of the Battalion thus devolved on Major J. Walker. " The Commanding Officer wishes all ranks to remember that in the work in front of us we are putting to the test our reputation as a Battalion and has absolute confidence that Officers, N.C.O's and men will worthily uphold the honour of the Regiment to which we belong," was his message to the troops on the eve of battle.

About midnight on June 30/July 1st, the Battalion marched out of Senlis. Though its role was still indefinite, everything had been prepared so that it could move into battle at a moment's notice. The transport moved to lines near Hedauville. The Battalion itself marched to B Assembly Trenches in Aveluy Wood, arriving long before dawn. There was none too much room in the trenches, but all the men were got in somewhere. The enemy was quiet. There can be no doubt that he knew full well what was impending, but he reserved his fire for the better targets which would soon present themselves. Few of the men even tried to sleep; excitement was far too high for that.

At zero hour—7-30 a.m.—the British artillery fire lifted from the enemy front line, and the British and French infantry " went over the top." Much has been written of that great assault, but nothing need be noticed here, except what took place on the X. Corps front. There the 36th and the 32nd Divisions went forward with a magnificent dash. They swarmed over the first enemy lines; they over-ran Thiepval and St. Pierre Divion, the Schwaben and the Leipsig Redoubts. Some of the Ulstermen even reached Grandcourt Railway Station. But their casualties were appalling. " Mopping-up " was then unheard of; counter-battery work was in its infancy; creeping barrages were unknown. Down came the enemy artillery barrage, and it was such as few had seen before. German machine gunners and riflemen, emerging from the security of their deep dugouts, took the attack in enfilade and in reverse. Men fell in thousands. The survivors were too few to maintain the positions they had reached. By an early hour the attack on the X. Corps front had failed.

Of course, all this was only learned by the Battalion later. From Aveluy Wood nothing could be seen of what was happening on the Corps front. The men knew that the attack had opened; for a time they knew nothing of its progress. They had nothing to do. They were not troubled by enemy shelling, for the hostile artillery had far better targets elsewhere. After some time, wounded began to pass, and also a number of prisoners. The former were eagerly questioned, and some news of the earliest stages of the attack was obtained; but it was not until much later that authentic information was received.

Towards 11-0 a.m., orders to move across the River Ancre arrived. The Battalion Intelligence Officer was immediately sent forward to reconnoitre the bridges and report on the safest; none envied him his job, but, as things turned out, it was simple enough. The enemy was paying no attention to the bridges. About 11-30 a.m. the Battalion moved off by platoons, at fifty yards' interval, A Company leading. Marching via Brooker's Pass, it reached the Southern Dugouts near Crucifix Corner, Aveluy, without incident. There it remained until the evening of the next day. The 6th Battalion Duke of Wellington's Regt. was also there and accommodation was very crowded; but otherwise the men were not uncomfortable. Aveluy was not shelled. Crowds of stragglers from different battalions of the attacking divisions were coming in to reorganise, and rumours of the failure of the attack were increasing. Apart from carrying wounded to the neighbouring dressing station, and helping men who came back from the line absolutely worn out, the Battalion had nothing to do.

About 7-0 p.m. on July 2nd the Battalion left Aveluy and moved up to relieve the 5th Battalion West Yorkshire Regt. in Johnstone's Post. This position was in the narrow and deep valley which lies along the south-eastern edge of Thiepval Wood. Two large cemeteries now occupy a great part of the valley, and the inscriptions on the weather-beaten crosses bear eloquent testimony to the presence of the 49th Division in that area. None who were there in July, 1916, will ever forget it. It was a point at which many trenches met, but, apart from these and a few shelters in the bluff along the edge of Thiepval Wood, there was no cover. When the Battalion arrived that evening, the enemy was putting down a terrific counter-preparation on Johnstone's Post, where he evidently suspected an assembly for the attack. A continual stream of 15 cm. high explosive shells poured into the hollow from the south-east. The cover of existing trenches was nothing like enough to accommodate the Battalion, and all that could be done was to get the men as close as possible to the steep south-eastern side of the valley, which afforded a little protection.

Very early the next morning, orders were received for the Battalion to support a fresh attack which the 32nd Division was about to make on Thiepval. These orders did not arrive until about half-an-hour before the attack was to begin. What was to be done? Very little was known of the ground; there was no time for reconnaissance; there was not even time to issue proper orders to companies. Fortunately, the instructions were cancelled before zero hour. The 32nd Division, however, made its attack. It had little success. One corner of the Leipsig Salient was taken, and was very useful two months later as a starting point in the operations which outflanked Thiepval on the south. It was also much used as a "show ground" in the next few weeks, as there were many fine enemy dugouts in the German line. Apart from this, the attack was a failure.

The whole Battalion remained at Johnstone's Post until the evening of July 4th, when two companies moved to the Northern Dugouts, Authuille Bluff. Throughout its stay it was never free from shelling, and frequently the enemy put down counter-preparations of exceptional intensity. Casualties were terrible. The Aid Post became frightfully congested, not only with the Battalion's own men, but with crowds from other units; and it is no exaggeration to say that the dead lay around it in heaps. None could have done more—few could have done half as much—than Capt. S. S. Greaves, R.A.M.C., did. Day and night he worked without ceasing. He might have been in a hospital, far from the scene of action, for all the excitement he showed. Many a man owed his life to the skill and care lavished on him by the 4th Battalion Medical Officer at Johnstone's Post. But the casualties of those first days on the Somme were so appalling that the medical staffs were quite inadequate to deal with them. Hour after hour the Battalion worked to clear the wounded, but fresh cases streamed in far more quickly than earlier ones could be evacuated. And all the time, into the midst of that deadly valley, the 5.9's screamed, taking their remorseless toll of human life and limb. Without a chance of a fight, scores of the Battalion went down. Chief among them was Capt. E. E. Sykes, M.C., an officer of magnificent physique and dauntless courage; one who had gone to France with the original Battalion, and whose men would have followed him "into the mouth of hell." Fearfully wounded in the abdomen, he died shortly after at the Aid Post, and his body rests in Authuille Military Cemetery, not far from the scene of his death.

But enough has been said of these horrors. Men who were there will ever remember them. Others who know what battle is can picture them, far better than words can describe. To those who have been fortunate enough never to see such things, no language can describe them.

On the evening of July 5th the Battalion relieved the 5th Battalion Duke of Wellington's Regt. in the front line, just in front of Thiepval village. It was responsible for a sector about a thousand yards in length, and all four companies held portions of the front line. These trenches were the very ones from which the attack had been launched on July 1st—no permanent advance had been made on that front, nor was there to be any until late in September. No Man's Land was thick

Capt. W. N. EVERITT, M.C.
(Killed).

Capt. C. HIRST.
(Killed).

Lieut. J. T. RILEY.
(Killed).

Capt. S. S. GREAVES, D.S.O., M.C.,
R.A.M.C.

JULY AND AUGUST, 1916

with dead; occasionally a wounded man, who had lain out for days, succeeded in crawling into the British lines. Trenches and shelters had been so terribly battered that all work had to be concentrated on the necessary repairs. The enemy artillery was extremely active, and many men were killed or wounded before the two days' tour came to an end. When the Battalion was relieved on July 7th, partly by the 6th Battalion Duke of Wellington's Regt., and partly by the 5th Battalion King's Own Yorkshire Light Infantry, it withdrew to the assembly trenches in Aveluy Wood, which it had occupied on the morning of July 1st. The relief was very late, everything was sodden with rain, and the one night which was spent there was little enough rest for anyone.

On the way back to Thiepval Wood the next night, a shell near Lancashire Dump wounded several men and killed Sec.-Lieut. W. S. Booth. He had been bombing officer for some time and was a tower of strength to the Battalion.

Then began the longest continuous stretch of duty, under battle conditions, which the men were ever called upon to perform.

Tucked away near the point of the angle, between the enemy front line and the River Ancre, was Thiepval Wood. It was bordered on the west by the marshes of the river, and on the south and south-east by the Johnstone's Post valley; on the east and north-east the ground sloped steeply up to the German lines on the heights above. With its trees, its thick undergrowth and numerous "rides," it must have been a pleasant spot in pre-war days. But, during the early weeks of the Battle of the Somme, it rapidly became a desolation little better than the woods in the Ypres Salient the following year. Such was the home of the Battalion from July 8th to August 19th. Never, during the whole of that time, did the men leave it. Reliefs were carried out every few days with the 5th Battalion Duke of Wellington's Regt.; but periods in Brigade Reserve were little improvement on those in the front line, for both were passed in the wood.

With the exception of its first tour, the Battalion always held the extreme left sector. Its left flank rested on the River Ancre

and its right on Union Street, the length of front being about
a thousand yards. All four companies held portions of the front
line, and, tour after tour, they returned to the same positions—
A, B, C, D from right to left. No Man's Land varied from about
250 to 400 yards in width. Along it, and roughly parallel to the
opposing lines, lay the sunken Thiepval Road. Crowded as it
was with the bodies of the Ulstermen, who had fallen or crawled
there to die on July 1st, this road was a ghastly place. The
British front line lay along the north and north-eastern edges
of Thiepval Wood. Hewn out of the chalk, the trenches had been
comparatively good up to the opening of the battle; but the
fearful hammering they had since received had almost obliterated
them in many places. There were some good deep dugouts,
but not nearly enough to accommodate all the men. The communication trenches, which led back to Battalion H.Q. and
the crossings over the Ancre, were badly constructed and sited;
the main ones lay along, or just beside, the chief rides in the wood,
and they were so straight that they could easily be enfiladed
by the enemy artillery.

Battalion H.Q. was at Gordon Castle. There, too, accommodation was scanty. Some attempts were made to improve it,
but these were greatly hampered by enemy shelling. In particular, a bath-house was planned and, after a week's hard work,
was completed, only to be demolished the following morning
by a shell. Nothing daunted, Lieut. J. T. Riley set to work
to rebuild it. But the second attempt had no more success than
the first. The very night the building was pronounced ready
for use, another shell knocked off one of the corners. That was
too much. The yearning for cleanliness had to remain unsatisfied, while the remnants of the building were used for the
holding of the numerous courts of enquiry which were so popular
about that time.

Throughout this period, though the role of the Battalion
was the purely passive one of holding a portion of the line, that
line was situated right in the middle of a furious battle. The
first attacks on Thiepval had failed; but the very substantial
successes, which were being gained further to the south, were
gradually turning the defences of that village on the east. The

enemy undoubtedly feared a repetition of the attack, made by the X. Corps on July 1st. His artillery was always active, and often regular barrages would fall on the wood. The front line came in for a great deal of attention, and it was only by much labour that posts at all fit for occupation could be maintained. Elgin and Inniskilling Avenues, the two chief communication trenches to Battalion H.Q., were often enfiladed by field guns. But the worst shelled area of all was the Ancre, in the neighbourhood of which ration-carrying parties had a very bad time. As the weeks dragged on the wood became thinner and thinner, until all the trenches were easily visible to aircraft and even to ground observers. Then artillery, from the heights north of the river near Beaumont Hamel, began to take the wood in enfilade, and caused much damage. But, apart from artillery fire the enemy was not very aggressive. There was not much rifle fire, and, except to repel a definite attack, machine guns were little used. Taking everything into account, the casualties suffered by the Battalion were not excessive. They were constant—it is doubtful whether a day passed without some men being killed or wounded—but they were not out of proportion to the enormous weight of artillery fire.

Since the early days of July, the direct attacks on Thiepval had been discontinued, and a defensive policy had been adopted on that sector, for the time being. Nevertheless, there was considerable activity, every effort being made to pin the enemy to his ground, and to distract his attention as much as possible from the operations of the Fourth Army on the right. The British artillery fire never slackened; day after day, and week after week, the deluge of shells was kept up. This fire was supplemented by the trench mortars, with which the troops were now much better supplied. Considerable use was made of the new Lewis guns, especially at night; and C.S.M. McNulty was again to the fore with his Winchester. Minor demonstrations were constantly being made, with the object of deceiving the enemy and making him believe that an attack was imminent. The following order, from 147th Infantry Brigade, is an example of what the Battalion was frequently called upon to do:—

"The Army Commander wishes everything possible to be

done to keep the enemy in front of the Division on the alert, make him man his parapets and get him under our shrapnel fire.

With this object the following demonstration will be made to induce the enemy to man his parapets. At 1-0 p.m. to-day as many bayonets as possible will be shown along the whole front of the Brigade as if assault is imminent and timed for 1-0 p.m. For five or ten minutes previous to this hour whistles should be blown at intervals along the front as if signals were being made. The tops of ladders or trench grids should be shown over the parapets. The artillery immediately after 1-0 p.m. will open bombardment on enemy front and support trenches, especially on those trenches which can be taken in enfilade.

Any other device which can lead the enemy in front line to expect an assault at 1-0 p.m. should also be employed and Machine guns will fire during the artillery bombardment."

On several occasions smoke barrages were put up by the Battalion. For this purpose, special emplacements were constructed about every twenty-five yards along the front line, and from these smoke bombs were thrown out into No Man's Land. Usually the wind changed just before zero hour and Thiepval Wood was enveloped in a wonderful haze of smoke. There can be no doubt that these activities met with a certain amount of success. This was amply proved by the speed with which the enemy put down his defensive barrages time after time.

Patrolling too was very active. It was mainly carried out by the Battalion H.Q. Scouts, and much very useful, and often dangerous, work was done by them. In particular, some extremely daring and skilful patrols were done by Sec.-Lieut. H. H. Aykroyd, the Battalion Intelligence Officer, in the Ancre valley, for which he was awarded the Military Cross. On one occasion, when visiting the neighbouring battalion's post at the Mill, he had the unpleasant experience of being mistaken for an enemy patrol, and was heavily bombed.

Reliefs were carried out with the 5th Battalion Duke of Wellington's Regiment every few days and soon became very simple, for companies always occupied the same positions, both in the

JULY AND AUGUST, 1916

front line and in reserve. Battalion H.Q. only had to move about two hundred yards from Gordon Castle to Belfast City. When in Brigade Reserve, two companies were in support to each of the battalions in the front line. During the day there was little to do, but at night working parties had to be found. It was a dreary life, though enlivened occasionally by the exploits of the Intelligence Officer. He it was who, whilst engaged in a scientific investigation of German flares, nearly burnt out Battalion H.Q. To him also was due the wondrous camouflaging of Belfast City, the remains of which may still be seen in Thiepval Wood.

The long and unbroken spell in Thiepval Wood caused much hardship to the men. There were no facilities for cooking, and so all food had to be sent up cooked from the transport lines. For six weeks, no one had a decently-prepared dinner. Supplies of clean clothing were not often available, and baths for the men were absolutely impossible. It can be imagined what an awful state they got into, living as they were under filthy conditions during the hottest season of the year, with never a chance of a good wash. At first some men bathed in the Ancre, but this was very dangerous owing to the thick weeds; after a man had been accidentally drowned there about the middle of July, all bathing was strictly forbidden. There can be no doubt that this long period of harassing and filthy conditions seriously affected the men physically.

Towards the end of July, Lieut.-Col. E. G. St. Aubyn came back to the Battalion. From that time, until August 19th, Major J. Walker and Capt. A. L. Mowat shared the duties of second-in-command, taking turns in the line and with the rear echelon.

During July work had consisted mainly of keeping the front line in a habitable condition, and repairing the communication trenches, which were continually being damaged by shell fire. Many bodies too were recovered from No Man's Land and decently buried. But, about the beginning of August, the digging of the famous parallels began. It had been decided to renew the frontal attack on the sector from Thiepval to the River Ancre, but, after the experience of July 1st, No Man's Land in that area was considered too wide to attack across successfully. Hence it was determined to push forward the British front line by digging a series of trenches in No Man's Land. These " parallels " stretched from the Ancre to the top of Inniskilling Avenue, the foremost being roughly along the line of the sunken road, though on the extreme right it crossed the road. In other words, the front on which they were dug corresponded almost exactly with the Battalion sub-sector. Practically none of the actual digging was done by men of the Battalion, but, whenever they were occupying the front line, they had to find covering parties for the work. Every night, as soon as it was dark enough to conceal movement, one platoon per company moved out into No Man's Land, and took up a line along the northern edge of the sunken road. There they remained so long as the work was in progress. Company Commanders took turns in charge of the whole covering party. The actual working parties—nearly a thousand men nightly—were provided by the 148th Infantry Brigade. Really this number was much too big. Heavy shelling had reduced the communication trenches in Thiepval Wood to a very derelict condition; the movement of large parties along them became very slow, and much time was wasted in coming and going. No Man's Land too became very congested. As a result, the amount of work done on the parallels was small compared with the number of men engaged.

The work of the covering parties proved tedious, but not particularly dangerous. The enemy infantry made practically no attempt to interfere with the digging, and only once was a party of Germans encountered. It happened in this way. An officer of A Company was on the right of the covering party one night. Following a not uncommon practice of his, he was moving about alone, when he saw a party of men, a little way off on the flank, who did not appear to be working. He went up and gently exhorted them to get on with their job. A chorus of gutterals was his answer, as an affrighted party of Germans made off. But though the enemy infantry was comparatively inactive, this cannot be said of his artillery. Even if the actual working parties were not observed the first night, the results of their labours cannot have escaped the German observers the next day, for the newly-turned chalk showed very white on

JULY AND AUGUST, 1916

the ground. From that time the enemy made a practice of putting down a barrage regularly soon after midnight, and there were many casualties among the crowds of men in No Man's Land. But the barrage did not seriously affect the covering parties, which escaped with very little loss. The parallels were nearly complete before the Battalion left Thiepval Wood, and had been absorbed into the front line system.

All things considered, there was not much recognition of the good work done by the men of the Battalion at this period. Mention has already been made of the Military Cross awarded to Sec.-Lieut. H. H. Aykroyd. The only other officer to receive that decoration was Sec.-Lieut. F. V. Blackwell, who was brought to notice by a daring daylight patrol, which resulted in the recovery of several machine guns lost by the British on July 1st. R.S.M. F. P. Stirzaker was also awarded the Military Cross, more for his continuous gallant work than for any specific act; throughout all this period he earned a magnificent name for hard work, devotion to duty and gallantry. But he was not the first warrant officer of the Battalion to receive the Military Cross. That honour had already been won by C.S.M. (now R.Q.M.S.) W. Lee, for conspicuous gallantry while the Battalion was near Ypres in 1915, particularly for his conduct on that never-to-be-forgotten December 19th.

The longest tour comes to an end at last. On August 19th the 9th Battalion Loyal North Lancs. Regt. relieved the Battalion, which moved back to billets near Raincheval. There it remained until August 27th. The 49th Division was at last to be thrown into the attack, and the time at Raincheval was mainly occupied with special assault training. A facsimile of the enemy trenches, which formed the objectives, had been taped out, and over this the men practised every morning. The rest of each day was occupied with the thousand and one preparations essential to the success of any operation.

When the Battalion first moved back to Raincheval, the operation was expected to take place within a very few days. But, like so many of the British attacks, it was postponed. It was a pity that the Battalion did not know from the very first how long a time it would have out of the line. The men were

F

very run down after their long spell in Thiepval Wood, and much might have been done to improve their condition. Instead, they were kept for many days in that nervous state which must precede every attack, and the period of rest could not be utilised nearly so fully as it might have been. Even after a move had been made to Forceville on August 27th, the exact date of zero day still remained for a time in doubt. At length the attack was definitely fixed for September 3rd.

Two days before the operation, the Battalion suffered a great loss. Lieut.-Col. E. G. St. Aubyn became so seriously ill that he was evacuated sick on September 1st, and soon afterwards was sent to England. So ended his connection with the Battalion, for which he had done so much. He returned to the 147th Infantry Brigade in the autumn, but took command of the 7th Battalion Duke of Wellington's Regt. Thus it fell to Major J. Walker to command the Battalion in its first big attack.

(b) September 3rd, 1916.

The attack made on September 3rd, 1916, is one of the most important events in the Battalion's history. Never before had it been selected for an operation of that kind. It is therefore very unfortunate that the difficulties of writing a strictly accurate account are so great. Yet, of all the operations in which the Battalion took part during the war, none is so obscure in many of its details, and around none has so much controversy raged. At the time, the higher commands certainly did not understand clearly what had taken place. Nearly all the officers and senior N.C.O's, who took part in the assault, were killed. Survivors' narratives differ considerably in matters of detail. In short, it is impossible to write an account which is absolutely exact in such details as the precise times at which certain events took place. The following account has been written after a careful study of all the available official documents, supplemented by the personal narratives of many of the survivors. Among the official papers, none is of greater interest and importance than a German narrative, which was captured two or three weeks after the event.

This is the report of the Officer Commanding the 1st Battalion 180th Infantry Regt.—the unit which was holding the line south of the Ancre when the Battalion attacked. In it are detailed the extent of the British success, the dispositions made by the Germans to counter-attack, and the operations which finally resulted in the recapture of the positions, which the enemy had temporarily lost.

The operation was part of a big attack, which was to be made about dawn, on both sides of the River Ancre. South of that river the 49th Division was attacking, with the 147th Infantry Brigade on the right and the 146th Infantry Brigade on the left. On the front of the 147th Infantry Brigade, the 4th Battalion on the right, and the 5th Battalion on the left, were detailed for the assault; the 6th and 7th Battalions were in support and reserve respectively. The Battalion was thus on the extreme flank of the divisional front, and, as no one was attacking further to the south, had its right " in the air." The following is a brief summary of the Operation Orders :—

1. Companies were to assemble in the parallels before dawn, in the positions shown on the map.

2. At zero hour A, B and D Companies were to advance simultaneously. As soon as B Company had taken the First Objective, A and D Companies were to go through it to the assault of their respective objectives.

3. Company objectives were as follows :—

B Company. Enemy front line from point 84 to point 54.

A Company. Enemy support line from point 95 to point 66.
> One platoon was to push up the Munster Gasse, and make a block in that trench beyond the support line.

D Company. Enemy communication trench from point 84 to point 95. Blocks were to be made in the enemy front and support lines towards the Schwaben Redoubt.

C Company was to remain in Battalion reserve.

4. A hurricane bombardment was to open at zero hour on the objectives; it was to remain on the enemy front line for three minutes, and on the enemy support line for eight minutes. Perhaps the greatest difficulty in the operation was the keeping of direction. A glance at the map will show that A and B Com-

panies had to advance approximately half right on leaving the parallels—an extremely difficult manœuvre to carry out in battle, in the half light of early dawn, and in a country where there were no landmarks. The task of D Company was even harder. Not only had the men to advance on an incline, but, on reaching point 84, they had to "right form," in order to occupy the communication trench, with their front towards the Schwaben Redoubt. Of course these manœuvres had been carefully practised over the " tapes " at Raincheval, but the carrying of them out in the excitement of battle, under heavy fire, was a very different matter.

The parallels, in which the Battalion was to assemble, were already very well known to many of the men. They were rough and narrow, and so deep that ladders had to be provided for the men to leave them by. The first objective—the enemy front line— was about two hundred and fifty yards from the foremost parallel. No Man's Land was to be crossed in quick time and three minutes were allowed for this, rather a short period when it is remembered that the ground was one mass of shell holes and debris, and that the advance was up a decidedly steep slope. The enemy front line, owing to the shape of the ground, was barely visible from the parallels. The Battalion's objectives lay in a re-entrant between the Schwaben Redoubt and the Pope's Nose, from which positions a deadly cross-fire could be brought to bear on the advance, unless it were well protected by the British artillery. The slope and condition of the ground, between the enemy first and second lines, was very similar to No Man's Land. The shelling of the past two months had so battered the enemy defences that it was extremely difficult to recognise definite points, or even stretches of trench.

During the afternoon of September 2nd, the Battalion marched from Senlis to Martinsart Wood, where it halted until evening. A hot meal was served at 8-0 p.m., and, about an hour later, the platoons began to move off to their positions of assembly. No smoking was allowed, and the strictest orders about silence had been issued. So, with no noise save the squelch of boots in the mud and the occasional rattle of equipment, the men passed through Aveluy Wood, along a specially taped line, drew bombs

SEPTEMBER 3RD, 1916

and other battle equipment at the bottom of Black Horse Road, and crossed the Ancre. During the crossing they were somewhat harassed by enemy shelling, and D Company suffered some casualties. But, apart from this, the march was not seriously hampered, and all were in position by 3-25 a.m. on September 3rd. Then followed two weary hours of waiting for the dawn and that hurricane burst of artillery fire, which was to be the signal for the assault. High as was the nervous tension, and great the excitement in those crowded parallels, some of the men actually slept. How few realised that, within the next few hours, scores would be sleeping for ever !

About 5-0 a.m. dawn was breaking. The enemy had been very quiet during the night, but he now began to show traces of nervousness and occasional bursts of machine gun fire clipped the parapets. The Battalion* stood to, and bayonets were quietly fixed. At 5-10 a.m. one great gun spoke, and then, to quote the words of one who took part in the attack, " the whole sky seemed to light up suddenly." The hour had come. Up rose the three companies like one man. There was no hesitation. Over the parapet they swarmed. The attack had begun.

The enemy was thoroughly on the alert. Flares went up all along the front, and, in spite of the British barrage, which was very good, a deadly cross fire of machine gun bullets opened from

---

*The following Officers and Warrant Officers went into action with the Battalion on September 3rd, 1916 :—

Battalion H.Q.: Major J. Walker (C.O.); Lieut. W. C. Fenton (Adjt.); Sec.-Lieut. H. H. Aykroyd, M.C. (I.O.); Sec.-Lieut. H. N. Taylor (L.G.O.); Sec.-Lieut. N. Mellor (Bombing O.); Capt. S. S. Greaves, R.A.M.C. (M.O.).
R.S.M. F. P. Stirzaker, M.C.

A Company: Lieut. W. N. Everitt, M.C.; Sec.-Lieut. A. E. Hirst; Sec.-Lieut. G. F. Robertshaw.
C.S.M. A. Stirzaker, D.C.M.

B Company: Capt. C. Hirst; Sec.-Lieut. V. A. Horsfall; Sec.-Lieut. H. E. Pohlmann.
C.S.M. W. Medley.

C Company: Capt. E. N. Marshall; Sec.-Lieut. F. Walker; Sec.-Lieut. W. Smith.
C.S.M. T. H. Greenwood.

D Company: Lieut. J. T. Riley; Sec.-Lieut. E. C. Mee; Sec.-Lieut. C. W. Tomlinson.
C.S.M. J. C. Walker.

Fighting strength of the Battalion on the afternoon of September 2nd :—

	Officers (including M.O.)		Other ranks	
Battalion H.Q.		6		121
A Company	,,	3	,,	127
B Company	,,	3	,,	127
C Company	,,	3	,,	127
D Company	,,	3	,,	127
Total		18		629

the directions of the Schwaben Redoubt and the Pope's Nose. There is some doubt as to the exact time when many of the officers and senior N.C.O's were hit; but it is practically certain that Capt. C. Hirst, Sec.-Lieut. A. E. Hirst and Sec.-Lieut. C. W. Tomlinson were all killed, and Sec.-Lieut. G. F. Robertshaw wounded, before the first objective was reached. Many men fell, but the lines went forward splendidly. Steadily they crossed No Man's Land, halted, and got down a few yards from the enemy front line, waiting for the barrage to lift. But already there was apparent one point, which seriously affected the success of the operation. Companies were becoming mixed. Some of the men of A and D Companies were mingled together; and many men of the 5th Battalion were in the ranks of the 4th Battalion. Also, in the half light, the rear waves of the attack did not notice quickly enough that the first wave had halted, and so they crowded up on it. The difficulties of keeping distance and direction had been too great.

The enemy artillery barrage did not open properly until nearly ten minutes after zero hour, but then it was very heavy. The old British front line and the first parallel received most attention, and were soon almost obliterated. Heavies rained down on the tunnel entrances; shrapnel deluged the communication trenches. The barrage embraced the whole of Thiepval Wood, and many casualties were suffered by the two reserve battalions of the 147th Infantry Brigade. But the foremost parallel and No Man's Land were not heavily shelled at first, and thus machine gun fire was the only serious danger to the men lying near the enemy front line.

Immediately the British barrage lifted, B Company charged and captured its objective without much difficulty. This line had been terribly shattered by the bombardment of the previous two months and in places had almost disappeared. It was so bad that most of the men did not enter it at all, but remained in shell holes in the open, where they began to consolidate. Their position was very exposed and, as time went on, they lost heavily from machine gun fire. Others, among whom C.S.M. W. Medley was most conspicuous, worked along the trench, bombing the deep dugouts with which it abounded, and collecting prisoners.

SEPTEMBER 3RD, 1916

The latter were sent back across No Man's Land, but only one is known to have arrived at Battalion H.Q. The rest probably perished under the fire of their own artillery and machine guns. One part of B Company worked a considerable distance along the enemy front line towards the Pope's Nose, bombing as it went. All that trench was thoroughly cleared, but the company, and the men of the 5th Battalion who were with it, were not strong enough to hold the whole, and it had to be left unoccupied. Numbers of Germans, some without rifles, were seen making off across the open on the left, and were heavily fired upon. It seems probable that, for some time, the Pope's Nose was evacuated by the enemy; but it was never occupied by the British.

Meanwhile, A Company had advanced, hard on the heels of B Company. Passing straight over the captured line, the men moved across the open until about fifty yards from the enemy support trench. There they halted, sheltering in shell holes, and waiting for their barrage to lift. Already they had suffered very heavy casualties. Some, in their over-eagerness, had advanced too far, and had been hit by their own shells. Only one officer—Lieut. W. N. Everitt, M.C.—had survived; C.S.M. A. Stirzaker, D.C.M., had fallen between the first and second objectives; and scores of N.C.O's and men had been killed or wounded. But they had been reinforced by some men of B Company, who had gone forward with them, and by Cpl. A. Denham's Lewis gun team, which had lost D Company and had advanced on the right of A Company. The men came under a very heavy fire from the German support line. Numbers of the enemy were seen making off across the open, and Cpl. Denham did some execution with his Lewis gun; but the bulk of the German garrison held its ground and fought well. For some time the Company lay in the open, exchanging shots with the enemy in his line. The British barrage had now lifted, and there was thus nothing to interfere with the German marksmen and machine gunners. Casualties were piling up, but the second objective was not yet taken. Lieut. Everitt, with Sergt. Bancroft, had already reconnoitred right up to the line, and had thrown some bombs among the enemy there. He now determined to try to rush the position, after a short burst of Lewis gun fire. Assisted by Sergts. Haigh and Bancroft, he crawled round and informed the men of his intention. They were told to charge as soon as the Lewis gun ceased fire. The gun opened, but stopped almost at once with a broken return spring; quite coolly the N.C.O. on the gun—his name is now unknown—changed the part, and reported to Lieut. Everitt that he was ready to reopen fire. One magazine was fired, and then A Company charged. Everitt himself was first in the trench, and was followed closely by Haigh. The bay they entered was unoccupied, but the next was full of the enemy. These were bombed, and either fled or dived into their deep dugouts. Parties then moved to right and left along the trench, bombing dugouts and collecting prisoners. The latter were sent back across the open, but none appear to have arrived. Many Germans were killed in the second objective. Of the parties which moved along the support line, that to the right got well beyond point 95, towards the Schwaben Redoubt, without encountering any of the enemy; but it could find no trace of D Company, which should have had a post near that point. The other party cleared and occupied the whole line to beyond point 66, where Sergt. H. Haigh got in touch with a small party of the 5th Battalion. Consolidation of the line, which was very wide and deep, then began. Only about forty of the Battalion had reached the second objective. These were organised in a line of posts from point 86, which was held by Sergt. Bancroft and Cpl. Denham, to beyond point 66. The second objective had been taken a little before 6-0 a.m. Soon after, the Germans began to bombard it heavily with artillery and trench mortars, and the discomfort of A Company was added to by some of the British guns, which had not "lifted" sufficiently and were firing into its back.

Meanwhile, except for such men as Cpl. Denham's Lewis gun team which had become detached from its company, no one had seen or heard anything of D Company since the opening of the attack. Like the rest it had advanced at zero hour, and had crossed No Man's Land on a right incline. Its two waves had halted near the enemy front line, waiting for the barrage to lift. Comparatively few casualties had been suffered in the advance, but these included Sec.-Lieut. C. W. Tomlinson missing, and

Lieut.-Col. J. WALKER, D.S.O.

Lieut. J. T. Riley and C.S.M. J. C. Walker wounded. Both of the latter refused to go to the rear to have their wounds dressed, and continued the advance with the rest of the company. When the barrage lifted, the men stormed the enemy front line, and some of them extended up a very battered communication trench, which they believed to be their objective. All dugouts were bombed, and several prisoners were taken; these apparently suffered the same fate as most of the other prisoners that day. The men set to work to consolidate what had been captured. They had not been long in their new position when the enemy made a weak counter-attack, from the direction of the Schwaben Redoubt. This was driven off without difficulty, but the men had very little opportunity to carry on with the consolidation. Their position was very exposed and the enemy defences, which had been captured, were so shattered that they afforded little cover. Very heavy rifle and machine gun fire, both from the Schwaben Redoubt and the east, was directed on them; and shells were soon bursting in their midst. But where was the Company ? The exact position it reached that day has been a matter for controversy ever since. No other company ever got into touch with it, and the German report, already mentioned, sheds no light on the mystery. It seems probable, indeed almost certain, that they inclined too much to the right in crossing No Man's Land, and entered the enemy front line to the south-east of point 84; in fact, it would appear that the Company actually captured, and held for some hours, the fringe of the Schwaben Redoubt. But it is only fair to say that Sergt. (now C.S.M.) W. Brooke, the only senior N.C.O. of D Company who got back to the British lines, is still convinced that the Company reached point 84, its correct objective.

It is convenient, at this point, to interrupt the narrative for a short time, in order to summarise the situation about 7-0 a.m. and to note what steps had been taken by the enemy to deal with it.

About 7-0 a.m. the positions of companies were as follows :—

A Company held the German support line from point 86, where there was an isolated post, to a little way beyond point 66. On both flanks the line was clear of the enemy for some considerable distance.

B Company held the German front line, from about midway between points 84 and 54, to beyond point 54. No enemy was in the line between the Company and point 84, nor for some distance on the left.

D Company held a position facing south-east, on the fringe of the Schwaben Redoubt; exactly where cannot be said. All companies were very weak and no reinforcements had arrived, for reasons which will be indicated later. Only one officer per company was left—Lieut. W. N. Everitt, M.C., with A Company, Sec.-Lieut. H. E. Pohlmann with B Company, and Lieut. J. T. Riley with D Company. Sec.-Lieut. V. A. Horsfall of B Company fell soon after the first objective was taken. Sec.-Lieut E. C. Mee of D Company was lying dead in the enemy wire. Supplies of S.A.A. were running very low, and bombs were almost exhausted. No carrying parties had been able to get up to the captured positions, and the only way to replenish was to collect from the dead and wounded who dotted the ground. But the most serious aspect of the situation was that the rest of the attack south of the Ancre had failed. By 7-0 a.m. the only British troops maintaining their positions in the enemy defences were those of the Battalion, with elements of the 5th Battalion—all hopelessly mixed up. The enemy, finding there were no British near the Pope's Nose, was re-occupying his front line there, and cautiously feeling his way along the trench towards B Company.

Meanwhile, energetic measures had been taken from the start by the German commander opposite. As soon as the situation began to develop clearly, he directed part of his reserve troops to counter-attack along, and parallel to, the Munster Gasse. The remainder were sent to the Schwaben Redoubt to strengthen the garrison there, and to counter-attack from that direction. There is no doubt that the enemy attached more importance to the holding of the Schwaben Redoubt than to anything else on that front. This is amply proved by the dispositions of his reserve troops on September 3rd. It is also borne out by men of the Battalion who were captured that day, and who have given accounts of their examinations by the enemy. And the enemy was right. With the Schwaben Redoubt still in his hands, he could dominate and enfilade practically all the objectives of the

49th Division. It would also appear, from their own account, that the Germans found it necessary to utilise the whole of their regimental reserve that day, before they succeeded in repelling the British; and that they even began to draw reinforcements from another unit—the 66th Infantry Regt.

Soon after 8-0 a.m., serious enemy counter-attacks began on A Company's position. For some time the barrage had slackened, and even rifle and machine gun fire had died down. What puzzled the men of A Company was to see Germans in the neighbourhood of the Pope's Nose, and in the support line in rear of it; for it must be borne in mind that no one knew anything of the situation on any other front than his own. These Germans, as has already been said, were cautiously working their way along the trenches towards the British, bombing as they went; but they were still a long way off. The real counter-attack at length came from enemy troops who advanced across the open, on both sides of the Munster Gasse. The post at point 86 had, by this time, completely run out of S.A.A. and bombs, and so was unable to offer any real resistance to the advance. The Germans came cautiously forward; avoiding a frontal attack, they worked round the right flank of the post until they were in its rear. Bombing it from this position, they caused many casualties. Sergt. Bancroft, Cpl. Payne and several men were killed; Cpl. Denham and a number of others were wounded. Having thus prepared the way for an assault, the enemy rushed the post, overwhelmed and made prisoners of the few survivors. This happened unbeknown to the rest of the men of A Company. The first indication they had of it was the enemy bombing along the second objective from the right. The situation soon became impossible. With no bombs and scarcely a round of S.A.A. left, they were forced slowly to withdraw towards their left. On arriving at point 66, they found themselves between two fires, for the enemy bombing party from the west was also approaching along the trench. The position was clearly untenable. Lieut. Everitt had only a handful of men left. He gave orders to withdraw down the communication trench to point 54. The withdrawal was conducted slowly and in good order, two or three men waiting at each bend in the trench to cover it. At length the front line was reached, but only a few isolated men of B Company could be found there; the enemy artillery and machine guns had done their work only too well. The party reconnoitred along the trench towards the Pope's Nose; another enemy bombing party was encountered. With so few survivors, and almost without ammunition, Lieut. Everitt could do no more. He gave the order to withdraw to the parallels. The men jumped out of the trench and started across No Man's Land, but they did not scatter sufficiently. Few ever reached the comparative safety of their own lines. A machine gun opened from the Pope's Nose, and most of them fell. Of the fate of Lieut. Everitt nothing certain is known. For some time it was hoped that he was still alive. But nothing definite was ever learned of what happened to him after he gave the order to withdraw. One of the most gallant, competent and hardworking officers the Battalion ever had, he probably fell when so many of his men went down in that last crossing of No Man's Land.

And what of D Company? Its fate was much the same as A Company's. Harassed by machine guns from the Schwaben Redoubt, and by rifle fire from snipers to the east, it beat off several counter-attacks. S.A.A. and bombs ran out, and the men searched the dead to replenish their supplies. Rapidly their numbers dwindled. Severely wounded and in great pain, Lieut. J. T. Riley fought fiercely until he was at length killed. C.S.M. J. C. Walker, who had carried on though wounded early in the action, was also killed. Yet, practically leaderless, the men still fought on, until an officer of the 5th Battalion, who had become mixed up with D Company, ordered a withdrawal. Then the remnants of the company—they did not muster twenty, all told—withdrew to the parallels.

Everything that had been gained was lost. Not a Britisher remained in the enemy lines, save the few men who had been captured. The number of these was very small. On the authority of the Germans themselves, only seven unwounded prisoners from the 4th and 5th Battalions were taken that day. Many men were still lying out in shell holes, and, during the rest of the day and night that followed, some of these crawled back into the lines. But there were far more lying out there who would never crawl again.

Throughout the action Battalion H.Q. was located in a deep dugout, near the junction of Inniskilling Avenue with Whitchurch Street; C Company was in Battalion reserve, either in or near the old British front line. All arrangements had been made for sending up stores soon after the objectives were taken. East Koyli Sap was to be improved, and used as a communication trench for that purpose. But this was never done. Early in the action it became so crowded with casualties and others that parties could not move along it. Even if they had been able to do so, it entered the enemy front line at the Pope's Nose, which was never occupied by the British on September 3rd.

Lack of reliable information was the most serious difficulty with which Battalion H.Q. had to contend during the battle, and the 5th Battalion was even worse off in that respect. Signallers had gone forward with the assaulting companies, but no message ever came back from them. Cpl. C. Landale, D.C.M. made gallant attempts to run a telephone line across No Man's Land, but it could not be maintained on account of the enemy barrage. Most of the runners who left with messages were killed. No information was ever received from the observation post. The result was that, during the whole operation, Battalion H.Q. was almost completely ignorant of what was happening.

For a long time the sole information obtained was from wounded men, and was very indefinite. At 5-55 a.m. it was learned that the first objective had been taken, that the second was being attacked, and that the two assaulting battalions were badly mixed. Ten minutes later a wounded man reported that A Company had taken its objective. Then there was little news for more than an hour and a half. Two carrying parties were sent forward, and it is believed that a few bombs did reach the German front line and were used by the 5th Battalion. Runners were twice sent out to get in touch with B Company, but none came back. Information that the attack of the 146th Infantry Brigade on the left had failed was received by the Battalion about 6-30 a.m. Knowing so little of the situation, the Commanding Officer naturally hesitated to throw any more troops into the battle; and, as events turned out, it is well he did not use his reserves, for they could have done little real good, and there would only have been more casualties.

At last a wounded runner arrived from B Company, bearing the following message from Sec.-Lieut. H. E. Pohlmann :—

"To I.R.

Am holding point 54 and to left 100 yds. In touch with 5th. Only remaining officer in B Coy. Bombs wanted. 6-40 a.m. 3.9.16. H. E. Pohlmann, 2 Lt. B Coy."

It had taken the runner two hours to come.

At once Major Walker ordered two platoons of C Company, and two of the reserve bombing teams, to advance across the open and reinforce B Company. But these orders were never issued. Before they could be written out the advanced signal station reported that the men of the 147th Infantry Brigade were withdrawing.

C Company had not been engaged, but it had suffered many casualties from shell fire. When it was clear that the attack had failed, Capt. Marshall was ordered to man the parallels, in case the enemy tried to counter-attack. But no such attempt was made.

At 11-50 a.m., more than four hours after it had been written, a message was brought in from Lieut. Everitt, by a wounded runner. Arriving so late, it was of no practical use ; the situation had entirely changed. But as evidence of the deeds of A Company that day, it deserves to be quoted in full :—

"To the Adjt.

My right is only at the communication trench point 86. I am partly in the fifth lines. I have only roughly 25 men including six from B Coy. Have no bombers. Short of bombs and Lewis Gun ammunition. Our artillery firing into our back especially on the right.

Don't know where D Coy. are.

W. N. Everitt, Lt.,
3.9.16. 7-40 a.m. O.C. A Coy."

About 5-0 p.m. troops of the 148th Infantry Brigade relieved the Battalion in the line. The weary men withdrew to Martinsart Wood to reorganise, but a party of C Company was left in for the night, to search No Man's Land for wounded, and to help in the evacuation of those who had already come in.

Only once—October 11th, 1918—has the Battalion had heavier casualties than on September 3rd. It went into action 18 officers and 629 other ranks strong; of these only three companies, each consisting of 3 officers and 127 other ranks, and a few Battalion H.Q. details, went " over the top." The total casualties that day were 11 officers and 336 other ranks. More than half were either known to be dead, or were missing; and as the number of prisoners taken by the enemy was very small, it may fairly be presumed that the Battalion lost, in killed alone, at least 150 other ranks. Of the nine officers who went over with the assaulting companies, only two, both wounded, returned; in addition, Sec.-Lieut. F. A. Innes was killed at 147th Infantry Brigade H.Q., and Sec.-Lieut. W. Smith was wounded with C Company. September 3rd is the blackest day in the Battalion's history, for, unlike October 11th, 1918, it had no success to compensate for its casualties. To-day, upon the very line of the first objective, which B Company carried that eventful morning and was later forced to evacuate, there stands a great cemetery. In it have been collected the remains of many men, from scores of solitary graves; and on the crosses the legend " Unknown soldier 1/4th Battalion Duke of Wellington's Regt." is one of the most common. There rest many of the gallant men who fell that day.

It is not the purpose of this book to criticise as a general rule, but some slight exception must be made in connection with the attack on September 3rd. At the time there was a widespread belief, which was certainly held by most of the higher authorities, that the Battalion never gained its objectives. This was wrong. A and B Companies reached, and cleared the enemy from, the whole of the first and second objectives; it is true they did not occupy the whole of them, but that was due simply to lack of men. For more than two hours there were no Germans in either of the lines which the Battalion was ordered to capture. These facts are clearly proved, not only by the evidence of the men who carried out the assault, but also by the German official report on the action. The men of D Company, as has been stated, seem to have got too far to the right; but even they fulfilled their role, for they successfully defended the Battalion's exposed right flank so long as there were men enough to hold the ground which had been won. During the next few weeks several divisions successively failed to carry the objectives of September 3rd. Even after Thiepval itself had fallen, it was some time before the Schwaben Redoubt and the defences north of it passed into British hands.

(c) The Leipsig Redoubt.

The day after the Battalion's unsuccessful attack on the German line, Major R. E. Sugden, D.S.O., rejoined and assumed command, being promoted Lieut.-Colonel a few days later. He had been in England for nearly nine months, as the result of his wound received near Ypres the previous December; but now, though he had not yet fully recovered the use of his hand and arm, he had returned to France. For nearly two years from this date he held command of the Battalion, only leaving it when he was appointed G.O.C., 151st Infantry Brigade, in June, 1918.

After a few days in Martinsart Wood, the Battalion moved back to bivouacs near Hedauville. Little work was done except reorganisation, which was very necessary. Not only had an enormous number of officers and N.C.O's become casualties, but three whole companies had been practically wiped out. Out of these companies no officers, only one warrant officer—C.S.M. W. Medley—and very few N.C.O's had survived. The elaborate B Echelons of later days were only in their infancy, and so little framework existed on which to rebuild. The only thing to do was to make use of the personnel of C Company to provide the necessary framework. Hence, many N.C.O's and specialists were transferred to other companies. Sec.-Lieut. F. Walker and Lieut. J. G. Mowat were appointed to the command of A and B Companies respectively. C.S.M. A. McNulty again became C.S.M. of A Company, and C.Q.M.S. A. L. Lord of C Company was transferred to D Company as C.S.M. The supply of men was simpler. Large drafts arrived within a few days, and, by the middle of September, the Battalion's fighting strength was practically the same as it had been at the beginning of the month. On September 21st a draft of eleven officers arrived, and several more joined a few days later. Among them were three or four who had already served with the Battalion abroad, either as officers or in the ranks, while others had seen active service elsewhere.

While the Battalion was at Hedauville, Brig.-General E. F. Brereton, C.B., D.S.O., came over to say farewell. The men were drawn up in a hollow square, and were first addressed by the Divisional Commander. Then the Brigadier spoke. In a magnificent speech, which deeply impressed all who heard it, he paid a glowing tribute to the dead and said good-bye to the living. The parade was dismissed and all rushed down to the road. Roar upon roar of cheering burst forth as the car passed slowly through the lines of men and, at length, disappeared from view. If he had ever doubted it, the demonstration must have proved to the General how much he was beloved in his Brigade. Brig.-General C. G. Lewes, D.S.O., assumed command of the 147th Infantry Brigade.

By September 15th the Battalion was considered ready for active service again; it moved up to Martinsart Wood and from thence, the next day, to Crucifix Corner, Aveluy. On September 17th it was in support to an attack, made by the 1/7th Battalion Duke of Wellington's Regt., on part of the Leipsig Redoubt. Unlike the bigger operation of September 3rd, this attack was planned to take place in the evening, zero hour being 6-30 p.m. Thus the assaulting troops would have the whole night for consolidation. The main duty of the Battalion was to provide a number of carrying parties, no less than 7 officers and 215 other ranks being detailed for that purpose. Of these, about half were to work with the assaulting troops, while the remainder were responsible for keeping the various dumps supplied. Profiting by the experience of September 3rd, Brigade H.Q. had decided that carrying parties should actually accompany the assaulting troops when they attacked. It was hoped, in this way, to get some supplies of ammunition up to the objectives before the enemy barrage came down. The men for this duty were divided into three separate parties, under Sec.-Lieuts.

H. N. Taylor, E. W. Flatow and E. Rawnsley respectively. A further party, under Sec.-Lieut. G. Rawnsley, was to carry up water in petrol tins.

Half-an-hour before zero all parties were in their assembly positions. Many of the men, who had only left England a few days, had never even been in the line before, and it must have been a particularly nervous time for them. The principal supplies to be carried up were Mills bombs, and every man had a box under each arm. When the assaulting troops went over, the carrying parties advanced immediately in rear of them. The ground was not easy to cross, being one mass of shell holes, and littered everywhere with the debris of shattered trenches and wire entanglements. Nevertheless, the men went well, and most of them succeeded in delivering their first load before the enemy barrage came down. Back they went for a second load, and this time the crossing was more dangerous. Though rather scattered, and not particularly heavy, the enemy barrage was most uncomfortable; and machine guns did not make the situation any pleasanter. But through it all the men worked splendidly. Backwards and forwards they went, time after time, until at length the unusual message came back " Enough bombs." That message is the best criticism that can be given of the way in which the carrying parties did their work. By this time they had naturally become very scattered. Many were being employed as messengers or guides; some had lost their bearings, for it was now quite dark; and there were many casualties. Altogether, the Battalion lost that day 12 other ranks, including C.S.M. T. H. Greenwood of C Company, killed, 7 missing, and 39 wounded. But the work had been well done. Officers collected all they could find of their parties, and rejoined the rest of the Battalion; but many men did not report back until long after dawn the next day.

The day after the attack the Battalion moved up into close support to the 5th Battalion Duke of Wellington's Regt., which had taken over the captured trenches. Three days later it took over the defence of the new line. D Company, with C Company in close support to it, held the whole of the captured ground; the other companies occupied the old British line. D Company's sector was a ghastly place. Rain and shell-fire had turned the ground into a mass of mud, littered with the awful debris of battle. Never had the Battalion seen so many dead Germans; and there were many British too. Bodies were lying all over the ground in the open; many more were exposed by the shovel, and hastily re-covered. A hot September sun beat down in the daytime, and the air was filled with the stench of decaying humanity. Water was scarce, as every drop of it had to be carried up, and had to be used very economically. Ration parties had a very hard task, for there were neither tracks nor proper communication trenches. Almost the only real comfort was provided by the excellent German tunnelled dugouts which abounded, and were sufficient to accommodate the whole company. These were from twenty to thirty feet down; they were splendidly built and, in some cases, quite comfortably furnished; and they were proof against the heaviest shell. This was as well, for the hostile artillery was very active. Though the Germans probably had a very hazy idea of the British positions, they knew where their own deep dugouts had been and persistently shelled those localities. Practically all movement could be easily observed, and there was much coming and going of staff officers and others in connection with the new attack on Thiepval which was planning. D Company came in for all the shelling, which was brought on by this movement, and also for the not infrequent barrages put down by the enemy. The other companies had an easier, though far from pleasant, time.

Much work was done by the Battalion while it was in the Leipsig Redoubt. Its role was to prepare the way for an attack on Thiepval by the 18th Division. Assembly trenches had to be dug; the dead had to be buried. Most of this work was done by the support companies, who sent up large parties each night. D Company's duty was restricted to holding the line—quite a sufficient task for the new men of whom the company was mainly composed. Casualties occurred almost hourly. It was a nerve-racking time.

At length the relief came on September 24th. A heavy bombardment of 15 cm. shells about 5-0 p.m., which at one time seemed likely to hinder the relief seriously, was stopped by the

British retaliation. An unusually quiet night followed. Soon after dark the 12th Battalion Middlesex Regt. began to arrive; and when, about midnight, D Company's relief was complete, the Battalion turned its back on the Somme battlefield for ever. B and C Companies had been relieved earlier and they marched straight through to Lealvillers. A and D Companies were to be met by buses at the bottom of Black Horse Road. The former got away after a long wait, but there were no conveyances for the latter. Wearily—few of them had had any sleep to speak of for three days or nights—the men dragged themselves along to Martinsart Wood, where they simply dropped down by the roadside and slept. About dawn buses did arrive, and the company was quickly taken to Lealvillers, where a halt was made for breakfast. Then it bussed straight through to Halloy, while the rest of the Battalion had to march. The ride was some satisfaction for the night spent on the road.

The day after its arrival at Halloy the Battalion learned of the fall of Thiepval. In the midst of the satisfaction caused by this news, there was naturally some little disappointment that, after so many months of work and fighting, it had not been " in at the death."

CHAPTER VI.

WITH THE THIRD ARMY.

(a) Hannescamps.

MANY expected, and all hoped for, a fairly long period of rest when the Battalion moved back to Halloy, after nearly three months of the Somme Battle. But it was not to be. The 49th Division was transferred to the Third Army, and, within five days of its relief in the Leipsig Redoubt, the Battalion was holding a front line sector again. Two days of easy marching, and a night each at Humbercamps and Bienvillers, had brought it to the Hannescamps sector, where it relieved the 2nd Battalion Royal Welsh Fusiliers, on September 29th.

The new sector lay astride the Hannescamps—Essarts Road, and was the longest front the Battalion had held up to that time. It was outside the area of the Somme Battle, had been quiet all the summer, and so had suffered little from shell fire. At a first glance the trenches appeared to be in splendid condition, and in places they really were—Lulu Lane, the communication trench on the left, was about as fine a piece of field engineering as the Battalion had seen. But the greater part of the front line and most of the communication trenches were far from good. The weather was dry when they were taken over and, fortunately, there was practically no rain while the Battalion was there. Very little of the work had been properly revetted, and it was obvious that the trenches would slide in as soon as the wet weather came. The front line was of the regulation type—six yard bays and four yard traverses—with two or three long saps running out into No Man's Land. It was fairly well provided with shelters, B Company in the centre being particularly well off with a number in the sunken Hannescamps—Essarts Road. It was garrisoned by three companies; the fourth was in reserve, with two platoons near Battalion H.Q. and two about halfway up Lulu Lane. Battalion H.Q. lived in shelters along the road, just south of the village of Hannescamps. These were moderately comfortable, except for the rats; but few would have been any good against shell fire.

The enemy was very quiet. Apart from a few light shells now and then, his artillery was practically inactive. Trench mortar, machine gun and rifle fire were almost unknown. This was due mainly to the extent of No Man's Land. On the extreme left, the opposing lines approached within about 250 yards of one another; but on the greater part of the front they were over 1,000 yards apart. The main activity of the Battalion was patrolling. In that department Sec.-Lieut. G. Crowther, who had succeeded Sec.-Lieut. H. H. Aykroyd, M.C. as Battalion Intelligence Officer, was extremely active. Night after night he penetrated deeply into No Man's Land in his efforts to secure an identification—but without success. On one occasion he did encounter the enemy—near the Osier Bed, which was his particular haunt—but he failed to make a capture, though he certainly wounded one German. Apart from this, the Battalion only came in contact with the enemy once. During their first night in the sector, some men of C Company, who were holding a sap-head on the left, were bombed, and suffered several casualties.

At Hannescamps, the Battalion had taken over the most elaborate and well-organised system of cooking they had ever seen in a front line sector. A good kitchen had been built in a sunken road not far from the village, and there hot meals were regularly prepared for the whole Battalion. These were carried up, in hot food containers, by the men of the reserve company, and living was almost as good in the front line as in rest billets. The only serious difficulties were the shortage of water, and the rats. Rats! Everyone who has seen much of trench warfare knows how prevalent rats are. But never, at any other time or place, has the Battalion had to contend with such a pest as it found at Hannescamps. Everywhere the trenches swarmed with them; but nowhere were they so bad as among the shelters near Battalion H.Q. They ate everything they could get their teeth into. The very first night the Battalion was there, not only were nearly all iron rations spoiled, but more than half the packs and haversacks of the men of D Company, who were in reserve, were ruined. Nothing could be done to cope with them and they had to be endured. The remaining packs and haversacks were only saved by taking them out nightly and hanging them on thin wires, which were stretched from tree to tree in a neighbouring orchard.

After four days in this sector, the Battalion was relieved by the 1/5th Battalion King's Own Yorkshire Light Infantry, and went to Souastre for a rest. There all efforts were concentrated on smartening up. This was very necessary. For practically three months there had been little opportunity for a man to keep himself bodily clean, much less smart; and there had been few proper parades. The result had been a distinct falling off in smartness; but, after one or two periods in Brigade Reserve, the improvement was very marked.

Only two tours were done in the Hannescamps Sector and then the 146th Infantry Brigade took over the line. While the remainder of the Battalion moved to Bienvillers for the night, D Company was sent to the Bluff, south of Fonquevillers, where it came under the orders of the 5th Battalion Duke of Wellington's Regt. There it provided shifts for work in the tunnels for two days, and then rejoined the Battalion at Humbercamps. After two more short moves, the Battalion arrived again at Souastre.

(b) Fonquevillers.

From the middle of October until the beginning of December, the Battalion was inter-relieving with the 5th Battalion Duke of Wellington's Regt. in the Y Sector, Fonquevillers. This sector had a frontage of rather over a thousand yards, and extended from the Fonquevillers-Gommecourt Road on the left, to the "Mousetrap," an unoccupied rectangle of ground opposite Gommecourt Park, on the right. It had been the scene of one of the most costly failures of July 1st, for from it the men of the

46th Division had started when they attempted to take Gommecourt in conjunction with the 31st Division. When the Battalion first took over the sector, it was held with two companies in the front line and two in support. But, before long, these dispositions were altered. The front line system was divided into three company sectors, each company finding its own immediate support; and the fourth company became battalion reserve. The front line had been continuous at one time, but now parts of it were practically derelict; communication along it was still possible without much difficulty, but there were unoccupied gaps between the three companies. The position was a strong one, though it was not to be compared with the magnificent defences which the enemy had constructed for himself round Gommecourt. Battalion H.Q. occupied a line of shelters and dugouts along the Fonquevillers—Hebuterne Road, commonly known as Thorpe Street. Chief among these was the Bairnsfather Dugout, so-called because it had once been occupied by the artist whose work is so well known to all readers of the *Bystander*. It was a comfortable little place, like several more in the vicinity. Its walls were lined with whitewashed timber and adorned with many drawings by the creator of "Old Bill," some executed in pencil, some apparently with the end of a red-hot iron.

Things were not so quiet in the neighbourhood of Fonquevillers as they had been at Hannescamps. The enemy did not make much use of heavy artillery, but his field guns were often active. These did not harass the front line troops greatly, but a good deal of shrapnel was fired on Thorpe Street, and various parts of the village frequently received attention. The most "unhealthy" spot was the Shrine, at the western entrance; it was never advisable to loiter near there for long. Trench mortars caused a lot of trouble. On the left in particular these often fired, and, though actual "minnies" were uncommon, there were plenty of "rum-jars." On one occasion the Commanding Officer was confined for some time in a dugout, the entrance to which had been blocked by one of these trench mortar shells. The roof of this dugout was at least fifteen feet thick, but it was bulged in by the force of the explosion.

As at Hannescamps, the offensive spirit of the Battalion was mainly confined to patrolling. No Man's Land varied from 200 to 400 yards in width. With the exception of the ruins of the Sucherie, which were really on the next battalion's front, there was little of interest between the lines. Sec.-Lieut. G. Crowther was again to the fore in his efforts to capture a prisoner, but he had no success. The enemy appeared to be quite willing to leave No Man's Land to the British ; at any rate, few patrols of his were encountered. At length, when all minor attempts to secure identification had proved unsuccessful, 147th Infantry Brigade H.Q. determined to make a raid—the first operation of that type to be carried out in the Brigade. It was undertaken by the 5th Battalion Duke of Wellington's Regt., who made the attempt one night through the 4th Battalion, which was then holding the line. The operation was well planned and executed ; the raiding party succeeded in entering the enemy lines and did a great deal of damage ; but they failed to secure an identification. Apart from a few minor duties, such as providing covering fire from Lewis guns and assisting in the evacuation of the wounded, the Battalion took no part. But some casualties were suffered from the defensive barrage which the enemy put down.

While the Battalion was in this sector, the successful attack north of the River Ancre, which resulted in the capture of Beaumont Hamel and other positions, took place. The battle was too far off to have any real effect on the Fonquevillers front, though, at one time, it was intended that a smoke barrage should be put up by the Battalion to distract attention from the real attack. Elaborate preparations had been made for this, but eventually the orders were cancelled and nothing was done.

At Fonquevillers, Battalion H.Q. once spent a very uncomfortable half-hour. "Authentic" information had been received from Brigade that the enemy had driven a mine right under H.Q. mess. The exact time at which this was to be exploded was known, and it was found that it came in the middle of a relief. This was most inconsiderate on the part of the Germans, for the necessity of handing over correctly prevented officers visiting their friends, or making expeditions "on duty" to distant parts of the line. There was an anxious minute when the time came to go into the air. Nothing happened.

Winter had begun soon after the Battalion came into the sector, and, with its coming, conditions became very bad. The trenches were in no condition to stand bad weather. Very little work had been done on them for months, probably because everyone hoped that the British would have advanced far beyond them ere winter set in. Now, when the rain came, they immediately began to cave in. But the Battalion had behind it the experience gained at Ypres the previous winter. There was indeed more work to do than could possibly be done; so parts of the line were allowed to become derelict, and one or two communication trenches fell into disuse. Work was concentrated on what was most necessary, and the battalion in the line had the assistance of large working parties sent up by the battalion in reserve. Long hours had to be worked, but excellent results were obtained. There was plenty of mud, but no part of the trenches in use ever became really water-logged. How well the men worked during one tour is shown by the following highly complimentary letter, which was received from the Brigadier :—

"O.C. 4th W. Riding Regt.

I wish to express to the Battalion under your command my great appreciation of the work done in your sector, and the excellent spirit shown by your men during the past 6 day tour in the trenches under circumstances of exceptional difficulty.

Your work was good, not shoddy, and when not working your men were trying to shoot Bosches.

My only regret is, that owing to circumstances, I was unable to spend more time with you, but it was a compliment that after what I saw on Wednesday, I knew I could leave the Battalion to do its best.

This excellent spirit of keenness and hard work in a Battalion is worth a great deal to its Brigade Commander.

Please circulate my remarks to your officers and men.

C. Lewes, B.-General,

Commdg. 147 Brigade."

Periods of Brigade Reserve were usually spent in Souastre, at which village the Battalion transport was permanently billeted. Most of the men occupied barns of the familiar French

type, those timber and clay structures so well known to all who
have served with the British Expeditionary Force. Generally
speaking, the troops were fairly comfortable. The barns were
in fairly good condition. There were plenty of civilians still
living in the village, though it was not far from the line. There
were plenty of estaminets, and there was a Y.M.C.A. hut. Little
training was possible owing to the large working parties which
had to be found. Needless to say, the men groused at these,
but, as they worked mostly on the trenches which they occupied
themselves in the line, they realised that the work was for their
own benefit. Sometimes only half the Battalion went to Souastre,
the rest stopping in billets in Fonquevillers, under the command
of Major A. L. Mowat. This arrangement was made in order
to have two companies on the spot to work under the direction
of the 57th Field Company, Royal Engineers.

For the greater part of this period the Battalion was very
short of officers. When it left the Somme area it was well over
strength, but, soon after its arrival in the Third Army, it had
been called on to transfer ten to other battalions of the Regiment.
No further drafts had been received, many officers were absent
on courses, and the usual wastage through sickness was going
on. The result was that, during the latter part of the time at
Fonquevillers, there were seldom more than two officers per company doing duty in the line.

On December 5th the Battalion was relieved in the Y Sector
by the 1/5th Battalion Sherwood Foresters—the battalion
which had gone " over the top " from those very same trenches
on July 1st. As each platoon was relieved it marched back to
Souastre, where a halt was made in a field for dinner, after
which companies formed up and marched to Warlencourt. The
next day the Battalion marched to Halloy, where it was to stop
until early in the New Year.

(c) Halloy.

Halloy was one of the worst places for billeting in the whole
of France. The barns were mostly in a bad state of repair.

The hutment camps were exceptionally muddy. The inhabitants of the village were far from sweet-tempered, as a general rule. To make matters worse, it seemed to be the invariable custom of the British authorities to crowd far more troops into the place than it could reasonably be expected to hold. The weather was not particularly bad for the time of the year, but December is never an ideal month. Hence the conditions, under which the Christmas of 1916 was spent, were none of the best.

There was not a great deal of training. Occasional battalion route marches were held, but the companies attempted little except specialist training. No. 5 Platoon of B Company won the 147th Infantry Brigade Platoon Competition; but it was not successful when it represented the Brigade in the 49th Divisional Competition. Towards the end of the time at Halloy, large working parties had to be provided for unloading stores at Mondicourt Railhead. Several large drafts of men arrived to replace the wastage of the previous autumn, and, by the beginning of January, the Battalion's " paper " strength was over 1,000 other ranks.

The chief event was Christmas Day. Great preparations were made as usual. A motor lorry was obtained to fetch additional supplies from Amiens. Cpl. F. Smith was, of course, very much to the fore; Sergt. Lockwood rose to the occasion, as he always did at that season of the year. Dinner accommodation was a difficulty. Only one suitable room, at an estaminet, could be obtained, and that would only hold one company at a time. So the dinners started at noon and ran on right through the afternoon, the men sitting down in four company shifts. But everything went off well, the usual smoking concerts helped to pass the time, and the anniversary was thoroughly enjoyed by all.

(d) Berles.

On January 7th, the Battalion left Halloy, and, moving by march route, relieved the 2nd Battalion Bedfordshire Regt. in Brigade Reserve to the B1 Sub-sector. Battalion H.Q. and two companies were accommodated in the village of Berles; the other two companies were at Humbercamps. These were to be the dispositions of the Battalion for the rest of the month, whenever it was out of the line, except on one occasion when the whole went to Humbercamps. Though very much nearer the enemy—the village was only about a mile from the British front line—the troops at Berles were far more comfortable than those at Humbercamps. Parts of the village had been very little shelled. Quite a number of French civilians were still living there and a few small shops were open. There were many very comfortable billets in private houses, some of which still contained a good deal of furniture; and the men were not at all crowded. Here and there extensive tunnels had been dug in the hard chalk, and to these the men had orders to retire if the enemy started shelling. Working parties had to be provided as usual, but these could be borne with ease in such comfortable surroundings.

The Battalion first took over the B1 Sub-sector on January 10th. Its dispositions were somewhat peculiar. The front line was divided into three company sectors, but one platoon was drawn from each to form a composite company, in reserve at Battalion H.Q. The fourth company lived in extremely comfortable billets in the village, where it was in reserve if needed; but it was mainly employed on working parties. Seldom has part of a battalion in the line been more comfortably off.

The sector was in an awful state. Laterally, each company was completely isolated from its neighbours by absolutely derelict trench. Long stretches of the communication trenches were deep in water, while portions of the front line fairly beggar description. It had been very badly constructed; in some places the revetments had bulged so much that there was scarcely room to force one's way along the trench; elsewhere, the sides had collapsed altogether, and the trench was nothing but a cavity, filled with mud and debris. The pumps were kept constantly at work, but were quite inadequate to deal with the water. So bad was the front line on the left company front that, during the moonless nights of the first tour, it took the subaltern on duty two hours to walk once each way along the line—and yet the company sector was only about two hundred yards in length. But the men stood it well. Kitchens, similar to those at Hannescamps, provided plenty of hot food; and thigh boots were available for all.

Artillery was fairly active on both sides. The vicinity of Battalion H.Q. received most attention and several casualties were suffered near there, the chief being R.S.M. T. Glover, who was wounded in the arm by a shell splinter. There was also a certain amount of trench mortar fire, particularly on the right, where the lines were not more than eighty yards apart; indeed, at one point, only about forty yards separated the saps of the opposing troops. The British had a heavy trench mortar which occasionally fired on the enemy defences, opposite to the left company. Owing to doubts as to the accuracy of this infernal machine, it was customary to clear a portion of the front line while it was firing. Certainly it produced most terrific explosions, and it provoked a good deal of retaliation until, one day, a " premature " destroyed not only the gun but the whole of the team which was working it.

Towards the end of the month an exceptionally hard frost began. Quickly, all the mud and water froze hard, and sheets of ice covered the bottoms of many trenches. Snow fell and the ground became white. It froze on the trench grids, making them so slippery that it was almost impossible to walk without sandbags tied over the boots. The change in the weather had its advantages as well as its disadvantages, and probably the former outweighed the latter. Iron-hard ground was a great improvement on the awful mud; ice was better than water; and the weather was dry. But the lot of the sentry was most unenviable. To stand on the fire-step, in the face of a biting north-easterly wind, with the thermometer registering as much as 28 degrees of frost, was a terrible task. Everything possible was done. Hot drink and rum were provided. Section commanders actually put their men through some of the exercises in bayonet fighting and physical drill in the front line. But the weather of early 1917 will not be forgotten by those who were in the trenches at that time.

During the earlier part of the month patrolling had been very active, in spite of the bad condition of No Man's Land. Little had been possible on the right company front, where the lines were so near together; but, further north, they were as much as five hundred yards apart in places. Sergt. J. Bancroft, of C Company, was particularly energetic. Twice he reached the enemy wire, reconnoitred it for several hundred yards, and brought back very valuable information as to its strength, the enemy dispositions, defences and working parties. On one occasion, finding his men rather " windy," he fell them in in No Man's Land, put them through some bayonet fighting drill, and then proceeded with the patrol. But the deed for which he won the Military Medal happened after the cold weather had set in, when the snow-covered ground shone white in the rays of the moon. Sec.-Lieut. G. Rawnsley, with Bancroft and two men, was out on patrol. He had reached a point about thirty yards from the enemy line when a flare revealed his presence, and he was shot through the head. In spite of the heavy fire maintained by the enemy, Bancroft remained with the body for some time, trying to get it back. Finding the task beyond his power, he returned to his own line, collected and led a party to the spot, and succeeded in bringing the body in. All this was done in the face of heavy fire, and his coolness and daring thoroughly merited the decoration which he received.

Before the frost set in, all work had been concentrated on keeping the trenches in a habitable condition. But, with the frost, such work became temporarily unnecessary, even had it been possible. Meanwhile, new theories of how a line should be held were developing. The gradual increase of fire power, due to the introduction of Lewis guns and the growth of the British artillery, made it unnecessary to keep so many men in the front line; the increase in the strength of the enemy artillery and trench mortars made it inadvisable to do so. Instead of a line in which practically every fire-bay was manned, the system of semi-isolated posts was coming in. To adapt the old trenches to this new idea of defence, now became the chief form of work. Derelict trenches had to be filled in; the trenches which were to be preserved had to be adapted for all round defence by platoon or section posts. This was mainly carried out by filling the disused trenches with wire, so that they could not be occupied by the enemy.

Bombing too had had its day, and the utility of the numerous saps, which covered most front lines, was discounted. Among other improvements in the Battalion's sector, it was decided to fill in the T head sap which lay only about forty yards from the enemy, on the right company front. This was a delicate task. The order was to fill it in with earth; but it approached so near to the German line that the least stroke of a pick on that iron-bound ground could easily be heard. What was to be done? As luck would have it, the enemy was engaged in wiring his sap just opposite; and so it became the nightly custom to assemble a working party in the British front line and wait until the enemy party was heard. Then the work of filling in the T head sap would begin, for no fire was likely to come from the enemy while his own party was out. This went on for several nights without incident; but the work progressed very slowly, owing to the frozen condition of the soil. On the last night the Battalion was in the line it changed its tactics. Instead of sending out a working party, it trained a Lewis gun on the enemy sap and opened fire as soon as the wiring party was heard. Whether any casualties were caused cannot be said; but the wiring came to an abrupt conclusion.

Had the Battalion remained longer in that sector, it would probably have been called upon to do a raid on the enemy line. Much time had been expended on reconnaissance for that purpose, and the order was fully expected. Perhaps it was due to its own intentions that the Brigade was so nervous about the enemy; whatever the cause, it seemed most anxious to ascribe to the Germans designs on the British line. A sign of this nervousness was the great interest taken in a gap in the enemy wire near the Berles-Monchy Road. It is probable that the gap was an old one, which had escaped notice up till then; but the amount of paper that flew about on the subject was enormous. Of course, nothing happened.

The Battalion's departure from the B1 Sub-sector was the result of a rearrangement of divisional fronts. The 46th Division was extending north and taking over the whole of the 147th Infantry Brigade sector, while the 49th Division was doing the same on its left. Hence, when the Battalion was relieved on January 30th, and moved to Humbercamps, it knew that it was not to return.

Brig.-Genl. R. E. SUGDEN, C.M.G., D.S.O., T.D.

(e) Riviére.

On February 1st the Battalion moved to Riviére, where it relieved the 8th Battalion King's Royal Rifle Corps, in Brigade Reserve to the F1 Sub-sector. The 1/5th Battalion Duke of Wellington's Regt. followed, and, throughout the next month, the two were inter-relieving as they had been at Berles. The accommodation in brigade reserve was very good, considering its nearness to the line. Three companies lived in billets in the village; the fourth garrisoned the Wailly Keeps, a reserve line of platoon posts. This latter was an ideal duty for an enthusiastic platoon commander. He had his own little command, nicely compact; he lived with his platoon, looked after its food, and supervised its work and training; and, except in one case, his company commander was not too near. What could a keen young subaltern want better ? The bulk of the Battalion in Riviére found working parties, so there was little chance for training. But the Battalion had a tour in the line to do before it was really able to taste the joys of brigade reserve. On February 2nd it took over the F1 Sub-sector from the 7th Battalion King's Royal Rifle Corps.

This sector was, in one respect, the most " perfect " the Battalion ever occupied. Students of the many official handbooks on " Trench Warfare," which were produced in the first two years of the war, will remember the excellent instruction on the planning of trenches—how each system should have a continuous front line, supervision trench, support line and reserve line, with numerous communication trenches from front to rear. They will remember too how each of these, except of course the supervision and communication trenches, was to consist of alternate bays and traverses, etc., etc. And those of them who knew the Western Front will remember how seldom, if ever, they saw these theories put into practice. Well, the F1 Sub-sector was an exception. The supervision trench did not, indeed, run the whole length of the front; but there were the continuous front, support and reserve lines, properly traversed and supplied with fire bays, and connected by numerous communication trenches. In fact, an aeroplane photograph of the sector might almost have been reproduced in one of the textbooks, as a perfect example of what ought to be done. The bombing expert had also been at work, and the protection of the main communication trenches was " beautiful,"—but was it effective ? Perhaps it was due to this theoretical accuracy of the sector that the authorities selected it as a training ground for embryo officers. At any rate, several privates from the Artists' Rifles were attached to the Battalion for instruction while it was in that area. So much for theory !

In practice also the line was not at all bad. The trenches were deep and narrow, and afforded good protection against shell fire. At the beginning of February everything was frozen hard, and so there was no trouble with the mud ; but when a thaw set in, shortly before the Battalion left the sector, the support line and several communication trenches soon became impassable. Accommodation was adequate ; most of the dugouts were sufficiently deep to withstand any ordinary bombardment and a few were really comfortable. In short, the line had been carefully constructed, in accordance with ideas now quickly becoming obsolete ; it had been well looked after, and might have been a pleasure to live in—but for the enemy. The archaic atmosphere was rather heightened by the presence of such " prehistoric " appliances as the West Spring Gun, and rifle batteries.

One of the most interesting features of the sector was a Russian sap, near the boundary between the centre and left companies. About 75 yards out in No Man's Land, and nearly parallel to the left company front, was a bank, behind which patrols could move quite out of sight of the enemy. The remains of a derelict sap ran out to its southern end, but this had been replaced by a Russian sap—that is, a covered-in passage—well revetted with timber. A listening post was permanently established at the end of this sap ; during the day it remained under cover, but at night it occupied a shell hole in the open. It was in touch with a second post, at the entrance to the sap, by means of a bell worked by a string. This apparatus was tested frequently to make sure that it was in working order. The existence of both listening post and sap was supposed to be unknown to the enemy ; probably he knew all about them, but, at any rate, he was not supposed to.

The front system, embracing both front and support lines, was divided into three company sectors. The fourth company was in battalion reserve. Battalion H.Q. was, of course, in its " correct " position, a little in rear of the reserve line. Companies did not always hold the same sectors, for the right was generally considered to be the most uncomfortable ; but there was not much to choose between them.

The F1 Sub-sector was the " liveliest " the Battalion held while it was with the Third Army, but it is not to be compared with such places as Thiepval Wood or Nieuport. Heavy artillery was not much used by the enemy, though the reserve company H.Q. had the reputation of being the datum point for 5.9's. But the German field guns were very active on many parts of the front. The most frequently-shelled spot was the top of Forest Street—the communication trench on the extreme right. That point was constantly and very accurately " whizz-banged," for the enemy could easily detect any movement there. All parts of the front line came in for attention. The enemy also used " rum-jars " and vane bombs very freely. The latter probably caused far more annoyance than casualties. However, Lieut.-Col. H. A. S. Stanton, D.S.O.,* was severely wounded by one of them.

There was also a good deal of back area shelling, and the transport was harassed more than once on its nightly journey with rations. Near Basseux its route led through the position of a 6-inch howitzer battery, which the enemy frequently shelled. There Pte. H. Bibby, while driving a limber up to Riviére one night, had his ride horse killed under him. He coolly cut it out of the traces and completed his journey with one horse, himself walking by the side and supporting the pole for a distance of a mile and a half. It was not the first time that he had been brought to notice, and the award of a Military Medal, which followed, was well deserved.

The British were not idle. Their artillery did plenty of work

*At that time O.C., 1/5th Battalion Duke of Wellington's Regt. ; formerly Adjutant of the 1/4th Battalion.

on that front, and their trench mortars were always ready to fire. There were some excellent and well-hidden Stokes mortar positions, and also some 2-inch in the line. Both of these were eager to retaliate, and it was soon found that the former quickly stopped the enemy's use of vane bombs. Targets for Lewis guns or rifles were not common, but C.S.M. A. McNulty did some excellent practice with his Winchester. His gory tale of how, after more than four hours' waiting, he saw the blood splash from the forehead of a German officer, was much appreciated by all who heard it. The snow made patrolling difficult at first, but it did not stop it. The higher authorities were clamouring for identification, and every possible means was tried. But enemy patrols were conspicuous by their absence. Once a working party was located near the head of the Russian sap, and a plan was made to secure a dead or wounded German. A party was to lie in wait in the sap, and, when it heard the enemy, to signal to the artillery, who would open a heavy burst of shrapnel fire; the party was then to rush out, pick up the killed and wounded, and return. But though Lieut. F. H. Kelsall waited in the sap for several hours, on more than one occasion, the enemy party did not again appear. So, when all other means of obtaining identification had been tried without success, the Battalion was ordered to make a raid on the enemy line.

Capt. J. G. Mowat was selected to command the raiders. Arrangements were made for the whole party to stop out of the line during the next tour, to rehearse the operation. Comfortable billets were provided for the men, they were not worked too hard, and they enjoyed themselves thoroughly. Once their billets were changed owing to a rumour about a spy. There may have been some truth in the report. Certainly the inhabitants of Riviére, in some unknown way, learned much about the operation beforehand. They even knew zero hour, a point which had been kept secret from nearly all the raiders themselves.

After careful consideration the enemy front line, immediately to the west of the Wailly-Ficheux Road, was selected as the objective for the raid. No Man's Land was thoroughly reconnoitred by Battalion H.Q. scouts. The operation was fixed for the evening of February 17th, and was planned to take place as follows :—

1. Zero hour was fixed for 10-0 p.m. Fifteen minutes before zero the raiders were to be assembled in No Man's Land, along the bank by the Russian sap, divided into the following parties :

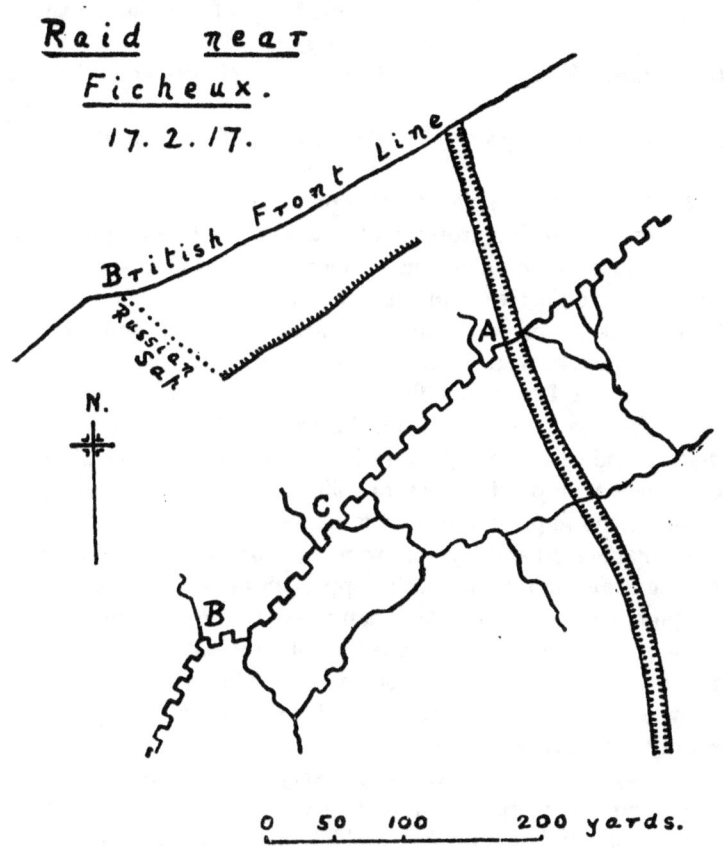

| (a) Right Flank Party. | Sec.-Lieut. R. C. Purvis and 12 other ranks. |
| (b) Left Flank Party. | Sergt. G. Moscrop and 12 other ranks. |

(c) Communication Trench Party.	Sec.-Lieut. E. V. Blakey and 12 other ranks.
(d) Dugout Clearing Party.	Sec.-Lieut. A. Butler and 15 other ranks. (Sub-divided into two parties under the officer and Sergt. F. Johnson respectively.)
(e) Parapet Party.	Capt. J. G. Mowat and 14 other ranks.
(f) Bangalore Torpedo Party.	Sec.-Lieut. W. L. Hirst and 5 other ranks.

2. At 10-0 p.m. a heavy shrapnel barrage would open on the enemy front line, from point A to point B (see map). After four minutes it would gradually open out to form a box barrage round the objective. Meanwhile, the enemy front line on both flanks, and all communication trenches and ground in the vicinity, were to be swept by artillery, trench-mortar, machine and Lewis gun fire.

3. The Bangalore Torpedo Party was to advance, immediately under the barrage, and blow a gap in the wire at point C. The other parties were to follow, in order as above, pass through the gap, and enter the enemy line.

4. Parties (a) and (b) were to move along the trench towards the right and left respectively, approach as near to the barrage as possible, and cover the flanks of the operation. Party (c) was to move down the enemy communication trench from point C, and establish a block in it. Thus protected, party (d) was to secure identification and do as much damage to the enemy trenches as possible.

5. Capt. J. G. Mowat, with party (e), was to remain on the parapet. Signallers were to run a telephone wire across No Man's Land so that he would be in direct communication with Battalion H.Q. When he considered that nothing further could be done, he was to give the recall signal and supervise the withdrawal.

6. The assembly was to be covered by fighting patrols, sent out by the 5th Battalion Duke of Wellington's Regt., then holding the line.

At length February 17th arrived, and, in the evening, the raiders began to move up to their positions. All were assembled, according to plan, before zero. Apart from an enemy searchlight, which swept No Man's Land during the assembly but did not reveal the men to the Germans, the preliminaries passed off without incident. Just before the barrage opened, Sec.-Lieut. W. L. Hirst advanced with his torpedo party. The torpedo was a cumbersome affair, twenty-two feet long, which required three men to carry it. As the party moved forward it laid out a tape, to show the direction to the raiders. The barrage had now opened, the enemy was thoroughly aroused, and the flares which he was firing considerably helped the party, as it hurried forward. The barrage was excellent. On reaching the enemy wire, the men pushed the torpedo well in, though not without difficulty, for it was heavy and the wire was very thick. They then withdrew, except the officer and one Royal Engineer who remained to light the fuse. As soon as this had been done, the two rushed back about thirty yards and threw themselves flat on the ground. Almost at the same moment the torpedo exploded with a terrific crash.

Meanwhile, the raiders, in column of parties, had advanced to a position about forty yards from the enemy wire. Immediately the torpedo exploded they rushed forward, only to find that much of the wire still remained uncut. Capt. Mowat, Sergt. Moscrop and others flung themselves upon it. Slashing at it with bill-hooks, and hurling great chevaux-des-frises to one side, they forced a passage. Sergt. Moscrop was the first to enter the trench, and he was quickly followed by all the men of the flanking parties. By 10-6 p.m. every man was in the trench and at work.

The left flank party came upon an enemy sentry post almost at once. One unwounded prisoner was taken and was passed out of the trench to Capt. Mowat, who was waiting on the parapet. The rest of the Germans were killed. The party then began to work its way along the trench to its left. A second enemy party was encountered, and, for a short time, held up the advance. But half of the British party was working on the parapet. Cpl. E. Jackson, who was in command of these, quickly worked round the Germans, dropped into the trench behind them, and attacked them from the rear. One was taken, the rest were killed. But the prisoner, after his capture, fired at and wounded Moscrop; so he was promptly killed. The party then continued its way towards the left, where it became engaged with some German bombers. These it successfully held at bay until the recall signal was heard.

The right flank party, under Sec.-Lieut. R. C. Purvis, moved along the trench in a similar manner. It had barely started when word was passed down that identification had been obtained. Sergt. J. S. Sheard led the way, and himself accounted for the first three Germans who were met. Moving further along, the party became heavily engaged with some of the enemy, who were bombing from the parados. Several casualties were suffered, including Sergt. Sheard severely wounded. But here, as on the other flank, the advantage of having a party on the parapet was apparent. This party, of whom Lance-Cpl. R. Knox shot two Germans, was able to hold the enemy bombers at bay; and the right flank was well covered until the end of the operation. When the recall signal was sounded, all began to withdraw. Before leaving the trench, Cpl. S. Jessop threw a petrol can, with Mills bombs attached, down a dugout entrance; great sheets of flame shot up the stairway and "the results appeared satisfactory," says the official report.

It would appear that the Bangalore torpedo had not been exploded exactly at the pre-arranged spot. As a result, the raiders entered the trench more to the left than had been intended. Sec.-Lieut. E. V. Blakey searched for the communication trench, which it was his duty to block and hold, but was unable to find it. He was able, however, to give assistance both to Sergt. Moscrop and to the dugout-clearing party; and, as the enemy does not seem to have made any attempt to counter-attack along the communication trench, the failure to find it did not affect the operation.

Both flanking parties had received strict orders to ignore all dugouts. These were left to Sec.-Lieut. A. Butler, Sergt. F. Johnson and their men. The former worked to the right, the latter to the left. Each party carried with it a plentiful supply of Mills bombs and short-fused Stokes shells. Every dugout was bombed, and the crashing explosions showed clearly how effective the Stokes shells were. No one can attempt to estimate the number of casualties which were inflicted, but they were certainly heavy. There is no doubt that many Germans were in the dugouts. A light flashed down the entrance to one showed four bodies lying on the steps. Lance-Cpl. H. Kane was particularly prominent in this work. He shouted down the entrance to one dugout and was answered by much talking; but as he did not understand the language he thought it best to drop a bomb down. So he did.

Meanwhile, Capt. J. G. Mowat was hard at work on the parapet. He was in communication with Battalion H.Q by telephone the whole time. He had to keep a careful watch on the operation, in order to be ready to deal promptly with any unforeseen development. Also he was largely occupied in improving the gap in the enemy wire, so that the return of the raiders might be easier. By 10-18 p.m. he saw clearly that enemy bombing attacks were becoming serious on the flanks, and, as identification had been obtained early on, there was no reason to remain longer in the enemy lines. He ordered the recall to be sounded. Two buglers were with him for that purpose. Their notes rang out and were heard by all. The pass-word " Mowat " was shouted everywhere. The withdrawal began.

Everything went well. The parties of Sec.-Lieuts. E. V. Blakey and A. Butler withdrew first, leaving the trench by means of light ladders which they had carried forward with them in the first advance. Their withdrawal was covered by the flank parties, who afterwards moved towards the point of entry, covered by their own parapet men. By 10-20 p.m. every man had left the trench, and " All Clear " was sent back along the wire. The artillery barrage again dropped on the enemy front line, to cover the withdrawal across No Man's Land. This was soon effected, Capt. Mowat bringing up the rear. In a few minutes every man, including all the wounded, was back in the British line. There were no " Missing."

The raid had been an unqualified success, and was therefore a great source of satisfaction to the Battalion. It was an example of what careful and thorough training can do. With the exception of the slight loss of direction in the first crossing of No Man's Land, which resulted in the trench being entered too much to the left and Sec.-Lieut. Blakey failing to find his objective, everything had worked like clockwork. Identification had been obtained, an enormous amount of damage had been done to the enemy defences, and many Germans had been killed or wounded— 17 dead Germans were actually counted, and there must have been many more in the dugouts which were bombed. All this had been done at a cost of only seven wounded, of whom, however, Sergt. J. S. Sheard died a few days later. All these casualties had been suffered in the enemy trench; not a man had been hit either during the advance or the withdrawal. There can be no doubt that the effect on the morale of the Battalion was very great. The raiders themselves were most enthusiastic and would have dearly liked to do another raid. Everyone else in the Battalion envied them their good luck.

Capt. J. G. Mowat shortly after received the Military Cross which he had thoroughly earned, both by his good work in training the party and by his gallant leadership. Sergt. G. Moscrop received the Distinguished Conduct Medal, and several Military Medals were awarded to the N.C.O's and men who had been most prominent in the operation.

The Battalion did two more tours in the same sector before it was finally relieved. Little of special note happened. The enemy artillery and trench mortars were rather more active than they had been earlier in the month, probably as a result of the raid. About this time one or two officers of the 62nd Division, which had only recently landed in France, were attached to the Battalion for instruction. The only event of real importance was a fire in the Assistant Adjutant's dugout; this consumed many "valuable" official documents, and was thus a great source of satisfaction to the Orderly Room for many weeks to come.

On the last day of February the Battalion was relieved by the 2/9th Battalion London Regt., and moved back to Bailleulval. As a parting message of hate, the enemy shelled the village that night and caused several casualties. But the Battalion had now finished with the Third Army. For a few days it marched and counter-marched about the district, never stopping more than a night at one place, except Halloy. None of these places was of much interest, except perhaps Neuvillette, where the billets were exceptionally good. On March 7th the Battalion marched to Doullens, and, after waiting in the streets all day, entrained in the evening. Soon after dark the train started on its slow northerly journey, and so, without interest and unnoticed, the Battalion left the Third Army.

CHAPTER VII.

WITH THE FIRST ARMY.

(a) Ferme du Bois Sector.

THE Battalion arrived at Merville about 8-0 a.m. on March 8th. A very cold night had been spent on the train, snow was falling on arrival, and the hot tea which was served at the station was very welcome. A short march brought the Battalion to the village of La Fosse, where the next night was spent in fairly comfortable billets. Apart from a little difference of opinion between the Commanding Officer and a very ill-tempered Frenchman, who said he would rather have Germans than British in his barn, the day was uneventful. The next day the Battalion relieved the 12th Battalion London Regt. in Brigade Reserve to the Ferme du Bois Sector. As the same billets were occupied on and off for over two months, some description of them is necessary.

Battalion H.Q. and one company were lodged at Senechal Farm, near Lacouture. This was one of the large moated farmhouses, so common in the district, and consisted of the usual hollow rectangle of buildings, surrounding a pond and a midden. It was supposed to accommodate 500 men, but never more than about half that number occupied it while the Battalion was in the area. A second company was quartered in a similar, but smaller, farm about half a mile distant; a third occupied billets in the village of Lacouture; and the fourth was in houses on King's Road, on the way to the trenches. Considering how near the Battalion was to the front line, these billets were quite comfortable. The country around was very flat and intersected by ditches; much of it was under cultivation, and the inhabitants hardly seemed to realise that there was a war. The owner of Senechal Farm, who was a very important man in the district, certainly did very well out of the troops ; not only did he receive considerable sums for billets, but an estaminet, which he ran on the premises, was well patronised, and must have been a very profitable concern. Dotted about the district were a number of fortified posts, some in a very bad state of repair. The Battalion was required to find " caretakers " for about ten of these posts, and the " flat cart "—that cart which carried on so long with the transport, in spite of its official " destruction " about once every three months—came in very useful for taking rations to these men.

On March 13th the Battalion relieved the 1/5th Battalion Duke of Wellington's Regt. in the Right Sub-sector of the Ferme du Bois Sector. Here it remained, inter-relieving with the same battalion, usually every six days, until the latter part of May. This period was very uneventful. The line was exceptionally quiet—almost the quietest the Battalion ever held. Casualties were very slight ; in fact, on occasion, a six-day tour in the line was carried through without a man being injured.

Owing to the low-lying and damp condition of the country trenches could not be dug, and the defences consisted entirely of breast-works. The material for these had been obtained from " borrow-pits," which quickly filled with water and so became additional obstacles to the enemy. Millions of sandbags must have been used in the building of this line. The shelters occupied by officers and men were built into the parados, and were comparatively comfortable. Such a line was quite satisfactory, indeed almost luxurious, in quiet times. But it was the worst type possible to occupy in a bombardment, for none of the shelters were more than splinter-proof, and breast-works are poor protection against shell fire.

The Battalion front was well over 2,000 yards in length—by far the longest it had held up to that time. Two continuous lines of breast-works, each garrisoned by two companies, formed the main defences. The front line was held by seven platoon posts, three on the right company front and four on the left. Each post was complete in itself, was well wired front and rear, and was only in communication with neighbouring posts by means of patrols, which moved along the unoccupied parts of the line at stated times. At night the entrances to these posts were blocked by chevaux de frise, and sentries challenged everyone who approached along the front line. Between the two companies there was an unoccupied gap, 500 yards long.

The support line was held rather more continuously, but long stretches were quite unoccupied. Three communication trenches connected the front line with the Rue du Bois—Rope Street, Cadbury Street and Cockspur Street. When the Battalion first took over the sector the hard winter weather was just breaking. The whole country-side was very wet and many of the trenches, particularly the communication trenches, were deep in water. But, before the Battalion left, the sector had dried up considerably.

Battalion H.Q. was in a nameless farm on the Rue du Bois. This farm had suffered little from enemy shelling and there were several quite comfortable rooms in it. All headquarter personnel lived either in the farm buildings or in shelters which had been erected in the orchard. Few of the latter were even splinter-proof, but the locality was never shelled. It was one of the most comfortable H.Q. ever occupied by the Battalion and much work was done to improve it. It was customary for the resting battalion to provide a platoon each day to work under the orders of the battalion in the line. During one of his tours, the Adjutant of the 1/5th Battalion made use of this working party to build a new sandbag dugout for himself. Apparently he was pleased with the work for he named the dugout "Deodar House," after the secret nomme de guerre of his own battalion, quite overlooking the fact that the work had been done by men of another unit. But the men of the 1/4th Battalion had their revenge. When they were next in the line they painted every scrap of the woodwork outside the Farmhouse red—their battalion colour—much to the disgust of the other battalion which preferred its own colour—green. At this time there was a perfect mania for naming places and nailing up notice boards so that there should be no mistakes. An energetic police corporal, having a prisoner for whom he wanted to find a job of work, built a small sandbag ammunition store, and was so pleased with the finished article that he placed upon it a big notice board—"The Binns Redoubt."

FERME DU BOIS SECTOR

The Transport Lines were at Vieille Chapelle and everything was so quiet that ration limbers were brought up nightly along the Rue du Bois, as far as Battalion H.Q. Each company had its trench kitchen in the support line and hot meals were provided for all men with little more difficulty than if the Battalion had been back in rest. The canteen was set up at Battalion H.Q., and a "hawker" went round the front line daily to sell cigarettes, etc. to the men, within two hundred yards of the enemy.

From the British front line the ground sloped very gently up to the Aubers Ridge, from which the Germans had good observation. But they made little use of this. Their artillery was very quiet, except on rare occasions. Canadian Orchard and the posts on the right got most attention; Sec.-Lieut. S. P. Stansfield was killed near Shetland Post. But, compared with what the Battalion had experienced elsewhere and was to encounter later, the shelling was almost negligible. Occasional salvoes would be fired on one of the communication trenches or some other part of the line, but these caused very little inconvenience. Rarely was anything of heavier calibre than the 10.5 cm. howitzer used. One noteworthy exception to this was the afternoon of May 12th, when the junction of Cadbury Street with the Rue du Bois was heavily shelled with what appeared to be 21 cm. armour-piercing shells. Though there were no casualties this caused great inconvenience, for the pump, which supplied all water for the companies, was seriously damaged, and it took about two days to get it into working order again. The reason for this bombardment was never understood, but, as it was the only occasion on which shells of such heavy calibre were used, it was probably only a visit from a "travelling circus." Occasionally the 15 cm. howitzer appeared; one day it heavily shelled the Rue du Bois near Sandbag Corner; on another occasion it wrecked the officers' mess of the A246 Battery, which lay about 1,000 yards behind Battalion H.Q.

In other ways too the enemy seemed quite willing to "live and let live," if he were not interfered with. He had both medium and light trench mortars in his lines, but seldom fired more than a few rounds at a time from them. His machine guns did little and sniping was almost unknown. Undoubtedly he held his front line thinly, though movement was observed almost daily in the vicinity of the Boar's Head, where much work was in progress. One day he gave very clear evidence that he was awake. An energetic platoon commander, who was trying to make things uncomfortable for the " Hun " with rifle grenades, unfortunately had a premature, and the loud cheering that was heard from the opposite side of No Man's Land showed that the enemy was on the watch and fully appreciated the incident.

The Battalion had two excellent observation posts on the Rue du Bois, which boasted the grandiloquent names of the " Savoy " and the " Trocadero." From these, and from smaller ones in the front line, excellent observation could be obtained of the whole enemy system and of much of the country in rear. The enemy seemed to make very little effort to conceal himself and so the sector was a regular " promised land " for the Battalion Intelligence Officer. The Sugar Factory at Marquillies, with its prominent chimney, was of particular interest, both for the large amount of enemy transport which moved about near it, and for the careful record which was kept of the times when the chimney smoked. This chimney also exercised a great fascination on the Commanding Officer, and the first thing that had to be done when the Battalion moved to neighbouring sectors was to identify this landmark from the new position. Indeed, it was almost a relief to some when the Battalion went to the coast and was quite out of view of Marquillies.

During the whole time the Battalion was on the Ferme du Bois Sector patrolling was very active. At first this was very uncomfortable, for the greater part of No Man's Land was badly water-logged. For a long time no brilliant success was gained. No Man's Land was thoroughly mapped, but practically all attempts to enter the enemy front line were unsuccessful. Until about the middle of April, the Battalion was faced by the 6th Bavarian Reserve Division—the Quinque Rue was one of its inter-regimental boundaries—which did practically no patrolling. With the exception of a patrol encounter on the night of April 18/19th, no enemy patrol was ever seen in No Man's Land. On the same night C.S.M. W. Medley, M.M., of B Company, entered the enemy front line south of the Quinque Rue, and made some

Capt. A. E. MANDER.
(Killed).

Capt. J. G. MOWAT, M.C.
(Killed).

Capt. E. N. MARSHALL, M.C.

Capt. N GELDARD, D.S.O., M.C.

FERME DU BOIS SECTOR

valuable observations, but failed to secure an identification.

Much permanent work was done while the Battalion was in this sector. The trenches were put into a thorough state of repair and were much improved, mainly by the construction of new shelters. A good deal of wire was put out. A series of concrete machine gun posts in front of the support line was begun. Front line and support companies inter-relieved in the middle of each tour, and, as tours were spent by companies on the right and left alternately, all officers and N.C.O's got a thorough knowledge of the whole line.

Reliefs were all carried out by daylight and with greater ease than in almost any sector the Battalion has occupied. The distance to billets was short, and a relief which began about midday would be complete, with the relieved troops settled in billets, by about tea-time. Periods of rest were taken up mainly with training, though a certain number of working parties had to be found. The training area was near Richebourg St. Vaast, less than two miles from the front line, but it was very rarely a shell dropped there. Platoon exercises were generally carried out in the neighbourhood of billets. While in rest many football matches were played, both within the Battalion and against neighbouring units. An excellent recreation room at Senechal Farm was used for smoking concerts and lectures, as well as for reading and writing.

April 14th—the second anniversary of the Battalion's landing in France—was celebrated at Vieille Chapelle. A dinner for all surviving officers of the original Battalion was held at the estaminet, best known for its associations with a lady named Alice. A smoking concert for the men who had come out with the Battalion was held in the Y.M.C.A. hut at Vieille Chapelle, the 49th Divisional Band coming over to assist in the programme. It was found that there were nearly two hundred survivors still serving with their old Battalion.

On April 27th Lieut.-General R. Haking, G.O.C. XI. Corps, presented medal brooches to a number of officers and other ranks of the 49th Division, including Major A. L. Mowat, M.C., Capt. J. G. Mowat, M.C., and ten other ranks of the Battalion. The ceremony took place at Merville and a guard of honour of 20 other ranks, under the command of Sec.-Lieut. A. J. Robb, was furnished by the Battalion.

Meanwhile, the first British offensive of 1917—the Battle of Vimy-Arras—had opened on April 9th. Lying only a few miles to the north of the battle area, the Battalion could clearly hear the roar of the artillery, and at night could see the glare of burning dumps and the flashes of the guns. Before long a current from the battle began to affect it ; the demand for identifications became more and more persistent. Early in May signs began to point to the presence of a different division on the Ferme du Bois front, and the Intelligence Department was most anxious to secure a prisoner. On the afternoon of May 10th, a particularly urgent memo. on this subject was received. Very early the following morning a Battalion runner arrived at 147th Infantry Brigade H.Q. and insisted on seeing an officer at once. When told that all were asleep he still insisted, saying that the officer would not mind having been awakened when he saw his message. This is what had happened.

About 10-30 p.m. on May 10th, C.S.M. W. Medley, M.M., with eleven other ranks of B Company, left the front line, crossed No Man's Land, and reached the enemy wire. There he left six men to form a covering party, and, cutting a passage through the wire, entered the enemy front line with the remainder of his patrol. About seventy yards to his right was an enemy sentry post, but he decided to attempt nothing against it as it was difficult for anyone to approach without being observed. He crossed over to the enemy second line, passed that also, and continued straight across country until he reached the third line. The patrol was now about six hundred yards in rear of the enemy outposts. Leaving the rest of his party in an old shelter, the patrol leader went forward alone to reconnoitre. He reached a communication trench, known as Serpent Trench, and saw a man walk along it. He returned and brought up his men, getting into the trench with two of them, and leaving the rest on the parapet. They were barely in position when three Germans—afterwards found to be a water-carrying party—came along the trench. C.S.M. Medley called on them to surrender and they at first laughed, probably thinking it was a joke of their own men ;

but, presently realising that they really were face to face with a British party, they turned and ran. The parapet party immediately opened fire and killed one German; Medley pursued and captured a second; but the fate of the third is unknown. The prisoner was promptly hoisted out of the trench and the patrol returned by the way it had come, reaching the British line without loss after an absence of more than four hours. The prisoner turned out to be a machine gunner of the 3rd Bavarian R.I.R. (1st Bavarian Reserve Division), a most valuable identification, since it proved that a relief had taken place opposite the Battalion front, and that one of the German divisions which had been shattered at Vimy was now holding the sector. It was to receive this news that Brigade H.Q. had been disturbed in the early morning.

Needless to say, this particularly daring enterprise—the enemy front had been penetrated to a depth of 700 yards—caused considerable stir, and C.S.M. W. Medley and the Battalion received many congratulations. Lieut.-General R. Haking, in forwarding the report to the Army Commander, wrote: "It is one of the best examples of good patrol work that I have ever heard of ... I am of the opinion that the whole operation was a model of how to carry out an enterprise of this nature." The Army Commander fully agreed, and spoke of it as "a very fine example of an offensive patrol." The G.O.C., 147th Infantry Brigade, in congratulating the Battalion on its success after so many disappointments, said "The skilful handling of the commander, and the courage of all ranks was only excelled by their spirit of determination to succeed in their task before returning. Men who have such a spirit cannot be beaten." For his work on this occasion C.S.M. W. Medley received the Military Cross, and the Military Medal was awarded to four other members of the patrol.

During the latter part of the Battalion's stay in the area the main feature was the arrival of two divisions of the Portuguese Expeditionary Force, which were to take over that part of the line. They had been excellently equipped by the British Government, but lacked the experience of trench warfare necessary before they could be trusted with the defence of a sector. The ront between the River Lys and the La Bassée Canal had always been considered a suitable one for the training of new troops, and so a number of Portuguese units were attached to the 49th Division for instruction. At first, only some officers and N.C.O's came up to the line for a few days at a time. But, towards the end of April, a whole company was sent up for 48 hours, and from that time, until the Battalion left the sector, there were usually some Portuguese in the line with it. As is usual with troops sent in for instruction, the Portuguese were not entrusted with the actual holding of any part of the line. When a company came up, one of its platoons would be sent to each of the four British companies; the company commander would attach a section to each of his platoons; while the platoon commander would arrange that every Portuguese soldier should be attached to a British soldier, should work with him everywhere, and thus get an idea of the routine of trench life. Language was a difficulty and interpreters were not always available; but, as many of the Portuguese officers and a few of the men had a knowledge of French, this was used whenever possible. Yet, on the whole, though they had no common language, the private soldiers seemed to be able to make themselves better understood than their officers. Another difficulty was accommodation—there was not room for two or three hundred additional men in the shelters; however, as the weather was fine and warm for the time of the year, this was overcome.

Some Portuguese transport men were also sent to the Battalion for instruction, but they learned little. Love of their animals and a high standard in turn-out were strong points with Sergt. Crossley's men. But the Portuguese were very different. Few of them cared anything for their animals and the majority were deliberately cruel; they knew nothing of "eye-wash" and the appearance of their transport on the road was a standing joke among the British. Their "A" and "Q" departments were also far from efficient. They never seemed to know how many men they had, nor what rations they ought to receive. Certain it was that the Battalion was better off for rations while the Portuguese were in the line with it than it had been before.

When the 147th Infantry Brigade finally left the sector it was taken over by the Portuguese and was held by them until the German offensive in April of the following year.

On May 16th the Battalion was relieved in the Ferme du Bois Sector for the last time and went back into Brigade Reserve.

(b) The Cordonnerie Sector.

Towards the end of May the whole of the 147th Infantry Brigade had been withdrawn from the line, but, as the relief of the other Brigades of the 49th Division by the Portuguese was not complete, the Division could not yet be made use of in any other sector. Just north of the 49th Division was the 57th Division—a Lancashire Territorial Division, recently out from England. The attack on the Messines Ridge by the Second Army was timed to begin early in June, and the 57th Division had to send two battalions to support the flank of that attack. To replace these in the line, the 1/4th and 1/5th Battalions, Duke of Wellington's Regiment were lent by the 147th Infantry Brigade.

On May 25th the Battalion marched to Estaires, where it remained for one night. The next day it moved to Sailly-sur-la-Lys, and on May 27th it took over the Cordonnerie Sector from the 2/5th Battalion Loyal North Lancashire Regt. Here it came temporarily under the orders of the 170th Infantry Brigade, 57th Division.

The Battalion sector was a very long one—about 2,800 yards—and the front line was very thinly held. It was divided into three company fronts, but each company had only one platoon in the front line, scattered in small posts. At night a second platoon was sent up to patrol between the posts on the company front. The other two platoons were in the support line for garrison and counter-attack. The fourth company also lived in the support line but was held in Battalion Reserve. The defences of this sector were very similar to those which the Battalion had just left, but were in better condition. The New Zealand Division had held the front recently and had done a great deal of work there ; the support line was well supplied in parts with concrete dugouts, and two very large dugouts, each of which would easily hold a company, had been constructed by the Maori Pioneer

Battalion. There were many communication trenches between the front and support lines, and there was an exceptionally comfortable Battalion H.Q. in a farmhouse which had been knocked about very little. There was a bath-house on the premises, and also a bakery—the pride of the 2/5th Battalion Loyal North Lancs.; but the latter was not used by the Battalion.

Perhaps the most interesting feature of the sector was that it included about half of the old No. 3 Section, Fleurbaix—the very first sector the Battalion had held on coming to France. Its present left extended almost as far as the Convent Wall, and the left communication trench was that very Dead Dog Alley which had been dug by it two years before. There, too, were the graves of the men who had been the first to lay down their lives; these were sought out and put in good repair, for it was always the practice of the Battalion to pay this tribute to its lost ones whenever it had the opportunity. Officers were able to revisit some of their old haunts, particularly Capt. W. C. Fenton who stood again on the Rue des Bassiéres, happily without stopping another machine gun bullet. But how changed were the conditions in other ways! In 1915 the Battalion held a 1,000 yard front with something like 700 men in the front line; in 1917 it was holding a front nearly three times that length with only about 100 men permanently posted in the front line. In 1915 troops depended almost entirely on their rifles to maintain their position; in 1917 they had Lewis and machine guns, artillery and trench mortars, and they preferred to defend their positions by counter-attack rather than by original fire effect.

On taking over the sector the Battalion learned from the outgoing unit that the enemy front line was practically unoccupied, and that patrols found little difficulty in entering it by night, or even in penetrating to the second line. Acting on the assumption that this information was correct, very vigorous patrolling was begun. It was gradually found, however, that the inactivity of the enemy had been much exaggerated. The boundary between two enemy divisions—the 38th Landwehr and the 79th Reserve—was opposite the Battalion's front. The morale of the former was low, its men kept an indifferent watch, and C Company's patrols had little difficulty in entering its line. But the front of the latter was always covered at night by a strong fighting patrol which effectually prevented the British approaching, though they made several attempts. It was there that a patrol experienced the effects of the gas which British projectors were throwing into Biez Wood, and had to beat a hasty retreat. Gas masks had to be worn. The officer in charge of the patrol, following his usual custom, had gone out with nothing but a P.H. helmet, and that had not been out of its satchel for many weeks. When he came to put it on, he found the eye-pieces so dirty that he was practically blind, and had to be led by his men. The incident caused a good deal of amusement in the Battalion at the time.

One day there was a most unfortunate accident on C Company's front. A trench mortar battery had arranged for a big "shoot," and, for this purpose, two large dumps of shells had been made in the front line. For some cause, which was never satisfactorily explained, as soon as the guns opened fire both dumps exploded, wiping out the gun crews. The Battalion was fortunate in having only one casualty, but two great holes were blown in the parapet, and, though C Company worked very hard to repair the damage, the task was not finished when they were relieved.

On the last day of the tour a very successful piece of work was carried out by a small patrol. Owing to the lie of the land and the height of the enemy parapet, it was very difficult to obtain observation of places immediately in rear of the enemy front line. To remedy this, it was determined to establish a temporary observation post on the front of the enemy parapet one morning. Such an operation would hardly have been possible in any ordinary line, but the Battalion was still working on the assumption that the enemy front line was practically deserted. The party chosen consisted of Cpl. E. Jackson, M.M. and two men of B Company, one H.Q. observer, with glasses and telescopic periscope, and two signallers, whose duty it was to lay a telephone line across No Man's Land and maintain communication with the British front line. As a precaution, arrangements were made for a box barrage to be put down by the artillery and

Stokes mortars if called for, and for Lewis guns to provide cross fire.

About 3-30 a.m., just as dawn was breaking, the party started. They crawled slowly through the long grass which covered No Man's Land, got through the enemy wire after much trouble, and Cpl. Jackson and the observer established themselves on the enemy parapet. The signallers succeeded in getting into telephonic communication with the British front line. After lying on the parapet for about an hour and a quarter, the N.C.O. and the observer entered the enemy trench and moved along it. Almost immediately they came upon a deserted, but recently occupied, sentry post. Continuing along the trench, they turned a corner and saw six rifles leaning just outside a dugout, from which very obvious snores were issuing. They immediately returned and summoned two more men to their assistance. The last—one had been sent back some time before—was posted on the parapet. The four proceeded along the trench and arrived just in time to find the Germans coming out of the dugout. One German fired, missing completely, and the British at once closed, calling on them to surrender. Without further resistance all the Germans—there were seven of them, including two N.C.O's—put up their hands. They were got over the parapet at once and hurried across No Man's Land. A few shots were fired by a neighbouring German post, but the whole party, including prisoners, reached the British lines unhurt.

It is recorded that a certain Company Sergeant-Major of the Battalion was walking quietly up towards the front line when he saw a number of Germans come rushing over the parapet. Thinking it was an attack, he dashed across the open, only to find on his arrival that the men he had seen were prisoners. His disappointment was great, but he revived his drooping spirits by clouting one of them over the head to put him in a proper frame of mind. The Commanding Officer was in his morning bath when the party arrived. So delighted was he that he rushed out in the somewhat scanty attire of a towel and a pair of slippers, and, in this garb, interviewed the seven well-drilled Germans, who stood stiffly to attention throughout. Physically the prisoners were a well-built lot of men, but their morale was very poor.

They were very willing to talk, and one of them said they had been talking recently of giving themselves up. At any rate, they were saved that trouble.

The prisoners were despatched to Brigade H.Q. in charge of the men who had captured them. Later, the Battalion received some highly complimentary messages from the higher authorities, particularly from the G.O.C., XI. Corps. He was so pleased with the operation that he not only strongly recommended Cpl. E. Jackson, M.M., for the Distinguished Conduct Medal, an honour which was awarded in due course, but bestowed Military Medals on all the other members of the patrol. It should be mentioned also that a congratulatory message was received by O.C. B Company, addressed to " The Body-snatching Company," from " The Working Company " (i.e. C Company—self-styled).

The next night the Battalion was relieved by the 5th Battalion Duke of Wellington's Regt. and went back into Brigade Reserve at Rouge de Bout. Here a very pleasant time was spent. The weather continued gloriously fine, as it had been in the line, and the billets were good. Each company provided one platoon to man a line of defensive posts; the others carried on training. There was great competition in turning out smart guards, B Company winning with a D.C.M., M.M., corporal and three M.M. men. Here news arrived that Capt. W. C. Fenton and Capt. C. Jones, the padre, had each been awarded the Military Cross, and the occasion was suitably celebrated. Plans were also completed for an operation which the Battalion was to carry out during its next tour in the line.

This operation was founded on the supposition that the enemy front line was practically unoccupied—a supposition which the Battalion had already begun to shake. The XI. Corps wished to impress the enemy with the idea that active operations were in preparation on the Corps front, and so hinder his sending troops away to the real battle areas. With this idea in view a scheme was drawn up for seizing the German front line and establishing a number of posts in it. The main points of the scheme were these :—

1. In conjunction with the 146th Infantry Brigade, which was still in its old sector on the right, and a Brigade of the

57th Division on the left, a stretch of the enemy front line was to be seized at night, and a number of fortified posts were to be established in it.

2. Each of the three companies in the front line was to establish one platoon post.

3. For purposes of this operation the four platoons of each company were known as W,X,Y,Z. Their respective duties were as follows :—" W " platoon was to seize the position in the enemy front line and cover it during consolidation ; " X " platoon was to consolidate and garrison the post ; " Y " platoon was to carry the necessary ammunition and stores across No Man's Land ; " Z " platoon was to garrison the old British front line during the operation.

4. Additional parties, provided by the 5th Battalion Duke of Wellington's Regt., were to dig three communication trenches across No Man's Land to connect the new posts with the old front line. These trenches were to be named " Halifax," " Brighouse " and " Hull." " Cleckheaton " had been suggested as one of the names, but was vetoed on the ground that the artillery would never understand it ; hence the introduction of " Hull," which was not thought to be beyond the intellect of the gunners.

5. The whole operation was to be carried out in one night.

When the Battalion took over the Cordonnerie Sector a second time the necessary preparations were started at once. One of the most important of these preliminary arrangements was the preparation of dumps of all necessary stores in the front line. To carry this out Capt. H. Hanson was attached to Battalion H.Q., and very hard he worked, perspiring freely in the sweltering weather, and often pushing trucks on the light railway, and carrying stores himself.

The night of June 15/16th had been fixed for the operation, and all was ready. But, in the early morning of June 15th, the orders were suddenly cancelled and the Battalion was warned to be ready for relief that night. What would have been the success of the operation, had it been carried out, can hardly be said. Judging from previous reconnaissance of the front, it is probable that C Company would have established its post without difficulty, and that B Company would also have succeeded though it might have had to fight ; A Company's task would, almost certainly, have proved the hardest, and it is doubtful whether its post could have been founded at all.

The Battalion was relieved on the night of June 15/16th by the 2/4th Battalion Loyal North Lancashire Regt., which had returned from the fighting near Messines, and marched straight through to billets at Estaires. A very pleasant three weeks had been spent in the sector, there had been very few casualties, and the Battalion took away with it the best of wishes from the 170th Infantry Brigade as the following letter from the G.O.C. shows :—

H.Q., 170th Inf. Bde.,
June 15th, 1917.

My Dear Sugden,

I should like you and all your battalion to know how sorry we are to part with you. I have not met a better organised battalion nor one in which work was more thoroughly and quietly done. You gave us a taste of your fighting qualities on Trinity Sunday and I am disappointed indeed that circumstances prevent you gaining the honourable distinction that your proposed operations would undoubtedly have conferred on you and your gallant fellows. At any rate your very complete preparations for them will give us valuable assistance in the future.

The 1/4th West Riding Regiment takes with it the heartiest good wishes of my brigade.

Yours sincerely,
F. G. Guggisberg.

(c) St. Elie Sector.

The Battalion spent three nights in Estaires and then moved by motor bus to Sailly Labourse. The next day it marched to billets in Philosophe, a mining village north-west of Lens. Here the 147th Infantry Brigade came temporarily under the orders of the G.O.C., 6th Division, relieving a Brigade of that division which was required for an operation near Lens. The first days were spent in Brigade Reserve at Philosophe, time being occupied in training and in reconnaissance of the sector which the Battalion was soon to take over. The country was typical of the Lens mining district and not unlike the Barnsley coalfield. An excellent view of it was obtained from the top of a neighbouring slag-heap.

On the night of June 25/26th the Battalion relieved the 6th Batt. Duke of Wellington's Regt. in the St. Elie Right Sub-Sector, where its right rested on the Hulluch-Vermelles Road. This sector was a most peculiar one, and quite different from any the Battalion had previously occupied. The country-side was all chalk, so that the trenches were comparatively easy to keep in order and were, on the whole, dry. The sector was approached from Vermelles by Chapel Alley, one of the longest communication trenches the men had ever seen, which ran alongside the road to Hulluch; but most people preferred to use the road or a cross-country route until they were about half way up to the line. The trenches lay entirely on the ground which had been captured from the enemy in the Battle of Loos. Battalion H.Q. was an old German dugout, just off the old German front line. From this point the route to the front line was up Devon Lane as far as St. George's Trench, and then along one or other of the tunnels. These tunnels were wonderful works of engineering. Cut out of solid chalk, lit up by electric light, ventilated by electric fans, and lying thirty to forty feet below the surface, they gave one a feeling of absolute security, except against gas. Indeed, this feeling was so strong that they exercised rather a demoralising influence—once inside, one hardly liked to leave them, for the heaviest shell or trench mortar could scarcely shake them. Here and there stair-cases led up to posts, the parapets of which were constructed from the sandbags of " spoil " obtained in the excavation of the tunnels. Except on the centre company front, nearly every post was reached in this way. Most of the old front line was derelict, little being held except the posts at the tunnel exits, and a few great mine craters.

A Company was on the right, B Company in the centre, and D Company on the left. C Company was in Battalion Reserve, in deep dugouts off St. George's Trench. Both the right and left

ST. ELIE SECTOR

companies lived almost entirely in the tunnels, but B Company had its H.Q. in a deep dugout, which was approached by the half-derelict Grimwood Trench, and its principal post in Newport Sap, a great mine crater garrisoned by one platoon by day and two platoons by night.

Fosse 8, an enormous slag-heap a little to the north of the St. Elie Sector, was the dominating feature of the district. Machine guns from this mound had been one of the main obstacles to the British advance in the Battle of Loos. Its possession gave the enemy excellent observation over a large area and was probably the main reason for his great artillery and trench mortar activity.

Never had the Battalion experienced such trench mortar activity. The Stokes mortar battery, which had been left in the line by the 6th Division, fired until its guns were red-hot. A heavy trench mortar, which had its home thirty to forty feet below the surface and fired up a sort of chimney, made things very lively for the Germans in Cité St. Elie with its "flying pigs." The enemy too was very active in this department. Opposite the Battalion's left were the St. Elie quarries and these were packed with trench mortars of all descriptions, which were able to carry on their deadly work in almost complete security. The enemy, when he thought fit, could put down such a trench mortar barrage as the Battalion had never known before. Deservedly, the sector bore a very bad reputation.

However, the first day passed quietly, and the night of June 26/27th was one of those glorious nights, with an almost full moon, which one sometimes gets at Midsummer. Dawn had almost come before the silence was broken. The Battalion was already standing to, and the additional platoon had just been withdrawn from Newport Sap, when, at 3-10 a.m., without any warning, the enemy opened a terrific bombardment. Trench mortar shells of all calibres rained down on the posts at Boyau 78, Newport Sap, "K" Dump and Devon Dump, and on the centre company H.Q. A heavy barrage of high explosive and shrapnel fell on St. George's Trench and Devon Lane. At the centre company H.Q. Capt. J. G. Mowat, M.C., Sec.-Lieut. I. C. Denby and four other ranks were instantly killed by a heavy trench mortar shell, just after the first had sent up the S.O.S. signal. The entrance to "K" Dump was blown in and Sec.-Lieut. H. Pollard wounded. All quickly realised that an enemy raid on a large scale was in progress.

At Newport Sap Sec.-Lieut. G. Crowther, in spite of the terrific bombardment which blew in the trenches in several places, got his men standing to and beat off a party of the enemy which appeared, with rifle and Lewis gun fire. The men at Devon Dump, which post was fortunately not hit, opened rapid fire to their front, but it was purely blind fire for they could not see more than twenty yards owing to the dust and smoke raised by the bombardment. Machine guns at Dudley Dump fired on a party of Germans who were seen in the vicinity of "K" Dump, and drove them off. But a third enemy party succeeded in entering Boyau 78. Here the platoon commander had withdrawn his men into the tunnels, as soon as the bombardment opened, in order to avoid casualties. Unfortunately, two men took a wrong turning and were come upon by the raiding party. One managed to escape into an old shelter, but the other was captured. The raiders then blew in the main tunnel exit with a mobile charge, and returned to their own lines, harassed in their retreat by the machine guns at Dudley Dump, and the excellent shrapnel barrage which the British artillery was putting down. By about 3-30 a.m. the raid was over and the barrage had ceased.

The total casualties in this raid were 2 officers and 4 other ranks killed, 1 officer and 12 other ranks wounded, and one other rank a prisoner. To the surprise of everyone the G.O.C., 6th Division, was pleased when he heard that a prisoner had been taken. It suited him well that the enemy should think his division had been relieved on that sector by the 49th Division. But this was little satisfaction to the Battalion which had suffered so seriously, particularly in the death of Capt. J. G. Mowat, M.C., one of the most gallant and competent officers in the Battalion. Its only real satisfaction was the knowledge that heavy casualties had been inflicted on the enemy. Early in the morning several German ambulances had left, crowded with wounded, and observers had seen a number of bodies laid out for burial in the cemetery near Cité St. Elie.

Early the following morning the Battalion was heavily bombarded with gas shells, the right company and Battalion H.Q. receiving most attention. Some of the gas got into the tunnels, but they were quickly cleared by the ventilating apparatus. This was the first real experience of enemy gas which the Battalion had had since the days of the Somme, and about twelve casualties, including Sec.-Lieut. C. E. Binns, were sustained. Many of these did not report sick until some hours after the bombardment, the gas poisoning apparently taking time to develop. The Commanding Officer had a slight touch of it, but remained in the line.

To assist more active operations, which were in progress further south, efforts were being made to attract the enemy's attention to the St. Elie Sector. The capture of a prisoner from the Battalion had already assisted this object. The next night, a patrol of the 6th Battalion exploded a Bangalore torpedo in the enemy wire opposite Boyau 78, and left marks of identification near the spot, in the hope that they would be found by the enemy. On June 28th companies had orders that unusual movement was to be shown in their lines, and arrangements were made for a smoke screen to be put up along the fronts of the two flank companies that evening. At the same time the artillery was to put down a heavy barrage. Actually, the smoke was not discharged, for the wind was in the wrong direction, but the artillery part of the programme was carried out. To save casualties all men, except a few sentries, had been withdrawn to the tunnel entrances before zero hour. The enemy replied to the barrage, shelling posts and communication trenches for the most part, but no casualties resulted except at Newport Sap. There the platoon commander had his men drawn up on the two stairways leading to the deep dugout which they occupied. He remained at the top of one stairway himself, with his platoon sergeant immediately behind him. During the enemy retaliation a shell burst on the parapet just in front, killing him and wounding the sergeant. Sec.-Lieut G. Crowther was a great loss to the Battalion; he was a most competent officer and very popular with everyone.

The remainder of the tour was fairly quiet. A good deal of

rain fell, flooding part of Devon Lane temporarily, but the water soon cleared. No one was sorry when the 9th Battalion Suffolk Regiment returned from the neighbourhood of Lens, and relieved the Battalion on the night of July 1st/2nd. The heavy casualties at the beginning of the tour had depressed everyone, especially after the quiet times which the Battalion had had for some months. The tunnels too exerted a depressing influence.

After two days in Brigade Reserve near Vermelles, the Battalion was relieved by the 9th Battalion Norfolk Regt., and, embussing at Philosophe, moved to L'Epinette, near Lestrem. Everyone was glad to leave, and the "Hulluch" sector, as it is known to most, represents a black page in the Battalion history. A little row of graves, in the military cemetery at Sailly Labourse, is the only lasting memorial of the Battalion's sojourn there.

CHAPTER VIII.

THE COAST.

(a) St. Pol and Ghyvelde.

THE Battalion arrived at L'Epinette early in the morning of July 4th, and there it remained for more than a week. After the recent depressing time which had been spent near Hulluch, the comfortable billets and the pleasant and highly-cultivated surroundings were indeed a welcome change. Some training was done, but the main feature of the stay was the Brigade Sports, which were held near Paradis. On the whole, the Battalion was not very successful in the events, but its canteen, the only one on the ground, did a roaring trade.

On July 13th the Battalion marched to Merville where it entrained. After a much quicker journey than was usual in France, it arrived at Dunkerque, and marched thence to a camping ground just outside St. Pol. Here tents had been pitched by the advanced party. The conditions were rather primitive, it being an entirely new site, and the number of tents was so small that about twenty-two men had to be crowded into each. The camp was pitched among the sand dunes which made an excellent training area, in view of the operations in which the Battalion expected soon to be engaged. Large tracts of these sand hills were covered with furze and other undergrowth, growing in places as high as six feet, and a highly interesting night march on compass bearing was carried out there. At first bathing was largely indulged in, but a particularly obnoxious variety of jelly fish infested the sea and caused so many casualties that it was practically given up, except by the few who patronised the deep ditch round Fort Mardyck.

At the end of five days the Battalion marched to Bray Dunes, where it was accommodated in a former Belgian camp. A further move into one of the front line sectors near the coast was expected, and an advanced billeting party actually went forward to Oost Dunkerque. But these orders were cancelled and the Battalion moved a mile or two inland to Ghyvelde, and settled down to hard attack training there.

When the Battalion first received orders to move up to the coast, the 49th Division was intended to take part in a big attack on the Dunes Sector, with its flank resting on the sea. This operation had been prevented by an enemy attack on July 11th, which had captured the whole of the Dunes Sector and pushed back the British line to the south side of the Yser Canal. Now the Division was detailed to make a frontal attack on the village of Lombartzyde. The 147th Infantry Brigade was to operate on the left, with its right on the Nieuport-Lombartzyde Road and its left on the Galeide Brook. The Battalion was to lead the attack on the right of the Brigade. The operation was a very complicated and difficult one. A large number of men had to be assembled on a very narrow front, and, after taking a series of objectives, which included the western half of the village of Lombartzyde, the Battalion was to consolidate a line on the light railway N.N.W. of the village, with another battalion of the Brigade on its left, facing nearly due west along the Galeide. With the enemy very much on the alert on that front, the assembly alone would have been fraught with great danger and difficulty.

A facsimile of the enemy trenches had been dug near at hand by another division, and this was used by the 147th Infantry Brigade. In order to approximate to the actual conditions of the operation, the Battalion used to fall in at 1-0 a.m. and march off to its assembly positions. All had to be assembled by half-an-hour before dawn. At dawn the "attack" would begin, and the Battalion would be back in camp about 8-0 a.m. Little was done during the rest of the day.

But this attack never took place. The Battalion never learned definitely why this was. Perhaps it was due to the severe casualties inflicted on the other Brigades of the Division by the enemy's first use of "mustard" gas. On the last day of July the Battalion moved to La Panne Bains, and took over coast defence duties from a Belgian battalion. In those days La Panne was a delightful place, and the three days spent there were much enjoyed by all. The town had suffered little from shell fire or bombing, and everything was going on much the same as in peace time. The coast defence duties were not heavy. Billets were mostly on the sea front, in good houses or hotels. The "Terlynk" and the "Continental" were well patronised. It was a regular seaside holiday for everyone.

(b) The Lombartzyde Sector.

On the night of August 3rd/4th the Battalion relieved the 1/5th Battalion King's Own Yorkshire Light Infantry in the Lombartzyde Right Sub-sector. Motor buses conveyed them to a point about midway between Oost Dunkerque and Nieuport, and from there they marched up to the line. The night was unusually quiet for that sector, but pouring rain hampered the relief and caused much discomfort.

The Lombartzyde Sector was a position of supreme importance. Since the enemy attack on July 11th had driven the British out of the Dunes Sector to a line on the south side of the Yser Canal, it had become the only British position north of the canal. It was simply a bridge-head, about 1,500 yards wide and 1,000 yards deep, bounded on the right by the flooded Bamburgh Polder, and on the left by the canal and the flooded Galeide Brook. Like the Dunes Sector it had been attacked on July 11th, but the enemy had only succeeded in maintaining a footing in the front, and part of the support, lines to the west of the Nieuport-Lombartzyde Road. To maintain this bridge-head as a "jumping-off" place for attack was of the utmost importance, and its capture was as much to be desired by the enemy. Hence, since July 11th, an enormous weight of artillery had been concentrated there by the British, and the Germans had been equally active on their side.

The 147th Infantry Brigade took over the defence of the sector from the 148th Infantry Brigade and had two battalions in the front line—the boundary being the road to Lombartzyde—one in support in the Redan, and one in reserve on the Nieuport side of the canal. The Battalion held the sub-sector east of the road, and never in its previous history had it held a front in such depth. The sector is of such interest that the Battalion dispositions are given in detail :—

1. A Company garrisoned all the three most forward lines ; one platoon held Nose Trench, a second held Nose Support, and two platoons were posted in Nasal Trench where the Company H.Q. was situated. To strengthen the defence, a Lewis gun team from other companies was attached to each of the two front platoons of A Company.

2. C Company garrisoned Nasal Support, where the Company H.Q. was, with two platoons ; the other two were in Nasal Walk, a trench between the two most northerly arms of the Yser Canal.

3. B Company had two platoons in Nasal Lane, but its other two platoons lived in the town of Nieuport, where they worked under the Royal Engineers.

4. The whole of D Company was in Battalion Reserve in the Redan.

It will thus be seen that the Battalion had garrisons in five successive lines of trench north of the canal, and a sixth line was held south of one of the branches of the canal.

The condition of the sector was appalling. Water lay so near the surface of the ground, that only breast-works could be constructed, and the borrow pits quickly filled. The heavy rains of the preceding days had made matters worse. The enormous volume of shell fire had damaged the trenches beyond hope of repair. There were only two communication trenches on the front—Nasal Avenue, which was dug by the side of the road right up to the front line, and Petit Boyau, better known as "Toute Suite Alley" from the general habits of people using it, between Nasal Support and Nose Support. Neither of these could be used for more than a few yards at a stretch as they had been so badly knocked about, and most people preferred to walk straight up the road as far as Nasal Support and then along the top of the ruins of Petit Boyau. Of course they could be observed from the enemy lines, but so also could they be if they tried to move along the trenches ; and one could move six times

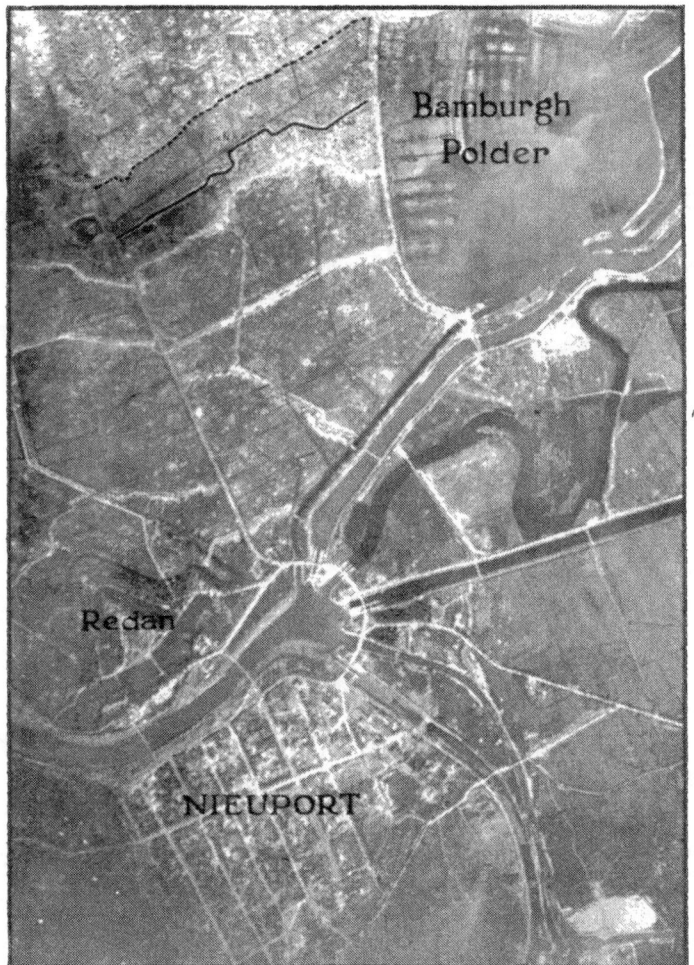

German Front Line ----------
British Front Line ———⌒———

THE LOMBARTZYDE SECTOR.
Aeroplane Map.

faster in the open, which was always considered an advantage. The defensive lines were in equally bad condition, and practically all movement was under observation. Except in A Company's area, accommodation was very scanty, especially in Nasal Support where it became worse almost daily, owing to the shattering of dugouts and shelters. The foremost lines, which had been the scene of heavy fighting on July 11th, were littered with dead and all the debris of battle. To crown all, the whole place was a mass of mud and the stench everywhere was sickening. Perhaps it was this last characteristic of the sector which suggested the very confusing system of trench names in use there.

Just north of the canal was an old fort, the former bridge-head of Nieuport; on the official maps it is called the "Palingbrug," but it was always known as the "Redan." The ramparts of this fort had been tunnelled into to provide accommodation for reserve troops, and these tunnels were fairly safe from ordinary shell fire. There were also a few pillboxes scattered about the Redan and one of these, which contained about six rooms, was occupied by Battalion H.Q. In dry weather it was fairly comfortable, but, as it had been cracked in numerous places by shell fire, the water fairly poured in when it rained. Just over the room which was occupied by the Commanding Officer was a great shell hole; a working party filled this in with much labour and it was lucky they did so, for, the very next night, another shell burst on the exact spot. Had the hole not been filled in, it would have been a bad look out for the Colonel.

The approaches to the sector were almost worse than the sector itself. To reach the south side of the canal one must pass through Nieuport, which was always a most "unhealthy" place. On arriving at the canal one had the choice of four bridges—perhaps! To the east was a series of six bridges, one after the other, crossing the different branches of the canal and called, for some unknown reason, the Cinq Ponts. All these were very heavily-built structures of masonry which could hardly be demolished by shell fire. Then, from east to west, came Vauxhall Bridge, Crowder Bridge and Putney Bridge. These were wooden structures, four to six feet wide, floating on the water of the canal. Parties of Royal Engineers were permanently stationed by these bridges to repair them as soon as they were shot away. The crossing of the canal was always an adventure. The man who wanted to get to the other side first noted the areas of enemy shelling, and, when he had decided which was the quietest bridge, rushed across it as fast as he could go. No one ever loitered on or near a bridge. At night things were even more uncertain. In the dark, the middle of a bridge might be missing without one knowing it, and several men had duckings as a result. Somewhere at the bottom of the Yser Canal lie the remains of a bottle of whisky and a dozen eggs, abandoned by a Battalion runner when he had to swim for it. When the tide was up the bridges lay level on the water; but at low tide the ends sloped at an angle of about forty-five degrees, and the quickest method was to sit down and slide to the bottom.

Whilst the Battalion was holding the sector its transport lines were at Coxyde Bains. It was quite impossible to do any cooking in the line. Apart from the fact that smoke would be almost certain to draw enemy fire, the men were far too short of accommodation for themselves to think of building trench kitchens. So all food was sent up ready cooked.

By far the worst feature of the sector was the great activity of the enemy artillery. This was mainly the result of two factors. In the first place, the weight of fire which could be brought to bear was exceptionally great. All the following artillery groups could be concentrated on Nieuport:—

1. The coast defence batteries between the line and Ostend. In the normal way these had little to do, and often they were switched round to fire into Nieuport.

2. The batteries on the Dunes Sector, which had little to do unless the British attempted an attack across the Canal.

3. The artillery on the Lombartzyde Sector itself, which was exceptionally powerful.

4. The guns covering the inundated Belgian front, where an attack by either side was practically impossible.

Also, the bridge-head was so small, and movement so restricted, that the enemy could hardly go wrong in his shelling. What was called "a quiet day" in the neighbourhood of Nieuport would have been described by some such phrase as "great activity on the part of the enemy artillery" on most other fronts.

It is hard to say which parts of the sector were most heavily shelled. No part was free from shelling. Even the transport lines at Coxyde Bains had their share on more than one occasion. Probably the worst localities were Nasal Support, the Redan, and the bridges. The quietest time of the day was the early morning, between 4-0 a.m. and 8-0 a.m. Just before dawn it was the enemy's general custom to put down a heavy barrage on Nasal Support, probably intended to overwhelm any troops who might be assembled for an attack. After that, most of the German gunners apparently took time off for breakfast and an hour or two's rest. About 8-0 a.m. things would begin to liven up, and there would be plenty of activity throughout the rest of the day. But the nights were the worst. Practically every night was one inferno, from dusk until dawn. High explosive rained down all over the sector, shrapnel burst above the bridges and the Lombartzyde Road, the neighbourhood of Battalion H.Q. and the Redan were deluged with gas shells, both mustard and diphosgene. Shells of every calibre were used, from the giant 15-inch, which came over with a roar like that of an express train into Nieuport, down to the "whizz-bang," which harassed one in the neighbourhood of the Aid Post. No attempt was made to keep telephone lines going except to Brigade H.Q. and to the Nasal Lane company, and these were continually broken. Practically all communication had to be done by the runners, who had a very hard time and suffered many casualties. There had been a long-standing discussion, between those who had been near Ypres in 1915 and those who had been at Johnstone's Post in the following year, as to which of these places was the worse shelled. But the Battalion had not been long in front of Nieuport before it was mutually agreed that the argument might be dropped. Nieuport beat all previous records.

But, with the exception of artillery fire, the enemy showed little activity. Machine guns were quiet; sniping was almost unknown. There was some trench-mortaring of the two front lines, but this was negligible compared with the artillery fire. The enemy front line was very lightly held, but on two occasions his patrols were seen in No Man's Land, though no encounter took place.

Heavy as was the enemy artillery fire, the activity of the British gunners was greater. The German attack of July 11th had caused great anxiety to the higher commands, and an enormous weight of artillery had been brought up. Behind Nieuport, the country was packed with guns of all calibres, and firing programmes were so arranged that some batteries would always be in action. As many as 18,000 shells were sometimes fired on that front in a single twenty-four hours. The protective barrage which could be put down by the eighteen-pounders was thicker than the Battalion had ever dreamed of; where it had been used to a single gun, there was here, not a battery, but a brigade. On one occasion, when a S.O.S. was sent up on the sector, the eighteen-pounders alone fired over 8,500 rounds in about half-an-hour. And on that sector every available gun fired on S.O.S.

Such was the Lombartzyde Sector in which the Battalion spent the first half of August, 1917.

As has already been said, the night the Battalion took over the line was particularly quiet. But a very clear warning was given by the outgoing battalion that this was not the normal state of affairs. The only casualty of importance that night was Capt. N. Geldard, O.C. D Company, who was wounded in the Redan. But the first complete day that the Battalion spent in the sector it had a taste of what was in store for it, suffering heavier casualties* than on any previous day since it left the Somme battle in September, 1916.

One of the main features of this tour in the line was the great patrol activity. Nightly, four standing patrols—one to every two hundred yards of front—were pushed out into No Man's Land, to give early warning of any attempt by the enemy to assemble for the attack. The whole of the enemy wire, or rather what remained of it for the British artillery had done its work well, was reconnoitred. But the main point of interest was a post† in the old British front line, which had been retained by the enemy after his abortive attack on July 11th. This post lay just to the west of the Nieuport-Lombartzyde Road, and it was hoped to regain it in connection with a raid which was pending. The position was carefully reconnoitred by Sec.-Lieut. A. J.

*7 killed, 24 wounded.   †Marked X on map.

Robb, of A Company, the officer detailed to carry out the operation.

The raid was to be carried out by a company of the 1/6th Battalion Duke of Wellington's Regt., and was to penetrate as far as the enemy second line, on the west of the Nieuport-Lombartzyde Road. It was arranged that Sec.-Lieut. Robb's platoon should form up and advance in rear of the raiding party. When the latter had captured the enemy post and advanced to its second objective, Robb was to occupy the post, consolidate and garrison it. Zero hour was fixed for 1-0 a.m. on August 8th, and, by 3-30 a.m., the whole platoon was to be withdrawn, with the exception of 1 N.C.O. and 6 men, who were to form the permanent garrison of the post. Thus only two hours and a half were allowed for the capture of the post and its consolidation, the carrying up of stores, and the opening up of communication with the left of A Company along Nose Trench.

At zero hour the raiders went over under a fine barrage. They captured the enemy post, penetrated to their second objective, and returned with a light machine gun and several prisoners of the 199th German Division. The 4th Battalion party was not so successful. Advancing in rear of the raiding party, most of them lost direction and did not arrive at the post at all; some of them went forward as far as the German second line and started consolidation there, thinking they had reached the right spot. Eventually, they discovered their mistake and withdrew with the 6th Battalion. The result was that Sec.-Lieut. A. J. Robb, on reaching his objective, found that he had only one N.C.O. (Cpl. J. Yates) and about six men with him. These he at once set to work, while he went out to seek the rest of his platoon. He failed to find any of them. Not long after the raiders had withdrawn an enemy party advanced to re-occupy its post. A bombing fight ensued in which Cpl. Yates succeeded in driving off the enemy; but when the fight was over he found he had only four unwounded men left. About 2-25 a.m. Sec.-Lieut. Robb returned to the post, and, as the number of men he had available was quite inadequate even for the defence of the post, and still more so for all the necessary work of carrying and consolidation, he ordered a withdrawal. Soon after, the enemy re-occupied the post. Dawn was now so near that there was no time to organise and carry out another operation, so the enemy was left in possession.

The following night a combined operation by artillery and gas projectors was carried out on the Lombartzyde Sector with no other result, from the Battalion's point of view, than to bring down heavier fire than usual. Then, on the night of August 9/10th, the 1/6th Battalion Duke of Wellington's Regt. took over the line, and the Battalion went into Brigade Reserve, in what were known as the Presque L'Isle Defences.

In the Presque L'Isle Defences a comparatively quiet and quite pleasant time was spent. A and C Companies lived in Nieuport, B Company had one platoon on Presque L'Isle itself—an island at high tide, a peninsula at low—while the rest of the Battalion occupied dugouts in the railway embankment, south-west of the Yser Canal. About 220 men were found daily for work in Nieuport or the trenches, but, apart from this, the Battalion had a complete rest. A number of men, who had remained out of the line for training, returned and were replaced by an equal number who had been through the recent tour. The only important drawback to the position was the almost continual roar of artillery on both sides. It was during this period that the Battalion witnessed the protective barrage which has already been mentioned. Suddenly one night, almost like a terrific clap of thunder, the whole of the British artillery opened fire. Men rushed out to see what was happening and found themselves standing in the middle of a half circle of light, caused by the flashes of the guns. This continued for about half-an-hour, and, in the rare seconds when one was not almost deafened by the roar, the screech of the "heavies," which were flying over from further back, could be heard. The officer who had sent up the S.O.S. signal believed he had seen the enemy massing for the attack. It is to be hoped he was correct, for troops in close order in the open must have been annihilated by such a storm of projectiles.

After four days' rest the Battalion returned to the same front as before, D Company occupying the forward positions, and B Company being in Nasal Support this time. The conditions were much the same as in the previous tour. Much time and labour were spent in wiring the front line, and, by the time the Battalion was relieved, an almost continuous double-apron fence had been put out along the whole front.

Throughout the time that the Battalion was in the Lombartzyde Sector the 147th Infantry Brigade was working under the orders of the G.O.C., 32nd Division. On the night of August 16/17th, the 20th Battalion Royal Fusiliers of that division took over the line. It was a night which will remain vivid in the minds of many, particularly certain officers and men of Battalion H.Q. Fortunately, the full volume of enemy artillery fire did not open until rather later than usual, and the majority of the troops were well on their way out before it reached its worst. But, long before relief was complete, high explosive and gas shells were raining down on the Redan, the vicinity of Battalion H.Q., and the bottom of the road to Lombartzyde. It was during this bombardment that Pte. H. J. Louth, of C Company, earned the high commendations of the Royal Fusiliers. Detailed as a guide to the incoming troops, he was wounded early on in the chest, but he remained at duty and did not report at the Aid Post until he had seen the troops he was responsible for safely into position.

When relief was complete, a small party of officers and runners left Battalion H.Q. The air was thick with diphosgene, but the night was so dark that movement in respirators was extremely slow and precarious. Hence, everything was risked, and the party rushed through numerous gas pockets to the Cinq Ponts. The first two bridges were passed without difficulty, but over the remainder the enemy was putting an intense barrage of shrapnel and high explosive. The trenches between these bridges were crowded with men awaiting opportunities to cross. Never before that night did some realise how fast a man can run when carrying a " tin " box of Lewis gun magazines, in addition to his ordinary equipment. One by one the bridges were rushed until the last had been crossed—and the party was still intact. Then the town of Nieuport had to be crossed, and, in the streets, one shrapnel shell burst so close on the top of everyone that all " ought " to have been hit ; yet, in some strange way, everyone escaped. At length Nieuport was left behind and a long dreary walk brought the party to Queensland Camp, near Oost Dunkerque, where the rest of the night was spent.

No one wept when he saw the last of Nieuport and the Lombartzyde Right Sub-sector.

(c) Coast Defence and Training.

For more than a month the Battalion remained on the coast under the XV. Corps, but it did not go into the front line again. The day after its relief in the Lombartzyde Sector it marched to Oost Dunkerque Bains, where coast defence duties were taken over from the 2nd Battalion Argyle and Sutherland Highlanders (33rd Division). It was the first time the two battalions had met, but they were destined to come in contact again on several occasions. The coast defence duties were not burdensome, two companies at a time providing all garrisons. The sector extended nearly up to Nieuport Bains, and one or two casualties were sustained from shell fire. Much amusement was provided by a number of French 37 mm. revolver guns which had been taken over as part of the defences. The men had never seen these weapons before and felt compelled to perfect themselves in the handling of them by frequent practice out to sea. The result showed itself in a few days in a scarcity of ammunition, and indents for more began to come in from companies, one Company Commander asking for a large supply of 37 cm. shells. As he was not known to have on his charge any guns of such high calibre, the indent was ignored. The shell cases also formed desirable souvenirs.

Many of the Battalion billets were in good houses or hotels along the sea front. On a clear day a good view could be obtained from the top storeys as far as Ostend. But this had its disadvantages, for the enemy also had the shore under observation, and so no movement was allowed on the sea front, nor bathing in the sea. While in this area, the Battalion was working under the orders of the 66th Division, who had quite a good concert party within easy reach.

Nearly a fortnight was spent at Oost Dunkerque Bains, the last two days at Surrey Camp just outside the town, and then the Battalion returned to La Panne. This time the billets were not nearly so good as they had been a month before. Since then, XV. Corps H.Q. had moved into the town and had appropriated all the good billets on the sea front, so the Battalion had to be content with greatly inferior billets about a mile inland. But the town was the same as ever, though occasionally visited by bombing planes; bathing was again possible; and there were now no coast defence duties to perform. Instead, some hard training was carried out, and several fierce " battles " were fought amongst the sand dunes. While at La Panne, the whole Brigade was one day reviewed on the sands by the G.O.C., XV. Corps, who presented medal ribbons to a number of officers and other ranks, and afterwards took the salute in the march past.

The most important event of the stay at La Panne was a visit from the G.O.C., 2nd Army, Gen. Sir H. Plumer. By this time, though the Battalion was still in the XV. Corps area, it had been transferred to the 2nd Anzac Corps, Second Army. There was no ceremonial parade. Instead, the Battalion paraded in fighting order, just on the French side of the frontier, and carried out a practice attack for the General's inspection. It was a time when many ideas on tactics were changing, owing to the experiences of the early part of the Third Battle of Ypres; in particular, the old practice of mopping-up by lines was giving way to the newer idea of mopping-up by areas. It was this point, more than any other, that the General insisted on when he spoke to the officers after the scheme was over. Incidentally, he gave the Battalion the first definite news of what it was destined for in the near future—to take part in the attack on the Passchendaele Ridge. It was the first time that most of the officers had heard the name—one now so well known to everyone, and conjuring up so many memories.

The Battalion left La Panne on the 13th of September, but only moved as far as Bray Dunes, where a camp was pitched among the sand hills. Training continued though the district was not so suitable as the last had been. Two night marches on compass bearings, which took place here, are worthy of record.

The first was for platoon sergeants, and was easily won by C Company, who received drinks round as their reward. The other was for officers and produced more amusement, though there was no prize. One Company, led by an experienced and fully-qualified surveyor in civil life, never got near its objective. A second company, trying to steal a march on the others, started from the wrong point and soon got into difficulty; after negotiating a precipitous cliff, at least two hundred feet high, and a mass of barbed wire, they threw up the sponge and retired to rest, calling down curses on the head of the unfortunate officer who had planned the march. It wasn't his fault, but perhaps it was fortunate for him that he was far away. It was at Bray Dunes too that Capt. N. T. Farrar celebrated his promotion, and rumour has it that a combination of A Company and the Q.M. Stores is not the best for a night march without a compass.

(d) En Route for Ypres.

Not until the latter end of September did the Battalion start on its march to Ypres. When it did take to the road its wanderings were so confusing that many wondered what really was to be done with it in the near future. Bray Dunes to Ypres should be marched with comfort in three days, or even two, for the distance is only about 25 miles. Actually the Battalion marched further than that in the first three days. Yet, it was not until the night of the twelfth day from starting that it passed through Ypres. In the intervening time it had marched about 75 miles, and had halted at various places for five complete days of rest. But the march had this advantage—it got the men into splendid condition.

The march was very uneventful. During the whole period up to the last day—October 4th—the weather was fine. The first few days were very hot, and the second day in particular, when the Battalion moved from Coudekerque to Wormhoudt, the march was extremely trying. A rather late start had been made so that the whole of the march took place in the heat of the day, and many men fell out. In the neighbourhood of

Buysscheure, where the Battalion remained for three nights, a football match between Battalion H.Q. and A Company resulted in a win for the former. As every officer who was qualified to play for either side turned out, the match provoked an unusual amount of interest. All who saw the match will remember the roar of cheers which went up when Capt. A. E. Mander—" Old Man "—headed a goal for his company.

About a week after leaving Bray Dunes the Battalion arrived in the Second Army training area, some miles to the west of St. Omer. This naturally fostered the idea that a period of intensive training was to be carried out before the men moved into battle. But, the very next day, advanced billeting parties were sent forward, and on the 30th of September the Battalion was again on the move.

On October 3rd the frontier was passed, the night being spent at Clyde Camp, not far from Watou. An early start was made the next morning, and, as the distance was short, it was still early when the Battalion arrived at Red Rose Camp near Vlamertinghe. That day the weather broke; it rained pretty steadily throughout the march, and was the beginning of a long spell of wet. The men were fairly comfortably housed in the camp, but accommodation for officers was very bad. As things turned out this mattered little, for only B Echelon and the Transport spent a night there. At last the Battalion was to be rushed into battle at the shortest possible notice.

CHAPTER IX.

THE BELLE VUE SPUR.

(a) October 4th—8th.

THE Third Battle of Ypres opened on July 31st, 1917, with an attack by two British Armies—the Second Army on the right and the Fifth Army on the left—supported by a French Army Corps to the north. At first a considerable advance was made, but the unusually wet weather of August greatly hampered operations. During September the weather improved and progress continued, but the fighting was exceptionally severe, the enemy stubbornly defending every inch of the ground. Notwithstanding all difficulties, by the beginning of October the Second Army was in touch with the Passchendaele Ridge, which was the last natural barrier between the British and the fertile, low-lying plains of Belgium. Though this ridge proved so serious an obstacle to the British advance, it is by no means conspicuous. At no point is it as much as sixty metres above sea level, and its average height is little more than fifty metres.

Some description of the battlefield, which the Battalion entered early in October, is necessary. For nearly three years the enemy had been fortifying the area east of Ypres, making use of every method and device known to modern warfare—and throughout the war the Germans were unsurpassed as field engineers. The result was a mighty fortress, covering many square miles of ground, second to none on the Western Front, or, for that matter, in the world. The ground was covered with trenches, constructed according to the latest ideas of fortification, and crammed with every device for offence and defence. Thousands of miles of barbed wire had been used in the construction of obstacles. Hundreds of " pill-boxes "—massive but low-lying structures of reinforced concrete, invulnerable unless they received direct hits from at least an 8-inch shell—covered the country-side and sheltered thousands of machine guns. The German artillery was extremely powerful and magnificently handled; and as every ridge, up to the battle of Messines, was in enemy hands, his gunners had all the advantages of superior observation. Such was the country that the British had been attacking, and slowly penetrating, during the last two months.

This country the British and German artillery had turned into a desolation unparalleled even on the Somme battlefield in the previous year. Literally, every inch of ground had been torn up by shell fire. The whole appearance of the country-side had changed—most of the roads had almost disappeared, thick woods had become nothing but collections of broken and distorted tree-stumps, of some villages there was scarcely a trace. Everywhere the ground was littered with the awful debris of war—dead bodies of men and animals, derelict tanks and guns, shattered wagons and every conceivable form of what was known to the men as "salvage." To crown all, the heavy rains of the late summer and early autumn had converted the whole area into a quagmire, the drainage system having been completely destroyed by artillery fire. Cross-country travelling was extremely difficult for a man on foot, for even when he picked his way carefully he was often bogged well above the knees; transport and animals could not move at all except by the newly-made roads and tracks. Every effort had been made to deal with the situation by the construction of plank roads, gridded tracks and light railways, but transport difficulties and the activity of the enemy artillery seriously interfered. Could the prophetic eye of Dante have looked so far forward into the future, he might readily have introduced this desolation as the setting to one of the lowest circles of Hell.

The Battalion was about to settle down for the night in Red Rose Camp when an urgent order from 147th Infantry Brigade H.Q. altered everything. In spite of the rain that day, a particularly successful attack had been made on a wide front; all objectives had been reached, and, in some cases, passed. Luck had been on the side of the British for once, for that same morning the enemy had planned a big counter-attack. Unfortunately for him his zero hour had been fixed a few minutes later than the British, whose barrage, 1,000 yards in depth, had passed slowly over three enemy divisions, assembled in close order in the open, and had almost annihilated them. So promising had been the situation at one time that the 147th Infantry Brigade was within an ace of being thrown into the battle that very day, to exploit it. This, however, had not been done, but the Battalion now received orders to move up and relieve the 1st Battalion Canterbury Regt., in reserve to the 2nd New Zealand Infantry Brigade. At once all was bustle and excitement, and, soon after 11-0 p.m. the Battalion, in battle order and at battle strength, marched out of camp to play its part in the battle for the Passchendaele Ridge.

The night was very dark and wet, and great difficulty was found in carrying out the relief. The route to Pommern Castle, where Battalion H.Q. was located and round which the whole Battalion was posted, lay along No. 5 Track—a single line of grids, in particularly evil condition, with fearsome mud on both sides. Relief was not complete until after dawn. Some anxiety was felt as to what should be done in case the enemy attacked, for not a man of the Battalion had any clear idea where he was, or where the front line lay. Accommodation was very bad. One or two low-lying, very wet, and extremely uncomfortable pill-boxes were occupied by Battalion H.Q.; but nearly everyone had to be content with a shell-hole over which he could spread his waterproof sheet. October 5th was spent mainly in trying to build habitable shelters.

On the night of October 5/6th the Battalion moved up to the line, where it relieved two New Zealand battalions. D and C Companies held the front line—D Company to the south of, and C Company along, the eastern edge of Berlin Wood; A Company was in support on Abraham Heights, and B Company in reserve near Otto Farm, where Battalion H.Q. was situated. Abraham Heights were rather heavily shelled at intervals, but, apart from this, nothing of importance happened during the twenty-four hours that were spent in the sector. The enemy was undoubtedly very disorganised after the attack of two days before, and was in no condition to be aggressive.

The night of October 5/6th was a particularly bad one for the Battalion transport men. Owing to the appalling condition of the ground, supplies could only be taken up on pack animals, and that night, for the first and last time, Texas packs were used. These proved most unsatisfactory, the loads could not be properly secured, and constant halts were necessary to readjust them. The amount of traffic on the roads was amazing. From Vlamertinghe to Ypres, and up beyond Wieltje, the whole road was packed with every conceivable form of vehicle and pack animal. Blocks were constantly occurring and causing wearisome halts. Soon after the convoy started it became split up, owing to vehicles pushing in between the animals. Beyond Ypres the conditions became even worse, and eventually the convoy returned to Red Rose Camp without having reached the Battalion. But soon after dawn a fresh convoy set out and succeeded in delivering the rations.

The next night the Battalion was relieved by the 2/5th Battalion Manchester Regt. (66th Division) and returned to Pommern Castle. The next two days were spent in active preparation for the attack which was to take place on October 9th. Large carrying parties were found for establishing forward dumps, and all officers reconnoitred routes up to the line and assembly positions for the attack.

This operation was on a very big scale. The 49th Division was to attack on the extreme left of the Second Army, with the Fifth Army attacking on its left and the 66th Division on its right. The main details of the attack were as follows:—

1. The 49th Division was to advance straight towards the point of the Belle Vue Spur, an offshoot of the main Passchendaele Ridge, on a frontage of about 1,500 yards.

2. Two objectives were to be captured and consolidated, the second objective being about 1,250 yards from the British Front Line.

3. The attack was to be made by the 148th Infantry Brigade on the right and the 146th Infantry Brigade on the left, each having two battalions in the front line. The 147th Infantry Brigade was to be in Divisional Reserve.

It was thus very uncertain what the role of the Battalion would be. Its orders were to be assembled at Pommern Castle by zero hour (5-20 a.m.) ready to move at a moment's notice. There it was to remain until further orders were received from Brigade H.Q., and, as it was the reserve battalion of the Brigade, these orders were not expected very early.

The morning of October 8th was bright and sunny, and the ground was drying up splendidly. But about the middle of the afternoon very heavy rain began to fall which continued, almost without a break, right through the night. The ground, already in very bad condition, was thus rendered almost impassable in many places, and the assembly of the attacking Brigades was seriously hampered.

(b) October 9th.

By 5-0 a.m. on October 9th the Battalion,* with the exception of most of B Company, who had not yet returned from a carrying party, was assembled at Pommern Castle ready to move. At 5-20 a.m. the barrage opened, several batteries near where the Battalion was assembled being in action, and all knew that the attack had begun. For about two hours nothing happened;

---

*The following Officers and Warrant Officers went into action with the Battalion on October 9th, 1917 :—

Battn. H.Q.: Lieut.-Col. R. E. Sugden, D.S.O. (C.O.); Capt. W. C. Fenton, M.C. (Adjt.); Lieut. H. S. Wilkinson (I.O.); Lieut. W. T. Scholes; Capt. J. M. Anderson, R.A.M.C. (M.O.).
R.S.M. F. P. Stirzaker, M.C.
Lieut. G. P. McGuire (Liaison Officer at 147th Infantry Brigade H.Q.).

A Company: Capt. A. E. Mander; Lieut. A. Kirk; Sec.-Lieut. J. R. S. Brabham.
Sergt. H. Gidley (A/C.S.M.)

B Company: Capt. S. Balme; Sec.-Lieut. L. L. Johnson; Sec.-Lieut. J. S. Watson; Sec.-Lieut. R. E. Stubington.
C.S.M. H. Haigh.

C Company: Lieut. E. V. Blakey; Sec.-Lieut. A. M. Luty; Sec.-Lieut. A. W. Nevile.
C.S.M. J. Parkinson.

D Company: Capt. N. Geldard; Lieut. W. L. Hirst; Sec.-Lieut. L. Gumby; Sec.-Lieut. W. Oldfield, M.M.
Sergt. W. Brooke (A/C.S.M.)

Fighting Strength of the Battalion on the morning of October 9th :—

	officers		other ranks
Battn. H.Q.	5	,,	59
A Company	3	,,	101
B Company	4	,,	86
C Company	3	,,	106
D Company	4	,,	108
Total	19	,,	460

R.S.M. F. P. STIRZAKER, M.C.
(Killed).

R.S.M. W. LEE, M.C.

C.S.M. W. MEDLEY, M.C., M.M.

Sergt. A. LOOSEMORE, V.C., D.C.M.

save for the noise of the guns, everything was quiet, and no news of the attack came through. About 7-30 a.m., orders were received for the Battalion to advance to the vicinity of Aisne Farm, some six or seven hundred yards west of Kansas Cross. B Company's carrying party had not yet returned, so guides were left behind for them, and the rest of the Battalion moved off in artillery formation, with platoons at fifty yards' interval. The ground was very wet after the heavy rain of the night before, and movement was slow and laborious. The Battalion had scarcely reached its destination when fresh orders arrived, directing it to proceed forthwith to the neighbourhood of Korek, where it would come under the orders of the 146th Infantry Brigade, whose advanced H.Q. was there. The route followed was along No. 6 Track, a single line of grids in none too good condition. Platoons had to move in single file, and, as they drew near to Korek, came under heavy artillery fire which caused several casualties—the first suffered that day. On arrival there the Battalion halted and began to dig in as the artillery fire was still heavy. While it was thus engaged, the remainder of B Company came up, so that the Battalion was again concentrated. The Commanding Officer went personally to the 146th Infantry Brigade H.Q. for orders and information as to the situation. The latter, he found, was very obscure. It was not definitely known where any of the Battalion H.Q. were situated; the 1/5th Battalion West Yorkshire Regt. was believed to be at or near Peter Pan, the 1/7th Battalion West Yorkshire Regt. somewhere between Kronprinz Farm and Yetta Houses. The only definite information was that both were in need of reinforcements, and the Commanding Officer was accordingly ordered to send up two companies in support of each. He returned to his Battalion H.Q. and orders, as definite as the situation would admit, were issued at 10-50 a.m. A and B Companies were placed under the command of Capt. A. E. Mander, whose instructions were to report to the 1/7th Battalion West Yorkshire Regt. and place himself under its orders. C and D Companies the Commanding Officer decided to lead in person to the assistance of the 1/5th Battalion West Yorkshire Regt.

At 10-55 a.m. Battalion H.Q. moved off, followed by C Company, with D Company bringing up the rear—all in artillery formation. Near Calgary Grange they came across Capt. Ablitt, of the 1/5th Battalion West Yorkshire Regt., who stated that his Commanding Officer was wounded and he was now in command. Most of his H.Q. personnel were casualties, he had no proper Headquarters and knew very little of the situation. The Commanding Officer informed Capt. Ablitt that he was moving up to Peter Pan with two companies, and then continued on his way. There was no protective barrage to cover the advance of the Battalion, and, as it came down the slope past Calgary Grange, very heavy machine gun fire was encountered from the pill-boxes on the Belle Vue Spur. The enemy artillery was also active, and, though the companies extended, many casualties were suffered before the old British front line was reached. Here a halt was made for about fifteen minutes to give companies an opportunity to reorganise, and to allow time for the reconnaissance of the crossings over the Ravebeke. In normal times this stream would have been a very slight obstacle, but the devastating fire of the British artillery and the recent heavy rains had converted its course into a formidable morass. Sec.-Lieut. A. M. Luty went forward to reconnoitre for practicable crossings. Under a heavy artillery and machine gun fire he carried out this duty, marked the possible places with sticks, and then returned to his own lines.

Lieut. H. S. Wilkinson, the Battalion Intelligence Officer, was also sent forward, not only to reconnoitre the crossings of the stream, but to try to get into touch with men of the 146th Infantry Brigade. Running from one shell-hole to another, he soon lost touch with the two men who had started out with him, and went on alone. Near the Ravebeke, a bullet lodged in his steel helmet, fortunately without wounding him. As he could find no other means of crossing, he waded through the stream, the water coming above his waist. He then advanced straight towards Peter Pan, across awful mud, and with machine gun bullets whistling all round. Soon he met a party of the 1/6th Battalion West Yorkshire Regiment, but they could tell him nothing of the situation. So he determined to reconnoitre as far as Peter Pan itself before returning to report. Not a dozen yards from the ruined building he was severely wounded. One bullet shattered his jaw; another went right through his left shoulder and fractured the arm. That was the end of his reconnaissance. He had established the very important fact that the enemy did not hold Peter Pan, but he was unable to return to give the information. In great pain and half covered with water, he lay in a shell-hole until the advance of the Battalion swept past him, and he was found and carried back.

Meanwhile, the Battalion was again advancing. C Company led the way, with D Company in close support. Under a hail of machine gun bullets, in the face of accurate sniping, and with shells bursting all round, they steadily advanced by section rushes, in extended order. The rear company gave covering fire to the leading one, and machine guns also assisted in keeping down the hostile fire. But many men went down, killed or wounded, in the mud, before the stream was reached. Then followed the crossing of the Ravebeke. Some of C Company had carried saplings with them which they threw across, others crossed on the fallen trees which were already lying there, yet others literally forced their way through the mud and water. On the far side of the Ravebeke the fire was, if anything, heavier; but the men pressed on to Peter Pan where many of them gained some temporary protection among the ruined buildings. It was in this crossing of the Ravebeke, and the advance to Peter Pan, that the Battalion suffered its heaviest casualties that day. Among others, Capt. N. Geldard, O.C. D Company, went down with a bullet wound in the ankle—his second wound in less than three months. Lieut. W. L. Hirst assumed command of D Company. Had the Battalion carried out its advance under a proper barrage the casualties would not have been nearly so heavy. But the Ravebeke had been crossed, which was, at the moment, the really important thing.

Battalion H.Q. was established in a newly-made shell hole, just in rear of the ruins of Peter Pan. C Company was pushed forward at once to get in touch with the West Yorks. and to gain contact with the enemy. Following a line slightly to the right of the direction of Wolf Copse, they came upon a number of West Yorks. who had dug themselves in, from two to three hundred yards in front of Peter Pan. Reconnoitring to their flanks, they also gained touch with a platoon of the 1/6th Battalion West Yorkshire Regt. So they set to work to consolidate on that line. There were rumours of other troops of the 146th Infantry Brigade still further out in front, but, apart from a few advanced men in shell holes, none were seen, and it is unlikely that any existed. D Company was also sent forward to prolong C Company's line to the left. Lieut. W. L. Hirst, with his C.S.M., first reconnoitred the ground, and, finding a company of the 6th Battalion Duke of Wellington's Regt. already in position there, brought up his company to prolong the line on its left. With the exception of the platoons found by C Company, no formed body of the 146th Infantry Brigade was ever found by the Battalion, though various isolated groups and stragglers were taken charge of by different companies. Meanwhile, machine gun fire from the Belle Vue Spur and from Wolf Copse was still sweeping the Battalion front, and extremely accurate sniping from the latter direction made individual movement very hazardous. Companies were doing what they could to keep this down with Lewis gun and rifle fire, but casualties were frequent. Two signallers, attached to C Company, were shot through the head as they were moving along a shallow trench. The Adjutant, Capt. W. C. Fenton, M.C., while reconnoitring the positions, was also wounded in the head. As Lieut. H. S. Wilkinson had already been wounded, only the Commanding Officer and Lieut. W. T. Scholes were left at Battalion H.Q. Such was the situation on the right about 3-0 p.m.

Meanwhile, A and B Companies had not moved with the rest of the Battalion. On receiving his orders to reinforce the 1/7th Battalion West Yorkshire Regt., Capt. A. E. Mander had sent out scouts to try to find out the location of the Battalion H.Q.; but, after some time, these had returned without any information. The companies were therefore kept in shell holes in the vicinity of Calgary Grange until something definite could be discovered. It was not until 12-20 p.m. that they got into touch with the Commanding Officer of the 1/7th Battalion West Yorkshire Regt., who was found moving his H.Q. back to Calgary Grange. He simply told them to stand fast for the present. They remained where they were until about 3-0 p.m., when they received orders to move up to Yetta Houses, and fill a gap in the line there. With A Company leading and B Company in support, they moved off in artillery formation, until they reached the swamps of the Ravebeke. Here heavy machine gun fire, and the same accurate sniping which had harassed the rest of the Battalion, forced them to extend. Capt. A. E. Mander was hit in the head by a sniper during the advance, and killed instantly. His death was a great loss to the Battalion, for he was not only a most conscientious officer, but a general favourite with all ranks; nothing was ever too much trouble for him if he thought it would benefit his men, and his only ambitions in life seemed to be to work hard and make others happy. On his fall, Lieut. A. Kirk assumed command of A Company.

A and B Companies reached their objective about 5-30 p.m. Like the rest of the Battalion, they found only stragglers of the 146th Infantry Brigade. A Company began to dig in to the right front of Yetta Houses, with B Company in support in an old trench in rear. Patrols sent out to the left failed to gain touch with any troops, save a few stragglers in shell holes, so Lieut. Kirk ordered the flank of his trench to be thrown back to protect his left. About dusk, patrols sent out by all companies succeeded in gaining touch with one another, and the line which was held for the night was as follows :—

Right :—C Company, facing N.E., and about 200 yards from Wolf Copse. It was in touch on the right with a platoon of the 1/6th Battalion West Yorkshire Regt., and had scattered men of the same battalion in shell holes in front of its position.

Right Centre :—A Company of the 6th Battalion Duke of Wellington's Regt., under Capt. Buxton.

Left Centre :—D Company, N. of Peter Pan, and facing Wolf Farm.

Left :—A Company, just to the right front of Yetta Houses, with its left flank thrown back as no touch had been obtained there. B Company was behind Yetta Houses, in support to A Company.

Battalion H.Q. was behind Peter Pan, still occupying its shell hole, " and very uncomfortable at that," according to the situation report sent in by the Commanding Officer. This line remained unchanged until the Battalion was relieved the following night.

Darkness brought a welcome relief from the harassing machine gun fire and the accurate sniping which had caused so many casualties during the day. Though heavy, casualties had not been sufficiently high to interfere seriously with the efficiency of the Battalion. C and D Companies combined had lost nearly 30 per cent. of their men, and A and B Companies about 20 per cent. These losses were, to a certain extent, made good by the temporary incorporation of numbers of stragglers. The men settled down for the night as best they could, tired out with their efforts of the day. Every officer and man was covered with mud from head to foot, and his clothes were thoroughly soaked with water. In these circumstances little comfort could be hoped for, especially as the Battalion failed to get in touch with the ration convoy. The night was very cold. Patrols were pushed out to maintain contact with the enemy, and these found the pill-boxes on Belle Vue Spur and the neighbourhood of Wolf Copse still held. One H.Q. scout unfortunately was captured by the enemy while out on patrol; he had become separated from the man he was working with, owing to the darkness and the very broken nature of the country. Suddenly he found himself right on the top of an enemy post; a bullet shattered one of his arms and paralysed his power of resistance, and, though he tried to run for it, he was easily taken.*

Throughout the day the enemy made no attempt to counter-attack, contenting himself by harassing the exposed British troops with his fire. About 7-0 p.m., a report that the Germans were massing for the attack caused some excitement, but it turned out to be incorrect. Towards midnight the Battalion was surprised by the opening of a heavy shrapnel barrage on its front. As everything was quiet at the time, no call for help had been sent back, and no operation was known to be in progress, the cause of this remained a mystery for some time. It was cleared up about 1-45 a.m. by the arrival of an order, from the 146th Infantry Brigade, to mop up a considerable area of ground on

---

*This man did not long remain a prisoner. Certified by a combined board of Dutch and German medical men as unfit for further service, he was repatriated through Holland.

the front. The barrage had been intended to cover this opertion, but so late did the order arrive, that it had long been over and nothing could be done.

The dawn of October 10th was ushered in by the customary German "hate," but after that things became fairly quiet for a time. A change was made in the Battalion dispositions at dawn. B Company was moved back to the vicinity of 146th Infantry Brigade H.Q. where it became Brigade Reserve. A Company thereupon withdrew one platoon from the line to form a company reserve.

Little of importance happened during October 10th. Very accurate sniping from Wolf Copse, as on the previous day, caused much inconvenience and several casualties. At various times during the day numbers of the enemy were seen on the Belle Vue Spur, and artillery fire was directed on them. About 4-0 p.m., Battalion H.Q. was subjected to a heavy and very accurate shelling. This was believed to be a result of the laying out of the Battalion ground sign, which had been called for by a contact aeroplane ; it was thought that this had been seen by enemy planes which were also up at the time.

Word had been received during the day that the Battalion was to be relieved that night by a New Zealand Battalion. About 10-0 p.m., these troops began to arrive. They did not take over in the ordinary way, but preferred to select their own position and dig an entirely new line for themselves. So, as the New Zealanders marched in and took up their position, the Battalion marched out. Relief was complete about midnight.

The orders issued to companies were that they should make for the Wieltje Road and follow it until they met the guides who were being sent up from the transport lines. All that night these guides were out on the road, directing men to X Camp, St. Jean, where they were to rest and where hot tea and rum awaited them. From about midnight until long after dawn, the troops of the 49th Division streamed down the road, some singly, some in groups of two or three, others in formed bodies. It is doubtful whether, before or since, the Battalion has been more thoroughly done up. After living in that waste of mud and water, with practically no shelter, for nearly a week, it had carried out an attack over the same appalling ground, and then consolidated and held its position in the face of violent artillery and machine gun fire.

The attack of October 9th had not been a complete success, but a very important advance had been made. The first objective had been carried practically in its entirety, and, in front of Peter Pan, a new line had been established some distance beyond it. But the second objective had not been reached. The most important success was the establishment of a line, well beyond the Ravebeke, along the whole front. This stream was a most serious obstacle, and the consolidation of a line to the east of it provided a good jumping-off ground for the troops who were to attack later on the same front. The difficulty of the operation may be judged from the fact that an attack launched from the new line a few days later by the New Zealanders failed to gain an inch of ground, and that the second objective of the 49th Division on October 9th was only just reached three weeks later by the Canadians, who had come up quite fresh to make the attack. The operation of October 9th was one of the first of that awful series of attacks on the Passchendaele Ridge which failed to obtain a full measure of success owing, not to the opposition of the enemy, but to the appalling condition of the ground.

That the work done by the 49th Division was appreciated by the higher commands is shown by the following message from the G.O.C., 2nd Anzac Corps, under whom the Division had fought :—

"Following message has been received by me from Army Commander, begins :—

'Please accept and convey to all your troops engaged to-day my heartiest congratulations on success achieved.

General Plumer.'

The Commander-in-Chief also called here to-day and wished specially to congratulate you and your Division.

I wish also to add my high appreciation and thanks to you personally and to all ranks of your Division on having done so much under such arduous and trying conditions.

General Godley."

The G.O.C., 49th Division, in a Special Order of the Day, wrote "Nothing could be finer than what the Division accomplished."

The G.O.C., 146th Infantry Brigade, in a personal letter to the Commanding Officer, said "I cannot thank you enough for the cheerful and thorough way in which all my orders were carried out." While the Battalion's own Brigadier, referring to the response of his troops when ordered up to support the other Brigades of the Division, said "Officers and men, though thoroughly exhausted, at once forgot their fatigue and advanced through the enemy barrage in the most gallant style worthy of the best traditions of the Army."

(c) Rest and Reorganisation.

Though a welcome change after the hardships of the Belle Vue Spur, X Camp, St. Jean, was far from a paradise. There were very few tents, and most of the men had to be content with small bivouacs or covered holes in the ground. The camp had been pitched hurriedly by a New Zealand battalion only a day or two before, and there had not been time to perfect it. It was not shelled, though the enemy paid attention to some neighbouring areas, and on several occasions his bombing planes were not far off at night. But the camp was made something like a home, and great regret was felt, and expressed, when a neighbouring Corps found that the Battalion was on the wrong side of the road and orders to move were issued. There was no other suitable camping site in the district. The best that could be found was a small field, pitted with shell holes, and covered with very long grass and rank weeds, all absolutely sodden by the rain. Into this field the tents and bivouacs were moved and repitched in the pouring rain, the men freely expressing their opinions, in language more forcible than polite, and the officers thoroughly sympathising.

On October 12th the New Zealand Division made its attack on the Belle Vue Spur, with the result already mentioned. One of the worst features of October 9th had been the difficulty of getting the wounded away; there had been far too few stretcher-bearers, and many of the wounded had suffered greatly by their long exposure. For the New Zealand attack each battalion of the 147th Infantry Brigade was asked to provide 200 men to assist in evacuating the wounded, and volunteers were readily forthcoming from among the men who had themselves learned the awful conditions. For two days these men worked in the battle area, fortunately with practically no casualties, and the gratitude of the New Zealand Division is shown by the following letter, written by its Divisional Commander to the G.O.C., 147th Infantry Brigade :—

"My Dear General,

Please express to the officers and men of your Brigade who came forward to assist in getting in the wounded, the very hearty thanks of myself and Staff, and the whole Division.

I have heard the warmest expressions of praise for the way in which your men volunteered to come forward and undertake what was certainly a very exhausting and maybe dangerous task.

I hope they did not suffer casualties, or if so, that they were light. The New Zealand Division will not forget the debt they owe to the officers and men of the 147th Brigade.

A. W. Russell, Major-General."

On October 16th the Battalion moved back to a hutment camp south-east of Vlamertinghe and here there was more comfort, though the huts were very crowded. In fact, at this time, there was not nearly enough accommodation, around and behind Ypres, for the enormous number of troops which had been brought up to take part in the battle of Passchendaele. Some training was done during the week the Battalion was there, particularly of specialists, the loss of whom had been very heavy in the recent battle. There, too, Major-General E. M. Perceval, C.B., D.S.O., said farewell to the 147th Infantry Brigade. He had commanded the 49th Division for more than two years, but was now returning to England to take up a home command. The Brigade paraded in hollow square and was inspected by the General, who afterwards thanked the men for all they had done and wished them farewell. The Brigade then marched past. Major-General N. J. G. Cameron, C.B., C.M.G., who had formerly commanded an infantry brigade of the 50th Division, succeeded to the command of the 49th Division.

REST AND REORGANISATION

The Battalion was now sent well back for a period of rest and reorganisation. On October 24th it moved by motor bus to tents near Winnizeele, a village famous for a restaurant which catered specially for officers. The camp site was not a good one, but three days later the Battalion moved to billets near Steenvoorde, where it remained for about a fortnight. Time was spent in reorganisation and training. Some interesting tactical schemes were worked out, one of which was attended by the new Divisional Commander. This was the first time the men had met him, though they were to see much of him in the future. He turned out to be a man of exceptional energy, who spent much of his time in the line, and seemed to have a peculiar preference for visiting the hottest places he could find. Here some drafts, both of officers and other ranks, joined the Battalion; but the heavy casualties sustained at Nieuport and the Belle Vue Spur were not made good until the reorganisation of the British Expeditionary Force at the beginning of the next year. The arrangement of billets did not allow of much social relaxation being organised. B Company, who occupied a large and comfortable barn, held a very successful concert, chiefly noteworthy for the dancing of a certain " Miss " Hey, who there made her début in that role. Another feature was the lecturing of the Area Commandant of Steenvoorde, whose comments on the strategy of the war were most interesting, even though his prophecies were sometimes rather wide of the mark.

On November 9th the Battalion moved by motor bus to the neighbourhood of Ypres where it was to remain, save for one period of rest, until the last great enemy offensive was launched in the following spring.

CHAPTER X.

WINTER ON THE PASSCHENDAELE RIDGE.

(a) Molenaarelsthoek and Keerselaarhoek.

THE battle for the Passchendaele Ridge was still raging when the Battalion returned to the neighbourhood of Ypres in November. To the south of the Zonnebeke Road the crest of the ridge was almost everywhere in British hands, but round the village of Passchendaele itself heavy fighting was to continue into December. The Battalion was not destined to carry out any further attacks; its role was the far more tedious, and almost equally difficult one of assisting to hold the ground which had been gained.

Ten days were spent in hutment camps at the back of Ypres. Winter was setting in and off the gridded walks, which ran round the huts, the camping areas were simply wastes of foul mud. About 200 men were found daily for work on light railways in the district. While the Battalion was encamped there news was received that the Commanding Officer had been awarded a Bar to his Distinguished Service Order, for good work during the attack on the Belle Vue Spur, and the occasion was suitably celebrated. Capt. W. C. Fenton, M.C., who had recovered from his wound, rejoined the Battalion here. About this time the allotment of leave improved considerably, so much so that, at the end of November, no less than 150 all ranks were away from the Battalion for that reason.

About the middle of November Lieut.-Col. R. E. Sugden, D.S.O., assumed temporary command of the 147th Infantry Brigade, during the absence of the G.O.C. on leave. As soon as the Brigadier returned, he went on a month's leave himself, so that Major A. L. Mowat, M.C., was in command of the Battalion until the latter part of January. On November 19th the 147th Infantry Brigade took over the defence of the Broodseinde

MOLENAARELSTHOEK & KEERSELAARHOEK

Sector, and the Battalion moved up into brigade right support on Anzac Ridge. Accommodation in this position was particularly poor. The tiniest of pill-boxes was all that was available for Battalion H.Q., and the same table had to serve for meals and office work by day, and as a bed for all H.Q. officers by night. On the night the Battalion took over, some gas shells burst just outside the shelters occupied by H.Q. details. C.S.M. A. Day, of A Company, who was Acting R.S.M., all the runners, and several others were so severely gassed that they had to be evacuated. A number of Battalion scouts, who had been left out of the line for training, had to be sent for to act as runners.

Four days later the Battalion relieved the 1/6th Battalion Duke of Wellington's Regt. in the Molenaarelsthoek Sector, which extended from opposite Justice Wood to about Flinte Wood. The relief was a stormy one. The tracks were heavily shelled and one platoon had eight casualties going into the line. The front was rather a long one and required three companies in the line. As it lay on the forward slope of the Broodseinde Ridge, which was under observation from the Keiberg Spur opposite, no movement was allowed by day. Accommodation was poor and there were no continuous trenches. At night much work was done, joining up front line posts, constructing supporting posts to the west of the ridge, digging a defensive communication trench on the right, and wiring. The influence of the battle further north made the front a lively one. Army barrages were continually being put down in the vicinity, in an endeavour to distract the enemy's attention from the real point of attack. Judging from the Battalion's experiences, these had a fair amount of success, for the enemy artillery was very active; frequently parts of the line were heavily shelled, and barrages on No Man's Land during the night were common. These latter greatly interfered with the work of patrols, which were out nightly. Fortunately, casualties were not heavy; but it was during this tour that Sec.-Lieut. J. S. Watson, a most promising young officer of B Company, was killed.

The Battalion transport too had a very rough time. The enemy was doing a great deal of back area shelling, and night after night the ration convoys had to pass through it. During this tour the transport lost the first of its number killed in action. But all ranks behaved with great gallantry, and, in spite of casualties to men and animals, rations were invariably delivered nightly.

There is no doubt that, by this time, the enemy had settled down to a defensive policy for the winter. The collapse of Russia had come too late to prevent the British gaining the Passchendaele Ridge, though German reinforcements from the Eastern Front had made that task far more difficult. For the next few months the enemy was content to leave things as they were, and quietly to perfect his plans for a great offensive the following spring.

On November 27th the Battalion was relieved by the 1/5th Battalion King's Own Yorkshire Light Infantry, and, after a night spent near Gordon House, moved to Vancouver Camp The day after its arrival Capt. H. Hanson, O.C. D Company, was so seriously wounded by a shell, just outside Vlamertinghe, that he died two days later in hospital. His death was a great blow to everyone. He was one of those men whom no one can help liking, possessing a most equable temper, and, though unsuited by age to the rigours of trench warfare, always trying to remain cheerful and to make the best of things. Sec.-Lieut. P. Donkersley was also severely wounded by the same shell.

In the next camp was a New Zealand Cyclist Battalion against whom a very vigorous " rugger " match was played. The result was one casualty—Sec.-Lieut. F. Irish with a dislocated elbow— and a win for the Battalion by two tries to a try. Little training was possible for, a few days after arrival at the camp, practically every available man was moved to Lancer Camp, near Potijze, for working parties. Little more than Battalion H.Q. remained at Vancouver Camp. Three days later the Battalion was again concentrated in Dragoon Camp, and the next night took over the Keerselaarhoek Sector from the 4th Battalion Suffolk Regt. (33rd Division).

This sector deserves more than a passing mention as it was one of the worst, if not the worst, ever held by the Battalion. The usual route to the line lay along a gridded track which seemed endless to the weary and heavily-laden soldier. The track was far from " healthy," particularly where it wound round Abraham Heights ; at this point several casualties were suffered by the advanced party, when the Battalion was first taking over the sector. But it was after Seine that the real trouble began. Just beyond that point the grids came to an end,* and for the rest of the way, over a mile in distance even if a direct line were followed, the troops simply wallowed among mud and shell holes, appalling even in that country. The front line posts were on either side of the Ypres-Roulers Railway, and their condition beggars description. Originally shell holes, attempts had been made to improve them by digging ; but so water-logged was the ground that all excavations filled with water almost at once, while the sides caved in as quickly as they were dug out. To the south of the railway another difficulty presented itself ; as often as digging was started anywhere, dead bodies, in a state of decomposition, were uncovered, and the hole had to be filled in quickly. It was extremely difficult to get R.E. material up to the front line at all. Owing to enemy observation no movement was possible by day, and the nights were so black, and usually wet, that a man could hardly see a yard in front of him. The man who had carried up one trench grid or revetting frame from Battalion H.Q. to the front line, had done a really hard night's work. The Ypres-Roulers Railway, which ran through a deep cutting and should have been an easy and direct route to the line, was absolutely impassable owing to the thick mud which covered it. No fires could be lit, and the only hot food or drink that could ever be obtained was that heated over Tommy's cookers. In short, the state of discomfort and misery in which the men lived had never been equalled in the history of the Battalion, except possibly in those ghastly days on the extreme left sector in December, 1915. An American officer, who was attached to the Battalion at this time, expressed amazement that men could exist at all under such conditions.

The front system was held by two companies, one on each side of the railway. A third company was in support round Hillside Farm, a prominent pill-box just below the crest on the west side

*While the Battalion was holding the Keerselaarhoek Sector the gridded track was continued as far as the crest of the Passchendaele Ridge.

of the ridge. The other company was in reserve in a number of shelters not far from Tyne Cottage. Battalion H.Q. was near Seine.

Fortunately the enemy was not very active on this front. His artillery made good practice on and around the village of Passchendaele, a little further to the north, but comparatively little attention was paid to the Keerselaarhoek Sector. Probably he realised that an attack there was practically impossible for either side. Patrols which pushed out in the direction of Tiber Copse and along the Railway reported the ground impassable; sheets of water covered much of No Man's Land, and where there was no water the mud was almost bottomless. The only route by which the opposing forces could come in contact was in the direction of Assyria, on the Keiberg Spur, and even there the ground was in an appalling condition. Only in the event of hard frost would an attack be possible anywhere. So, apart from harassing fire, there was little activity.

Three days were considered a long enough spell for any troops to hold that line, so, on the night of December 10/11th, the 1/5th Battalion Duke of Wellington's Regt. came up to relieve, and the Battalion returned to Dragoon Camp. It was not much of a rest. The camp was, on the whole, comfortable, considering that it was to the east of Ypres. But nearly every man was required for working parties daily, and these were often in badly shelled areas. Rather to the surprise of everyone, the Battalion remained at Dragoon Camp for five days. The 1/5th Battalion had asked and been allowed to remain in the line for an extra two days, preferring to do this rather than have the fatigue and discomfort of going out and then coming in again for another tour. But every man was heartily sick of it by the time his five days were over.

One point in connection with the relief is worthy of note. The advantages of the Zonnebeke Road, as a route to the line, had been so much praised by one officer of the Battalion that the Commanding Officer determined to try it. All went well until he was nearing Zonnebeke, and then, without any warning, a 5.9 burst in the middle of the road about seventy yards away. It was almost immediately followed by a second, which burst within ten yards of the party, luckily just off the road. That was enough! With one accord everyone made off straight across country as fast as he could go. This was not very fast, for all were heavily laden and often sank up to the knees in mud. But they got away from the road, over country which no one would have dreamed of attempting in ordinary circumstances. And none of them ever tried the Zonnebeke Road again.

Little need be said of the second tour in this sector except that it only lasted 48 hours. If such a thing were possible, the conditions were even worse than before. Some snow fell during the tour, but it melted almost as it fell and simply helped to make things more miserable. When the 1/7th Battalion West Yorkshire Regt. came in to relieve, it was with the greatest joy that the Battalion bade farewell to the Keerselaarhoek Sector.

The next rest period was spent at Halifax Camp, which adjoined Vancouver Camp. About this time the weather changed and bright days, with hard frost, supplanted the constant rain which had helped to make things so miserable of late. Though much colder, the change in the weather was a great improvement. On December 23rd, when the time came for another tour in the front line, the Battalion was taken up in the morning by broad gauge railway as far as Hellfire Corner, and halted there until the middle of the afternoon. Cook kitchens had been brought up to this point and hot dinners were served before the men started again. Shortly before dusk the Battalion marched off, via Mole and Jabber Tracks, to the Molenaarelsthoek Sector, where it relieved the 1/5th Battalion King's Own Yorkshire Light Infantry.

Since the Battalion had held this part of the line a month before, the length of the front had been reduced by the New Zealanders taking over part on the right flank. It was now only necessary to have two companies in the front line. Of the other two, one garrisoned a line of posts on the western slope of the ridge, and the other lived in shelters and pill-boxes near Battalion H.Q. Companies inter-relieved after three days in the front line.

This tour was the pleasantest the Battalion had on the Passchendaele Ridge. The frost, which continued throughout, had made the ground everywhere passable. Though colder, it was quite dry, and so far more comfortable than the damp had been. Snow covered the ground, but not to any great depth. Except for some further snow occasionally, the weather was bright. The nights were wonderful. The moon was at the full, and, assisted by the reflection from the snow, the light was so bright at midnight that observers on the crest of the ridge were able to use ordinary glasses for observing the Keiberg Spur, more than 2,000 yards away. The days were often misty, which made it possible to move about freely to the east of the ridge where, before, all movement had been forbidden in daylight.

Advantage was taken of the bright nights to do a great deal of work. Much wire was put out in front, posts were improved and shelters built therein, and a lot of work was done on the support posts west of the ridge. Since the Battalion had last occupied the sector, two communication trenches had been cut through the ridge nearly up to the front line, and these made movement both safer and easier. Enemy artillery was not very active, and, with one important exception, most of the shelling was very scattered. It was one of these scattered shells that wounded Capt. E. V. Blakey, M.C., and C.S.M. J. Parkinson, as they were going the round of their company posts in the support line. The exception was a small but prominent pill-box on the crest of the ridge, which the Battalion used as an observation post, and the enemy apparently as a registration point. Fortunately this pill-box was very strong and had a cellar, to which the observers retired when things became too lively. The nearest enemy posts were a long way off; indeed, later information goes to show that the nearest post was at least a thousand yards east of Celtic Wood.

Christmas Day, for the first and only time during the war, was spent by the Battalion in the front line. In the circumstances, little could be done to celebrate the occasion. Messages of goodwill were telephoned to the Brigadier and the Divisional Commander. One Company Commander, after laboriously putting a message of seasonable greetings into B.A.B. code, sent it over the wire to another company. The O.C. that company, delighted with his success in deciphering the first few letters of it, repeated it to Battalion H.Q. and to the remaining companies, in his own name. Rumour has it that one company, not very expert in B.A.B. code, spent a dreadful night wondering what operation was to take place; perhaps the mistakes which had been made in encoding the message accounted for the inability of these officers to read it. Many visitors called at Battalion H.Q. and visits were exchanged with the 1/6th Battalion Duke of Wellington's Regt., which was holding the sector on the left. Apart from a present of shells, despatched to the enemy on the stroke of midnight, there was little activity on either side.

The nights were so bright, and movement over the snow visible at so great a distance, that special white overalls were worn by men when patrolling. Unfortunately, no change was made in the colour of the equipment which had to be worn over them. The result was that, though the men of a patrol were practically invisible at no great distance, sets of equipment could be seen moving about in No Man's Land. There was much patrol activity on both sides, rendered necessary by the hard frost which had made No Man's Land easily passable. There is also no doubt that the enemy was as anxious to secure identification as the British were. So patrols, both defensive and offensive, were out practically the whole of every night. On the night of December 23rd/24th Sec.-Lieut. J. W. Lumb, while reconnoitring in the neighbourhood of Flinte Farm, narrowly escaped being surrounded by a large enemy patrol. After that, nothing further was seen of the enemy in No Man's Land for several nights. About 11-0 p.m. on December 28th, a small defensive patrol of one N.C.O. (Cpl. Aspin) and three men left the right company front. They had not been out very long, and were near the north-west corner of Celtic Wood, when they saw a party, about twenty strong, moving towards them along the northern edge of the wood. At first they believed this to be a New Zealand patrol from the battalion on the right, but soon they found it was a party of the enemy. All were clad in long white coats and a few were wearing belts filled with bombs; most were armed with revolvers. The German party tried to surround the small British patrol, and succeeded in cutting off one man and capturing him. The other three broke through the cordon and made for their own line, with the enemy in pursuit.

On reaching the wire there was a scuffle in which one man was killed, but Cpl. Aspin and the other succeeded in forcing their way through the wire and gaining one of their own posts. The garrison of this post, warned by the noise, was standing to, but had hesitated to fire for fear of hitting its own men. It now opened a heavy fire with Lewis guns and rifles, and the enemy immediately made off. As soon as one could be organised, a strong fighting patrol was sent out; but the enemy had disappeared. It is probable that the German party was on its way to raid the British line and that the patrol had served its object, though it had been unfortunate enough to lose one man killed and another captured. This mishap was undoubtedly due to the carelessness which had developed owing to previous immunity, and was a salutary lesson to many in the Battalion.

The next night the Battalion was relieved and went back into Brigade Reserve. The relief did not pass off without casualties. A shell exploded among a party of H.Q. scouts, as they were crossing the Hanebeek Valley on their way to Westhoek Ridge, killing one and wounding six. In Brigade Reserve the Battalion was very scattered, dispositions being as follows :—

    Battn. H.Q. : Garter Point.
    A Company : Tokio.
    B Company : Westhoek Ridge.
    C Company : Tunnels near Moulin Farm.
    D Company : Distributed between Anzac Ridge, Tokio and Retaliation Farm.

About this time the lessons learned in the recent battle of Cambrai were beginning to take effect, and an elaborate system of defensive lines was in course of construction in the Ypres Salient. While in Brigade Reserve, all men were kept hard at work on these rear lines of defence, and on tunnels which were being made near Moulin Farm. The birth of the New Year passed almost unnoticed at Garter Point. On January 4th, 1918, the Battalion was relieved by the 1/8th Battalion West Yorkshire Regt. and moved to Infantry Barracks, Ypres. Several casualties were suffered during the relief. So ended the first period of the Battalion's defence of the Passchendaele Ridge.

To Face Page 184.

THE YPRES SALIENT, WINTER, 1917-18.

(b) Work and Training.

In pre-war days Infantry Barracks had been one of the permanent barracks of the Belgian Army. It must have been rather a bleak building, but it had been built on such solid lines that, in spite of heavy shelling, parts of it were still habitable. It was not an ideal billet for troops to occupy in January, being extremely draughty. Several of the rooms had been fitted up with wire beds and there was ample accommodation for the whole Battalion. There was also quite a good little concert room on the premises. During the time the Battalion was at Infantry Barracks it was engaged in work on the Corps Line, particulars of which are given later.

After four days, the Battalion was relieved by the 2/6th Battalion Lancashire Fusiliers (66th Division), and moved back to Devonshire Camp, between Busseboom and Ouderdom. This camp was in very poor condition and had actually been condemned some time previously. But the number of troops in the Ypres Salient was so great that its use could not be dispensed with. The weather had again turned to rain and the huts leaked badly. At Devonshire Camp the 147th Infantry Brigade Concert Party—the " Ducks "—began its activities. The Battalion contributed several performers, chief amongst whom was the " low comedian," commonly known as " Jenks."

While at Infantry Barracks and Devonshire Camp, nearly all available men were working on the Corps Line. This was part of the new defensive system which was being constructed all over the Ypres Salient, and consisted of a line of strongly fortified posts on the Westhoek Ridge. Three of these were allotted to the Battalion, which re-allotted them to companies as follows :—

  Frezenberg Post :   D Company.
  Kit and Kat Post : A and B Companies.
  Sexton Post :   C Company.

By this means, the same company always worked at the same post, and soon men began to take a great pride in making their particular post better than anyone else's. The work was very hard. Sixty men per company were sent up daily ; the company commanders took turns in charge of the party; and either the Commanding Officer or the Second in Command went up daily. The men had to rise long before daybreak in order to get breakfast and catch the train at Brandhoek Station. At first they marched to the station, but, shortly before the Battalion left Devonshire Camp, the system of conveying them by motor bus was started. The train took them as far as Hellfire Corner, from which point they marched up to their work. Only haversack rations were taken, but tea was made on the spot. Hot dinners were ready on their return to camp, which was not until fairly late in the afternoon. The working parties were occasionally troubled by enemy shelling and on one occasion C Company suffered casualties. Most men were ready for bed very early in those days.

The divisional arrangement was that one Infantry Brigade should remain up near Ypres for this work, while the other two were back for rest and training. The 147th Infantry Brigade had been the first for work. On January 26th the 148th Infantry Brigade came up to take over the work and the Battalion, which had already done its day's work on the Corps Line, moved by train direct from Hellfire Corner to Caestre, whence it marched to the billets that awaited it at St. Sylvestre Cappel. Here it remained, except for a few days spent on the rifle ranges near Moulle, for nearly a month.

Only the billets occupied by Battalion H.Q. and the officers of C Company were in the village itself. All the rest were in scattered houses and farm-buildings, some well over a mile away. But the billets were comfortable, and the troops found the French inhabitants well disposed towards them. Many still look back on the time spent there as one of their happiest times in France. Training was entirely by companies; the men were too scattered, and there was no ground available, for Battalion training. Much of the training was in connection with a divisional competition scheme, but the Battalion was very unlucky in its results. As companies were so scattered they kept mostly to themselves, and there was little opportunity to organise social functions. Towards the end of the stay, a highly successful "convivial" was held by the warrant officers and sergeants

WORK AND TRAINING

at the "Brown Cow" in the village. Most of the officers were present, and, among them, Capt. Allen, V.C., M.C., particularly distinguished himself.

In January a big reorganisation of the British Expeditionary Force took place, the strength of each Infantry Brigade being reduced to three battalions. In the 147th Infantry Brigade the 1/5th Battalion Duke of Wellington's Regt. was broken up, and a draft of 10 officers and 250 other ranks was posted to the Battalion from it, late in January. A few days later, a further draft of two officers and about 80 other ranks arrived from the 8th Battalion Duke of Wellington's Regt. (11th Division), which had also been dissolved. These reinforcements brought the Battalion to full strength again, for the first time since the beginning of August, 1917. Both the officers and men of these drafts quickly settled down, and many of them soon rendered very valuable services to their new battalion. It has always been a matter of pride in the Battalion that new officers and men, from wherever they came, were quickly assimilated, and in a short time regarded the Battalion as their own.

Early in February the Battalion moved by train to Moulle for four days' shooting. All day was spent on the Second Army ranges, and the training culminated in a big Battalion field practice. A special "bullet and bayonet" competition was held there for the best platoon from each company in the 147th Infantry Brigade, and this the Battalion was very unlucky to lose. D Company's platoon was at first placed top, but afterwards was defeated when it had to compete again against the best platoon of the 1/7th Battalion Duke of Wellington's Regt. In spite of rather unsettled weather, the time at Moulle passed very pleasantly, musketry at long ranges being quite new to the Battalion since it came to France. At the end of the time, the return to St. Sylvestre Cappel was made by road, two days being taken on the journey.

On February 20th the G.O.C., XXII. Corps (the new title of the old "2nd Anzac Corps") inspected the Battalion at training. Great preparations were made for his arrival and a scout, posted at a useful point of observation along the road, gave early warning of his approach. His entry upon the training field was greeted with a volley of rifle grenades (not *at* him) ; Lewis guns and rifles opened rapid fire on the miniature rifle range, the marksmen all being arrayed in small box respirators ; while a platoon, with many lurid epithets and a most unusual amount of energy, attacked a row of sacks with the bayonet. It is hoped that the G.O.C. was suitably impressed. At any rate he ought to have been. But his only comment after this great display of the Battalion's offensive spirit was " How are the men's boots ?" Later in the day he presented medal ribbons, at a ceremonial parade, to a number of officers and other ranks of the 147th Infantry Brigade.

This was the end of the Battalion's period of rest. The next day it marched to Caestre, entrained there for Ypres, and spent the night at Infantry Barracks. A very strenuous time was in store for it, and much was to happen, ere it went back into rest again.

(c) Reutel Sector.

This was the first time the 49th Division had held a part of the front line since the strength of a brigade had been reduced to three battalions, and naturally, defence schemes and systems of relief required revision. The Divisional Sector was divided into two Brigade Sectors ; the left, which was much the narrower front, was held always by the 146th Infantry Brigade with only one battalion in the front line at a time. On the right, the 147th and 148th Infantry Brigades inter-relieved every eight days. Here, all three battalions of the brigade held sub-sectors of the front line. The Reutel Sector, which was on the extreme right of the Division, abutting on the 33rd Division, was allotted to the Battalion, which, throughout the time it was there, inter-relieved with the 1/5th Battalion York and Lancs. Regt.

When in Divisional Reserve, the Battalion usually lived at Maida Camp, near Belgian Chateau. To reach the Reutel Sector the men were taken by light railway trains as far as Birr Cross Roads, and from thence marched straight up the Menin Road as far as Hooge Crater. At this point they bore to the left, through the desolate remnants of Chateau Wood, and then moved along Jargon Track to the vicinity of Polygon Butte; companies then followed separate routes to their respective positions. Although this route had its fair share of shelling, the Battalion was generally fortunate in its reliefs.

The front line was rather over a thousand yards in length, and the sector was held as follows :—

Front Line : Two Companies, each having two platoons in the front line, one in the support line, and one available for immediate counter-attack. The front line was the main line of defence.

Support Company : One platoon in Patu Support and the remainder of the Company in the reserve line near Battalion H.Q. In the event of enemy attack the whole company was to move up into Patu Support.

Reserve Company : In pill-boxes and dugouts to the north of the Polygon de Zonnebeke. In the event of enemy attack this company was to move up into the reserve line, vacated by the support company.

Battalion H.Q. was in a pill-box about two hundred yards from the Butte. Inter-company reliefs were carried out in the middle of each tour.

The sector was one of the most varied and interesting that the Battalion had ever occupied. It was taken over from the 1st Battalion Otago Regt. (New Zealand Division) on February 22nd. This division had occupied it for a long while and had done an extraordinary amount of work there. Like all the sectors on the Passchendaele Ridge, it was very wet, and the Battalion found it quite impossible to drain certain parts of the trench system, particularly Plumer Trench, the communication trench on the left. Except for one gap in the middle, where all attempts to get the water away had failed, there was continuous communication along the front line. This line had been well and deeply dug, and was well provided with fire bays, shelters, and all the necessary provisions for trench life. The right rested upon the valley of the Polygonbeke which, like all streams in the district, was an impassable morass. The centre ran through the ruins of the village of Reutel, whose existence would probably have been overlooked had not the trenches in places been cut through the actual foundations of the houses. Near the centre of the front line, the parapet had been built over the village well; this provided the water supply for both front line companies. There had once been a continuous support line, but the centre was now derelict, and only the two flanks were occupied. Each Company H.Q. was comfortably housed in a pill-box which gave practical immunity from shell fire. The front line faced roughly southeast, the ground, except on the extreme left, falling away to the Reutelbeke. On the left a spur ran out from the main ridge, near the point of which had been the village of Becelaere, now marked only by some prominent pill-boxes.

Behind the front system of defences lay Jetty Warren, once a tributary of the Polygonbeke, but now a filthy, noisome and impassable quagmire. It was crossed in two* places by gridded bridges, and these were the only means of communication with the front line, except a very roundabout route through the area of the next battalion. This fact was well known to the enemy, who swept them with machine gun fire at frequent intervals during the night. On the forward slope of the hill, overlooking Jetty Warren, was Patu Support Line, a well-constructed fire trench but rather short of accommodation for men. About five hundred yards further back lay the reserve line and Battalion H.Q., the latter in a small but very strong pill-box, the chief drawback to which was the lowness of the roof. When the Battalion first took over the sector all communication with the front line companies was across the open; but before it left a good communication trench had been dug from Patu Support to the right company H.Q., and a second had been started from the reserve line to Patu Support.

The main feature of the countryside was Polygon Butte, popularly supposed to be the ruins of the race course stand. This stood out so prominently that it naturally became a registration point for the enemy artillery, and people did not generally linger near it. Here Capt. A. J. Robb, of D Company, was wounded, when returning from his inspection of the line before the Battalion took over.

*Before the Battalion left the sector, a third had been built.

All the ground behind Jetty Warren was overlooked from Polderhoek Chateau. That commanding position lay about 1,000 yards due north of Gheluvelt and an equal distance from the Battalion's right. It had been the scene of terrific fighting the previous autumn and had changed hands more than once; but finally the enemy had kept possession of it. From the Reutel Sector nothing but a great pill-box could be seen. This was a favourite mark for the British artillery. Guns of the heaviest calibre were constantly firing at it, and sometimes splinters from the explosions were hurled right into the Battalion's lines. Attempts were even made to smash it in with 12-inch "duds." But apparently no serious damage was done to it. Occasionally enemy snipers from that position fired on men moving to and fro between Patu Support and the Butte; but the range was too great for this to be really dangerous.

Like all sectors which had been occupied by the New Zealanders, the Reutel Sector was a very active one. It was not so much the hostile artillery. This was certainly not quiet, especially round the Butte, on Patu Support, and near the well in the front line. But most of the activity came from the infantry. The Germans had posts much nearer the British line than the Battalion had been used to of late. Although the crest of the ridge was in British hands, the enemy had retained a hold on the slope instead of withdrawing to the far side of the valley. Some of his posts were only about a hundred yards from the British line. When advanced parties from the Battalion first visited the line they were surprised at the amount of firing which was going on; and when the New Zealanders finally handed over they were most anxious that their old front should be kept lively. The Battalion did its best to oblige, and not without success. At night the amount of Lewis gun and rifle fire was extraordinary. Capt. A. M. Luty was particularly energetic in this respect, and C Company got through more ammunition in a night than the average battalion in the line fired in a month. The enemy retaliated with plenty of machine gun fire, sometimes making it very uncomfortable for parties working on the top. Some patrolling was done, but the enemy was so close, and his positions were so well known, that this was not a very important feature. Most active of all was the sniping by day. The enemy had no continuous line and he seemed to take comparatively little trouble to hide himself. Men could be seen at almost any hour of the day, and the front line garrisons became tremendously keen on sniping. Not many hits were made, so far as is known, but this caused no slackening of the fire. A low pill-box near Juniper Wood, little more than a hundred yards from the British front line and opposite to the right company, was the main centre of the sniping. Here there was one little German who became very well-known to everyone. He was bald-headed, and something of a sportsman. Many men spent hours trying to snipe him, and he was only too ready to retaliate. He fired over the top of the pill-box, but was careful not to show himself too often in the same spot. A man watching for him would see a rifle barrel slowly appear over the top, followed by a bald head. Sometimes he might succeed in getting in a shot; at other times, the bald head would disappear too quickly. Then the situation would be reversed; the little German would be up first, and it would be the turn of the Britisher to duck quickly. And so things went on day after day, with little execution on either side, and " honours easy."

The enemy made considerable use of vane bombs, and it was by one of these that Sec.-Lieut. R. B. Atkinson was wounded. Stokes shells were the ordinary form of retaliation. Gas shells too were used, though in no great number, except in the neighbourhood of the Butte. In this sector the Battalion first met with the enemy Blue Cross Gas—comparatively harmless, but causing violent sneezing.

Needless to say, much work was done in the sector. The wire in No Man's Land was much improved, a good deal of revetting was done in the front line, and great efforts were made to drain Plumer Trench, though without much success. Most important was the work further back. This was carried out under the supervision of Major E. Jackson, M.C., of the 458th Field Company, Royal Engineers, a very competent officer with whom the Battalion was on excellent terms. It was under his direction that the new communication trench was dug from Patu Support to the Right Company H.Q.

The period too was one of fads which, though they sometimes irritated, often provided a certain amount of amusement. Chief among these were the "Silent Days," and the wearing of small box respirators. At first the term "silent day" was not very well understood. One company, it is said, suspended all firing, and did not even retaliate when fired upon. But the real purpose was to compel battalions to use means of communication other than the telephone. For twenty-four hours the use of the telephone, either for speaking or buzzing, was forbidden, except in cases of emergency. So pigeons, power buzzers, Lucas lamps, and all the other devices, which had formerly been looked upon as things for signallers to learn but never to use, were pressed into service. The increased use of the power buzzer and wireless speedily showed up the ignorance of certain ciphers, which all officers were supposed to be acquainted with. The wearing of small box respirators was another fad, intended to familiarise all with their use. About every other day, orders would be received that they were to be worn continuously by all ranks during certain hours, and that work was to be continued as if nothing unusual were happening. The practice was mildly resented by some, who thought they had to wear them quite enough when there actually was gas about, without being put to the discomfort of wearing them needlessly. Elaborate precautions were taken to ensure that everyone did wear them at the times stated, and there was unholy delight in the Battalion when two Brigade runners were caught one day not complying with the orders.

During the time the Battalion was holding the Reutel Sector the weather was, on the whole, good. Though trench strength was high, accommodation was not very crowded. All companies had their trench cook-houses, and hot meals were as regular as if the Battalion had been in rest. The transport men were having an easy time, for rations were brought up to Crucifix Dump, not far from the Butte, by light railway. The Quarter Masters of the Brigade took it in turns to come up in charge of the ration train.

The first tour of duty in the Reutel Sector was not a specially eventful one. On February 25th the enemy heavily shelled the front line near the well, blowing in the parapet, causing several casualties, and burying the garrison of a machine gun post. C.S.M. W. Brooke was among the wounded. On this occasion Cpl. H. Kane, M.M., of D Company, behaved with the greatest gallantry. Going to the assistance of the buried men, he quietly set to work to dig them out, and succeeded in doing this, in spite of the heavy bombardment which continued round him, and the fact that he was in full view of an enemy pill-box only about a hundred yards away. For this gallant act he was awarded the Distinguished Conduct Medal. Early on the morning of February 28th a heavy counter-preparation was put down in front of the line, the higher commands fearing an enemy attack from the direction of Polderhoek Chateau. Except for a certain amount of enemy retaliation, nothing happened. Much attention was paid to the enemy pill-box in front of the Right Company, which has already been mentioned. The Battalion had been detailed to carry out a raid during its next tour, and this pill-box had been selected as the objective.

On March 2nd the Battalion was relieved by the 1/5th Battalion York and Lancs. Regt., and moved to Maida Camp. Here training was carried on as well as possible, but was much hampered by lack of suitable ground. The platoon which had been selected to carry out the raid was sent to the 147th Infantry Brigade School to train, as it was to be left out of the line until the night before the raid. When the Battalion returned to the line, after its six days' rest, preparations for the raid were completed. The plan was as follows :—

1. The objective was the enemy pill-box already described, which lay rather more than a hundred yards from the line. To the right of it lay an old British tank, stranded and abandoned in one of the attacks of the previous autumn, and known to be occupied by the enemy sometimes.

2. The raiding party was to consist of Sec.-Lieut. L. Gumby and 31 other ranks (one complete platoon) of D Company. Two men of the 147th Light Trench Mortar Battery accompanied the party, carrying with them short-fused Stokes mortar shells, to damage the pill-box.

REUTEL SECTOR

3. At zero hour (7-0 am.) the party was to advance in four sections, one on each flank of the pill-box, one towards it, and one towards the tank.

4. A creeping barrage was to cover the advance, while enemy positions in the vicinity were to be engaged by artillery and trench mortars.

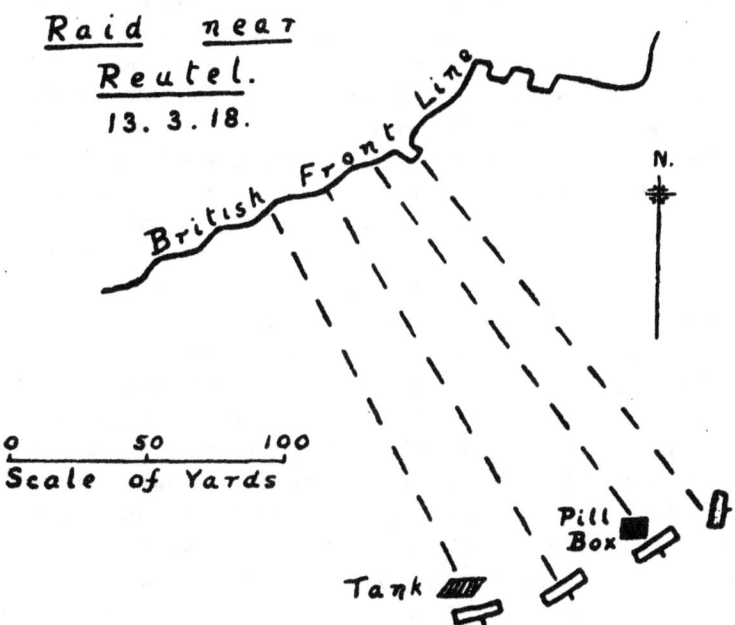

Zero hour had been fixed after dawn as the broken nature of the ground made an advance in the dark extremely difficult.

On the evening of March 12th the raiding party came up by light railway, and was accommodated with the reserve company for the night. During the night final preparations were made; steps for each of the four sections were cut in the parapet of the front line trench opposite the pill-box, and four gaps were cut in the wire. By dawn on March 13th the whole party was assembled in the front line, waiting for the barrage to open. There too was the Commanding Officer, in communication with Battalion H.Q. by a telephone wire, laid specially for the occasion.

At 7-0 a.m. the barrage opened, and the raiding party went over in line of sections in file. From the start, the flanking sections went well and reached their positions without difficulty ; but the section under the direct command of the platoon commander, whose special objective was the pill-box, was delayed by the short firing of one of the barrage guns. In the meantime, about twenty of the enemy got out of a trench in rear of the pill-box and tried to escape. They were heavily fired on by the flanking sections, and many were brought down. As soon as the barrage lifted off the pill-box, two of the enemy mounted a light machine gun on the top ; but both were shot down before they could open fire. By this time the centre section had got forward, worked round the pill-box, and captured one or two prisoners in rear of it. The pill-box itself was then attacked. A Mills bomb was inserted through a loophole and a M.S.K. grenade was dropped down the ventilating shaft. The latter immediately had its effect, about thirty Germans coming out with their hands up. How so many had been able to crowd into so small a space cannot be conceived. They were immediately directed to run across to the British line, where now the greatest excitement prevailed ; everywhere men were standing on the parapet waving to them to come in. A Stokes shell was thrown into the pill-box and then, about 7-20 a.m., the withdrawal was ordered. A few minutes later the raiding party, with the exception of two dead near the pill-box and some wounded still in No Man's Land, was back in its own lines.

When the captures came to be totalled up it was found that there were no less than 37 prisoners, and, in addition, three enemy machine guns had been brought back by the raiding party. Among the prisoners was the little bald-headed man, who had been the source of so much amusement to the front line troops the previous tour. Also, many dead and wounded were lying about round the pill-box, not counting a number who had certainly been wounded in escaping to the rear. All this had been accom-

To Face Page 196.

Major W. C. FENTON, M.C.

Capt. N. T. FARRAR, M.C.

Capt. A. KIRK, M.C.

Capt. P. G. BALES, M.C.

plished by a total force of one officer and thirty-three other ranks—less than the total number of prisoners—with a loss of only two killed and eight wounded. Unfortunately, two of the wounded afterwards died. The greatest loss to the Battalion was Cpl. H. Kane, D.C.M., M.M., who was severely wounded in the back and, after dragging on for several weeks in hospital, died. He was one of the most gallant N.C.O's the Battalion ever had—the sort of man who would have won the Victoria Cross had the chance come his way.

So great had been the success of the raid that, when the first estimate of prisoners—30—was telephoned through to Brigade H.Q., they were too sceptical to forward the news to the Division. When the prisoners began to appear over the crest line, they were seen by some artillery observers who, never dreaming that such success had been gained, sent frantic messages through that the enemy was counter-attacking. When this was denied they declared that they could see the enemy in crowds coming down the hill.

But much still remained to be done. A number of wounded were lying out in No Man's Land and these had to be brought in. This business was taken in hand by Major A. L. Mowat, M.C., who had gone up to the line immediately the Commanding Officer returned. Some of the enemy meanwhile had hoisted a white flag, and, under its protection which had not been violated by the British, were collecting their wounded. Seeing this, Major Mowat ordered a white flag to be put out, and stretcher-bearers to go over and bring back the wounded. This was done but, no sooner did they appear on the top of the parapet than every enemy machine gun in the district opened fire on them. It was a typical "Hun" trick—to make use of the white flag to collect their own wounded and then to open fire at once when it was used by their opponents. The flag was quickly hoisted down and fire was opened in retaliation. It is unlikely that any man in the Battalion ever respected a German flag again. In spite of this failure, it was not long before every wounded man was brought in. Lce.-Cpl. A. Moon, of D Company, particularly distinguished himself in this work. He had already done yeoman service during the raid ; though not himself one of the party, he had taken a Lewis Gun out into No Man's Land on his own initiative, and with it had provided covering fire during both the advance and the withdrawal. Now he twice went out, and on each occasion succeeded in bringing in a wounded man. For these actions he afterwards received the Distinguished Conduct Medal.

Later in the morning, a large party of the enemy was seen advancing to reoccupy the empty pill-box. Attempts to bring artillery fire to bear on them failed, but a heavy fire was opened with rifles and Lewis guns. Eventually the enemy artillery put down a protective barrage, under cover of which the Germans were able to rush forward and enter the pill-box. Apart from artillery activity, the rest of the day passed quietly, but during the night Patu Support was heavily shelled and several men of B Company were killed or wounded.

Needless to say, the Battalion received many messages of congratulation and commendation, for the raid had been one of the most successful on record. The Commander-in-Chief sent his congratulations, an unusual thing in connection with a minor operation, while the following wire was received from Second Army H.Q. :—

"General Plumer was delighted on his arrival to hear of the successful raid this morning of West Riding, 49th Division, and wishes to convey his congratulations to all concerned."

This was the first intimation the Battalion had that General Plumer had returned from Italy. Perhaps the most delighted people, though no message came from them officially, were the New Zealanders, who realised that their wishes were being carried out and that their old front had been left in good hands. For this operation, Sec.-Lieut. L. Gumby was awarded the Military Cross, Sergt. H. Binns and Lance-Cpl. R. A. Hudson the Distinguished Conduct Medal ; Cpl. H. Kane, D.C.M., M.M., received a bar to his Military Medal, and eleven other ranks the Military Medal.

The remainder of the tour was marked by a considerable increase in the volume of enemy artillery fire. This was probably partly a result of the raid, but it may also have been an attempt to pin British troops to that area while the enemy concentrated for his attack elsewhere. The areas chiefly affected were the usual ones, with the addition of Peter Trench; this trench had been named after the Commanding Officer's youthful son, the father later expressing the hope that his son would have better fortune than his trench had had.

On the night of March 17/18th a S.O.S. test was arranged which had a rather amusing sequel. In order to ensure that S.O.S. signals should be seen by the artillery if they were sent up, a chain of repeating stations had been arranged. A S.O.S. sent up in the front line was to be repeated from the left company H.Q., then from Battalion H.Q., and thence further back. To test the efficiency of this chain, green Very lights were supplied by Brigade, and it was arranged that, at 9-0 p.m., two of these should be fired from the front line, and repeated backwards as ordered. Everything went off well; the signals were seen, promptly repeated and—down came an enemy barrage. Brigade had overlooked the important point that a double green was the enemy S.O.S. Capt. N. T. Farrar who, as O.C. Left Company, was responsible for repeating the signal, in order not to give away the location of his Company H.Q., had gone down to Jetty Warren to fire his lights. Now Jetty Warren happened to be one of the enemy barrage lines, and Capt. Farrar soon found matters so lively there that he decided to run for it. As the scheme was only a test the British artillery was not intended to fire, but frantic appeals for retaliation soon got them going. Similar tests should have been carried out by the other battalions of the Brigade later in the night, but these orders were cancelled owing to the result of the first test.

On the night of March 18/19th the Battalion was relieved. Instead of going back to Maida Camp, two companies moved to Westhoek Dugouts and two to Railway Wood Dugouts on Cambridge Road. The relief was much hampered by heavy gas shelling, but the Battalion escaped with practically no casualties.

The period which followed was one of anxious expectation. For the last month signs had been accumulating of the imminence of a great enemy offensive. It was known that many of his best divisions had been brought over from the Russian Front, and that his armies had never been so strong in the West before. In the early months of the year attack training had been carried out on an unusually large scale. And now the information obtained from almost every prisoner pointed to a great attack in the very near future. Every possible precaution had been taken in the Second Army to meet an attack, should it come on that front, and all were anxiously waiting for the enemy to make his first move. One minor attack had been made on the 33rd Division north of the Menin Road, about a fortnight before. But as the enemy had made no further attempt there, it was probably only a " blind."

On March 21st the storm broke, though far away to the south. Never since stationary warfare had taken the place of movement, had a single attack been made on so wide a front in the West. From the neighbourhood of Arras to far south of St. Quentin, the whole front was ablaze. The news which reached the Battalion during the first few days was brief, but it was enough to make clear to everyone that practically the whole force of the enemy's offensive was directed against the British, and that the situation was desperate to a degree. On March 24th the Commander-in-Chief published his, now famous, Special Order of the Day ; and in forwarding it to Battalions the G.O.C., 49th Division, himself issued an Order which is so characteristic of the man that it is worth repeating in full :—

"In forwarding the attached copy of a Special Order of the Day by Field Marshal Sir Douglas Haig, I wish to say at once that I have complete confidence that the 49th (West Riding) Division will acquit itself gloriously in whatever circumstances it may be placed.

Remember that other Divisions elsewhere are at this moment holding up splendidly the most strenuous efforts of the enemy to force a decision.

Remember also that if we are called upon to fight here, we shall be fighting on the historic ground where the ' contemptible little British Army' fought and defeated the enemy's first great effort to destroy it in 1914. In that year we defeated him with the rifle. With the rifle we can and will defeat him again—the more thoroughly this time, as we have our wire to give our rifles a better opportunity than they had in 1914.

Go on improving your wire, look carefully to your rifles, Machine Guns, and Lewis Guns, and ammunition, exercise vigilance every moment of the day, to see that every yard of your front is watched and can be shot into. We can then beat off any attack.

So much for the defensive.

We must also be aggressive. Every front line company must send out at least one fighting patrol every night to look for opportunities for killing or capturing enemy patrols or posts. Identifications are of great importance, but more important still is the object of making ourselves masters of No Man's Land, and inducing the enemy to increase his strength against us on this portion of the front, thus helping to reduce the pressure against our comrades further South.

N. G. Cameron, Major-General,
March 24th, 1918.   Commanding 49th (W.R.) Division."

The Battalion chafed at its inactivity. It was well up to strength and in magnificent condition. After a month's rest and training, it had spent another month in a line where, though it had suffered comparatively few casualties, things had been sufficiently active to keep it in good condition. Furthermore, the highly successful raid of little more than a week before had raised its morale to such an extent that it felt fit to tackle anything. All leave had been stopped and officers, who were in England, recalled. The news that the New Zealand Division was moving south rather added to the excitement. On March 27th a warning order was received to be prepared to move at the shortest notice ; but that very night the Battalion again took over the defence of the Reutel Sector.

The tour which followed—the last the Battalion was to do in that sector—was wonderfully, almost uncannily, quiet. It was rarely a shell fell at all, and the standing joke of the tour was that, if the enemy division opposite wanted a concentration of fire on its front, it would have to ring up the neighbouring divisions and ask each to switch its "gun" round. This was not so correct of the enemy machine guns ; wiring was the main work carried out that tour, and several casualties were caused to men working on the top.

On April 3rd the tour came to an end, the Battalion being relieved by the 1st Battalion Leicestershire Regt. (6th Division). This division had just come up from the south-east of Arras, where it had been in the line when the enemy first launched his offensive. It had acquitted itself well, as it always did, but had been terribly cut up. From the men of this battalion something was learned of the battle in the south.

The Battalion said farewell to the Reutel Sector and moved back to Maida Camp again. Here several days passed quietly and nothing was heard of an early move. Indeed, so far did the Battalion seem from battle, that orders were received to relieve the 146th Infantry Brigade on April 9th. That Brigade was now holding the sector astride the Menin Road, facing Gheluvelt and Polderhoek Chateau, where it had relieved part of the 33rd Division. It was a disappointed party of officers and N.C.O's who went up to inspect the line on April 8th. But the Battalion was never to hold that sector. The same night orders for the relief were cancelled, and fresh orders were received to move the following day to a camp near Reninghelst.

The next day was crowded with incident. In the morning the G.O.C., Second Army, presented medal ribbons to a number of officers and other ranks, the Battalion providing three officers and 150 other ranks for the guard of honour. During the parade the General received several telegrams, and when he addressed the troops he referred to the probability that they would soon be in battle. In the afternoon the Battalion marched to the neighbourhood of Reninghelst, where it expected to remain for two or three days, and then to move to the southern battle. As the column wound its way along the road that bright spring afternoon, the dull but continuous roar of guns was such as had never been heard in that area since the battle of Passchendaele. Something was happening much nearer than the Somme, but none knew what. On arrival at the camp everyone quickly settled down, and arrangements were made for the night. But no night was to be spent by the Battalion there. The time had come when it was to write what is probably the finest page of its history.

CHAPTER XI.

THE ENEMY SPRING OFFENSIVE.

(a) Erquinghem and Le Veau.

ON April 9th the enemy launched his great offensive between the La Bassée Canal and Armentiéres. Preceded by an intense artillery bombardment, the German infantry broke right through the centre of the line which was held by the Portuguese ; and all was confusion there. It was the sound of this battle that the Battalion had heard as it marched along the road towards Reninghelst.

At the moment the 49th Division was too scattered for immediate combined action. Divisional H.Q. was still at Chateau Ségard, and in the same area the 148th Infantry Brigade was concentrated. The 147th Infantry Brigade had all arrived in the neighbourhood of Reninghelst by the evening of April 9th. But the 146th Infantry Brigade was still holding the line astride the Menin Road. It was due to this that, during the first fortnight of the operations which followed, the Division was not able to act as a unit.

When the Battalion arrived in camp, on the evening of April 9th, everyone expected to remain there for two or three days. It was the general idea that the Division would concentrate in that area, and then move down to the Somme battlefield. Hence, preparations were made for spending the night. The Commanding Officer was dining with Lieut.-General A. J. Godley, at Corps H.Q., and was not expected back until late. The Battalion was turning in for the night when he suddenly returned, bringing early information of an immediate move. He had heard of the disaster on the Portuguese front, and brought the news that the 147th Infantry Brigade was to be pushed into the battle at once. Immediately, all was bustle and excitement in the camp, and never had the men been in better spirits than when they heard that the Battalion was for battle at last. Little time was needed for preparation. Soon after midnight all were in motor buses hurrying south. At Neuve Eglise, through which the buses passed, the gravity of the situation was apparent. Transport vehicles and guns were being hurried back, while already enemy shells were dropping in the village. At La Crêche, which was reached at 3-15 a.m., the Battalion debussed, and marched through the darkness to Le Veau, arriving at 4-30 a.m. Here some empty huts and stables were found, and into these the men were put to get what rest they could. Picquets were posted, for the situation was so obscure that no one knew how soon the enemy might be upon him. And the Battalion waited for orders.

About 6-30 a.m. orders were received from 147th Infantry Brigade H.Q., to move up to a position of readiness near the cross roads at L'Epinette. Packs were dumped in a hut at Le Veau, a hurried selection was made of the personnel of B Echelon who were not to go into battle, and about 7-0 a.m. the Battalion* moved off. All along the road was witnessed one of the most pitiful sights of warfare, common enough in the early days of 1914, but never before seen by the Battalion. Everywhere civilians were leaving their homes and flocking to the rear; old people, women, and young children, some driving an odd cow or two, others pushing a few of their most valued household goods in barrows, plodded wearily along. Fortunately the

*The following Officers and Warrant Officers went into action with the Battalion on April 10th, 1918 :—
Battn. H.Q.: Lieut.-Col. R. E. Sugden, D.S.O. (C.O.); Capt. W. C. Fenton, M.C. (Second in Command); Lieut. P. G. Bales (A/Adjt.); Lieut. J. C. Walton (I.O.); Sec.-Lieut. H. A. Loudoun (Sig. O.); Capt. F. C. Harrison, R.A.M.C. (M.O.).
R.S.M. F. P. Stirzaker, M.C.
Sec.-Lieut. H. Rosendale (Liaison Officer at 147th Infantry Bde. H.Q.).
A Company: Capt. A. Kirk; Sec.-Lieut. B. H. Huggard; Sec.-Lieut. E. Clarke; Sec.-Lieut. J. C. Whitaker.
C.S.M. T. S. Sherwood.
B Company: Capt. N. T. Farrar; Sec.-Lieut. L. L. Johnson; Sec.-Lieut. S. R. Norton; Sec.-Lieut. F. Akroyd.
Sergt. A. Smith (A/C.S.M.).
C Company: Capt. A. M. Luty; Sec.-Lieut. T. T. Gilroy; Sec.-Lieut. F. D. Chippindale; Sec.-Lieut. M. C. O'Dowd; Sec.-Lieut. H. E. Burgoyne.
C.S.M. N. Hobson.
D Company: Lieut. B. M. Machin; Sec.-Lieut. J. W. Lumb; Sec.-Lieut. J. Turner; Sec.-Lieut. J. H. Kitson; Sec.-Lieut. W. Oldfield, M.M.
C.S.M. C. Naylor.
Owing to casualties and fresh officers coming up from B Echelon, many changes took place in the personnel during the next ten days. The Battalion went into battle so hurriedly that no record of the exact strength was made, but it was approximately 650 other ranks.

enemy was not shelling the road, so the troops were able to advance without hindrance, except from one low-flying aeroplane. L' Epinette was reached before 8-30 a.m. and the men began to dig in. Little was known of the situation, but from observation it appeared that the British were withdrawing to the north bank of the River Lys, particularly about the loop to the west of Erquinghem.

The Battalion had been placed at the disposal of the 101st Infantry Brigade (34th Division), and about 9-30 a.m. the G.O.C., Brig.-General B. C. Gore, came up, explained the situation, and issued his orders as follows :—

1. The 101st Infantry Brigade was holding a line south of the Bac St. Maur-Armentiéres Railway, with the 16th Battalion Royal Scots on the right and the 11th Battalion Suffolk Regt. on the left. This line the enemy had penetrated near the Rue Delpierre, between the two battalions.

2. The Battalion was ordered to send up two companies to close this gap in the line, and to place its remaining companies in positions north of the railway, in support of the Royal Scots and Suffolks respectively.

Company commanders were immediately summoned and the situation was explained to them. C Company, with D Company in support, was ordered to move up by the Rue Delpierre and close the gap. B Company, with A Company in support, was to assemble near the Rue du Moulin and advance to the assistance of the Royal Scots.

About 10-0 a.m. all companies moved off and Battalion H.Q. went forward to Wigan Post, some 500 yards north of the river. Enemy shells were already bursting around, and several direct hits were made on the road. The numbers of wounded who were streaming back showed only too clearly how severe the fighting was. Yet, quietly and in perfect order, the companies marched down to the River Lys by platoons. The main bridge was destroyed, but B Company, which was leading, succeeded in crossing by a wooden bridge near by, though this was also badly broken and only possible for men in single file. All the other companies crossed by a wooden bridge near the church. From this time, except A and B Companies which were in close touch throughout the day, companies were separated and their doings must be told individually.

On arriving in Erquinghem, B Company marched along the main street of the village, and took cover at the west end, while Capt. N. T. Farrar and Sergt. R. G. Brunt went forward to reconnoitre. They soon found that the situation was very different from what had been reported. Not only was the enemy to the north of the railway, near the Rue du Moulin, but he also appeared to be occupying the whole of the ground in the loop which the river makes to the west of Erquinghem. His outposts were in farms, only about 200 yards west of the village, and there was no sign of any formed body of Royal Scots. In these circumstances any attempt to advance south would almost certainly have led to disaster, so Capt. Farrar decided to take up a position covering the west end of the village. Between the river and the Rue du Moulin was an R.E. yard, with piles of trench grids and other stores; this B Company garrisoned with three platoons, pushing out its fourth platoon about a hundred yards in front. Its left was covered by a Lewis gun section which could fire, either along the road to the west, or down the Rue du Moulin; to protect its right and cover a bridge over the Lys, which was its main line of retreat, A Company sent up a platoon and a half, under Sec.-Lieut. E. Clarke, between the R.E. yard and the river. These dispositions opposed an enemy advance either from the west or up the Rue du Moulin, and remained unchanged for five hours—until the order to withdraw was received. During that time, two separate attacks were made by the enemy on the village; but so heavy was the fire kept up by A and B Companies that these had no success. Parts of Erquinghem were heavily shelled, and many buildings were set on fire; but the R.E. yard escaped the attentions of the hostile artillery. The men were much harassed by machine gun and rifle fire. In particular, A Company's platoon was heavily fired on from a farm house, only about a hundred yards away. Careful observation of this place through glasses revealed the fact that a large store of Mills bombs and Stokes shells was in an outhouse against the wall of the farm. Lewis guns were trained on this dump and fired for some minutes without success; but, suddenly, the whole dump blew up, completely destroying the farmhouse. As the place was packed with Germans, there is no doubt that they suffered very heavily. The British had excellent cover behind the piles of R.E. material, and, as a result, comparatively few casualties were suffered; but heavy losses were certainly inflicted on the enemy.

Late in the morning, an officer of the 11th Battalion Suffolk Regt. asked for reinforcements to close a gap in the line near the Rue du Moulin. In response, A Company sent up a platoon, which Sec.-Lieut. B. H. Huggard saw into position. This platoon was never seen again, and its fate was a mystery until after the armistice. Then, returned prisoners told how it had been surrounded by the enemy, and, after suffering heavily, the few survivors had been captured.

Meanwhile, what was happening to C and D Companies ? After crossing the Lys, C Company assembled near the top of the Rue Delpierre, while Capt. A. M. Luty, with Sec.-Lieut. T. T. Gilroy, C.S.M. N. Hobson and two N.C.O's, went forward to reconnoitre. The ground was swept by machine gun fire, and it was only by crawling that the party was able to reach the point where the road crosses the railway. Capt. Luty at once realised that it was impossible for him to get to his objective, and decided to hold the line of the railway. He returned to his company which, by this time, had suffered several casualties from enemy artillery fire. The company moved down the road by platoons and took up a position along the railway line, with its right turned back to face south-west. The position was a bad one as the straight line of the railway was heavily enfiladed by machine guns near the Rue du Moulin. Losses were heavy from the very first. Sec.-Lieut. M. C. O'Dowd and several men had been hit coming down the road. C.S.M. N. Hobson was wounded soon after the line of the railway had been taken up. After a short time, one platoon was sent across the railway to take up a more advanced position. Here, except for sniping, this platoon was not much worried for some time, but the rest of the company was suffering appalling casualties. The numbers of wounded were soon far greater than the company stretcher-bearers could deal with. It was then that Pte. A. Poulter earned the highest decoration that a soldier can win—the Victoria Cross. Hour after hour he toiled, in the greatest danger, tending the wounded and carrying them into safety.*

About 1-0 p.m. the situation became even worse. The enemy brought up a field gun which enfiladed C Company's position at a range of only a few hundred yards. Within half-an-hour scarcely twenty men were left unwounded. The position on the railway was clearly untenable, and soon it was decided that a move was necessary, if any were to escape unhurt. The few survivors crossed the railway and took up a position a little to the south of it. Here they suffered much less. About the middle of the afternoon the men of the 11th Battalion Suffolk Regt., who had been on the left of C Company all day, withdrew, having written orders to do so. As he had received no orders, Capt. Luty remained. It should be mentioned that orders to withdraw had been sent to him from Battalion H.Q. some time before, but the runners had become casualties and the orders never arrived. But before long the enemy was seen to be advancing rapidly, both from the south and west, and the position became hopeless. A withdrawal was ordered. Sec.-Lieut. F. D. Chippindale went forward to warn No. 9 Platoon, which was lying out in front ; a hail of machine gun bullets was sweeping the ground, and he had barely given the order when he was struck down. The few survivors of this platoon were surrounded and captured. The rest of C Company made a dash for the railway, but only about twelve ever reached it. One by one they rushed across, suffering two more casualties before all were over, and then made for Erquinghem. Many wounded were collected on the way, practically every man of the party assisting one along. They found the bridge near the church destroyed, and, before another crossing

---

*Extract from the 6th Supplement to the " London Gazette," dated June 25th, 1918 :—
" 24066 Pte. Arthur Poulter awarded Victoria Cross.

For most conspicuous bravery when acting as a stretcher-bearer. On ten occasions Pte. Poulter carried badly wounded men on his back to a safer locality, through a particularly heavy artillery and machine gun barrage. Two of these were hit a second time whilst on his back. Again, after a withdrawal over the river had been ordered, Pte. Poulter returned in full view of the enemy who were advancing, and carried back another man who had been left behind wounded. He bandaged up over forty men under fire, and his conduct throughout the whole day was a magnificent example to all ranks.

This very gallant soldier was subsequently seriously wounded when attempting another rescue in the face of the enemy."

Private A. POULTER, V.C.

ERQUINGHEM AND LE VEAU

could be found, enemy skirmishers were already in the village. At last another bridge was discovered, about half a mile towards Armentiéres, and over this the miserable remnants of the company crossed, remaining on the northern bank until the bridge had been demolished. Of the Company, 5 officers and 139 other ranks strong, which had crossed the Lys about six hours before, little more than the strength of a section remained.

D Company had crossed the Lys in rear of C Company in the morning, and had taken up a position in support, south of Erquinghem and astride the Rue Delpierre. Here they had come under heavy artillery and machine gun fire, and had suffered considerably. About 1-30 p.m. they received orders to support the 11th Battalion Suffolk Regt., and moved up to a position in rear of La Rolanderie Farm, where the H.Q. of that battalion was situated. They had not been there long when they received their orders to withdraw, and so returned to the north of the river.

Throughout the day Battalion H.Q. was at Wigan. It had originally been intended to move across the river, but, owing to the uncertainty of the situation, this was never done. The position had not been occupied long before it was realised that the enemy had crossed the Lys, away to the right. Indeed, it is very possible that German troops were actually across, a little to the west of Erquinghem, before any of the Battalion entered the village. By the middle of the morning the situation on that flank was rapidly becoming serious, and the Commanding Officer recommended that troops should be sent up to the neighbourhood of the line Lancashire—Jesus Farm. By 12-20 p.m. A Company's signallers had established communication by means of a visual station in one of the houses, and throughout the day they and B Company remained in touch with Battalion H.Q. But no reports were received from C and D Companies until the afternoon. About mid-day the neighbourhood of Wigan began to receive attention from the enemy artillery, and, though few casualties were suffered, great inconvenience was caused by the destruction of the officers' rations. At 12-40 p.m. orders were sent to D Company to move up in support of the 11th Suffolks, these orders anticipating a very urgent appeal from the Commanding Officer of that unit which arrived a little later. The first report from C Company, timed 1-7 p.m., arrived about 2-0 p.m., but gave no idea of Capt. Luty's desperate situation. However, it was rapidly becoming clear that Erquinghem was untenable, though the real gravity of the situation was not known at the time. As a matter of fact, while the Battalion was still fighting in and to the south of Erquinghem, the enemy was right in its rear at Le Veau, looting the packs which had been dumped there in the morning, and fighting with the men of B Echelon who had been left behind. Early in the afternoon, machine gun bullets from the west began to fall about Wigan. But, by this time, the order to withdraw to Nieppe had been received, and had been passed on to companies. B Company and part of A Company withdrew by the bridge which they had been covering all day; the others crossed by bridges further to the east. Battalion H.Q. remained at Wigan until the early evening. Many buildings in Erquinghem were burning furiously, and numbers of the enemy could be seen moving about in the village.

All the companies had passed long before Battalion H.Q. moved. About 6-0 p.m. the line at Wigan was left in the hands of a very mixed garrison of Royal Scots, Suffolks, Australian tunnellers and others, and the Commanding Officer started for Nieppe. It was only then that the full gravity of the situation was realised. Enemy machine gun bullets were whistling across the road as the party moved along, and, when the level crossing by Nieppe Station was reached, it was found that an enemy machine gun was on the railway line to the north-west, shooting straight down the line. One or two casualties were suffered by H.Q. details in crossing the line. Near the entrance to Nieppe, the whole of D Company was met marching out towards the Station, and Lieut. B. M. Machin stated that he had received orders from the G.O.C. himself to seize and hold that point. Away to the north troops could be seen in extended order attacking towards Le Veau. These troops were A and B Companies, though this was not known at the time. From what he knew of the enemy's position on the railway, near the station, it was obvious to the Commanding Officer that the left flank of this attack was in danger. To cope with the difficulty H.Q. details, organised in two platoons under Sec.-Lieut. H. A. Loudoun, and one platoon of D Company, were sent down the road to the Station. Two platoons of D Company were directed to prolong the left flank of the attack on Le Veau, and the other platoon was kept in reserve.

It is now necessary to return to A and B Companies. On reporting at 147th Infantry Brigade H.Q. in Nieppe they had been told to occupy some old trenches at Les Trois Arbres. They had not been there long before they were ordered to fall in and move along the Nieppe-Bailleul Road towards Pont d'Achelles. Here they were drawn up by Maj. A. L. Mowat* and directed to attack and expel the enemy, who was established in the farmhouses and enclosures at Le Veau. A Company was on the extreme left with B Company on its right; beyond B Company were some Royal Engineers and other troops, mainly Northumberland Fusiliers. Neither side had any artillery to support it.

The advance started and at first progress was easy; but, when the attacking force was about six hundred yards from the enemy, very heavy machine gun and rifle fire opened on it. Progress could now only be made by section rushes with covering fire, and even this became impossible when the line had got to about three hundred yards from the enemy. It was at this point that the arrival of the two platoons of D Company on the left restored the situation. These did not meet with strong opposition, and were able to push forward and gain a footing on the railway. Taken now in flank the Germans began to withdraw, and this enabled A Company to continue its advance and reach the railway on its whole front. Meanwhile B Company had met with strong resistance from the farms and enclosures of Le Veau. A sniper, firing from an attic window, had been particularly obnoxious. For a short time they too had been held up, but Sec.-Lieut. F. Akroyd, supported by heavy covering fire from the rest of the company, managed to push forward on the right and establish a footing, with his platoon, in the enclosures. The enemy then withdrew on this front too, and B Company advanced to the railway. As the H.Q. details had established themselves firmly

*Throughout the operations in April, 1918, Major A. L. Mowat, M.C., was attached to 147th Infantry Brigade H.Q. as Assistant Brigade Major.

in the neighbourhood of the Station, the Battalion now held the whole of the railway line from that point nearly up to the Steenwerck Road. The men dug in a few yards in front of the railway line and there settled down for the night, after a most strenuous and exciting day. During this attack A Company had suffered heavy casualties, but both B and D Companies had come through comparatively lightly. In all, the Battalion had lost nearly two hundred men since it had left Le Veau early that morning.

(b) Nieppe.

During the night of April 10/11th Battalion H.Q. was established in the Hospice at the south-west end of Nieppe, and here it remained until the following evening. With the exception of the pitiful remnants of C Company, and one platoon of D Company, the whole Battalion was manning the line which had been established in front of the railway, between Nieppe Station and the Steenwerck Road. In spite of the uncertainty of the situation, everyone whose duties would allow of it slept soundly, tired out with the activities of the previous day and night. The night passed quietly, the enemy, after his set-back at Le Veau, making no further attack.

Early the next morning, the Commanding Officer made a personal reconnaissance towards L'Epinette, and nearly reached the village before he saw anything of the enemy. He was then heavily fired on by a party of Germans and forced to withdraw. Other patrols were pushed out well to the west of the railway without encountering the enemy. From French civilians, who had remained in their homes all through the fighting, they learned that large numbers of Germans had been there, but had withdrawn towards the south-west after the successful attack of the Battalion at Le Veau. The only actual encounter that took place near the railway was with a German artillery officer, who rode nearly up to the line with a mounted orderly about 8-30 a.m. He was shot and fell from his horse dead, but his companion escaped. The numbers of German dead littering the ground in front of the railway showed that, in spite of its own heavy losses, the Battalion had made the enemy pay even more heavily. About 9-0 a.m., units of the 101st Infantry Brigade relieved the Battalion, and the men were concentrated in houses near the Hospice.

The Battalion was now in Brigade Reserve, the other battalions of the Brigade manning the Nieppe System to the east of the town. The day was a very confused one. Continually the situation was being reported obscure at some part of the front, and frequently a company, or two platoons, or some other force, had to be sent off to clear it up. The only part of the front where the situation was never reported obscure was that held by the 147th Infantry Brigade. Such duties proved very tiring, though for some time no serious fighting resulted. By now the enemy was everywhere well across the Lys, the entrenched line of which Wigan formed a part had been entirely given up, and the railway and the Nieppe System were the outpost lines of the British. Incidentally, it should be mentioned here that the 1/5th Battalion York and Lancaster Regt. did the 147th Infantry Brigade a very good turn that day. By a highly successful counter-attack in the neighbourhood of Steenwerck, they held up the enemy's advance, and barred his approach to the main line of retreat from Nieppe—the road to Bailleul.

Nothing serious, so far as the Battalion was concerned, happened until after mid-day. But about 12-30 p.m., a message arrived from Brigade H.Q. stating that the situation was very obscure on the left of the 6th Battalion Duke of Wellington's Regt., near Bruna Gaye ; the remnants of C Company were already on their way there ; and an additional company was to be despatched at once. A Company was detailed for this duty, and the Commanding Officer himself accompanied it, leaving Capt. Fenton in charge at Battalion H.Q. Lieut.-Col. Sugden found matters in a very critical state ; artillery and machine gun fire were very heavy, and a strong German attack was being directed against a battalion of the Cheshires. The arrival of the 4th Battalion detachment restored the situation, but hard fighting continued there until the evening. One Lewis gun of A Company did great execution ; it was concealed in the upper storey of a house, found excellent targets among the masses of the enemy, and was apparently never discovered by them. The Commanding Officer remained at Bruna Gaye to direct operations.

Late in the afternoon there was again trouble on the right, and two platoons of B Company were sent to the neighbourhood of Nieppe Station. Here they had hard fighting for two hours, but held their ground successfully.

About 7-0 p.m. the Commanding Officer returned from Bruna Gaye. He had called at Brigade H.Q. on his way back, and had received orders for a further withdrawal, which was to be made that night. This withdrawal was rendered necessary by a fresh attack which the enemy had launched at Wytschaete that day, for there was now great danger that, unless all the troops in and around Nieppe withdrew at once, they would be surrounded. The withdrawal was to start at 7-30 p.m. and the difficulty was to get orders through to A and C Companies. Runners managed to reach them just in time, when they were in imminent danger of being cut off.

At 7-30 p.m. B and D Companies, followed by Battalion H.Q., left the Hospice and started towards Bailleul. Enemy machine gun bullets were sweeping the ground, and, before he had gone more than a hundred yards, R.S.M. F. P. Stirzaker, M.C., was hit in the throat, and died within five minutes. His death was a great blow to the Battalion which he had fought with continuously for three years ; he was a most hard-working, conscientious and gallant man, whose place could never be filled. It was impossible to remove the body, and he would have been the last to wish any risks to be run by others on his account. So he was left like a soldier on the spot where he had died, and the remainder of the party continued sorrowfully on its way.

The sight on the Nieppe-Bailleul Road that night was such as none of the Battalion had seen before, nor any wished to see again. Of vehicles there were practically none, but the whole road was crowded with men hastening to the rear. It was an army in retreat. But the crowd of men was not disorderly ; there was no panic. As each one reached his allotted station he quietly fell in, ready to hold a fresh line. Mercifully the enemy, for some unknown reason, scarcely attempted to shell the road. Had he done so the casualties must have been awful, for no shell dropped among those masses of men could have failed to hit many. One gruesome spot, where a 15 cm. shell had burst among a number of Royal Engineers, gave the passer-by an idea of what might have been. All along the left of the road the enemy flares, approaching nearer and nearer, showed how near the British troops were to utter disaster. But they escaped. And never again had the enemy such an opportunity. By about 11-0 p.m. the Battalion was again concentrated in a position near Bailleul.

(c) Bailleul.

About a mile from Bailleul the road to Armentiéres almost touches the railway. It was at this point that 147th Infantry Brigade H.Q. was established, the battalions occupying positions in the fields just to the south of the railway. The position was not really intended to be a defensive one, for other troops were well out in front of the Brigade. Nevertheless, the men dug in, and patrols were pushed out down the roads. The rest of the night passed quietly.

On April 12th, though there were some mild alarms during the morning, nothing special happened until after mid-day. Occasional shells burst near the Battalion's positions, one of which wounded Sec.-Lieut. F. Akroyd. But about 1-0 p.m. a heavy bombardment opened, and quickly drove Battalion H.Q. from its cottage to seek a hole in the ground, among the slits which had been dug the previous night. Intermittent shelling went on for the whole afternoon and caused several casualties, among them being Lieut. B. M. Machin and Sergt. F. Firth, the pioneer sergeant.

About 4-0 p.m. the Commanding Officer, who had been to Brigade H.Q., returned with the alarming news that the enemy had entered Bailleul from the west. The Battalion was ordered to move at once and expel him. Company commanders were summoned, and columns were detailed to enter the town by different roads. The operation was carried out with unexpected ease. The report was found to be incorrect. Nothing of the enemy could be seen in Bailleul ; in fact, the town was deserted, except for an Australian corporal who had just set fire to the Australian Comforts Store, much to the disgust of the Battalion which could have done with many of the articles thus destroyed. The companies moved through the deserted town and established a picquet line in the fields to the west of it, roughly along the line of the Becque de la Flanche, and covering all the roads in that direction.

Up to this time there had been little activity in the area occupied by battalions of the 147th Infantry Brigade. But early in the evening the advanced troops began rapidly to retire through them. Numbers of stragglers of different units entered Bailleul from the south, and the situation began to look serious. It was restored by Capt. Fenton, who took charge of a number of stragglers and posted them with D Company, in and around Bailleul Station. About this time the enemy began to shell the town, possibly attracted by the fire at the Australian Comforts Store, which was now burning furiously. One shell burst near a group of H.Q. details, as they were marching up the Station Road, killing one and wounding about fifteen of them.

When darkness fell the dispositions of the Battalion were as follows :—

D Company, with a number of stragglers of other units, was holding the railway line on both sides of the Station. The 6th Battalion Duke of Wellington's Regt. was holding a line in front of it.

A Company had a line of posts along the Becque de la Flanche, from the railway west of the Station, where it was in touch with the right of the 6th Battalion Duke of Wellington's Regt., to Steam Mill.

B Company continued this line due north as far as the Meteren Road.

Battalion H.Q. and C Company, which was in Battalion Reserve, occupied houses on the Station Road.

Reconnaissance soon showed that a composite force, which had been organised at the 22nd Corps Reinforcement Camp and went by the name of the 22nd Corps Reinforcement Battalion, was holding a line of posts from Steam Mill towards Meteren. Beyond these troops was the 19th Infantry Brigade (33rd

Division) covering Meteren itself. Thus, only A Company was actually in the front line.

The night passed quietly. A patrol of A Company, from Steam Mill along the Oultersteene Road, did not gain touch with the enemy until more than a mile down the road. During the night A Company was relieved by the 9th Battalion Northumberland Fusiliers, so that, by dawn, both A and C Companies were in Battalion Reserve in the town.

The morning of the 13th was also uneventful. A well-stocked Y.M.C.A. canteen was found in Bailleul, and a guard was placed over it to stop looting; the supplies there were taken charge of, and many were issued to the troops to supplement rations. Early in the afternoon the enemy began to shell the town heavily, and continued to do so for about two hours. Buildings proved a very bad protection against high explosive. The house occupied by Battalion H.Q. did not receive a direct hit, but windows were smashed and considerable damage caused by shells bursting just outside. Here Sec.-Lieut. H. A. Loudoun, the Signalling Officer, was wounded in the arm; and Cpl. A. R. Mitchell, the stout and popular N.C.O. in charge of the Battalion runners, was so badly hit in the body that he died shortly afterwards in hospital. It was deemed advisable to move Battalion H.Q. to a neighbouring house which had a small but substantial cellar.

Meanwhile, the other units of the Brigade were having serious fighting to the south of Bailleul. About dusk, the Battalion received orders to send up two companies to hold the line of the railway on either side of the Station, as it was feared the enemy might break through. A and C Companies were sent up, under the command of Capt. Fenton. These occupied a line to the south of the railway, covering the Station, on a frontage of about half a mile. During the night another withdrawal took place, contracting the defences to the south and south-east of the town. The 6th Battalion took over the defence of the railway line and Bailleul Station, while the 7th Battalion was brought back into the town in Brigade Reserve. D Company relieved the 9th Battalion Northumberland Fusiliers between the railway and Steam Mill. Its left should have been in touch with the right of the 6th Battalion, but there was found to be a considerable gap which it could not fill without dangerously weakening its front. A Company was moved up to close this gap. The withdrawal had, of course, automatically brought about the relief of the two companies south of the railway. At dawn the Battalion was disposed as follows :—

A Company was astride the railway, west of Bailleul Station, and in touch with the right of the 6th Battalion.

D Company held the line of the Becque de la Flanche from the right of A Company to Steam Mill, where it was in touch with the left of the 22nd Corps Reinforcement Battalion.

B Company was still in its old position behind the 22nd Corps Reinforcement Battalion.

C Company was in Battalion Reserve in houses on the Station Road.

Two days had now passed without the Battalion being drawn into any really serious fighting. There had been plenty of anxiety and much changing of dispositions, but, compared with the activities of April 10th and 11th, it had been a rest period. The attacks which the enemy had made to the south of Bailleul on April 13th had not been very successful for him, and he now determined to try his luck to the west of the town. Already, on the night of the 13th, his troops had been seen dribbling up towards Steam Mill.

The night of April 13/14th passed quietly, as did also the following morning. But early in the afternoon a bombardment, far heavier than on the previous day, opened on the town and on the positions along the Becque de la Flanche. B and D Companies were both shelled out of their H.Q. and forced to take to the fields ; in this shelling Sec.-Lieut W. Oldfield, M.M., of D Company, was severely wounded, and had the grave misfortune to lose the sight of both eyes. Meanwhile, observers reported that large numbers of the enemy were dribbling forward and massing about three hundred yards from the Battalion's outpost line. It was obvious that a heavy attack was impending. Fire was opened upon all movement, but did not appear to interfere much with the assembly. Little could be done but wait. As a precautionary measure, all available reserves of A Company were placed at the disposal of D Company.

BAILLEUL CHURCH AFTER THE BOMBARDMENT.

Bailleul was still being heavily bombarded, and about six big fires were raging in the Station Road alone, without anyone to check them, when, about 4-0 p.m., the attack came. Masses of the enemy advanced against the fronts held by D Company and the 22nd Corps Reinforcement Battalion. The latter gave way without much resistance, and the enemy was able to occupy Steam Mill. This seriously threatened the right flank of D Company, along the whole of whose front heavy fighting was going on. For a time its centre was pressed back, but the men soon regained the ground without assistance. Unfortunately, in this fighting, Sec.-Lieut. J. H. Kitson was killed.

The whole situation was extremely critical. The 22nd Corps Reinforcement Battalion had ceased to exist as a fighting unit though, luckily, B Company was in its rear, and held up the further advance of the enemy on that front. The loss of Steam Mill seriously threatened the right flank of D Company, who had only just been able to beat off the attack on its immediate front. The only battalion reserves available were the few survivors of C Company and the Battalion H.Q. details. Fortunately, something of the state of affairs was quickly known at 147th Infantry Brigade H.Q., and the G.O.C. promptly placed two companies of the 7th Battalion at the disposal of the Commanding Officer of the 4th Battalion. Battalion H.Q. details were assembled ready for any eventuality near the huts of the Officers' Rest Camp, while C Company and the companies of the 7th Battalion were warned to be prepared to counter-attack.

About 5-30 p.m. a heavy counter-attack was launched from the north-east towards Steam Mill, by Capt. Fenton with one and a half companies of the 7th Battalion, and Capt. Luty with C Company. The attack met with almost complete success. With the single exception of Steam Mill, the whole of the ground which had been lost by the 22nd Corps Reinforcement Battalion was regained. But Steam Mill itself was firmly held by the enemy, and could not be retaken. Everywhere else the enemy withdrew in confusion. During this fighting Capt. A. M. Luty was twice wounded, once while leading his men near Steam Mill, and a second time while he was being carried away on a stretcher. About 7-30 p.m., the Commanding Officer was able to report to Brigade H.Q. that the situation was again quiet.

Had the enemy been able to make a second attack, the situation would have been serious indeed. Save for the H.Q. details, the Battalion now had absolutely no reserves, while the companies of the 7th Battalion which had counter-attacked had to be used to man the line formerly held by the 22nd Corps Reinforcement Battalion. But, after the failure of their attack, the Germans attempted nothing further that day. In all, on April 14th, the Battalion lost one officer and 14 other ranks killed, two officers and 51 other ranks wounded, and two other ranks missing.

The occasional crashes of burning buildings were almost the only sounds which disturbed the night. It was not free from alarms, but nothing came of any of them. Towards midnight, the joyful news arrived that the Battalion was to be relieved by troops of the 59th Division, who were already on their way. The whole of both the 4th and 6th Battalions were to be relieved by the 5th Battalion North Staffordshire Regt., but as this Battalion was about 900 fighting strength, and the total effective strength of the battalions to be relieved was only about 600, no great difficulty was anticipated by 147th Infantry Brigade H.Q. There was, however, considerable difficulty in handing over the line, owing to the great extension of front which the dispersal of the 22nd Corps Reinforcement Battalion had rendered necessary. As a result, relief was not complete until some time after daybreak. Then the Battalion, delighted at the prospect of a rest, moved back to a position about half a mile south of St. Jans Cappel, where the site of a new line had been taped out the previous day.

(d) St. Jans Cappel.

On being relieved in Bailleul, the 147th Infantry Brigade passed into IX. Corps Reserve, but was to be prepared to move at half-an-hour's notice. The 7th Battalion was in reserve in or near St. Jans Cappel; the 4th and 6th Battalions bivouaced in the open about a thousand yards south of the village, where the new line had been taped. Everyone was tired out with the exertions of the past week, and the opportunity for a sound and unbroken sleep was welcomed. No one guessed how short the period of rest would be.

A few alarming rumours came through during the day, but little was thought of them at first. Then, about 4-30 p.m., came the order from Brigade which disillusioned all—the Battalion was to stand to at once, and work on the taped-out line was to be pressed on with as hard as possible. It was hinted that this line would probably be the front line before morning. Everyone responded with the greatest readiness and cheerfulness. Few shovels were available, but farm implements were seized and many of the men set to work with the long-handled spades of the district. The Battalion was responsible for a line, about half a mile in length, on the western side of the Bailleul—St. Jans Cappel Road. The 6th Battalion held a similar front on the opposite side of the road, but, apart from some Lewis guns manned by a battalion of the Tank Corps, there appeared to be no one for several hundred yards on the right. "When positions are taken up all ranks must definitely understand that no withdrawal is to take place excepting under written orders" was the Commanding Officer's message to companies. The strength of the Battalion was very low—only 19 officers and 307 other ranks all told—little enough to hold half a mile of front. It was then that the Commanding Officer, thinking the extreme urgency of the situation warranted the step, ordered up practically the whole of B Echelon.

The night which followed was one of the most depressing in the whole history of the Battalion. About 8-30 p.m. a message had arrived from Brigade H.Q. to warn everyone that the 59th Division would probably withdraw through the new line. But the message was unnecessary. The men of the 176th Infantry Brigade were already coming along the road, and it was clear that Bailleul, the town which the Battalion had helped to defend for three days in spite of heavy losses, had fallen. Many of the men of the 5th Battalion North Staffordshire Regt. stopped to assist in the defence of the new line; but most of their Brigade passed through to Locre to reorganise. The Battalion was again holding the front line. Picquets were pushed out well in front, a wiring party under the 57th Field Company, Royal Engineers, did valuable work, while through the night the men dug hard, and by dawn there was quite a good line.

The chief anxiety was the gap in the line, on the Battalion's right. This was eventually filled by the 5th Battalion North Staffordshire Regt. About 350 men of this battalion had remained in the line when the rest of their Brigade passed through, and these were now transferred to the right, where they took over the front under their own Commanding Officer. But, in accordance with the instructions of the G.O.C., 147th Infantry Brigade, Lieut.-Col. R. E. Sugden, D.S.O., retained supreme command of that part of the front, as well as of his own battalion.

The night passed without any enemy action. At dawn the next day, patrols pushed out well in front of the line, and located the enemy on the Becque de la Flanche. It was certain that he would soon make an attempt to continue his advance, but the Battalion now felt ready for him. Quite a respectable line had been dug during the night. This was held by B Company on the right and C Company on the left; D and A Companies were in support on the right and left respectively; B Echelon, which had arrived during the night, was kept at Battalion H.Q. in reserve. As time went on movement among the enemy became more and more pronounced, and early in the afternoon it was obvious that an attack was imminent. Large numbers of Germans were seen dribbling down the hedge-rows, from the direction of Bailleul, and massing about 500 or 600 yards from the Battalion front. Two companies of the 7th Battalion had been placed at the disposal of the Commanding Officer, to strengthen his right flank, and all ranks quietly awaited the enemy's move.

About 4-0 p.m. the storm burst. The desultory shelling of the earlier part of the afternoon changed to a barrage, and large numbers of the enemy advanced to the attack. The Battalion settled down to fight. On the right such a hail of bullets was poured into the advancing masses by B Company that the attack scarcely succeeded in debouching from the hedge, behind which the assembly had been carried out. On the left C Company, whose line was packed with Lewis guns, brought the advance to a complete standstill 300 yards from the line. A detachment of the 176th Light Trench Mortar Battery, which was covering

ST. JANS CAPPEL

the road to Bailleul, was able to burst shell after shell in the midst of the enemy. The attack had hardly opened before it had failed. Nowhere did a German get within 300 yards of the British line. To the east of the road it was much the same tale ; there the 6th Battalion Duke of Wellington's Regt. first held up the attack by Lewis gun and rifle fire, and then, issuing from its trenches, collected a number of prisoners. Within half-an-hour, of the whole German regiment which had made the attack, nothing was to be seen but the little group of prisoners moving to the rear, and the scores of dead who littered the battlefield. "Well done all ranks" was the message received from the Brigadier ; and "Well done old 147 Brigade" was the affectionate greeting of Major-General N. J. G. Cameron when he received the news.

Though the men of the Battalion knew it not, this was the last attack they were to sustain on that front. After eight days of almost continuous fighting, they had at length succeeded in bringing the enemy's advance to a full stop. The line which they had started to dig late in the afternoon of April 15th, and which they had defended so successfully the following day, was to remain the front line until the beginning of the victorious British advance in the late summer. Through it the enemy was never to penetrate ; and while the Battalion was in the neighbourhood he never again tried. For the time being the Germans had had enough of the 147th Infantry Brigade. But, at the time, the Battalion knew nothing of all this.

The days that followed were very anxious ones. So weak was the Battalion that it could not be expected to withstand many more attacks. Time after time reports came in that reinforcements were coming up, that French troops would soon be there. But as the days went by, and the Battalion still remained in that all-important part of the line, some began to doubt whether relief ever would come. At length one day a French cavalry officer arrived at Battalion H.Q., and informed the Commanding Officer that he had come for liaison purposes. His regiment was the advanced guard of considerable numbers of French troops, and was already bivouacing in the neighbourhood. He was authorised by his Commanding Officer to say that, although the regiment was not intended to take part in any fighting without orders from higher authority, if help were needed the Battalion need only let him know and the regiment would come.

Meanwhile the Battalion was hard at work improving the line. Patrols were active on the front, and were seldom interfered with. Two days after his unsuccessful attempt towards St. Jans Cappel, the enemy launched an attack further to the west, on the front which had been occupied by the men of the 5th Battalion North Staffordshire Regt. As luck would have it, these had been relieved the previous night by the 2nd Battalion Argyle and Sutherland Highlanders, who gave the enemy so warm a reception that afterwards he left that front severely alone. During these days the Battalion was not much troubled, except by intermittent artillery fire.

On the night of April 18/19th the Battalion was relieved by the 7th Battalion Duke of Wellington's Regt., and went into Brigade Reserve. Battalion H.Q. was situated in the Convent at St. Jans Cappel which had large, though not very strongly built cellars. The Aid Post was in a brewery on the opposite side of the road, where considerable stocks of beer, rather better in quality than the normal French variety, were much appreciated. Most of the men held a new switch line, which had been dug to the south-west of the village.

Only twenty-four hours were spent in the new location, for the next night the whole Brigade was withdrawn into Divisional Reserve. The Battalion was relieved by the 1st Queens and withdrew to Mont Noir; here the only billets available, with the exception of one estaminet occupied by Battalion H.Q., were slits in the ground.

By this time the French were coming up in force and were taking over the whole sector. Long before dawn on the morning of April 21st, the Battalion marched out and proceeded in the darkness, through batteries of French 75's which were already in action, to a hutment camp on the top of Mont des Cats. Here the men slept until the middle of the afternoon. It was the first real piece of comfort they had had since they were hurried into battle nearly two weeks before.

(e) Poperinghe.

The Battalion only stopped on Mont des Cats for a few hours and then it moved off to Poperinghe. On the way, it passed the G.O.C., IX. Corps, who had come to take a last look at the men who had served him so well. Though a sorry remnant of the Battalion, which had embussed so cheerfully at Reninghelst only twelve days before, they were well worth a second glance. Ragged, unshaven and unkempt, with nothing clean about them but their rifles, bayonets and ammunition, they were yet a body of veterans whom anyone would have been proud to command. Thrown into the battle when the enemy was flushed with success, they had fought and beaten him time after time. It was the proud boast of the Battalion that it had never withdrawn without definite orders to do so, and that the enemy had never won from it an inch of ground.

Messages of thanks and congratulations had poured in to the Brigade from all quarters—from the Commander-in-Chief, from General Plumer, and from the IX. Corps. The G.O.C., 34th Division, on parting with the 147th Infantry Brigade, wrote to the G.O.C., 49th Division, in the following terms :—

"The G.O.C., 34th Division, wishes to place on record his great appreciation of the services rendered by 147th Infantry Brigade during the period it has been attached to the Division under his command. The action of the 4th Battalion Duke of Wellington's South of the Lys on 10th April, the skilful rearguard fighting under cover of which the Division withdrew from the Nieppe position, the stubborn defence of the right of the Division at Steam Mill (S. of Bailleul) and the complete defeat of a whole German Regiment on the 16th April, are exploits of which the Brigade may well be proud.

Throughout the period the steadiness, gallantry and endurance of all ranks has been worthy of the highest traditions of British Infantry and the G.O.C., 34th Division, is proud to have had such troops under his command."

At Poperinghe the Battalion was housed in the Rest Camp by the Railway Station, but most of the officers slept in the Convent not far away. No training was attempted. The men were given as much rest as possible. Time was spent in reorganisation, of which every company stood much in need. A draft, about two hundred strong, joined the Battalion; but this was not sufficient to bring it to full strength, for over four hundred casualties had been suffered during the past fortnight. Here the 147th Infantry Brigade came again under the 49th Division, as did also the 148th Infantry Brigade.

The days were fairly peaceful, but the nights were rather disturbed by high velocity guns, which fired into the town. During the last night, several bombing planes visited Poperinghe and caused great excitement. Some bombs were dropped very near the camp, one in particular narrowly missing the Battalion Transport and stampeding some of the animals.

It was fully realised that the period of rest would almost certainly be short. The Germans had already captured the low range of hills about Neuve Eglise, and it was certain they would make a bid for the chain, of which Mont Kemmel is the highest point. Hence, there was little surprise when, early in the morning of April 25th, the Battalion was put on half-an-hour's notice to move.

(f) Kemmel.*

About 8-45 a.m. on April 25th, the order to move arrived. The Brigade was proceeding at once to Ouderdom in support of the 9th Division. The Battalion was to move by march route

*The following Officers and Warrant Officers went into action with the Battalion on April 25th, 1918 :—
Battn. H.Q. : Lieut.-Col. R. E. Sugden, D.S.O. (C.O.) ; Capt. W. C. Fenton, M.C. (Second in Command) ; Lieut. P. G. Bales (A/Adjt.) ; Lieut. J. C. Walton (I.O.) ; Lieut. L. J. Smets (Sig. O.) ; Capt. F. C. Harrison, R.A.M.C. (M.O.).
R.S.M. T. S. Sherwood.
Capt. H. N. Taylor (Liaison Officer at 147th Infantry Brigade H.Q.).
A Company : Capt. A. Kirk (O.C.) ; Sec.-Lieut. E. Clarke ; Sec.-Lieut. J. C. Whitaker ; Sec.-Lieut. G. Campbell.
Sergt. W. D. Foster (A/C.S.M.).
B Company : Sec.-Lieut. R. B. Broster (O.C.) ; Sec.-Lieut. C. T. Applewhaite ; Sec.-Lieut. S. R. Norton.
C.S.M. B. Haigh, D.C.M.
C Company : Lieut. W. G. Mackie (O.C.) ; Sec.-Lieut. T. T Gilroy ; Sec.-Lieut. A. C. Edwards.
C.S.M. J. E. Yates.
D Company : Capt. S. Balme (O.C.) ; Sec.-Lieut. H. Rosendale ; Sec.-Lieut. E. Turner; Sec.-Lieut. L. Gumby, M.C.
C.S.M. C. Naylor.

as it was to remain in Brigade Reserve, but motor buses were provided for all the rest of the Brigade. However, so quickly did the Battalion fall in and move off that it arrived at Ouderdom long before the buses appeared.

The situation was very obscure. A great battle was in progress to the south and it was believed that the enemy had captured Mont Kemmel ; but nothing was definitely known. The 6th and 7th Battalions were moved forward to form a defensive flank from Beaver Corner to Millekruisse, as the Cheapside Line was thought still to be in British hands ; but touch had been completely lost with the troops on the right. All that day the Battalion remained inactive in the fields near Ouderdom. They were little troubled, except by an occasional aeroplane. One of these dropped a bomb which caused one or two casualties, but otherwise the Battalion escaped unscathed.

In the evening the Battalion moved up to positions in some old trenches a little to the north of Millekruisse, and here it settled down for the night. But it was not to rest for long. About 2-30 a.m., Major A. L. Mowat arrived from 147th Infantry Brigade H.Q. with orders for an immediate attack. The situation and details were as follows :—

1. A big counter-attack was to be launched, by French troops on the right and the 25th Division on the left, to recapture Mont Kemmel and establish a line to the south of it.

2. The Battalion was to co-operate on the left of the 25th Division. It was to assemble on the Cheapside Line and attack in a south-easterly direction, on a front of about six hundred yards, with the trench system on the York Road as its objective.

3. In the event of the 25th Division not being able to advance, the Battalion was to conform to its line.

4. Zero hour was fixed for 4-25 a.m., when a creeping barrage would come down.

From the Battalion point of view, this operation was extremely difficult. No one had any knowledge of the ground, and the assembly was to take place and the attack to open before dawn. As the companies were much below full strength, the Commanding Officer decided to attack on a three-company frontage— B Company was to attack on the right, D Company in the centre, and A Company on the left. C Company was in support, and was to advance about two hundred yards in rear of the assaulting troops.

At once the Battalion fell in and marched off. Owing to the darkness of the night and the fact that everyone was completely ignorant of the ground, companies did not quite reach their assembly positions by zero hour, but were drawn up about the line of the Kemmelbeke. At 4-25 a.m. the barrage—a very thin one—opened, and the Battalion advanced. It passed through a deserted camp and came to a road, along the line of which were some old trenches. These had been occupied by the enemy, but he retired when the British advanced. The trenches were occupied and a halt was made there. This was due to the failure of the next battalion to advance.

The 74th Infantry Brigade of the 25th Division was attacking on the Battalion's right. One of its battalions did extremely well, forcing its way right into Kemmel village, and taking about 150 prisoners there. But the battalion on the immediate right of B Company failed to get forward. The 4th Battalion had met with very little resistance up to that time. Enemy machine gun fire was extremely heavy, but, as the morning was misty, very few casualties were caused by it at first. There is no doubt that the Battalion could have advanced further without much difficulty, but its orders were to conform to the 25th Division, and, as the men on its right were not advancing, it halted. For several hours it was believed that the line of Sackville Street had been reached, and this was the situation reported by the Commanding Officer to Brigade H.Q. at 5.5 a.m. Later it was found that the men had only got as far as Cheapside.

For about an hour things were comparatively quiet, except for enemy machine gun fire. Soon after 6-0 a.m. the battalion on the right began to withdraw, and before long the situation was becoming serious on that flank. The mist had cleared considerably, and the enemy was making better use of his machine guns. Taking advantage of the weakness of the troops there, he began to work round the Battalion's right flank, by Beaver Corner and R.E. Farm. To cope with this menace, first half, and later the whole, of C Company had to be sent over to the right to form a defensive flank, facing south-west. On the rest of the Battalion front there was little anxiety. All three companies were well in touch, and A Company was connected up with the 9th Battalion King's Own Yorkshire Light Infantry (21st Division) on its left. Enemy machine gun fire was heavy, but the troops had good cover.

As time went on, the situation on the right became more and more serious. Here enemy machine gun fire was particularly heavy, and his sniping very accurate. He was making determined attempts to advance to the west of the Milky Way, and there was great danger that he might get across the Battalion's line of retreat. The whole of C Company had been committed to the defence of this flank, and later, two guns of the Machine Gun Company and a detachment of the 147th Light Trench Mortar Battery had also been sent up. Thus, the whole available battalion reserve, except a few H.Q. details, was engaged. C Company had done some very useful work. They had driven the enemy from R.E. Farm, though they were unable to occupy it themselves; but they were suffering heavily from the enemy's very accurate sniping. At 9-25 a.m. a message was sent to the 6th Battalion asking it to send up a company to reinforce the right.

By about 11-0 a.m. the strength of C Company had been very much reduced. Man after man had been shot in the head by enemy snipers, among the casualties being Pte. A. Poulter, the stretcher-bearer who had so greatly distinguished himself two weeks before at Erquinghem. Lieut. W. G. Mackie, who was commanding C Company, was also wounded, and Sec.-Lieut. T. T. Gilroy assumed command. Soon after noon, two platoons of the 6th Battalion arrived and were sent up to strengthen C Company. This helped to restore the situation on the right flank, and, for a time, things were much quieter, though the enemy sniping and machine gun fire continued.

It was hoped that the 25th Division would take action to restore the situation on its left, and about 1-30 p.m. a message was received that a battalion of the South Lancashire Regt. was coming up to get in touch there. Meanwhile, there was great difficulty in supplying the forward troops with ammunition, owing to the heavy fire kept up by the enemy. Everything had to be carried across the open, and there was very little cover. In this connection, splendid work was done by some of the H.Q. batmen, who crawled up to the line with bandoliers slung over their backs.

During the afternoon the enemy made a further attempt to work round the right flank. Considerable numbers of them were seen moving along the side of a hedge, but the situation was satisfactorily dealt with by C Company. Sec.-Lieut. T. T. Gilroy had seen them himself. He quickly got two Vickers guns into position, and, when the enemy appeared at a gap in the hedge, so heavy a fire was opened at close range that the party was almost wiped out. This was the last attempt to advance that the enemy made that day.

By this time the discovery had been made that the Battalion was not in Sackville Street at all, but in Cheapside. This was at once reported to 147th Infantry Brigade H.Q., as it altered the situation considerably. The battalion of South Lancashires had come up, but was halted by the Milky Way and did not go into action. It was now night. Arrangements were made for wiring and other work to be done on the front; but this was not to be. The higher authorities had realised that the counter-attack had failed, and had decided to withdraw the troops, who had carried it out, from their advanced positions. About 11-0 p.m., the order for the withdrawal was received, and the operation began at 12-30 a.m. All went smoothly. The night was dark and the enemy remained inactive. A Company withdrew first, and was followed by the others in order from left to right, C Company moving last and bringing out with them the few men who were left of the next battalion. All the ammunition, which had been sent up during the day, was got away. The Battalion moved back along the Milky Way, through the line held by the 6th Battalion, and reoccupied the same positions near Millekruisse which it had left in the early morning of April 26th.

For the next two days the enemy made no further infantry attack, but his artillery was often active, particularly round Millekruisse cross roads. Not far from this spot Sec.-Lieut J. C.

Whitaker, of A Company, was killed by a shell on April 28th. There can be no doubt that, between April 25th and 29th, the Germans were replenishing their ammunition dumps, and making preparations for their next big attack. During this time the Battalion was in Brigade Reserve. Much work was done on a new line a little to the south of Millekruisse, and A Company moved up to garrison it. Otherwise, there was no change in dispositions.

On April 28th the enemy put down a heavy barrage on the British front, from 7-30 p.m. to 9-0 p.m., and desultory shelling continued through the night. About 3-0 a.m. on the morning of April 29th this suddenly changed to a barrage, the intensity and depth of which can seldom have been equalled. From Mont Vidaigne on the right to Zillebeke Lake on the left, the whole front was ablaze. On the sector held by the 147th Infantry Brigade the whole country, from the front line to beyond Ouderdom, was deluged with shells. High explosive and gas literally rained down everywhere. Practically the first shell of the bombardment burst in the roof of the farm house, which was occupied by Battalion H.Q., and mortally wounded both the orderly room clerks ; the R.S.M., who was in the same room, had a wonderful escape, and fragments actually penetrated the roof of the cellar, in which the Commanding Officer was sleeping at the time. By a great stroke of luck the barrage almost entirely missed the front line, so that its garrison, though extremely uncomfortable, was practically unharmed. No one doubted that this was the prelude to another mighty attack.

After about two hours of this bombardment, the German infantry advanced in great numbers to the attack. They gained nothing. Caught by the British barrage, mown down by Lewis gun and rifle fire, they suffered enormous casualties. It is said that, on one part of the front, they were so demoralised that they put out a white flag and tried to come in, but could not pass through the barrage. On the whole front attacked they only gained a footing in the allied line in two places, and from both of these they were ejected almost immediately by counter-attacks. All this time the barrage continued.

Meanwhile, the Battalion was in Brigade Reserve, anxiously awaiting information which could be acted upon. The Millekruisse Line had been strengthened by the addition of D Company, but B and C Companies were both available for any action. All telephone lines had been broken within a few minutes of the opening of the bombardment, and it was extremely difficult to obtain any news. Lieut. J. C. Walton, the Battalion Intelligence Officer, was sent up to get in touch with the H.Q. of the 7th Battalion, which was in the line; but he was blown to pieces by a shell before he had gone more than two hundred yards. About 7-0 a.m. it was learned from wounded men who had come down, that the 7th Battalion had been heavily attacked, but that they had held their ground and still had a company in reserve. On receipt of this news, the Commanding Officer immediately communicated with Brigade H.Q., asking whether he should send a company to assist them. About 9-0 a.m. a wounded N.C.O. of the 7th Battalion reported a fresh massing of the enemy for the attack. Lieut.-Col. Sugden waited no longer, but at once ordered up B Company to reinforce. Though the barrage was almost as thick as ever, the company succeeded in finding a route by which it reached its objective with very few casualties. It arrived just in time to stop an urgent message which was being sent, asking for the assistance of a company. But the reinforcements were never required. The worst of the battle was over. After two violent attacks all along the front, the enemy made only local and spasmodic efforts for the rest of the day. His force was broken; he had been beaten to a standstill; and he had gained—nothing. As the Divisional Commander wrote shortly after—" It was a great day for British Arms."

The battle of April 29th was far more than an ordinary defeat for the enemy. It was the final collapse of his offensive. During the next three months he was to launch other great attacks against the French, further to the south. But never again was he to try conclusions with the British in a great battle, until they took the initiative into their own hands, and, after driving him headlong from position after position, forced him to sue for an armistice from the men he had professed to despise. For the second time in less than three weeks the 147th Infantry Brigade had assisted in bringing the German attack to a standstill, and had consolidated and held a line which was to remain unbroken until all lines were left behind in the victorious advance of the autumn.

The following days were uneventful. Work continued on the Millekruisse Line, in which two companies were now permanently stationed. B Company remained under the orders of the 7th Battalion. Enemy artillery was active, but was as nothing compared with the barrage of April 29th. The 147th Infantry Brigade was strengthened by the temporary addition of a composite battalion, made up of the remnants of the 146th Infantry Brigade and the 19th Lancashire Fusiliers, each battalion furnishing one company. Among the many congratulatory messages, which poured in after the victory of April 29th, not the least appreciated was one from the G.O.C., IX. Corps, who had not forgotten the work of the 147th Infantry Brigade while serving under his command so recently.

On the night of May 1/2nd the Battalion relieved the 7th Battalion Duke of Wellington's Regt. on the left of the Brigade Sector. The front held was a peculiar one, and lay almost at right angles to the general line. Its left rested almost on Cheapside, where A Company had been on April 26th. From that point it ran nearly due north to and across the Kemmelbeke, and then turned at right angles across the Milky Way. Three companies held this line, the men occupying small slits in the ground; the fourth and a company of the 6th Battalion, which had been relieved by the 146th Composite Battalion, were in support. There was still plenty of hostile shelling but it was very scattered, and the little slits in the ground were difficult targets to hit.

The labours and troubles of the Battalion were now nearly over for the time being. A French Army had come up and was gradually taking over the front, along the chain of hills. On the night of May 3/4th the Battalion was relieved by the 3rd Battalion, 80th Infantry Regt., of the 32nd French Division. This Battalion, which was very strong, took over the whole front of the 147th Infantry Brigade. They were a magnificent body of men, and the British were much struck with their fine appearance. While the relief was in progress some anxiety was caused by a heavy enemy bombardment, but, apart from this, everything went smoothly. Capt. Fenton, with a few N.C.O's, was left in the line for twenty-four hours to assist the French; and the Battalion started on its march through the night to a well-earned rest.

It was daylight before the first halting-place was reached. This was a camp which, it was rumoured, had recently been occupied by a Chinese Labour Company. This fact did not altogether commend itself to the Battalion, but all men were so weary that it scarcely disturbed their sleep. In the afternoon a short march brought the Battalion to a hutment camp at St. Jans ter Biezen, where the rest period was to be spent.

The part taken by the Battalion, in what is generally known as the Battle of the Lys, is the most glorious chapter in its history. Never before nor since did the men fight so long continuously, nor against such overwhelming odds. They faced the enemy in the full flush of his successes on the Somme, when his morale was at its highest. They fought him again and again, and never yielded an inch of ground in battle. They taught him that he was no match for a British soldier, either in attack or in defence. They helped to pave the way for his crushing defeat a few months later.

And the men learned many things too. They learned that the German will never push home an assault in the face of a really determined resistance ; that infantry fire alone is sufficient to stop his most violent attacks. In the many engagements that they fought during April, 1918, no man of them ever used a bayonet, for never did the enemy reach their lines. They learned too—those of them who did not know it well before—that the spade, almost as much as the rifle, is the infantry man's weapon. And, perhaps most valuable lesson of all, they learned that what appear to be the blackest and most hopeless situations can be restored by men, if only they possess the necessary determination.

Throughout the most trying and uncomfortable conditions all ranks continued cheerful, and morale never declined. In spite of appalling casualties, the Battalion never became in the least disorganised. Camaraderie and good-fellowship were never more conspicuous. Though the Battalion was only about three hundred strong, a draft of two hundred was incorporated so thoroughly that the men of it fought, only two or three days later, as if they had never served with any other unit.

The Transport and Stores too did magnificent work. Frequently shelled, and on one occasion at least under machine gun fire, constantly on the move and often surrounded by disorder, they carried on their work in a way which earned the admiration of everyone. At a time when one was continually hearing of battalions who had had no rations for days, the 4th Battalion had never lived in such plenty. There is no doubt that this happy state of affairs increased the fighting efficiency of everyone enormously.

The work of the 49th Division, in which the Battalion had played no inconsiderable a part, was recognised on all sides. On the night of April 29th, the Commander-in-Chief expressed himself in the following terms :—

"I desire to express my appreciation of the very valuable and gallant services performed by troops of the 49th (West Riding) Division since the entry of the 147th Infantry Brigade into the battle of Armentiéres. The courage and determination showed by this Division has played no small part in checking the enemy's advance, and I wish to convey to General Cameron and to all officers and men under his command my thanks for all that they have done."

Among the many other messages, too numerous for reproduction, which were received, the following, expressed in the inimitable manner of the French, deserves special notice :—

"The G.O.C., 2nd Cavalry Corps, warmly congratulates the brave British troops who have heroically assisted in the defence of the chain of hills, and who, by their admirable resistance have broken down the enemy's effort and barred the way to Dunkerque.

Shelterless under a bombardment of the heaviest description, surrounded by poisonous gases of various description, stubbornly disputing every foot of ground, they have held their own against repeated attacks by greatly superior numbers, and though at first overwhelmed by weight of numbers they were obliged to give ground, they have inflicted such heavy losses on the enemy that his forces have been exhausted.

Once more the Germans have seen their hopes dashed to the ground. France will remember that.

Robillot."

It was a matter of the deepest regret to all that the 49th Division could not work as a whole during a great part of the operations; and none felt it more than General Cameron. In the confidential summary of operations, which he circulated a few days after the Division was withdrawn from the battle, one can clearly see his disappointment that this should have been so. One can also distinguish clearly his pride in the record of his men on so many different fronts. The concluding paragraph of that summary, as looking to the future, may fittingly end this chapter :—

"The reputation which you have won for courage, determination and efficiency, during recent operations, has its very joyous aspect, and it is deeply precious to us all.

It has also a serious aspect for us.

It lays on each one of us a great responsibility—a personal responsibility for doing all he can to ensure that the next time the Division is engaged it will perform even better service than it has in the past.

We shall shortly, we hope, be filling up with new men.

Let every old hand put his shoulder to the wheel in the task of instilling into our new blood the spirit of courage, determination and efficiency which has carried you through your recent trial so successfully.

Never fail to impress on all new hands what the rifle and bayonet can do in the hands of a determined British soldier who knows how to look after them and use them.

N. G. Cameron, Major-General."

CHAPTER XII.

THE LAST OF YPRES.

(a) May, 1918.

FOR nearly a month the Battalion was out of the line, and most of this time was spent at Road Camp, St. Jans ter Biezen. At first the accommodation was adequate, but, towards the end of May, the huts were becoming very crowded. This was due to the arrival of new drafts, and the return of a number of lightly wounded men. By the time the Battalion went into the line again nearly 200 had joined. Many of these were young soldiers, who had been hurriedly despatched from England to make good the very heavy losses suffered during the enemy's violent attacks in March and April. They were splendid material and quickly developed into fine soldiers. A large draft of officers also arrived towards the end of April. Here, too, Sergt. A. Loosemore, V.C., joined the Battalion.

The first days were spent almost entirely in reorganisation. This was very necessary after the enormous casualties of the last few weeks. But the organisation of the Battalion had never broken down, and there was a solid framework on which to build. New officers and men were quickly assimilated; new specialists were trained. Long before the rest period came to an end, the Battalion was almost as efficient a fighting unit as it had been at the beginning of April.

On May 14th the 147th Infantry Brigade moved by bus to St. Martin au Laert for four days' shooting. Tents were pitched about a mile from the town, and, as the weather was gloriously fine, a very enjoyable time was spent there. St. Omer was within easy walking distance of the camp, and the rather unusual experience of having a large town near at hand was thoroughly enjoyed. Enemy bombing planes were common at night, but they restricted their activities mainly to Arques, and never troubled the camp.

Soon after its return to Road Camp, the Brigade moved to Penton Camp, near Proven, for four days' work on the East Poperinghe Line. At this time an immense amount of labour and material was being used in the construction of defences between Ypres and Poperinghe. Everyone expected that the enemy would make a further attack in that direction, and no less than four defensive systems were in course of construction or improvement between the two towns. The East Poperinghe Line was the most westerly of these systems. A definite sector was allotted to each battalion, and every available man was sent to work on it. Parties paraded early in the morning and were taken up to the work by light railway trains. They did not return until late in the afternoon, so there was not much time for recreation. At Proven, officers met an old friend. Francois, well known to most officers who have seen much of Poperinghe, had transferred his restaurant business to Proven, when the German advance made Poperinghe too warm. As always, dinner at Francois' was very popular.

The Battalion returned to Road Camp on May 26th, and another week was spent there. At the end of May Lieut.-Col. R. E. Sugden, D.S.O., went on leave. He had scarcely arrived in England when an urgent wire recalled him, to take command of the 151st Infantry Brigade, 50th Division. He had no time to return to the Battalion, but went straight down to the neighbourhood of the Marne, where his Brigade awaited him. Everyone was delighted to hear of his promotion, for it was looked upon as an honour to the Battalion—few Territorial officers attained such high rank during the war. Another source of great satisfaction to everyone was that Major A. L. Mowat, M.C., was appointed to the command of the Battalion ; few had seen more service with it, and none had done more for its good than he.

While at St. Jans ter Biezen, permission was given for a photograph to be taken of all the " old originals " still serving with the Battalion. Four officers and 114 other ranks were included in the group. This should have been done on April 14th—the anniversary of the Battalion's landing in France. But circumstances over which the Battalion had little control—the battle of Steam Mill was fought on that day—had prevented any celebrations.

(b) Zillebeke Sector.

When the enemy broke through to the south of Armentiéres, and, still more, when he captured the Messines Ridge, the situation of the British troops in the Ypres Salient became very critical. Their whole right flank was laid bare, and they were in imminent danger of being cut off. The whole line was therefore withdrawn to a position a little in front of Ypres. With the exception of the Pilkem Ridge, all the ground gained in the terrific fighting of 1917 was thus given up. Indeed, astride and south of the Menin Road, the line was further back than it had been in 1915.

Early in June the 49th Division took over the line, from a point a little north of the Zonnebeke Road, to Zillebeke Lake. This line was divided into two brigade sectors, the third brigade being in divisional reserve. Thus brigades had sixteen days in the front line and eight days in rest. Each brigade had two battalions in the front line so that, now there were only three battalions to a brigade, one battalion had to do a continuous tour of sixteen days.

On the afternoon of June 3rd the Battalion moved by light railway to near Vlamertinghe Chateau, where it detrained. As soon as it was getting dusk, the men marched off to carry out the relief. That night the enemy artillery was extremely active; in fact, it was the " liveliest " night the Battalion had near Ypres the whole summer. Rome Farm was being very heavily shelled as the men went past towards the Menin Road, and when they reached Kruisstraat they passed into an area thick with mustard gas. A heavy bombardment of Warrington Road and the vicinity of the Lille Gate, with 8-inch gas shells, was in progress. This greatly hampered the relief, as respirators had to be worn for considerable distances ; but, luckily, the Battalion got in with practically no casualties.

The front line was about a line in length and was held by three companies, disposed as follows :—

Right : B Company, from Zillebeke Lake to the Warrington Road. Only one platoon occupied the front line posts, the remainder living in the dugouts along the western edge of the Lake.

Centre : D Company, from the Warrington Road to a point north-west of Moated Grange.

Left : A Company, from the flank of D Company to the Ypres—
Roulers Railway, about 300 yards west of Hellfire Corner. C Company was in reserve in a line about 500 yards in rear of the front line.

Battalion H.Q. was in the Ramparts of Ypres, not far from the Lille Gate. Never had such a commodious place been occupied before. When preparations were in progress for the Third Battle of Ypres in 1917, two divisional H.Q. had been constructed in the Ramparts, one near the Lille Gate and one near the Menin Gate. Now that the line had been withdrawn so far, these had come into use for battalions. There were rooms and to spare, lit up with electric light and comfortably furnished. Every H.Q. officer had his separate room, and there were also a fine large mess and a good office.

The front line was not very satisfactory. On the left it was continuous and good, but on the right posts were completely isolated. It was fortunate too that the weather was fine, for the ground was very low and would quickly have become waterlogged. The dugouts on the west side of Zillebeke Lake provided any amount of good accommodation for B Company, but the other companies were not nearly so well off in that respect. The reserve line occupied by C Company was also inferior.

When the Battalion took over the line there were no communication trenches, and all movement was across the open. The out-going unit—the 15th Battalion King's Royal Rifle Corps—stated that no movement in the open was advisable by day as enemy sniping was very accurate. This did not suit the Battalion at all, and, right from the start, officers began to make the usual tours of inspection. At first these were carried out with extreme care, all movement being done by crawling; but soon it was found that the enemy was very inactive, and, even before communication trenches were dug, movement in ones and twos became general.

The sector turned out to be a very quiet one. The 1st Land-

Capt. H. H. AYKROYD, M.C.

Capt. W. N. BROOMHEAD, T.D.

Capt. W. GRANTHAM.
(Died of Wounds).

Capt. S. BALME.

wehr Division was holding the line opposite, and these troops were of poor discipline and low morale. If left alone they remained very quiet, and there was little machine gun or rifle fire. The enemy artillery was rarely active. Nothing approaching the bombardment, which had taken place on the night of June 3rd/4th, ever occurred again. The chief feature of the artillery fire was the use of Blue Cross gas shells, which caused violent sneezing but were practically harmless.

From the Ramparts good observation could be obtained of much of the area occupied by the enemy. It was very tantalising to see Germans moving about in the neighbourhood of Kit and Kat Post, upon which A and B Companies had expended so much labour the previous January. All this ground, which was under observation, was well known to the Battalion, from its experiences of the previous winter. Very little movement was observed near the front line.

No Man's Land was covered with thick grass and was ideal for patrolling, either by night or day. In this department there was great activity. It was not that identifications were needed, for these were well known; but the more activity the Battalion could display, the less likely the enemy would be to weaken the front. Before long, the whole of No Man's Land, to a depth of several hundred yards, was well known. Several patrols were seriously interfered with by Blue Cross gas.

The first tour was not without excitement. On the night of June 10/11th a strong patrol, consisting of two officers (Sec.-Lieut. F. Woodward and Sec.-Lieut. A. Charlesworth) and 12 other ranks, moved out towards Hill 40. As they drew near to it, they thought they detected movement behind a hedge. They halted and, soon after, were challenged by a sentry in German. Sec.-Lieut. F. Woodward fired at him with his revolver, and at once the whole patrol opened rapid fire. The enemy, who was evidently there in strength, retaliated with a shower of bombs, wounding Sec.-Lieut. Woodward and three of his men. The action continued for some minutes, but at length Sec.-Lieut. Charlesworth, finding he could make no impression on the hostile position, withdrew the patrol. It was afterwards found that the enemy had a very strong post on Hill 40, from which good observation was obtained of the British line.

The next night the Battalion was relieved and went back into Brigade Reserve. Two companies garrisoned part of the Brielen Line, astride the Ypres-Poperinghe Road. The other two companies held a reserve line south of Ypres, from Kruisstraat to near the Lille Gate. At this time the Battalion was somewhat depleted in strength, owing to a mild form of influenza, commonly known as "Chink Fever."

(c) The Zillebeke Raid.

The one absorbing interest of this period of Brigade Reserve was the raid, which eventually came off on the night of June 19/20th. There was little opportunity for rehearsal or training, as the companies were scattered, and many men were tied down to certain posts. But the plan was worked out most carefully, down to the minutest detail, by the Commanding Officer, who made nearly all the arrangements and wrote the orders himself. The plan was as follows:—

1. The object of the operation was to secure identification and to do as much damage to the enemy as possible.

2. Twelve platoons of the Battalion* were to take part, and these were divided into three parties:—

(a) Two platoons of C Company, whose task was to seize and hold Hill 40, thus guarding the left flank of the main operation.

---

*The following Officers and Warrant Officers took part in the raid:—
Advanced Battn. H.Q.: Lieut.-Col. A. L. Mowat, M.C. (C.O.); Lieut. P. G. Bales.
Rear Battn. H.Q.: Major W. C. Fenton, M.C.; Sec.-Lieut. L. Gumby, M.C.
A Company: Sec.-Lieut. B. H. Huggard (O.C. Company).
C.S.M. F. Gledhill.
Sec.-Lieut. A. Charlesworth (No. 1 Platoon).
Sec.-Lieut. J. E. Bentley (No. 2 Platoon).
Sec.-Lieut. R. M. Leddra (No. 3 Platoon).
Sec.-Lieut. H. M. Marsden (No. 4 Platoon).
Sec.-Lieut. J. W. Entwhistle (No. 14 Platoon).
B Company: Capt. N. T. Farrar, M.C. (O.C. Company).
C.S.M. H. Haigh, D.C.M.
Sec.-Lieut. H. R. Newman (No. 5 Platoon).
Sec.-Lieut. R. E. Jones (No. 6 Platoon).
Sergt. F. J. Field (No. 7 Platoon).
Sec.-Lieut. W. G. Bradley (No. 8 Platoon).
Sec.-Lieut. H. Rosendale (No. 16 Platoon).
C Company: Sec.-Lieut. B. Crickmer (No. 10 Platoon).
Sec.-Lieut. H. E. Burgoyne (No. 12 Platoon).

THE ZILLEBEKE RAID 243

(*b*) A Company, operating north of the Warrington Road.

(*c*) B Company, operating south of the Warrington Road. A and B Companies were each reinforced by a platoon from D Company.

3. Objectives :—

(*a*) B Company : The line Hellblast Corner—Tuilerie—Tuilerie Chimney.

(*b*) A Company : 1st Objective : Enemy posts about 100 yards east of Cavalry Road.

2nd Objective : Halfway House.

4. All platoons were to be assembled in No Man's Land by 11-30 p.m. At 12-0 midnight the advance was to begin. First objectives were to be taken by the front platoons of companies. When B Company had gained all its objectives, Capt. N T. Farrar was to fire a red light as a signal to A Company, the support platoons of which would then advance on Halfway House.

5. The whole were to withdraw at 1-30 a.m.

6. The artillery was to open fire at 12-15 a.m. and put down a standing barrage along the line of Leinster Road. If the wind were favourable, it was also to put down a smoke barrage to cover the advance. But there was to be no creeping barrage.

Late in the evening of June 19th, the troops who were to take part marched into Ypres. As soon as it was dark enough to conceal movement they assembled in the British front line, and, about 11-0 p.m., moved out into No Man's Land. The night was very bright, the moon being almost at the full, and there was some anxiety that the enemy might detect the assembly and put down a barrage. But everything went well and not a shot was fired. All were in position by 11-45 p.m. Battalion H.Q. was established in a dugout in the British front line, and from there the Commanding Officer was in telephonic communication with Major Fenton, who was in the Ramparts. At 12-0 midnight the advance began, and, by a great stroke of luck, almost at the same moment, the moon disappeared behind a thick bank of clouds.

About 12-10 a.m. the left flank of C Company made contact

with the enemy. As they were approaching the post on Hill 40, they encountered a working party, about thirty strong. Shots were exchanged, and the Germans retired a short distance; but the post had, unfortunately, been warned. The flank party was heavily fired on, and Sec.-Lieut. H. E. Burgoyne was wounded. Sergt. R. Wilson was also wounded in the left arm, but remained at duty for some time, until the pain and loss of blood from his wound weakened him so much that he was forced to give up. Long grass and the broken nature of the ground impeded the advance, and, by the time the post was reached, its garrison had withdrawn. Sec.-Lieut. B. Crickmer, who had now assumed command of both the platoons, took up a position facing north-east, about fifty yards beyond the post. Here he became heavily engaged with large numbers of the enemy. All attempts to advance were met by heavy machine gun and rifle fire, and by bombs; and although several casualties were undoubtedly inflicted, he was unable to secure an identification. About 1-0 a.m. artillery fire began to harass the party, but the men held on to their position until it was time to withdraw, and successfully carried out their duty of covering the left flank of the raid. At 1-30 a.m. they withdrew, covered by a small rearguard, and regained their lines.

Meanwhile, the major part of the operation was going extremely well. At 12-15 a.m. the British barrage opened, the bursting shells showing up splendidly against the thick wall of smoke, which was soon built up. It was a picture. Apparently this was the first warning the enemy artillery had, that anything unusual was happening. Shortly after, the enemy barrage came down, and then the wisdom of starting to advance fifteen minutes before zero hour was clearly proved. By the time the German guns got into action all the raiders were beyond the barrage lines, and, that night, the Battalion did not suffer a single casualty from shell fire.

On the extreme right, Sergt. F. J. Field's platoon reached its objective with very little opposition; Vickers and Lewis guns were then brought into action, effectually guarding the right flank of the attack. In the centre Sec.-Lieut H. R. Newman, with No. 5 Platoon, advanced along the C3 Line and became

THE ZILLEBEKE RAID

engaged about fifty yards in front of the Tuilerie. This post was strongly held and wired; but the men cut through two belts of wire, crept up to within ten yards, and rushed the position. Four prisoners and a light machine gun were captured, several casualties were inflicted, and the remainder of the garrison made off. A little later, Sec.-Lieut. R. E. Jones came up south of the Tuilerie, and the line from that point to Hellblast Corner was firmly held until the end of the operation.

But the left platoon of B Company—No. 8 under Sec.-Lieut. W. G. Bradley—had a very rough time. When about 150 yards from its objective, the Tuilerie Chimney, three machine guns opened on the leading section at only a few yards' range. So heavy were the casualties that only two unwounded men were left in the section after the first burst. The other sections were also heavily engaged by an enemy post further to the left. Three attempts were made to rush the position, but without success. The platoon was harassed by machine guns and trench mortars, and had become so reduced in strength, owing to casualties, that Sec.-Lieut. Bradley was forced to break off the action and simply hold on to the position already reached.

Capt. N. T. Farrar was anxiously awaiting the signals from his platoon commanders, which would show that their objectives had been reached. These were received from his right and centre platoons, but not from his left, for the reasons already given. However, from his own position well forward in No Man's Land, he judged that the right flank was sufficiently secure for A Company to advance; and so, at 1-0 a.m., he fired his red signal light.

Meanwhile, A Company in the centre had been even more successful. The earlier part of its advance had been quite uneventful, and contact with the enemy had not been made until near Cavalry Road. Here a few bombs had been thrown, but the Germans had quickly withdrawn. The two leading platoons, under Sec.-Lieuts. R. M. Leddra and J. E. Bentley, crossed the road and occupied a line of trenches, about 200 yards beyond. Near the road Sec.-Lieut. Leddra came across a large dugout, which he bombed with M.S.K. grenades; three Germans came out and were promptly made prisoners. The Company Commander, Sec.-Lieut. B. H. Huggard, had gone well forward to keep in touch with the situation; with the assistance of no one but his runner, he himself rounded up four of the enemy who were trying to escape. Considerable numbers of Germans were seen making off to the rear, and some were shot while doing so. But at this point the smoke screen, which had been of great assistance in covering the earlier stages of the advance, helped the enemy. Many, who otherwise would almost certainly have been captured, were completely lost sight of in the smoke.

By 12-45 a.m. all five platoons of A Company had crossed Cavalry Road and were drawn up ready to advance on Halfway House, as soon as the signal should be fired by B Company. As has already been said, this signal was sent up at 1-0 a.m. But it was not seen owing to the smoke. This was very unfortunate for A Company was quite ready, and there was ample time for the second part of the operation to be carried out. So, no further advance was attempted, but the positions reached were maintained by all parties until the withdrawal.

At 1-30 a.m. the withdrawal began, and was carried out very successfully. White tapes marked the gaps which had been cut in the wire, and rockets were sent up from the Ramparts at Ypres, to direct any who had lost their direction. About 2-0 a.m. patrols went out to search for wounded, the Commanding Officer personally assisting in this work. Several wounded were brought in and the work was certainly well done, for the Battalion had only one man missing out of over 350 who had gone "over the top." Platoons moved back to their former stations in Brigade Reserve, where a well-earned sleep awaited them.

Though the second part of the operation—the attack on Halfway House—was not attempted, the raid was a great success. Eleven prisoners and a light machine gun had been captured, and considerable casualties had undoubtedly been inflicted on the enemy. The total casualties of the Battalion were 3 other ranks killed, one officer and 16 other ranks wounded, and one other rank missing. This was extremely light, considering that three quarters of the Battalion had spent one and a half hours in the enemy's lines. But by far the most satisfactory result of the raid was its effect on morale. Many of the officers and men who took part had only been with the Battalion a very short

THE ZILLEBEKE RAID

time, and a large number of the latter were very young and had seen no fighting before. The old soldier has learned to take things as they come, but success or failure have great effect on inexperienced and young soldiers. So it was with this raid. They went into action boys; they came out almost veterans.

For their services in connection with this raid, Sec.-Lieuts. B. H. Huggard and H. R. Newman were each awarded the Military Cross. Sergts. A. Loosemore, V.C., R. Wilson and F. J. Field received Distinguished Conduct Medals; and sixteen other ranks gained the Military Medal.

(d) Quiet Days in the Ypres Salient.

The night after the raid the Battalion was relieved in Brigade Reserve, and went to Siege Camp for rest. This camp lay on the east side of the Vlamertinghe-Elverdinghe Road. It consisted mainly of Nissen huts, but there were also a number of sandbag shelters and one or two pill-boxes. The surroundings were very pleasant. All the time the 49th Division remained in the Ypres Salient, the Battalion's rest periods were spent at Siege Camp. One period was much like another. Of the seven complete days out of the line, the first was devoted to baths and interior economy, and then three days were occupied with training and three were spent at work on one or other of the defensive lines in the neighbourhood.

All the work, of whatever nature, was allotted by tasks. If the men could finish in two days, they had a day off. But the tasks were heavy. Some very good work indeed was done by the Battalion during these rest periods, and, looking back now, it seems a pity that all this work was unnecessary; for none of the lines, so carefully constructed and strongly fortified, ever had to be held against an enemy attack.

Training was carried out mainly under company arrangements, but, on one or two occasions, battalion schemes were worked out, particularly one in which the Vlamertinghe Line was used as an objective. The Battalion had its own miniature rifle range and its own football field. The latter was much used. Not many hundred yards away was a Belgian detention camp, with the officers and N.C.O's of which the Battalion was on very good terms. Enemy shelling was not serious. There was a good deal of searching for the many gun positions which covered the area, but it was seldom that shells dropped dangerously near Siege Camp. One unlucky shot severely wounded Sec.-Lieut. A. Charlesworth during a tactical tour.

The main form of relaxation was dancing. For this the Battalion band was in nightly demand, and the absence of ladies did not interfere with the enjoyment. The first dance hall was an old ammunition store, the floor being covered with a large tarpaulin. When this store was pulled down, the band was ejected from a wooden platform which had been built for it near the orderly room, and had to perform on the bare earth while the dancers monopolised the floor. All ranks took part; the Regimental Sergeant Major could usually be seen affectionately encircling the waist of a signaller, while the Medical Officer and others have been known to grace the floor.

Gradually the nightmare of the enemy offensive was passing away. At first the days were full of rumours and alarms. Most elaborate defence schemes had been worked out, and heavy artillery counter-preparations were common at night, and in the early morning. Reports came through of the attacks on the French down south, but it gradually became clear that the enemy's power of attack was being worn out. From the first news of his attack on July 15th, it was obvious that little success had been gained. Then, three days later, came word of Marshal Foch's great counter-stroke on the flank, which not only robbed the Germans of the little ground they had gained south of the Marne, but drove them headlong to the Vesle. Almost at once everyone realised that the danger was past, and that soon it would be the turn of the British to attack. But this is anticipating.

On June 29th the Battalion returned to the line, relieving the 1/7th Battalion West Yorkshire Regt. This time it was holding the right of the Left Brigade Sector. The front extended from near White Chateau to the vicinity of Dragoon Farm. It was held by three companies, each having its platoons distributed

QUIET DAYS IN THE YPRES SALIENT

in depth in three lines. The fourth company was in battalion reserve, occupying a line in front of the civilian cemetery near the Menin Gate—the cemetery in which lie the remains of Prince Maurice of Battenberg. Battalion H.Q. occupied the old divisional H.Q. near the Menin Gate.

For sixteen continuous days the Battalion held this front. It was the longest unbroken trench tour that it had ever done, and most men were heartily sick of it by the time it came to an end. The tour was not particularly exciting. The enemy remained quiet, and, until the last few days, little but defensive patrolling was done. Almost nightly raids by the 148th Infantry Brigade had put the enemy so much on the alert that there was little hope of success for minor enterprises. During the last few days patrols became more active. Early one morning Sec.-Lieut. J. W. Entwhistle penetrated deeply into No Man's Land and located some enemy posts, which he believed were held at night. The following evening he took out a fighting patrol, hoping to occupy these posts before the enemy arrived. But he was not early enough. The Germans were there first, were thoroughly alert, and received him with a hail of machine gun bullets. Fortunately he succeeded in withdrawing without casualties. It was afterwards thought that the enemy might have discovered the visit paid to his posts in the early morning, owing to the removal of " souvenirs " by members of the British patrol. On another occasion Sec.-Lieut. J. A. Steele occupied West Farm, a ruined building about 500 yards out in No Man's Land, for a whole day, with no result, except that his party suffered torments from the bites of the horse flies which swarmed in the long grass. On the night of July 9/10th there was a terrific thunderstorm, with drenching rain. One platoon, which was carrying R.E. material up to the front line along F Track—the left boundary of the Battalion sub-sector—was struck by lightning. Two men were killed instantly, but the rest, though thrown violently to the ground, escaped with a severe shaking.

Messenger dogs were in use on this sector and some were even stationed at Company H.Q. This gave an opportunity to the sporting spirits among the officers, who backed their dogs to arrive with messages first. For some time the same dog always won, and by so big a margin that no one could understand the reason. At length the mystery was solved. A sentry had made friends with the losing dog, which was in the habit of stopping daily to see him when it passed his post.

The most important feature of this long tour was the appearance of American troops. The 30th Division of the American Expeditionary Force had been attached to the 49th and 33rd Divisions for instruction. This division was recruited entirely from North and South Carolina and Tennessee. Some of its companies boasted continuity from units of the Confederate Army in the American Civil War, and many of the officers and men were descendants of those who had fought under Lee and Jackson; indeed, the Intelligence Officer of one of the regiments of this division was a grandson of General Robert E. Lee. Physically the men were very fine, and the standard of education among them was very high. They were mostly recruited from agricultural districts, and were magnificent rifle shots. During the tour many officers and other ranks—or, as they are called in the American Army, " enlisted men "—were attached to the Battalion for instruction in trench duties. They proved themselves very keen to learn, and the Battalion got on well with them.

On July 15th the Battalion went back for its second period of rest at Siege Camp. After eight days it went into brigade reserve to the Right Sector. But the same night, before the relief was carried out, the men were engaged in an operation of, to them, an entirely new type. This operation was always known as Scheme B. It was a cloud gas discharge, and was to be carried out as follows :—

1. Nine light railway trains, each consisting of seven trucks, all loaded with gas cylinders, were to be brought up to Austral Dump by light engines. Here they were to be taken over by the Battalion, six men to a truck, and pushed out into No Man's Land in front of White Chateau, along an old light railway which ran there.

2. The men were then to withdraw into the support line, and the gas from all the cylinders was to be discharged simultaneously by a system of detonators, exploded electrically.

QUIET DAYS IN THE YPRES SALIENT

3. When sufficient time had been allowed for the gas to clear, the men were to go out again and push the trucks back to Austral Dump, where they would be taken charge of by the light railway men again.

The Battalion's part in the operation sounded simple, but it was to prove far otherwise.

On the night of July 23/24th the Battalion was brought up by light railway trains to near Ypres, and marched from there to Austral Dump. The first part of the operation went off smoothly. Apart from one burst of enemy machine gun fire, which wounded two men at Austral Dump, nothing exciting happened. The trains were pushed into position in No Man's Land without great difficulty, and the men withdrew according to plan. The gas was liberated and a dense white cloud floated slowly across No Man's Land. The enemy made no sign. Fifteen minutes after the discharge, the men went out again to remove the trucks. Then the trouble began. The trucks should have been much lighter after the discharge, but they were undoubtedly much harder to push. The air was thick with the gas, but so hard was the work that respirators could not be worn properly, and most men simply had the nose-clip and mouth piece adjusted. The oil of the wheels was clogged by the gas, the ground was slippery from the recent rains and afforded little foothold, and there was not sufficient room to move properly between the railway line and the barbed wire fences beside it. The first part of the way was up an incline, and trucks were continually derailed. To get these latter on to the lines again, the cylinders had to be unloaded, and then replaced. It was found impossible to move whole trains, and trucks had to be uncoupled, and pushed in twos and threes. Even then they could only be moved by officers and N.C.O's shouting to the men to "heave," as in a tug-of-war. It was almost daylight before the last trucks crossed the British front line. Every man was thoroughly exhausted, and many were suffering more or less from the effects of the gas. It had been a terribly anxious time for the Commanding Officer, who had himself been working as hard as anyone.

Strange to say, through it all the enemy remained completely inactive. The moon was very bright, and the noise must have been audible several hundreds of yards away. Yet, not a shot was fired; not a shell burst anywhere near. Could the gas have had so deadly an effect? Little was ever heard of the result of the operation. Patrols reported many dead rats in No Man's Land. Later, prisoners from the 6th Cavalry Division, which relieved the 1st Landwehr Division, spoke vaguely of the latter having been withdrawn owing to the use of a new gas by the British. But nothing more definite was ever learned by the Battalion.

After nine days in Brigade Reserve, the Battalion again took over the Zillebeke Sector, this time relieving the 2nd Battalion, 118th Regiment of the 30th American Division. This Division was now undergoing the last stage of its instruction, and during the whole tour the Battalion had an American company in the line with it. Each company came in for three days, the system of instruction being as follows :—

1st Day : Every American officer and other rank was attached to his British " opposite number," went with him everywhere, and shared all his duties.

2nd Day : An American platoon, under its own officer, relieved one British platoon in each company, and for twenty-four hours worked under the orders of the British company commander. The American platoons, during this time, carried out exactly the same duties as the British would have done had they been there.

3rd Day : The four American platoons were again concentrated under their own company commander, and relieved one of the British companies in the front line. For twenty-four hours the American company was responsible for its sector, and carried on the usual work, patrols, sentry duties, etc.

It will thus be seen that, quite early, American troops were placed in more responsible positions than the Portuguese had been, when they were undergoing similar training. Throughout this tour Major Callen, the Commanding Officer of the 3rd Battalion, 117th Regiment, whose companies were in the line, lived at the 4th Battalion H.Q.

Several minor events marked the tour. On August 3rd the

dugouts along the west side of Zillebeke Lake were heavily shelled, and B Company H.Q. was demolished. This was believed to be a result of the unusual movement caused by the American troops. It was the custom at this time for all front line troops to move about two hundred yards into No Man's Land early in the morning, and remain there until nearly dawn. This was done to avoid the enemy barrage, which would be put down on the British front line if an attack were intended. But apparently the enemy discovered this manœuvre, for he began to shell No Man's Land in the early morning, and several casualties were suffered. A relief too had taken place opposite. The 1st Landwehr Division had gone and the 6th Cavalry Division, which had been dismounted for some time and had seen service as infantry in Alsace, was holding the front. These troops proved to be of much higher morale, and stubbornly resisted all attempts to secure prisoners. But, the last morning the Battalion was in the line, a young Dragoon was captured near Moated Grange, by two officers of A Company.

On the night of August 7/8th the 3rd Battalion, 117th American Infantry Regt., relieved the Battalion, taking over the line completely for forty-eight hours. After one night in the Brielen Line the Battalion went back to Siege Camp for the third and last time. Its stay in the Ypres Salient was nearly over. It again held the line from August 16th to August 20th, but, on the latter date, it was relieved by the 5th Battalion Argyle and Sutherland Highlanders (34th Division), and, moving back to a camp near Oosthoek, said good-bye to the Ypres Salient for ever.

CHAPTER XIII.

THE LAST STAGE.

(a) Movements and Training.

ON the 23rd of August the Battalion moved by light railway to Proven, and from thence by train to Audruicq. From there it marched to billets in Nielles-lez-Ardres—some of the finest it had ever occupied. The weather was glorious, the country delightful, and a pleasant spell of rest and training was anticipated. But great events were happening in the south. On August 8th the Fourth Army, with a French army on its right, had started a brilliant offensive south of the Somme; when the situation became more or less stationary there, the Third Army had taken up the attack further north; and now it was time for the First Army to play its part. Fresh troops were needed and the 49th Division was ordered south. Moving from Nortkerque to Wavrans by train, the Battalion went into billets at Siracourt and Beauvois. There it had its first experience of training with tanks. A few days later it bussed to Camblain L'Abbé, where it occupied a hutment camp for nearly a fortnight.

At Camblain L'Abbé Brig.-General C. G. Lewes, C.M.G., D.S.O., left the Brigade which he had commanded for almost exactly two years. He had come to it in the latter days of the Somme battle, but was now appointed to a home command. He had been a good friend to the Battalion and there were many regrets when it paraded to say farewell. The men were drawn up in a hollow square and addressed by the G.O.C., who thanked them for their loyal support in the past and wished them the best of luck in the future. He left amid ringing cheers. Brig.-General H. H. S. Morant, D.S.O., who had formerly commanded a Brigade of the 1st Division, assumed command of the 147th Infantry Brigade.

The time at Camblain L'Abbé was well and pleasantly spent. Much training in the attack was carried out under the supervision of the new Brigadier. Various divisional concert parties at the Corps Theatre provided welcome relaxation; and the excellent Officers' Club, under the management of the Canadian E.F.C., was well patronised. Perhaps the most criticised part of the local arrangements was the exceptionally hard type of wire bed in use in the camp ; all who slept there will remember these.

On September 13th the 49th Division took over the line immediately north of the River Scarpe, and the Battalion moved to Roclincourt, where it was in divisional reserve. Time still passed pleasantly. Tanks were again to the fore in training. An inter-company Rugby football competition was played, and provoked much enthusiasm. The 147th Infantry Brigade never went into the front line here. After about ten days, the 49th Division was relieved by the 51st Division, and the Battalion moved to Feuchy.

" Old timers " saw in Feuchy some resemblance to the Johnstone's Post of Somme memory—but without the shelling. There was the same chalk soil, and similar shelters and dugouts were built on the sides of a similar valley. Accommodation was not of the best. Feuchy was in the middle of the country over which the battle of Arras had been fought in 1917, and the Battalion area was almost where the British front line had been for about five months of the summer of 1918 ; so good billets could hardly be expected. On the whole the weather was good, and the neighbourhood ideal for training. The River Scarpe, with its surrounding marshes, was useful, not only for swimming, but more than once for the working out of bridge-head schemes. One night all officers and platoon sergeants carried out a rather intricate compass march which will not soon be forgotten, particularly by those who, at one point, found themselves sitting on horses' backs in a wide trench. Altogether the time at Feuchy passed very happily.

Meanwhile, things were moving so quickly that, almost daily, one looked for fresh victories. On August 26th the First Army had attacked on both sides of the Scarpe and on that, and the following days, the British line had been pushed forward some miles, particularly south of the river. On September 2nd the Canadian Corps had broken right through the famous Drocourt—Queant Line, south of the river, and had pushed on almost to the Canal du Nord. On September 27th the passage of that great obstacle was forced, and, during the next few days, the high ground to the north of Cambrai was seized and held after terrific fighting.

The time had come for the 49th Division to play its part in the final adventure. On October 6th came the orders to move. When, late in the afternoon, B Echelon, under the command of Major W. C. Fenton, M.C., marched out en route for the Divisional Reception Camp at Mont St. Eloi, the Battalion knew that at last it was for battle; and perhaps, during all its years of active service, it had never been fitter. An hour or two later the Battalion,* over 650 strong, moved off and, in the darkness, bussed through the historic Queant—the pivotal point of the Hindenburg Line—to the neighbourhood of Buissy, where it bivouaced. For two days it lay idle. Its exact role had not yet been definitely settled. So unlikely did a move seem on the morning of October 9th that the adjutant, and most of the company commanders, rode up to reconnoitre the forward area. They rode on and on, until they came to the point where they expected to find the front line; it was occupied by a battery of 6-inch howitzers. Then they heard the news. Cambrai had fallen that morning, and the Canadians were already well beyond it. In haste they returned, only to meet the Battalion already two miles forward on the road. Beyond the Canal du Nord was a sight to be remembered by anyone who had seen the same ground on the previous day. Then the country had been covered with transport lines, the camps of ammunition columns, and all

---

*The following Officers and Warrant Officers went into action with the Battalion in October, 1918 :—

Battn. H.Q.: Lieut.-Col. A. L. Mowat, M.C. (C.O.); Capt. H. H. Aykroyd, M.C. (Adjt.); Lieut. P. G. Bales (I.O.); Lieut. H. A. Loudoun (Sig. O.); Capt. F. C. Harrison, R.A.M.C. (M.O.).
R.S.M. W. Lee, M.C.

A Company: Capt. A. Kirk, M.C. (O.C. Company); Sec.-Lieut. J. E. Bentley; Sec.-Lieut. T. E. Jessop; Sec.-Lieut. H. M. Marsden.
Sergt. W. D. Foster (A/C.S.M.).

B Company: Capt. W. Grantham (O.C. Company); Sec.-Lieut. H. Bamforth; Sec.-Lieut. R. E. Jones; Sec.-Lieut. A. F. Wenham-Goode.
C.S.M. H. Haigh, D.C.M.

C Company: Capt. R. B. Broster (O.C. Company); Sec.-Lieut. H. R. Newman, M.C.; Sec.-Lieut. F. Maley; Sec.-Lieut J. L. Hyland.

D Company: Capt. T. Hutton, M.C. (O.C. Company); Sec.-Lieut. J. W. Lumb; Sec.-Lieut. A. H. W. Mallalieu; Sec.-Lieut. H. Rosendale.
C.S.M. C. Naylor.

Lieut.-Col. A. L. MOWAT, D.S.O., M.C.

MOVEMENTS AND TRAINING

the details to be found immediately behind the line. Now it was deserted, save for the few odd men left behind to clear up. While over the hill in front, in that rolling grass-covered country, line after line and column after column could be seen moving slowly towards the east. The whole B.E.F. seemed to be on the march.

The night was spent in some deserted enemy shelters and dug-outs, in a sunken road to the west of Sancourt. Arriving after dark, there was little opportunity to make oneself comfortable. The following morning passed quietly but, about 1-0 p.m., came the orders to move again. Early in the afternoon the Battalion started. It crossed the Canal de l'Escaut at Escaudœuvres—the bridge had been in enemy hands barely twenty-four hours before, but he had left too hurriedly to destroy it. Yet he had found time wantonly to destroy in his usual manner; the houses were full of furniture senselessly damaged—chairs broken to bits, feather beds ripped open, crockery and glass lying smashed on the floors. An occasional shell was still falling as the Battalion marched through the village.

A halt was made by the railway embankment to the east of the village. Rifles were piled, hot tea was served, and the men lay down to get what rest they could. As darkness fell the scene was one never to be forgotten—the long rows of piled arms, the hundreds of men lying around sleeping or talking in whispers, the occasional glimmer of a light. It was a scene such as one sees in pictures of old-time warfare, and perhaps nothing showed more plainly that the long wearisome days of trench warfare were past. The stars shone brightly overhead and, to complete the picture, a small group of Canadian machine gunners sang song after song in the gloom.

(b) October 11th and After.

About 8-0 p.m. the Commanding Officer was summoned to Brigade H.Q. He was away for about two hours and, on his return, all officers were summoned. By the light of three candles stuck in the ground, he marked upon each officer's map the objectives and boundaries of the attack which was to be delivered the next morning, and then explained the plan of operations :—

    1. The Battalion was to assemble and dig in before dawn on the line of the Iwuy—Rieux Road, on a frontage of about 500 yards. The 7th Battalion Duke of Wellington's Regt., with its right on the Naves—Villers-en-Cauchies Road, would attack on the Battalion's right; the 146th Infantry Brigade on its left.

    2. A Company was to be on the right and D Company on the left. B and C Companies were to be in support on the right and left respectively.

    3. It was believed that the enemy was too shaken to put up a vigorous resistance. Hence it had been decided to attack without any artillery support.

    4. At 9-0 a.m. the attack was to begin, the first objective being the railway line midway between Avesnes-le-Sec and Villers-en-Cauchies, and the second objective the high ground east of the La Selle River.

The attack was part of a very big operation on a wide front and the task of the 49th Division was a most important one. Opposite to the Battalion's front, with its crest line about a mile from the assembly position, lay a long ridge. This was held by the enemy. The Canadians were to make an attack on the ridge that very night. If they succeeded, the Battalion would advance through them the next morning, and the first part of its task would be easy. But if they failed, the ridge must be captured by the Battalion, on its way to the first objective. *The ridge must be taken at all costs.* This was the definite order of the Divisional Commander. It was a point of extreme tactical importance, and its possession by the enemy was holding up the whole flank of the attack. Such were the orders issued by the Commanding Officer.

An advanced party was sent forward to reconnoitre routes to the assembly positions. Tea was served out and the Battalion waited only for rations to arrive. Time passed, there was no sign of the convoy, and the Commanding Officer became very anxious. It was imperative for the men to reach their assembly positions and dig in before dawn. The Battalion was on the point of moving off rationless when the limbers were announced. The delay had been no fault of the transport. Throughout the operations they always served the Battalion well. But the roads were crowded with vehicles of all kinds, and they had had to fetch the rations from a great distance. It was simply one of the difficulties which had to be faced in the new warfare of movement.

Shortly after midnight the Battalion moved off. It passed through Naves, which was thick with mustard gas, and was met about a thousand yards beyond by Battalion scouts, who had gone forward to reconnoitre the routes. Leaving the roads, companies crossed the Erclin River at points where the bed was dry, and moved independently to their positions of assembly. These were not reached without difficulty. The night was very dark and the ground strange. Troops of the 146th Infantry Brigade were using the same route, and there was some confusion. To make matters worse, the enemy put down a fairly heavy counter-preparation on the field which the companies were crossing, and about ten men were wounded. But, by 4-0 a.m., all were up and digging in. Everything was quiet when daylight came, and the hours dragged slowly on.

From the road on which the Battalion was assembled, the ground sloped gently upwards to the ridge, already mentioned. The land between was mostly under cultivation and afforded no cover to attacking troops. Near the top of the ridge was a stack of bean straw which formed a very useful landmark, as it was almost on the boundary between the two companies. The night attack of the Canadians had been unsuccessful and the enemy still held the all-important position. It was therefore decided that the first hour of the attack should be supported by a thick barrage. For half-an-hour this was to fall on the crest of the ridge; after that, it would move forward at the rate of 100 yards in three minutes for a further half hour. This information did not arrive at Battalion H.Q. until about 8-20 a.m., and there was barely time to inform the attacking troops before zero hour.

At 9-0 a.m., prompt to the second, the British artillery opened fire and the Battalion went "over the top." The advance was magnificent. Never, either in action or at training, had it been done better. In artillery formation, with sections in file and keeping perfect intervals, the men went quietly and steadily forward. If there were a fault, it was that of over-eagerness. The leading troops advanced rather faster than had been expected, and they were on the top of the ridge before their barrage had lifted.

Almost immediately the enemy barrage came down, consisting mainly of high explosive. Fortunately, the bulk of it fell just behind the assembly position and did little harm. Then the enemy machine guns opened, and these caused more trouble than the artillery. Sections were forced to extend in order to minimise casualties, but the rate of advance was scarcely affected. Near the straw stack on the hill, Sergt. A. Loosemore, V.C., D.C.M., of A Company, went down, shot through both legs; and the Battalion thus lost a magnificent leader who was liked by every one and almost worshipped by the men of his platoon. By 9-45 a.m. all four companies had disappeared from view over the crest line. The enemy's artillery fire had weakened considerably, many prisoners were coming in, in charge of lightly wounded men, and everything seemed to be going well. Battalion H.Q. moved up from the position it had occupied in the dried-up bed of the River Erclin, and temporarily established itself on the road where the Battalion had assembled. The Commanding Officer immediately went forward to the crest of the ridge to see for himself how the attack was progressing.

The Battalion was now meeting with much stiffer resistance and the advance had become slower. The British barrage had ceased and the enemy was better able to get his machine guns into action. Ground could now only be gained by infiltration, and by manœuvring sections round the flanks of enemy posts. Casualties were becoming heavier. At one point the attacking infantry came up against field guns, firing point blank at them. The 7th Battalion on the right was also meeting with strong opposition from the enemy in the village of Villers-en-Cauchies. But the advance still went on. The field guns were captured. It seemed as if the resistance would gradually be worn down.

Then, about 10-45 a.m., came the great enemy counter-attack. Appearing from the low ground to the south of Avesnes-le-Sec enemy tanks, eight in number, advanced against the attacking troops. All men of the Battalion agree that these tanks were of German pattern, and not captured British ones. The main force of their first attack fell upon the 146th Infantry Brigade on the left, which gave way before them and began to retire. Capt. R. B. Broster of C Company and Sec.-Lieut. H. Rosendale of D Company were shot down by machine gun fire from a tank, whilst trying to rally the left flank. Sec.-Lieut. T. E. Jessop of A Company, with the greatest gallantry, collected several Lewis guns and, by a concentration of their fire, actually forced one tank to withdraw. He was seriously wounded a little later and was carried to safety by the men of his platoon. An unknown man of C Company was seen running behind another tank, bomb in hand, trying to find an opening into which to throw it; he too was shot down. Capt. W. Grantham of B Company was so seriously wounded that he died a few weeks later—a prisoner in enemy hands. But all was of no avail. With its left flank "in the air," heavily pressed by the tanks in front, with no artillery—almost the only weapon which would have been effective—to support it, the Battalion began to withdraw. The withdrawal was slow and there was no panic. But all the hard-won ground, with its killed and wounded, its field guns and other trophies, was lost.

The Battalion halted a little in front of the road from which it had started little more than two hours before. All companies had become hopelessly mixed; the 6th Battalion, which had advanced in rear of the attacking troops, had become engaged, and its men were mingled with the men of the 4th Battalion. Furthermore, men from the battalions on the flanks had also wandered into the area in the confusion. The enemy, following hard on the rear of his tanks, had reoccupied the ridge, and was getting his machine guns again into action. His tanks, however, did not appear over the crest of the ridge; perhaps they were satisfied with the success gained, and feared to come into view of the British artillery. There was intense disappointment and not a little confusion everywhere.

Into the midst of this confusion the Commanding Officer threw himself. By his presence, personal energy, and utter disregard for danger, he quickly restored order. Time did not allow of separating the men into their proper companies, but officers and N.C.O's, assuming command of whatever men were near them, including men of other battalions, resolved confusion into order, disappointment into hope; and the Battalion was a fighting force again. Then it advanced to the attack once more.

This second advance was not so orderly as the first had been, but, in some ways it was, perhaps, finer. Without a gun to support it, through a hail of machine gun bullets, with men falling in scores, the line went forward. The Colonel led, his Battalion followed. "*The ridge must be taken at all costs.*" Those had been the words of the Divisional Commander the night before. And Lieut.-Col. Mowat and his men meant to take that ridge. Slowly, at first by section rushes and later, when casualties became heavier and heavier, by infiltration, they pressed on towards the crest. Conditions were much worse, in every way, than they had been earlier in the day. Losses were appalling. Sec.-Lieuts. J. E. Bentley and H. M. Marsden, both of A Company, with many N.C.O's and men, went down. But the advance never stopped. For a time the enemy maintained his position well, but, as the attack came nearer and nearer, his resistance began to weaken, and at length he gave way and retired. For the second time that day, about 1-0 p.m., the ridge was won. But at what a cost! Of the Battalion, over 650 strong, which had bivouaced by the railway at Escaudœuvres on the previous evening, little more than 250 remained.

The rest of the day passed comparatively quietly. The enemy made no further attempt to restore the situation, but any movement on the ridge was promptly shelled. There was much work to be done. During the afternoon the 6th Battalion was withdrawn to reorganise as Brigade Reserve. Companies were reorganised, their own men returning to them, and rectifications were made in the line. For a time there was some anxiety about the left flank, the next Brigade not being so far forward as the Battalion; this was, to some extent, met by sending up two H.Q. Lewis gun teams to strengthen that flank. In all this reorganisation Capt. A. Kirk, M.C., of A Company, was the right-hand man of the Commanding Officer. He established

OCTOBER 11TH AND AFTER

his Company H.Q. by the, now famous, straw stack, and exercised a general supervision over the whole of the front line.

When darkness fell the new line had been firmly established. Rain had fallen during the afternoon, all were thoroughly weary, and a deep sense of disappointment oppressed everyone. No one yet understood how great a success had really been gained; this it remained for the morning to show.

During the night active preparations were in progress for the advance to be continued the next day. The 6th Battalion relieved the 7th Battalion on the right, the latter becoming Brigade Reserve. Guns were pushed forward in the most daring fashion—some actually into No Man's Land—ready to deal with hostile tanks should they again appear. The advance was to start at 12-0 noon, under cover of a heavy barrage. In the early hours of the morning the enemy heavily shelled the neighbourhood of Battalion H.Q. with "whizz-bangs," but the meaning of this was not realised until the next morning. Actually, he was shooting away the ammunition before withdrawing his guns to the east of the La Selle River.

Next morning everyone was about early, though there was plenty of time before zero hour. The damp and cold of the night, and the discomfort of the narrow slits, which were the only cover available, were no inducement to late rising. The sun rose bright, but a thin mist hung about the ground. Preparations for the attack were leisurely made and the quietness of the enemy was commented on. But it was not until an officer's patrol had pushed far out in front of the line, and the Brigadier himself had ridden nearly to Villers-en-Cauchies, that the situation was realised. The capture of the ridge on the previous day had made the enemy's position untenable; he had withdrawn during the night, and all touch with him had been lost. Fresh orders were immediately issued—the Brigade was to advance at once, without any barrage, and make good the line of the railway which had been its first objective the day before. On the right the 24th Division had already started, and was well forward.

By 10-15 a.m. the Battalion was on the move. Covered by an advanced guard, consisting of the H.Q. scouts and the remnants of a platoon of B Company, it moved forward in artillery formation, two companies in front and two in support. The 6th Battalion maintained the alignment on the right, but some difficulty and delay were caused by the 146th Infantry Brigade, which did not move on the left until some time later. At first the advance led over the ground that had been won and lost on the previous day. Everywhere was evidence of the stern fight that had been made. The tracks of the tanks were clear in the grass, and the ground was strewn with the bodies of those who had fought and died. Only then was it realised how far the advance had, at one time, reached. The fate of many a man was cleared up. At one point a German machine gunner was found sitting behind his gun, dead; by his side lay the man who had killed him, also dead, with his bayonet right through the German's body. The inevitable " booby trap " was also in evidence—a brand new German machine gun, with a wire running from it to a spot a few yards away; but there was no time to examine the appliance.

On went the Battalion, across valleys and over ridges—and never a shell nor a bullet from the enemy. By noon the advanced guard was almost on the railway, but here the advance was again delayed for about half-an-hour. During the night the 51st Division had relieved the Canadians on the left, and was to have taken part in the attack timed for noon. Unlike the 49th Division its orders were not cancelled, and down came its barrage, promptly to time, a number of 4.5 inch howitzer shells falling about the area which the Battalion advanced guard had reached. However, about 12-30 p.m., the advance was resumed. The Battalion reached its objective, the line of the Avesnes-le-Sec—Villers-en-Cauchies Railway, without further incident about 1-30 p.m. Orders were issued for three companies to dig in on that line, with the fourth in reserve in a sunken road west of the railway.

Meanwhile, the advanced guard had pushed forward more than a thousand yards beyond the railway and had, at length, gained touch with the enemy. On approaching Vordon Wood, near the La Selle River, it was met by rifle and machine gun fire, not only from the wood in front but also from a small copse on the left flank. Numbers of the enemy were seen on the high ground south-west of Haspres. It was obvious from the volume of fire that the enemy was present in some strength, and that, without support, further progress by the advanced guard was impossible.

About 4 p.m. orders to advance and capture Vordon Wood were received. Half-an-hour later the Battalion, preceded by an advanced guard as before, moved forward. As the leading troops approached the wood they were again held up by hostile fire, and had to halt until two companies of the Battalion came up. The 146th Infantry Brigade had occupied Avesnes-le-Sec, but had not pushed far beyond it. As a result the small copse on the left was still held by the enemy, and seriously menaced the attack on Vordon Wood. To counteract this the reserve company, C Company, was moved up to form a defensive flank, facing north.

By this time darkness had fallen. The right of the wood was attacked, and was taken without much difficulty. The enemy rearguard did not put up much of a fight, but withdrew as soon as the situation looked serious, leaving two prisoners in the Battalion's hands. The wood, though narrow, was very thick with undergrowth, and provided excellent cover. Had they been willing to put up a better fight, the Germans might have caused far more trouble there than they did. The left, or northern, end of the wood lay outside the Battalion boundary, and no attempt was made to enter it until the next day. Dispositions for the night were taken up as follows :—

> B and D Companies dug in on the eastern edge of the wood.
>
> A Company was in support on the western edge.
>
> C Company formed a defensive flank, facing north, from the wood to the railway.
>
> Battalion H.Q. dug in on the railway.

During the night a strong fighting patrol reached the La Selle River and reconnoitred its banks for more than half a mile, without gaining touch with the enemy.

Early the next morning it was found that the enemy had been occupying the northern end of the wood during the night. A small party was seen to leave it in the morning and retire towards

Haspres. About 7-0 a.m. another party of Germans approached D Company's posts, but was driven off by rifle and Lewis gun fire.

October 13th was, more or less, an " off " day for the Battalion. At 9-0 a.m. the 19th Battalion Lancashire Fusiliers, with the 6th Battalion Duke of Wellington's Regt. on its right and the 148th Infantry Brigade on its left, attacked through the Battalion. The attack was unsuccessful. It came under heavy artillery and machine gun fire from the high ground east of the river, which was strongly held by the enemy, and was unable to make any progress. Throughout the day the Battalion maintained the positions it had won on the previous night. Several casualties were suffered from the defensive barrage put down by the enemy, among them being Capt. F. C. Harrison, the popular and cheery little Medical Officer. His slit in the railway cutting was hit by a shell, and he was so severely wounded that he died before he could be got to the advanced dressing station. Apart from this the day was uneventful, though there was one false alarm of tanks.

That night the ration convoy met with serious misfortune. Coming into the village of Villers-en-Cauchies, it was heavily shelled. Company Quartermaster Sergts. E. Walsh and B. Little, of A and B Companies respectively, were killed. Two horses were also killed, and the rations were scattered. Lieut. F. Irish, the Transport Officer, though himself wounded in two places, acted with great gallantry and coolness, and succeeded in collecting the rations and delivering them at his destination.

The next day was warm and sunny. Not long after dawn Sec.-Lieut. E. Maley, of C Company, was killed by a chance shell, in the rear of the wood, while he was taking round rum to his men. Since the 148th Infantry Brigade had come into the line it had pushed forward and secured the Battalion's left flank; but a gap still existed between the two Brigades, the north end of the wood being held by no one. As C Company was no longer necessary to form a defensive flank, it was moved up at dusk to occupy that part of the wood and fill the gap. The wood was very thick and tangled and bore evident signs of recent enemy occupation ; among other things, a tank had been hidden there not many days before.

OCTOBER 11TH AND AFTER

During the day, Major-General Lipsett, G.O.C. 4th Division, came up to make a personal reconnaissance of the front, as it was expected his division would soon relieve the 49th Division. He went right out in front of Vordon Wood, in full view of the German posts south-west of Haspres, was shot through the mouth by the enemy and instantly killed. His body was brought into the British lines by Lieut. J. Spencer, Intelligence Officer of the 147th Infantry Brigade, assisted by men of the Battalion.

On the night of October 14/15th the Battalion was relieved by the 1/7th Battalion West Yorkshire Regt. While waiting for the completion of the relief, Battalion H.Q. was surprised by the arrival of numbers of French civilians on the railway. They had escaped from the village of Saulzoir, had found their way through the lines, and were only too pleased to be at liberty again. What to do with them was the difficulty, and, in the midst of the excitement, the enemy opened upon the railway with mustard gas shells. This caused much anxiety for a time, but eventually they were got to the rear, apparently unharmed. When the line had finally been taken over the Battalion withdrew into divisional reserve, in the fields south-west of Avesnes-le-Sec, where there were some old enemy shelters and dugouts.

For two days the Battalion rested. Accommodation was very poor, but at such a time no one was particularly fanciful. What all wanted was rest—the chance of lying down without the probability of being awakened in a few minutes to stand to. For five days and nights there had been little rest for anyone, and all were thoroughly done up. There were no parades and no working parties. Sometimes the enemy shelled the locality, and a few casualties were suffered.

On the night of October 16/17th the Battalion went back into the line, taking over the front which it had previously held, with the addition of some three or four hundred yards on the right. Three companies were needed to hold this line, and even then it was very thinly held. Battalion H.Q. lived in the cellars of some houses at the east end of Villers-en-Cauchies. These were far more comfortable than the slits in the railway cutting had been, but they had disadvantages too, as the next night was to show.

Compared with the strenuous activity of the past week, the two-day tour which followed was quiet. Both the wood and the village were frequently shelled, and there were several casualties. But worst of all was the gas shelling. The night after the relief Villers-en-Cauchies was deluged with mustard gas. All the 6th Battalion H.Q. officers and details were gassed, and Major Clarkson, M.C., had to be summoned from the Divisional Reception Camp to take command. Over forty of the 4th Battalion H.Q. details were also so seriously gassed that they had to be sent down. The cellars occupied by the officers and the Aid Post were saved only by the lighting of great fires of straw at the entrance. Box respirators had to be worn for a great part of the night.

Nightly, the enemy was expected to fall back to a fresh rearguard position. Everyone was very much on the alert for signs of a withdrawal, in order that the operation might be harassed by a rapid British advance. The early morning of October 17th was very misty, the enemy was exceptionally quiet, and the Commanding Officer, who was up in the line at the time, began to fear that a withdrawal actually had taken place. About four hundred yards in front of Vordon Wood, and lying roughly parallel to it, was a sunken road, from which the ground sloped gently to the river. This Lieut.-Col. Mowat determined to reconnoitre in person, with the object of locating the enemy if possible. Setting out from the right flank of the Battalion with four others, he reached the road and proceeded along it. The mist had lifted considerably by this time, and, as the patrol came round a slight bend, it almost ran into an enemy post. Not more than fifty yards away was a German sentry. With rifle slung over his shoulder, and wearing greatcoat and soft cap, he was pacing up and down the road like a sentry in front of the guard-room. Fortunately, when first seen, he had his back turned, which gave the patrol a moment's grace. Withdrawing a few yards down the road, the men climbed the bank and made off towards the wood. The Germans, who proved to be about twelve strong with a light machine gun, opened fire, but their shooting was very bad. Retiring by bounds and covered by the fire of individual men, the patrol reached the wood without loss. Machine and

Lewis guns were immediately brought to bear on the German post, its garrison was driven from its position and retired towards the river. The encounter had established the fact that the enemy had not yet withdrawn.

Next day the Battalion was visited by Major-General N. J. G. Cameron. Usually sparing of words, he was, on this occasion, profuse in his congratulations on the success which had been gained. Particularly was he anxious that the men should realise how much they had done on October 11th—that their fearful losses had not been in vain, but had made possible a great British success. His views cannot be better expressed than by quoting his own words when he forwarded to battalions the congratulations of the Corps Commander, on October 13th :—

"It is with feelings of great pride and pleasure that I forward to you the attached copy of a message received from the XXII. Corps Commander. Evidence accumulates to show that your attack on the 11th October was a very real success. It cost the enemy heavily and dealt him a severe and much needed blow. It entirely turned the enemy's position at Iwuy, the possession of which was necessary to the further advance of the right wing of the First Army in the required direction. My heartiest congratulations to you all.

N. G. Cameron, Major-General,
Commanding 49th (W.R.) Division."

The Divisional Commander had only just left when the Battalion suffered another serious loss. The experience of the previous night had shown the danger of cellar accommodation, and it had been decided to return to the open. The few available men at Battalion H.Q. set to work digging slits in an enclosure not far from the building. Foremost among them was R.S.M. W. Lee, M.C., whose gallantry, tireless energy and exceptional strength had been conspicuous during the operations. While at work he was seriously wounded by a chance shell which burst near.

That night the Battalion was relieved by the 1st Battalion Royal Warwickshire Regt. (4th Division), and withdrew to billets at Naves. The relief was not carried out without loss. One party of D Company, while on its way out of the line, was caught by enemy gas shelling. Both Sec.-Lieut. J. W. Lumb and Sec.-

Lieut. A. H. W. Mallalieu were hit by fragments, the former so badly that he died in hospital about ten days later, while the latter lost a leg.

During the night the enemy carried out his long-expected withdrawal, so that the next day the 4th Division was able to push forward almost to the River Ecaillon. From one point of view this was very disappointing to the Battalion. After the hard work of the last week, and the gradual wearing down of the enemy's power of resistance, the men would have liked to reap the benefits themselves. Yet, by that time, all were so fatigued that probably they could not have taken such full advantage of the enemy's retirement as a fresh division was able to do.

While the Battalion had been in the neighbourhood of Villers-en-Cauchies the transport lines had been established near Rieux. Capt. H. N. Taylor who, though left out of the battle, had not gone to the Divisional Reception Camp, organised a party of men, consisting mainly of the Battalion Band, to search the battlefield of October 11th. The ground was gone over systematically, the dead were collected and were properly buried in a cemetery by the cross roads near Rieux. The cemetery is called the "Wellington Cemetery," and there lie the remains of most of those who perished in this series of actions. Their graves are well tended. French women of the neighbouring village have taken upon themselves the duty of paying this tribute to the men who sleep in their midst.

(c) Reorganisation.

For three days the Battalion lived in fairly comfortable billets at Naves. The village had not suffered very severely in the recent fighting and, since the enemy had fallen back to the River Ecaillon, was out of range of anything but long distance artillery fire. While the Battalion was resting there it was never shelled. The urgent business was reorganisation, for it was probable that the 49th Division would soon be back in the fighting line. Casualties could not be replaced, so each company was reorganised on a two-platoon basis. The loss of the many specialists, who had

WELLINGTON CEMETERY, Near ROEUX.

In the background is the ridge which the Battalion captured on Oct. 11th, 1918.

been gassed in Villers-en-Cauchies, was very serious. To a certain extent these could be replaced by the men who were at the Divisional Reception Camp, but even then the deficiency was great. However, what could be done was done.

On the 21st of October the Battalion marched to Le Bassin Rond, a small village at the junction of the Canal de l'Escaut with the Canal de la Sensée. Its appearance was not at first inviting. No one had lived there since the Germans had left it a few days before. The houses were all filthy and full of debris. However, a few hours' work made a wonderful improvement. The material structure of most of the houses had not been injured, and many wire beds and stoves had been left behind by the previous occupants. Before long the Battalion was comfortably settled, and a very pleasant week was spent there. The canals were full of fish, and one of the most popular forms of amusement was "fishing." The Germans had been good enough to leave behind them a large dump of hand grenades, and many of their "potato-mashers" came in very useful for this purpose. All the sportsman had to do was to drop a bomb into the canal and then select what he desired in the way of fish from those which came to the surface, stunned by the explosion. A fleet of small boats was collected, and, in the delightful autumn weather which lasted the whole time, many hours were spent on the water. A ferry was rigged up across the canal between Battalion H.Q. and the companies, and it became customary, when company commanders were due to attend at Orderly Room, for the adjutant and his understudy to defend the crossing. It was seldom that one arrived without a splashing. The Germans had also left behind them a plentiful supply of fuel, and " colliers " regularly plied on the deep, between the local " Newcastle " and the consumers on the other side of the water.

At the same time, much solid work was done. Everyone knew that, at any moment, the Battalion might be ordered to take its place in the fighting line. Already the 51st and the 4th Divisions had forced the passage of the River Ecaillon, and they were now facing the enemy near the left bank of the La Rhonelle River. Further north the Canadians, on both banks of the Canal de l'Escaut, had pushed forward nearly to the western outskirts of Valenciennes, where they were held up temporarily by the extensive floods. These floods made a direct attack on the town from the west extremely difficult, and it was therefore decided to outflank it on the south. To assist in this the 49th Division was ordered forward.

(d) November 1st—2nd.

On October 27th the 147th Infantry Brigade marched to Douchy, where it was billeted for the night. The next day it moved on, marching straight across the open country, to take over the line which had been established by part of the 51st Division. Here it was disposed very much in depth. The 6th Battalion held the front line to the south-east of the village of Famers, about a thousand yards west of the La Rhonelle River. The 7th Battalion was in support among the sunken roads to the south of Maing. The 4th Battalion was in reserve, occupying slits in the sunken road between Thiant and Monchaux-sur-Ecaillon, just east of the river. There was only one house on this road between the villages, but it had quite a good cellar. Of course this was allotted to Battalion H.Q., and, with the help of two large trusses of straw, it was soon made very comfortable. Round about were the wagon lines of several batteries, all camping in the open. During the first evening Major W. C. Fenton, M.C., who was commanding the Battalion in the absence of Lieut.-Col. A. L. Mowat on leave, had an unusual number of callers from the gunners. Each would drop in in the ordinary way, and, after a few minutes' general conversation of the usual type, would casually ask when the Battalion was going. Before long it dawned on the occupants that it was not so much their company that was sought after as their cellar. There were so many applicants for the first refusal that the Battalion decided, when the next move did come, to slip quietly away and leave them to fight it out among themselves. As events turned out, most of them moved before the Battalion.

The next attack, which was in preparation, was delayed for some days. Originally planned for October 28th, it was three times postponed for a period of twenty-four hours, and eventually came off on November 1st. The main plan of attack was as follows :—

1. The 49th Division, with a Canadian division on its left and the 4th Division on its right, was to attack in the direction of Saultain, force the passage of the La Rhonelle River, and outflank the defences of Valenciennes on the south.

2. On the 147th Infantry Brigade front, the 6th Battalion was to attack from a position south of Famers straight towards Saultain, with the 7th Battalion in support. The final objective for the first day was the line of the Marly-Préseau Road, south-west of Saultain.

For a time the role of the 4th Battalion was uncertain. At first it was feared the men would have to dump all arms and act as stretcher-bearers. But in the end, it was decided to keep them in Brigade Reserve, ready to exploit the situation should the attack go well. Preparations for this operation, and reconnaissance of the forward area, kept everyone fully occupied for the next few days. Only an occasional shell fell near, and no casualties were suffered.

Zero hour for the attack was 5-15 a.m. on November 1st. The evening before, as soon as it was dark, the Battalion moved up into the area south of Maing, where it occupied slits in the sunken roads. These had just been vacated by the 7th Battalion, which had gone forward to the neighbourhood of Caumont Farm, in support to the attack. Here the night was spent, the Battalion having orders not to move without direct word from 147th Infantry Brigade H.Q.

At zero hour the men of the 6th Battalion went forward under a splendid barrage. They crossed the river, partly on fallen trees, and partly over light bridges, which were carried forward with the assaulting troops by parties from the 19th Battalion Lancashire Fusiliers. They captured and held the Aulnoy—Préseau Road, which was their intermediate objective, and some of them even reached their final objective. But the 4th Division on their right had not been so successful ; after getting into the village of Préseau, it was heavily counter-attacked by two regiments of a fresh enemy division from reserve, and was driven out again. Thus, with its right flank uncovered, and having suffered heavy casualties, the 6th Battalion could not hold its final objective. Instead, it dug in on a line in front of the intermediate objective.

But the success gained was very great. Several hundreds of prisoners had been taken by the 6th Battalion ; indeed, the number of prisoners captured was almost double the total number of assaulting troops, on that part of the front. The first party to arrive at Battalion H.Q. was about 200 strong, and its size caused some uneasiness to the corporal and five men of the 4th Battalion, who were the only escort available. Really they had no cause to worry, for the prisoners were only too glad to be out of it, and all they wanted at the moment was to get well away from the fighting. As soon as they were marched off they started running at such a rate that the escort had hard work to keep up with them. These prisoners were a very mixed lot. Some were fine-looking men, but the majority were of poor physique, and the proportion of quite young boys was considerable. Perhaps nothing showed more clearly the straits to which German man-power had been reduced than the poor specimens who were captured from the 6th (German) Division—one of the active divisions which had invaded Belgium at the beginning of August, 1914, and which had been, throughout the war, one of the enemy's most famous assault divisions.

The 4th Battalion did not take any real part in the fighting on November 1st. Soon after 8-0 a.m. it moved up to positions of readiness near Caumont Farm, which then became Battalion H.Q. About the middle of the afternoon, when an enemy counter-attack was expected, two companies were moved further forward. But none ever came into action. A weak counter-attack did develop in the afternoon, but it was easily repulsed by the front line troops, who actually advanced their line some hundreds of yards as a result of it. The enemy indulged in some scattered shelling, mainly about the river, but no casualties were suffered by the Battalion.

It was expected that the Brigade would be relieved that night by the 148th Infantry Brigade. In fact, not only had all preparations been made for the relief, but practically the whole of the relieving troops had come up, and some details of the Battalion were on their way out. Then a sudden alteration was made, and a fresh attack was arranged for the next morning. During the night the 7th Battalion relieved the 6th Battalion in the front line, and the 4th Battalion moved up into support. A and C Companies occupied the intermediate objective ; B and D Companies were on the road just east of the river. The 148th Infantry Brigade relieved the 146th Infantry Brigade on the left. The objective was the final objective of the previous day.

At 5-30 a.m. on November 2nd the 7th Battalion attacked and easily gained its objective, which was not a distant one. Nevertheless, nearly one hundred prisoners were captured during the operation. As soon as news of the success arrived, D Company was pushed forward into some old rifle pits behind the intermediate objective, to be ready to assist should the enemy counter-attack. About 1-30 p.m. an urgent warning arrived—the R.A.F. had reported that the Mons—Valenciennes Road was packed with transport and guns moving west, and that masses of troops could be seen in the neighbourhood of Saultain ; a heavy counter-attack was expected. But nothing happened. The Mons—Valenciennes Road was crowded with columns ; but the R.A.F. had mistaken their direction. They were moving eastward, not westward. The enemy was in full retreat.

That night the Brigade was relieved by units of the 56th Division. As these intended to attack at daybreak, exact dispositions were not taken over, but troops were considered to be relieved as soon as others had arrived. For the second time within a fortnight the Brigade had just missed reaping the full reward of its efforts. That night the enemy retired well behind Saultain, and the " attack " of the 56th Division the next morning was little more than a promenade.

Perhaps, as the Battalion marched slowly through the night towards Haulchin, where comfortable billets awaited it, no one realised that he had seen his last fight—that so far as he was concerned the war was finished.

CHAPTER XIV.

DEMOBILISATION.

(a) Auby and Douai.

AFTER a night at Haulchin and a second at Douchy, the Battalion embussed for Auby. The road lay entirely through the country which had recently been evacuated by the enemy. Everywhere were signs of his occupation and departure. The route was necessarily a circuitous one, for there were many canals in the district and every bridge had been destroyed by the enemy during his withdrawal. Only a few temporary military bridges were in existence, the bare minimum necessary to supply the advancing British armies. Auby was almost deserted when the Battalion arrived, and, as it was a large village and the Battalion was small, there were ample billets. Like all villages recently vacated by the Germans, it was in a filthy condition; but the actual billets were fairly clean, having been occupied for a few days by troops of the 63rd Division. The church was in ruins, as was also the chemical works which was the mainstay of the place. But, otherwise, not much damage had been done, for there had been no protracted fighting in the district.

Reorganisation and training were begun at once. Though the Battalion was very low in strength, it might soon be called on to fight again. For fighting was still in progress, and, though the enemy retreat was quickly becoming a rout, few realised before the armistice how thoroughly beaten the Germans were. Only two platoons per company could be organised, but large drafts were hoped for soon. On November 8th the Battalion was inspected by the G.O.C., 147th Infantry Brigade, who commended it on its good turn-out, and also on its recent fighting record.

On the morning of November 11th came news of the armistice, which had been concluded with the enemy. Hostilities were to cease at 11-0 a.m., and all troops were to remain in the positions occupied at that hour. The news came rather as a surprise to most. Sweep-stakes on the date of the cessation of hostilities had been got up in the last few days by both the 4th and 7th Battalions ; officers of the former netted the proceeds of both. There was little time to make preparations for celebrating the occasion. At 11-0 a.m. the Battalion Band turned out and paraded the streets. A Battalion concert was hurriedly arranged for the evening and went off very well, in spite of the total absence of beer, which could not be procured in time. Brigadier-General H. H. S. Morant, D.S.O., was present, and said a few words to the men ; his pious wish that the armistice had been postponed a little, in order that he might have seen the Battalion again in action, was greeted with many cries of dissent. Though, of course, everyone was glad that the war was over, there were undoubtedly some who viewed the event with rather mixed feelings. To those who had lived for more than four years with the one great purpose of defeating the enemy, it seemed almost that the object of their lives had been taken away. And there is also a spirit of camaraderie and good-fellowship on the battlefield and in the trenches which no peacetime conditions can wholly reproduce.

The Battalion had come to Auby expecting to remain for, at most, a week or two. As events turned out it spent four months and a half there—by far the longest period it ever spent at one place abroad. The time was marked by few events of importance. Towards the end of November a draft, about 200 strong, arrived. This was rather a surprise, particularly as many of the men were farmers who, it was expected, would be in one of the earliest classes for demobilisation. Early in December it was decided to bring the Battalion Colours out to France, and a colour party* was sent to England to fetch them. The Colours had been deposited in the Parish Church of Halifax since the summer of 1915. On December 8th they were handed over to the colour party by the Rev. Canon A. E. Burn, D.D., after the morning service, and were safely conveyed to France.

*The Colour Party consisted of Lieut. P G. Bales ; Sec.-Lieut. T. T. Gilroy ; C.S.M. H. Haigh, D.C.M., M.M. ; Sergt. A. Meskimmon, M.M. ; Sergt. T. Chilton, M.M.

During the earlier part of December, ceremonial drill was the main occupation. On December 16th the 49th Division was inspected by the G.O.C., XXII. Corps, under whom it had served so long, though, at the time of the review, it was in the VIII. Corps. This was the first and only time that the whole division paraded together in France.

Christmas was celebrated with due honours. As was the general custom, the officers' dinner was held on Christmas Eve and the sergeants' dinner on Boxing Day, in order that Christmas Day itself might be wholly devoted to the men. A Rugby match between the officers and sergeants of the Battalion was played during the afternoon. The "form" of the officers was not very convincing; possibly this was the result of the festivities of the previous night. Altogether, the festive season passed very happily.

A few days after Christmas the 147th Infantry Brigade gave a "treat" to the children of Auby, and never until then was it realised how many youngsters there were in the village. Indeed, it was suspected that many had come in specially from the neighbourhood. A cinematograph show in the afternoon was followed by a tea, after which a real Father Christmas—the Medical Officer's store of cotton wool had been heavily drawn upon, and few would have recognised Sergt. E. Jones in the benevolent-looking old man—helped to hand out a present to each child. But the most striking event of the entertainment was the wonderful enthusiasm of the children as they joined in the singing when the band struck up the "Marseillaise."

Meanwhile, the Battalion had not been idle. Some work was carried out, trying to restore the damage done by the enemy in the district. Much of the country had been flooded and attempts were made to reduce the water, though without much success. Trenches were filled in, barbed wire entanglements were removed, and roads were improved. An area was allotted to the Battalion for salvage work, and a certain amount of useful material was collected. In connection with this work, a most unfortunate accident occurred early in December. During their removal to the salvage dump some trench mortar shells exploded, killing two men of A Company and wounding several more.

About once a week one whole company moved into Douai, which was about four miles away, to provide guards at the station there for forty-eight hours.

Some training was carried out every morning, and the afternoons were entirely devoted to games. The Battalion had a fairly good football field at its disposal, and this was in use every fine day. Much of both the training and recreation was in connection with the Divisional Competition, for the shield presented by Major-General N. J. G. Cameron. In these competitions the Battalion finished second, and was very unlucky not to do even better. Its greatest triumph was the winning of the competition for the best platoon in the Division. The Battalion was represented by No. 5 Platoon of B Company, under Sec.-Lieut. W. G. Bradley, with Sergt. F. B. Birtwhistle as platoon sergeant. After winning the Brigade eliminating competition with ease, this platoon came up against the platoons of the 1/5th Battalion West Yorkshire Regt. and 1/4th Battalion York and Lancaster Regt., winners in their respective brigades. The competition was most comprehensive and occupied three whole days. The platoons were inspected in drill order and fighting order; they had competitions in marching, firing with rifle, Lewis gun and revolver, close and extended order drill, ceremonial, and guard mounting. The competition ended with a small tactical scheme. Right from the start good shooting put No. 5 Platoon ahead, and it never lost this position, winning comfortably.

A Company won the Brigade inter-company Association football competition, but came down rather badly when it played a company of the D.A.C. in the divisional competition. Both Battalion teams reached the finals in the tug-of-war, but neither won. In the Brigade boxing championships the Battalion had two firsts and a second, but its representatives did little afterwards. About the middle of January several successes* were gained in the 147th Infantry Brigade Gymkhana. An officers' Rugby XV. was started and had great success, though most of the players had had no experience of the game before. The Battalion Rugby XV. was the best in the Brigade, but, unfor-

*4 Firsts; 1 Second; 1 Third.

tunately, the divisional Rugby competition was never played. Altogether, the Battalion was well to the fore both in military training and in sports.

With the armistice, the army education scheme was taken up strongly. The lack of trained teachers and the deficiency in books and stationery were serious obstacles, but they did not prevent a great deal of useful work being done. At least one hour a day was set apart for education, and classes were attended by everyone. General subjects were taught by platoon commanders, with the help of any competent N.C.O's or privates they could discover. Special classes were started in French and Spanish, mathematics and commercial subjects. Many lectures were given, mainly by outside lecturers; in particular, three lectures on the recent history of Egypt, which were given by the Brigadier and were largely based on his personal experiences, were much enjoyed. A Battalion debating society was started and had several successful evenings, the chief being a mock court-martial of "William Hohenzollern," carried out by the officers. Major W. C. Fenton's rendering of the title part, and Sec.-Lieut. R. M. Leddra's impersonation of "Little Willie," fairly brought down the house.

Reading and recreation rooms were opened in the village. The Battalion canteen continued its activities, but found the competition of the numerous estaminets which were being opened very strong. Whist drives were introduced and proved very popular; the Battalion was particularly fortunate in the receipt of large numbers of splendid prizes from the *Halifax Courier* Fund. For a short time an officers' club was in being, but it was not a great success.

The Battalion had not been long at Auby before the civilian inhabitants began to return. This had its advantages, but it had disadvantages too. On the whole the men got on very well with the natives, and the opening of shops and estaminets was very much appreciated. But, as more and more people returned, the billeting question for a time became rather serious.

Early in January demobilisation on a large scale began. Though much desired by most, this had also its melancholy aspect. It was sad to see the men, who had been so much to the Battalion, gradually melting away. Especially was this realised when a farewell whist drive was held on January 20th, in honour of Major W. C. Fenton, M.C., Sergt. F. Smith, and many men, who were to leave the next morning. Day after day, as one saw the lorry-loads of friends leaving for the Corps Concentration Camp, one realised how quickly a chapter of one's life was drawing to its close. By the end of February over 270 had left, besides a large number who had been demobilised on leave. Towards the end of February a draft of 8 officers and 169 other ranks left to join the 13th Battalion Duke of Wellington's Regt. at Dunkerque. By the middle of March the Battalion was but a skeleton, its effective strength being below 100.

On March 20th, what remained of the Battalion was moved to Douai, where the cadres of the 49th Division were being concentrated. Here the Battalion was soon reduced to cadre strength —4 officers and 46 other ranks. Before the cadre started for England it had been reduced still lower. Time hung very heavily on the hands of the few people who were still left. There were not enough to do any training, the necessary duties did not occupy much time, and there was practically nothing to do in Douai. Apart from one or two cinemas, and the estaminets, there were few forms of amusement. Even the strongest adherents of military life began to long for demobilisation. Almost daily there were rumours that the Battalion was to leave at some early date. But the weeks dragged on until May was past before the first move was made.

(b) The Return of the Cadre.*

*The cadre of the Battalion consisted of the following officers and other ranks :—
Lieut.-Col. A. L. Mowat, D.S.O., M.C. (C.O.).
Capt. W. N. Broomhead, T.D. (Q.M.).
Capt. P. G. Bales, M.C. (Adjt.).
Sec.-Lieut. J. A. Steele.
R.S.M. S. Flitcroft, D.C.M., M.M.
R.Q.M.S. P. Barker.
C.Q.M.S. E. Elsey.
Sergts. E. Ashworth, D.C.M.; E. L. Collinson; C. H. Shaw.
Cpls. J. W. Rider, M.M.; S. Barker, M.M.
Lance-Cpls. C. Walsh, M.M.; F. E. Thompson; A. Cobbold.
Privates N. Crowther, T. Langan, C. Charnock, C. Hipwood, H. B. Nelson, H. Pope, A. Tordoff, W. Steele, T. Walton, H. Wilkinson, H. Whiteley, W. H. Redman, F. Wade, F. Everett, E. Newsome, J. E. Walker, N. Rawson, S. J. Hawkes, H. Waite, C. Andrews.

On June 7th, after many false rumours and one lot of cancelled orders, the cadre at last left Douai. For the past month the weather had been very hot and dry, and it was a broiling morning when the Battalion vehicles and stores were entrained. The officers, with the loose baggage, occupied one of the well-known cattle trucks, which was made quite comfortable with a table, some forms and chairs; the men occupied third-class compartments. Early in the afternoon the train started. On the way to Arras a glimpse was obtained of the old camping ground at Feuchy. Then, circling round the ruins of Lens and passing Bethune and Hazebrouck, the cadre arrived at a siding near Dunkerque, just before dusk. The night was spent at what was known as the "dirty" camp—the blankets provided certainly deserved the name. The next morning the Battalion moved to No. 3 Camp where it remained for nine days.

No. 3 Camp was the centre through which passed all men and cadres on their way for demobilisation by the Dunkerque route. It was managed entirely by the 13th Battalion Duke of Wellington's Regt., so the cadre found itself in the midst of friends. Officers' and Sergeants' Messes were thrown open; everything that was wanted was immediately forthcoming, if available. Two very pleasant officers' reunion dinners were held in Dunkerque, and the Officers' Mess of the 13th Batt. Duke of Wellington's Regt. held a special guest night for the officers of the 147th Infantry Brigade. Altogether, the tedium of the stay on the coast was very much relieved. Strange to say, No. 3 Camp was pitched on the exact site which the Battalion had occupied in July, 1917. But how changed was the country! Then the Battalion had seen nothing but a flat grass patch and a waste of sand hills, on which to pitch its tents. Now the whole area was covered by immense camps, mostly of huts, which would accommodate many thousands of men. The time near Dunkerque passed uneventfully. The cadre remained there rather longer than was usual, partly as a result of a violent wind storm which delayed sailings for two or three days.

On June 16th the cadre sailed. The morning was spent in loading the vehicles on to the cargo vessel—S.S. "Clutha"—which was to carry them to Southampton. Among the loading

THE RETURN OF THE CADRE

party were several transport men who had assisted in a similar operation at Southampton, more than four years before, when the Battalion sailed for France. In the afternoon the cadre embarked on S.S. "St. George," and, about 3-0 p.m., the vessel moved away from the quay. Among her passengers was Capt. W. B. B. Yates, who had that morning arrived at Dunkerque on leave from the Murman Coast. Slowly the ship passed out of Dunkerque harbour and moved along the French coast, until opposite Calais. The day was perfect. A bright sun blazed down upon the deck, and there was scarcely a ripple on the water. Every now and then a fountain of water would rise at some miles' distance, followed by the sound of a deep 'boom,' as some mine was destroyed. Opposite Calais the ship turned north towards the English coast, and, in the early evening, the coast of France dipped from view, and all said good-bye to the land which held for them so many memories. A run along the English coast brought the "St. George," in the early morning, into Southampton Water, where it anchored off Netley until about 8-0 a.m.

Soon after breakfast the cadre landed at Southampton Docks and the work of unloading began. As the vehicles were slung by the great cranes out of the ship, they were run by the men into a large covered shed to await entrainment. A change had been made in the programme. When it left France, the cadre had expected to go to a camp at Fovant and remain there until stores had been checked over. But on arrival in England, it was found that only the stores were to go to Fovant, while the cadre was to proceed direct to Halifax. As soon as the vehicles were loaded the cadre might leave. Everyone worked with a will, and, by tea time, everything was on the train. Then all marched to Southampton West Station to entrain for London. While the cadre was waiting there, the train carrying the battalion's vehicles passed through the station on its way to Fovant, and a shout of unholy glee was the farewell of the transport men to their beloved (?) limbers. An uneventful journey brought the party to London where all spent the night at the Buckingham Palace Hotel.

Shortly after 3-0 p.m. on June 18th, the cadre reached Halifax. On the platform Brigadier-General R. E. Sugden, C.M.G., D.S.O.,

Lieut.-Colonel H. S. Atkinson, T.D., Lieut.-Colonel J. Walker, D.S.O., and many other old officers of the Battalion were waiting to meet the party and give it a rousing welcome. Outside the station was Sergt.-Drummer H. Deane, with a band which he had collected. A colour escort had been sent down from the depot of the 3rd Battalion Duke of Wellington's Regt. But, best of all, hundreds of demobilised men of the Battalion—the men who had made its history—had paraded there to welcome their old comrades. " Demobilised men of the 1/4th Duke of Wellington's Regt. rally round their old Battalion " was the inscription on the banner which they carried.

The cadre was photographed at the Station, and then it fell in and moved off. Notice of its coming had been very short, but the streets were gay with flags and packed with cheering crowds. Preceded by the band, and followed by the Colours with their escort and the demobilised " Dukes," who once again " moved to the right in fours," the cadre marched up Horton Street and round to the Town Hall, where it was welcomed home by the Mayor. The Commanding Officer thanked the Mayor for all the town and district had done for the Battalion while overseas, and for the day's welcome home. Then, turning to the men, he said farewell to them in words which all will remember :—

" The Battalion will now pass to another command, and I take this opportunity of thanking the men for their loyalty to me, to the regiment, and to the town and district they have represented. Those of us who have been spared to come through this great conflict hold a very sacred trust. We must ever remember the comrades we have left lying on the battlefields of France and Flanders. Let us try to prove worthy of their sacrifice. They have died that we might live ; and on our return to civilian life we must continue to serve our country, our town, and our homes in the same spirit of loyalty, cheerfulness and trust that pulled us through four years of war. If you do that you can look to the future with happiness, certain that your great efforts of the last few years have not been made in vain."

The cadre was then entertained by the Mayor at the Drill Hall, and afterwards the men dispersed to their homes for the night.

THE CADRE AT HALIFAX, JUNE 18th, 1919.

To Face Page 284.

The next day the men paraded for the last time and went to Ripon for dispersal. And when the time came to say the last good-bye there were many who regretted that, henceforward, their paths would lie apart. With the warmest of handshakes, and the deepest feelings of friendship and respect, we parted one from another, and the history of the 1/4th Battalion Duke of Wellington's (West Riding) Regiment in the Great War came to an end.

APPENDIX I.

ITINERARY OF THE BATTALION.

Date of Move.	Move to.	
4.8.14.	Halifax	Mobilisation of the Battalion.
5.8.14.	Hull	By train.
11.8.14.	Immingham	By boat.
13.8.14.	Great Coates	By march route.
15.9.14.	Riby Park	By march route.
17.10.14.	Marsden	By train.
5.11.14.	Doncaster	By train.
14.4.15.	St. Martin's Camp, Boulogne	By train to Folkestone; by S.S. "Invicta" to Boulogne.
15.4.15.	Estaires	By march route to Hesdigneul; by train to Merville; by march route to Estaires.
22.4.15.	Doulieu	By march route.
24.4.15.	La Croix Lescornez	By march route.
26.4.15.	No. 3 Section, Fleurbaix Sector	Relieved 3rd Bn. Worcestershire Regt.
29.4.15.	La Croix Lescornez	⎫
2.5.15.	No. 3 Section	⎬ Inter-relieving with 1/6th Bn. D. of W. Regt.
5.5.15.	La Croix Lescornez	⎭
8.5.15.	Croix Blanche	By march route.
9.5.15.	No. 3 Section	⎫
13.5.15.	La Croix Lescornez	
17.5.15.	No. 3 Section	
21.5.15.	La Croix Lescornez	
25.5.15.	No. 3 Section	⎬ Inter-relieving with 1/6th Bn. D. of W. Regt.
29.5.15.	La Croix Lescornez	
2.6.15.	No. 3 Section	
6.6.15.	La Croix Lescornez	
12.6.15.	No. 3 Section	
18.6.15.	La Croix Lescornez	⎭
25.6.15.	Sailly-sur-la-Lys	⎫
26.6.15.	Doulieu	
27.6.15.	Farms near Bailleul	
29.6.15.	Flêtre	⎬ By march route.
30.6.15.	Wood near St. Jans ter Biezen	
7.7.15.	Canada Wood, near Elverdinghe	⎭
8.7.15.	Lancashire Farm Sector	Relieved 2nd Bn. Royal Dublin Fusiliers.
13.7.15.	Canal Bank (Bde. Res.)	⎫
18.7.15.	Lancashire Farm Sector	
24.7.15.	Wood near Oosthoek (Divl. Res.)	⎬ Inter-relieving with 1/5th Bn. D. of W. Regt.
30.7.15.	Lancashire Farm Sector	
5.8.15.	Canal Bank (Bde. Res.)	⎭

APPENDIX I.

Date of Move.	Move to.	
11.8.15.	Glimpse Cottage Sector	Inter-relieving with 1/7th Bn. D. of W. Regt.
16.8.15.	Saragossa Farm (Bde. Res.)	
18.8.15.	Ypres Left Sector	Inter-relieving with 1/5th Bn. D. of W. Regt.
21.8.15.	Malakoff Farm (Bde. Res.)	
24.8.15.	Ypres Left Sector	
26.8.15.	Coppernollehoek (Divl. Res.)	Relieved by 1/4th Bn. Y. and L. Regt.
8.9.15.	Turco Farm Sector	Relieved 1/6th Bn. W. Yorks. Regt.
15.9.15.	Canal Bank (Bde. Res.)	Inter-relieving with 1/5th Bn. D. of W. Regt.
21.9.15.	Turco Farm Sector	
27.9.15.	Elverdinghe (Bde. Res.)	
2.10.15.	Camp near Woesten-Poperinghe Road.	
14.10.15.	Glimpse Cottage Sector	Relieved 1/5th Bn. W. Yorks. Regt.
21.10.15.	Canal Bank (Bde. Res.)	Relieved by 1/4th Bn. K.O.Y.L.I.
30.10.15.	Ypres Left Sector	Relieved 1/7th Bn. D. of W. Regt.
3.11.15.	Coppernollehoek (Divl. Res.)	By motor bus. Relieved by 1/6th Bn. D. of W. Regt.
11.11.15.	Ypres Left Sector	Inter-relieving with 1/5th Bn. D. of W. Regt.
15.11.15.	Malakoff Farm (Bde. Res.)	
19.11.15.	Ypres Left Sector	
23.11.15.	Malakoff Farm (Bde. Res.)	Relieved by 1/6th Bn. D. of W. Regt.
27.11.15.	Coppernollehoek (Divl. Res.)	
5.12.15.	Malakoff Farm (Bde. Res.)	
9.12.15.	Ypres Left Sector	Relieved 1/5th Bn. D of W. Regt.
13.12.15.	Malakoff Farm (Bde. Res.)	Inter-relieving with 1/6th Bn. D. of W. Regt.
17.12.15.	Ypres Left Sector	
20.12.15.	Elverdinghe	
27.12.15.	Coppernollehoek	
30.12.15.	Poperinghe	
31.12.15.	Camp near St. Jans ter Biezen	By march route.
1.1.16.	Houtkerque	
15.1.16.	Wormhoudt	
2/3.2.16.	Camps En Amienois	By march route to Esquelbecq; by train to Longueau; by march route to Ailly; by motor bus to Camps En Amienois.
11.2.16.	Picquigny	
12.2.16.	Molliens-au-Bois	By march route.
13.2.16.	Warloy Baillon	
28.2.16.	Right Section, Authuille Trenches	Relieved 1/4th Bn. K.O.Y.L.I.
4.3.16.	Bouzincourt	
5.3.16.	Authuille Defences	
6.3.16.	Mailly-Maillet	By march route.
29.3.16.	Harponville	
30.3.16.	Naours	

APPENDIX I.

Date of Move.	Move to.	
23.4.16.	Hedauville	By motor bus.
12.5.16.	Aveluy Wood	
1.6.16.	Martinsart Wood	
15.6.16.	Aveluy Wood	By march route.
20.6.16.	Vadencourt Wood	
27.6.16.	Senlis	
28.6.16.	Vadencourt Wood	
30.6.16.	B Assembly Trenches, Aveluy Wood	By march route, via Senlis.
1.7.16.	Crucifix Corner, Aveluy	By march route.
2.7.16.	Johnstone's Post	Relieved 1/5th Bn. W. Yorks. Regt.
5.7.16.	Right Sub-sector, Thiepval Wood	Relieved 1/5th Bn. D. of W. Regt.
7.7.16.	B Assembly Trenches, Aveluy Wood	Relieved by 1/6th Bn. D. of W. Regt. and 1/5th Bn. K.O.Y.L.I.
8.7.16.	Thiepval Wood, Right Sub-sector	Relieved 1/6th Bn. D. of W. Regt. and 1/5th Bn. K.O.Y.L.I.
11.7.16.	,, Bde. Res.	Relieved by 1/5th and 1/7th Bns. D. of W. Regt.
14.7.16.	,, Left Sub-sector	
17.7.16.	,, Bde. Res.	
21.7.16.	,, Left Sub-sector	Inter-relieving with 1/5th Bn. D. of W. Regt.
25.7.16.	,, Bde. Res.	
31.7.16.	,, Left Sub-sector	
6.8.16.	,, Bde. Res.	
12.8.16.	,, Left Sub-sector	
19.8.16.	Raincheval	Relieved by 9th Bn. Loyal North Lancs. Regt.
27.8.16.	Forceville	By march route.
2.9.16.	Martinsart Wood	By march route.
2/3.9.16.	Thiepval Wood, Assembly Parallels	For attack on German line.
3.9.16.	Martinsart Wood	By march route.
7.9.16.	Hedauville	
15.9.16.	Martinsart Wood	By march route.
16.9.16.	Crucifix Corner, Aveluy	
18.9.16.	Leipsig Redoubt (Support).	
21.9.16.	Leipsig Redoubt (Front Line)	Relieved 1/5th Bn. D. of W. Regt.
24.9.16.	Lealvillers	By march route. Relieved by 12th Bn. Middlesex Regt.
25.9.16.	Halloy	
27.9.16.	Humbercamps	By march route.
28.9.16.	Bienvillers-au-Bois	
29.9.16.	Hannescamps, Left Sub-sector	Relieved 2nd Bn. Royal Welsh Fusiliers.
3.10.16.	Souastre	Inter-relieving with 1/5th Bn. K.O.Y.L.I.
9.10.16.	Hannescamps, Left Sub-sector	
16.10.16.	Bienvillers-au-Bois	Relieved by 1/6th Bn. D. of W. Regt.

T

APPENDIX I.

Date of Move.	Move to.	
18.10.16.	Humbercamps	⎫
19.10.16.	St. Amand	⎬ By march route.
21.10.16.	Souastre (Bde. Res.)	⎭
24.10.16.	Y Sector, Fonquevillers	Relieved 1/6th Bn. W. Yorks. Regt.
30.10.16.	Souastre	⎫
5.11.16.	Y Sector	⎪
11.11.16.	Souastre	⎬ Inter-relieving with 1/5th Bn. D. of W. Regt.
17.11.16.	Y Sector	⎪
23.11.16.	Souastre	⎪
29.11.16.	Y Sector	⎭
5.12.16.	Warlincourt	By march route. Relieved by 1/5th Bn. Sherwood Foresters.
6.12.16.	Halloy	By march route.
7.1.17.	Berles-au-Bois and Humbercamps	By march route. Relieved 2nd Bn. Bedfordshire Regt.
10.1.17.	B1 Sub-sector, Berles-au-Bois	⎫
14.1.17.	Humbercamps	⎪
18.1.17.	B1 Sub-sector	⎬ Inter-relieving with 1/5th Bn. D. of W. Regt.
22.1.17.	Berles-au-Bois and Humbercamps	⎪
26.1.17.	B1 Sub-sector	⎪
30.1.17.	Humbercamps	⎭
1.2.17.	Riviére (Bde. Res.)	By march route. Relieved 8th Bn. K.R.R.C.
2.2.17.	F1 Sub-sector, Riviére	Relieved 7th Bn. K.R.R.C.
7.2.17.	Riviére	⎫
11.2.17.	F1 Sub-sector	⎪
16.2.17.	Riviére	⎬ Inter-relieving with 1/5th Bn. D. of W. Regt.
20.2.17.	F1 Sub-sector	⎪
22.2.17.	Bailleulval	⎪
26.2.17.	F1 Sub-sector	⎭
28.2.17.	Bailleulval	Relieved by 2/9th Bn. London Regt.
1.3.17.	Souastre	⎫
2.3.17.	Halloy	⎬ By march route.
6.3.17.	Neuvillette	⎭
7/8.3.17.	La Fosse	By march route to Doullens; by train to Merville; by march route to La Fosse.
9.3.17.	Senechal Farm (Bde. Res.)	By march route. Relieved 12th Bn. London Regt.
13.3.17.	Ferme du Bois Sector	⎫
17.3.17.	Senechal Farm	⎪
23.3.17.	Ferme du Bois Sector	⎪
29.3.17.	Senechal Farm	⎪
4.4.17.	Ferme du Bois Sector	⎪
10.4.17.	Senechal Farm	⎬ Inter-relieving with 1/5th Bn. D. of W. Regt.
16.4.17.	Ferme du Bois Sector	⎪
22.4.17.	Senechal Farm	⎪
28.4.17.	Ferme du Bois Sector	⎪
4.5.17.	Senechal Farm	⎪
10.5.17.	Ferme du Bois Sector	⎪
16.5.17.	Senechal Farm	⎭

APPENDIX I.

Date of Move.	Move to.	
25.5.17.	Estaires	By march route.
26.5.17.	Sailly-sur-la-Lys	By march route.
27.5.17.	Cordonnerie Sector	Relieved 2/5th Bn. Loyal North Lancs. Regt.
3.6.17.	Rouge de Bout (Bde. Res.)	} Inter-relieving with 1/5th Bn. D. of W. Regt.
11.6.17.	Cordonnerie Sector	
15.6.17.	Estaires	Relieved by 2/4th Bn. Loyal North Lancs. Regt.
18.6.17.	Sailly Labourse	By motor bus.
19.6.17.	Philosophe (Bde. Res.)	Relieved 1st Bn. Leicestershire Regt.
25.6.17.	St. Elie Sector	Relieved 1/6th Bn. D. of W. Regt.
1.7.17.	Tower Keep, Vermelles	Relieved by 9th Bn. Suffolk Regt.
3.7.17.	L'Epinette	By march route to Philosophe; by motor bus to L'Epinette.
13.7.17.	Mardyck Camp, St. Pol	By march route to Merville; by train to Dunkerque; by march route to St. Pol.
18.7.17.	Bray Dunes	} By march route.
20.7.17.	Ghyvelde	
31.7.17.	La Panne Bains	
3.8.17.	Lombartzyde Right Sub-sector	By motor bus to beyond Oost Dunkerque; by march route to trenches. Relieved 1/5th Bn. K.O.Y.L.I.
9.8.17.	Presque L'Isle Defences	} Inter-relieving with 1/6th Bn. D. of W. Regt.
13.8.17.	Lombartzyde Right Sub-sector	
16.8.17.	Oost Dunkerque	By march route. Relieved by 20th Bn. Royal Fusiliers.
17.8.17.	Oost Dunkerque Bains	By march route. Relieved 2nd Bn. Argyle and Sutherland Highlanders on coast defence.
27.8.17.	Surrey Camp	
29.8.17.	La Panne	
13.9.17.	Bray Dunes	
23.9.17.	Coudekerque	
24.9.17.	Wormhoudt	
25.9.17.	Buysscheure	} By march route.
28.9.17.	Audenthun Area	
30.9.17.	Longue Croix (Staple Area)	
3.10.17.	Clyde Camp, near Watou	
4.10.17.	Red Rose Camp, Vlamertinghe	
4.10.17.	Pommern Castle (Bde. Res.)	Relieved 1st Bn. Canterbury Regt.
5.10.17.	Front Line near Abraham Heights	Relieved 3rd Bn. Canterbury and 3rd Bn. Auckland Regts.
6.10.17.	Pommern Castle	Relieved by 2/5th Bn. Manchester Regt.
9.10.17.	Peter Pan	Attacked in support of 146th Infantry Brigade.
10.10.17.	X Camp, St. Jean	Relieved by New Zealand Div.

APPENDIX I.

Date of Move.	Move to.	
16.10.17.	No. 3 Area, Vlamertinghe	⎫
24.10.17.	A Camp, Winnezeele	⎬ By march route.
27.10.17.	Farms near Steenvoorde	⎭
9.11.17.	Canal Area, near Ypres	By motor bus.
12.11.17.	Swan Area, near Ypres	By march route.
19.11.17.	Anzac Ridge (Bde. Res.)	Relieved 1/7th Bn. W. Yorks Regt.
23.11.17.	Molenaarelsthoek Sector	Relieved 1/6th Bn. D. of W. Regt.
27.11.17.	Gordon House Area	Relieved by 1/5th Bn. K.O.Y.L.I.
28.11.17.	Vancouver Camp	By march route.
6.12.17.	Dragoon Camp	By march route.
7.12.17.	Keerselaarhoek Sector	Relieved 4th Bn. Suffolk Regt.
10.12.17.	Dragoon Camp	⎫ Inter-relieving with 1/5th Bn.
15.12.17.	Keerselaarhoek Sector	⎭ D. of W. Regt.
17.12.17.	Argyle Camp	Relieved by 1/7th Bn. W. Yorks. Regt.
18.12.17.	Halifax Camp	By march route.
23.12.17.	Molenaarelsthoek Sector	By train to Hellfire Corner; by march route to trenches. Relieved 1/5th Bn. K.O.Y.L.I.
29.12.17.	Garter Point (Bde. Res.)	Relieved by 1/5th Bn. D. of W. Regt.
4.1.18.	Infantry Barracks, Ypres	Relieved by 1/8th Bn. W. Yorks. Regt.
12.1.18.	Devonshire Camp	By march route.
26.1.18.	St. Silvestre Cappel	By train from Brandhoek to Caestre; by march route to billets.
5.2.18.	Moulle	By march route to Ebblinghem; by train to Watten; by march route to billets.
10.2.18.	Buysscheure	By march route.
11.2.18.	St. Silvestre Cappel	By march route.
21.2.18.	Infantry Barracks, Ypres	By march route to Caestre; by train to Ypres.
22.2.18.	Reutel Sector	Relieved 1st Bn. Otago Regt.
2.3.18.	Maida Camp	⎫
10.3.18.	Reutel Sector	⎪ Inter-relieving with 1/5th Bn.
18.3.18.	Westhoek and Railway Wood Dugouts	⎬ Y. and L. Regt.
27.3.18.	Reutel Sector	⎭
3.4.18.	Maida Camp	Relieved by 1st Bn. Leicestershire Regt.
9.4.18.	Camp near Reninghelst	By march route.
10.4.18.	Erquinghem	By motor bus to La Créche; by march route, via Le Veau, to Erquinghem.
10.4.18.	Nieppe	⎫
11.4.18.	S.E. of Bailleul	⎪
12.4.18.	Bailleul	⎬ By march route. (Battle of the Lys).
15.4.18.	S. of St. Jans Cappel	⎪
18.4.18.	St. Jans Cappel	⎪
20.4.18.	Mont Noir	⎭

APPENDIX I.

Date of Move.	Move to.	
21.4.18.	Mont des Cats	By march route.
21.4.18.	Poperinghe	By march route.
25.4.18.	Ouderdom	
25.4.18.	Millekruisse (Bde. Res.)	By march route. (Battle of Kemmel.)
1.5.18.	Millekruisse (Front Line)	
3.5.18.	Camp S. of Poperinghe	
4.5.18.	Road Camp, St. Jans ter Biezen	By march route.
14.5.18.	Camp near St. Martin-au-Laert	By motor bus.
19.5.18.	Road Camp, St. Jans ter Biezen	By motor bus.
22.5.18.	Penton Camp, Proven	By march route.
26.5.18.	Road Camp, St. Jans ter Biezen	By march route.
3.6.18.	Zillebeke Sector	By light railway to Vlamertinghe; by march route to trenches. Relieved 15th Bn. K.R.R.C.
11.6.18.	Bde. Res. near Goldfish Chateau	Relieved by 1/7th Bn. D. of W. Regt.
20.6.18.	Siege Camp (Divl. Res.)	Relieved by 1/5th Bn. Y. and L. Regt.
29.6.18.	Sector N. of Menin Road	Relieved 1/7th Bn. W. Yorks. Regt.
15.7.18.	Siege Camp	Relieved by 1/5th Bn. Y. and L. Regt.
23.7.18.	Bde. Res. near Goldfish Chateau	Relieved 1/6th Bn. W. Yorks. Regt.
1.8.18.	Zillebeke Sector	Relieved 2nd Bn. 118th American Inf. Regt.
7.8.18.	Brielen Line	Relieved by 3rd Bn. 117th American Inf. Regt.
8.8.18.	Siege Camp	Relieved by 1/4th Bn. K.O.Y.L.I.
16.8.18.	Menin Road Sector	Relieved 1/5th Bn. Y. and L. Regt.
20.8.18.	Wood near Oosthoek	Relieved by 5th Bn. Argyle and Sutherland Highlanders.
23.8.18.	Nielles-lez-Ardres	By light railway to Proven; by train to Audruicq; by march route to billets.
28.8.18.	Siracourt and Beauvois	By march route to Nortkerque; by train to Wavrans; by march route to billets.
1.9.18.	Camblain L'Abbé	By motor bus.
13.9.18.	Wakefield Camp, near Roclincourt	By march route.
23.9.18.	Feuchy	By march route.
6.10.18.	Bivouacs near Buissy	By motor bus.

APPENDIX I.

Date of Move.	Move to.	
9.10.18.	Sunken road S. of Haynecourt	⎫
10.10.18.	Railway embankment near Escaudœuvres	⎬ By march route.
11.10.18.	Assembly positions on Iwuy—Rieux Road	⎭
11.10.18.	Ridge S.E. of Iwuy	Captured in battle.
12.10.18.	Vordon Wood, W. of La Selle River	Following up retreating enemy.
14.10.18.	Area S.W. of Avesnes-le-Sec	Relieved by 1/7th Bn. W. Yorks. Regt.
16.10.18.	Vordon Wood	Relieved 1/7th Bn. W. Yorks. Regt.
18.10.18.	Naves	Relieved by 1st Bn. Warwickshire Regt.
21.10.18.	Le Bassin Rond	⎫
27.10.18.	Douchy	⎪
28.10.18.	Thiant—Moncheaux Road	⎬ By march route.
31.10.18.	Sunken Road S. of Maing	⎪
1.11.18.	Bde. Support near La Rhonelle River	⎭
2.11.18.	Haulchin	Relieved by units of 169th Inf. Bde.
3.11.18.	Douchy	By march route.
4.11.18.	Auby	By motor bus.
20.3.19.	Douai	By march route.
7.6.19.	A Camp, near Dunkerque	By train.
8.6.19.	No. 3 Camp, near Dunkerque	By march route.
16/17.6.19.	Southampton	By S.S. "St. George"; transport on S.S. "Clutha."
17.6.19.	London	⎫
18.6.19.	Halifax	⎬ By train.
19.6.19.	Ripon Dispersal Camp	⎭

APPENDIX II.

NOMINAL ROLL OF OFFICERS WHO SERVED WITH THE BATTALION ABROAD.

In compiling the list of officers, the following rules have been adhered to :—
1. In the case of officers who went out with the original Battalion, the rank stated was that held on April 14th, 1915.
2. In the case of officers who joined the Battalion after April 14th, 1915, the rank stated was that held at the date the officer reported for duty.
3. Decorations, a list of which will be found in Appendix V., have been omitted, except the following :—
    (a) Territorial Decoration.
    (b) Decorations won by officers before they joined the Battalion.
4. This record is a Battalion record. Hence, only service with the Battalion is shown.
5. The names of the officers of the original Battalion are marked*.

AKROYD, F., Sec.-Lieut. Joined, 25.11.17. Wounded near Bailleul, 12.4.18.

*ANDERTON, W. L., Sec.-Lieut. Bn. Bombing Officer (May—August, 1915). Killed in action near Ypres, 21.8.15.

ANDERTON, R., Sec.-Lieut. Joined, 14.8.16. Transferred to 2nd Bn. D. of W. Regt., 23.10.16.

*ANDREWS, M. P., Capt. O.C. A Coy. (May—August, 1915). Killed in action near Ypres, 14.8.15.

APPLEWHAITE, C. T., Sec.-Lieut. (6th Bn. Norfolk Regt.). Joined, 20.8.17. To hospital sick, 16.6.18.

*ATKINSON, H. S., Lieut.-Col. (T.D.). O.C. Bn. (August, 1914—May, 1915). To hospital sick, 24.5.15.

ATKINSON, R. B., Sec.-Lieut. Joined, 29.1.18. Wounded near Reutel, 16.3.18.

*AYKROYD, H. H., Sec.-Lieut. Bn. I.O. (January—September, 1916). 147th Inf. Bde. I.O. (September, 1916—July, 1917). To hospital sick, 12.7.17. Rejoined, 24.6.18. Adjt. (June, 1918—January, 1919). Second in Command (January—February, 1919). Left Bn. for demobilisation, 6.2.19.
Lieut., 30.5.16. Capt., 1.6.16. A/Major, 22.1.19.

BALDWIN, S., Sec.-Lieut. Joined, 21.9.16. Transferred to 8th Bn. D. of W. Regt., 26.10.16.

BALES, P. G., Sec.-Lieut. Joined, 21.9.16. Bn. I.O. (March—September, 1917 and May—November, 1918). A/Adjt. (September, 1917—May, 1918). Adjt. (January—June, 1919). Demobilised with Cadre of Bn., 19.6.19.
Lieut., 1.6.16. A/Capt., 22.1.19.

APPENDIX II.

*BALME, S., Lieut. Bn. Signalling Officer (1915). O.C. D Coy. (February—November, 1918). Left Bn. for demobilisation, 29.1.19.
Capt., 10.4.17.

BAMFORTH, H., Sec.-Lieut. Joined, 29.4.18. Demobilised on leave, 3.12.18.

*BELL, B. A., Lieut. Wounded near Fleurbaix, 26.5.15.

BENSON, G. W., Sec.-Lieut. Joined, 4.1.16. Transferred to R.F.C., 10.7.16.

BENTLEY, J. E., Sec.-Lieut. Joined, 29.4.18. Killed in action near Roeux, 11.10.18.

BESWICK, N.S., Sec.-Lieut. Joined, 22.6.15. Bn. M.G.O. To hospital sick, 15.8.15.

BIDDLE, V., Sec.-Lieut. Joined, 16.10.18. Transferred to 13th Bn. D. of W. Regt., 26.2.19.

BINNS, C. E., Sec.-Lieut. Promoted from the ranks; joined as an officer, 16.2.17. Wounded (gas) near Hulluch, 28.6.17. Rejoined, 9.10.18. Left Bn. for demobilisation, 7.2.19.
Lieut., 16.8.18.

BLACKWELL, F. V., Sec.-Lieut. Joined, 7.1.16. Transferred to 147th T.M.B., 12.8.16.

BLAKEY, E. V., Sec.-Lieut. Joined, 28.5.17. Wounded at Johnstone's Post, 4.7.16. Rejoined, 21.9.16. O.C. C Company (October—December, 1917). Wounded near Molenaarelsthoek, 27.12.17.
Lieut., 1.6.16. A/Capt., 20.7.17.

BOOTH, W. S., Sec.-Lieut. Joined, 25.5.15. Bn. Bombing Officer (1916). Killed in action near Thiepval, 8.7.16.

BRABHAM, J. R. S., Sec.-Lieut. (6th Bn. Norfolk Regt.). Joined, 20.8.17. Struck off strength of Bn. (sick in England), 27.1.18.

BRADLEY, W. G., Sec.-Lieut. Joined, 29.4.18. Left Bn. for demobilisation, 21.3.19.

BRICE, A. E., Sec.-Lieut. Joined, 16.10.18. Transferred to 13th Bn. D. of W. Regt., 26.2.19.

BROOMHEAD, W. N., Hon. Lieut. and Q.M. (T.D.). Joined Bn. from 6th Bn. Sherwood Foresters, 15.2.17. Demobilised with Cadre of Bn., 19.6.19.
Capt., 23.12.17.

BROSTER, R. B., Sec.-Lieut. Joined, 1.3.17. O.C. C Coy. (May—October, 1918). Killed in action near Roeux, 11.10.18.
A/Capt., 30.12.17. Lieut., 19.6.18.

BURGOYNE, H. E., Sec.-Lieut. Joined, 29.1.18. Wounded near Zillebeke, 20.6.18.

BUTLER, A., Sec.-Lieut. Joined, 8.8.16. Bn. and 147th Inf. Bde. Bombing Officer. Wounded (gas) near Nieuport, 10.8.17.

CAMPBELL, G., Sec.-Lieut. (4th Bn. East Yorks. Regt.). Joined, 18.9.17. Struck off strength of Bn. (sick in England), 30.8.18

*CHAMBERS, E. P., Major. Second in Command (August, 1914—May, 1915 and September, 1915—April, 1916). O.C. Bn. (May—September, 1915). Appointed Claims Officer, 49th Div., 3.4.16.
T/Lieut.-Col., 24.6.15.—15.9.15.

CHARLESWORTH, A., Sec.-Lieut. Joined, 29.4.18. Wounded near Vlamertinghe, 26.6.18.

APPENDIX II.

CHIPPINDALE, F. D., Sec.-Lieut. Joined, 19.5.17. Killed in action near Erquinghem, 10.4.18.
CHISNALL, F., Sec.-Lieut. Joined, 13.1.16. Transferred to 147th M.G. Coy., 4.2.16.
CLARKE, E., Sec.-Lieut. Joined, 29.1.18. Left Bn. for demobilisation, 18.3.19.
COPELAND, J., Sec.-Lieut. Joined, 21.9.16. To hospital sick, 19.11.16.
COURT, G. B., Sec.-Lieut. Joined, 28.12.15. Shell shock, 5.7.16.
CRICKMER, B., Sec.-Lieut. Joined, 29.4.18. Transferred to 13th Bn. D. of W. Regt., 22.4.19.
CROWTHER, G., Sec.-Lieut. Promoted from the ranks; joined as an officer, 14.3.16. Bn. I.O. and A/Adjt. (September, 1916—Mch. 1917). Killed in action near Hulluch, 28.6.17.
DENBY, I. C., Sec.-Lieut. Joined, 25.9.16. Killed in action near Hulluch, 27.6.17.
*DENNING, W. F., Capt. O.C. D Coy. (June—December, 1915). To hospital sick, 9.12.15.
DONKERSLEY, P., Sec.-Lieut. Joined, 19.5.17. Wounded near Vlamertinghe, 29.11.17.
DREW, E. B., Hon. Lieut. and Q.M. Joined, 25.11.16. To hospital sick, 31.1.17.
EADE, W. M., Hon. Capt. and Q.M. (6th Bn. Suffolk Regt.). Joined, 18.5.18. Transferred to 1/4th Bn. Seaforth Highlanders, 20.7.18.
EDWARDS, A. C., Sec.-Lieut. Joined, 28.10.17. Attached to 147th T.M.B., 6.5.18.
ENTWHISTLE, J. W., Sec.-Lieut. Joined, 29.4.18. To hospital sick, 25.9.18.
EVERITT, W. N., Sec.-Lieut. Joined, 13.9.15. O.C. A Coy. (December, 1915—September, 1916). Killed in action N. of Thiepval, 3.9.16. T/Lieut., 31.12.15. T/Capt., 24.6.16.
FARRAR, N. T., Sec.-Lieut. Joined, 17.2.16. O.C. B Coy. (June, 1917—February, 1919). Second in Command (February—April, 1919). Left Bn. for demobilisation, 3.4.19.
Lieut., 1.6.16. A/Capt., 12.7.17. A/Major, 7.2.19.
*FENTON, W. C., Sec.-Lieut. Wounded near Fleurbaix, 30.4.15. Rejoined, 8.1.16. Adjutant (February, 1916—June, 1918). Wounded on Belle Vue Spur, 9.10.17. Rejoined, 23.10.17. Second in Command (June, 1918—January, 1919). Left Bn. for demobilisation, 21.1.19.
T/Lieut., 10.2.16. Capt., 1.6.16. A/Major, 4.6.18.
FENTON, D. H., Sec.-Lieut. Promoted from the ranks; accidentally killed before commission announced, 8.9.15.
*FIELDING, T., Hon. Lieut. and Q.M. To hospital sick, 21.8.16.
FLATOW, E. W., Sec.-Lieut. Joined, 15.11.15. Wounded near Nieuport, 9.8.17.
Lieut., 1.6.16.
FLEMING, F. W. O., Sec.-Lieut. Joined, 25.9.15. Gassed near Ypres and died in hospital, 19.12.15.
FLETCHER, J., Lieut. Joined, 25.11.18. Transferred to 13th Bn. D. of W. Regt., 26.2.19.

APPENDIX II.

GELDARD, N., Sec.-Lieut. (6th Bn. D. of W. Regt.). Joined, 25.9.16. O.C. D Coy. (October, 1916—October, 1917). Wounded at Nieuport, 4.8.17. Rejoined, 11.9.17. Wounded on Belle Vue Spur, 9.10.17. Capt., 30.11.16.

GILROY, T. T., Sec.-Lieut. Joined, 15.10.17. Wounded (at duty) near Kemmel, 25.4.18. Transferred to 13th Bn. D. of W. Regt., 22.4.19. Lieut., 1.2.19. A/Capt., 13.2.19.

GRANTHAM, W., Lieut. Joined, 9.12.17. Wounded and missing near Roeux, 11.10.18. Died of wounds, a prisoner in enemy hands. A/Capt., 29.4.18.

GUMBY, L., Sec.-Lieut. Joined, 9.9.17. A/Adjt. (May—September, 1918). Attached to 147th Inf. Bde. H.Q., 13.9.18.

HANSON, H., Capt. (5th Bn. D. of W. Regt.). Joined, 23.5.17. Wounded near Vlamertinghe and died of wounds, 1.12.17.

HARTLEY, J. A., Sec.-Lieut. Joined, 22.6.15. Gassed near Ypres and died in hospital, 19.12.15.

HATCH, H. S., Sec.-Lieut. Joined, 8.8.16. To hospital sick, 3.12.17. Rejoined, November, 1918. Left Bn. for demobilisation, 3.4.19. Lieut., July, 1918.

HILL, G.M., Sec.-Lieut. Joined, 21.9.16. Transferred to 2nd Bn. D. of W. Regt., 23.10.16.

HINTON, W. E., Sec.-Lieut. Joined, 20.11.15. Wounded near Ypres, 11.12.15. Rejoined, 8.6.16. To hospital sick, 24.7.16.

*HIRST, C., Lieut. Bn. T.O. (April—August, 1915). O.C. B Coy. (December, 1915—September, 1916). Killed in action N. of Thiepval, 3.9.16. T/Capt., 22.1.16.

HIRST, A. E., Sec.-Lieut. Promoted from the ranks ; joined as an officer, 26.3.16. Killed in action N. of Thiepval, 3.9.16.

HIRST, W. L., Sec.-Lieut. Joined, 25.11.16. Left Bn. for demobilisation, 1.2.19.
Lieut., 1.7.17.

HOLME, R. E., Sec.-Lieut. Joined, 29.4.18. Transferred to 147th T.M.B., 18.7.18.

HOLT, J. W., Sec.-Lieut. Joined, 25.9.16. Transferred to 8th Bn. D. of W. Regt., 26.10.16.

HORSFALL, V. A., Sec.-Lieut. Joined, 15.7.16. Killed in action N. of Thiepval, 3.9.16.

HOTHERSALL, T., Sec.-Lieut. Joined, 16.10.18. Left Bn. for demobilisation, 28.1.19.

HUGGARD, B. H., Sec.-Lieut. Joined, 2.11.17. Wounded near Nieppe, 11.4.18. Rejoined, 4.5.18. Left Bn. for demobilisation, 2.3.19. Lieut., February, 1919. A/Capt., February, 1919.

HUTTON, T., Lieut. (M.C.). Joined, 19.8.18. O.C. D Coy. (November, 1918—February, 1919). Re-posted to 2nd Bn. D. of W. Regt., 12.2.19. A/Capt., 26.10.18.

HYLAND, J. L., Sec.-Lieut. Joined, 29.4.18. Transferred to R.O.D., 31.12.18.

ILLINGWORTH, A. C., Sec.-Lieut. Joined, 14.4.16. To hospital sick, 26.10.16.

APPENDIX II.

INNES, F. A., Sec.-Lieut. Joined, 25.9.15. Wounded near Ypres, 16.10.15. Rejoined, 23.10.15. Attached to 147th Inf. Bde. H.Q., 9.8.16. Killed in action in Thiepval Wood, 3.9.16.

IRISH, F., Sec.-Lieut. Joined, 28.3.17. Bn. T.O. (October, 1917—May, 1919). Left Bn. for demobilisation, 5.5.19.
Lieut., 25.7.18.

JESSOP, T. E., Sec.-Lieut. Joined, 25.5.18. Wounded in action near Roeux, 11.10.18.

JOHNSON, L. L., Sec.-Lieut. (6th Bn. Norfolk Regt.). Joined, 20.8.17. Wounded near St. Jans Cappel, 17.4.18.

JONES, R. E., Sec.-Lieut. (6th Bn. Manchester Regt.). Joined, 15.5.18. Transferred to 13th Bn. D. of W. Regt., 26.2.19.

JURY, R., Sec.-Lieut. Joined, 19.5.17. Wounded by enemy bomb at Dunkerque and died of wounds, 6.10.17.

KELSALL, F. H., Sec.-Lieut. Joined, 7.12.15. Wounded near Authuille, 29.2.16. Rejoined, 28.5.16. To hospital sick, 22.7.17.
Lieut., 25.6.16.

*KING, M. H., Lieut. Went to France as 147th Inf. Bde. I.O. and was extra-regimentally employed continuously from that time.

KIRK, A., Sec.-Lieut. Joined, 21.9.16. A/Adjt. (September—December, 1916). O.C. A Coy. (October, 1917—January, 1919). Demobilised on leave, March, 1919.
Lieut., 1.6.16. A/Capt., 28.10.17.

KITSON, J. H., Sec.-Lieut. Joined, 29.1.18. Killed in action near Bailleul, 14.4.18.

*LEAROYD, G. W. I., Lieut. Bn. M.G.O. (July, 1915—February, 1916). Transferred to 147th M.G. Coy., 4.2.16.

LEDDRA, R. M., Sec.-Lieut. Joined, 29.4.18. Transferred to 13th Bn. D. of W. Regt., 26.2.19.

*LEE, E., Lieut. Bn. M.G.O. (April—July, 1915). Killed in action near Ypres, 10.7.15.

LOUDOUN, H. A., Sec.-Lieut. Joined, 8.2.18. Wounded at Bailleul, 13.4.18. Rejoined, 24.5.18. Bn. Signalling Officer (June, 1918—February, 1919). Transferred to 13th Bn. D. of W. Regt., 26.2.19.
Lieut., 28.9.18. A/Capt., 6.2.19.

LUMB, J. W., Sec.-Lieut. Joined, 2.11.17. Wounded near Bailleul, 14.4.18. Rejoined, 27.4.18. Wounded near Villers-en-Cauchies, 18.10.18. Died of wounds, 30.10.18.

LUTY, A.M., Sec.-Lieut. Joined, 8.1.17. O.C. C Coy. (December, 1917—April, 1918). Wounded near Bailleul, 14.4.18.
Lieut., 25.4.18. A/Capt., 20.3.18.

MACHIN, B.M., Lieut. Joined, 29.1.18. Wounded near Bailleul, 12.4.18.

MACKIE, W. G., Lieut. Joined, 8.2.18. Wounded near Kemmel, 26.4.18.

MACKINTOSH, J. D. V., Sec.-Lieut. Joined, 28.5.16. Transferred to 2nd Bn. D. of W. Regt., 23.10.16.

MALEY, F., Sec.-Lieut. Joined, 30.4.18. Killed in action near Villers-en-Cauchies, 14.10.18.

MALLALIEU, A. H. W., Sec.-Lieut. Joined, 30.8.18. Wounded near Villers-en-Cauchies, 18.10.18.

APPENDIX II.

MANDER, A. E., Sec.-Lieut. Joined, 28.12.15. Wounded near Thiepval, 11.7.16. Rejoined, 8.8.16. Bn. T.O. (September—November, 1916). O.C. A Coy. (June—October, 1917). Killed in action on Belle Vue Spur, 9.10.17.
Lieut., 1.6.16. A/Capt., 10.7.7.

MANDER, P. G., Sec.-Lieut. Joined, 8.11.15. To hospital sick, 12.12.15. Rejoined, 16.6.16. Wounded near Thiepval, 17.8.16.

MARSDEN, H. M., Sec.-Lieut. Joined, 29.4.18. Killed in action near Roeux, 11.10.18.

*MARSHALL, E. N., Lieut. Wounded (at duty) near Ypres, 16.10.15. O.C. A Coy. (October—December, 1915). Wounded (gas) near Ypres, 19.12.15. Rejoined, 14.8.16. O.C. C Coy. (August, 1916—December, 1917). Appointed Chief Instructor XXII. Corps Lewis Gun School, 15.12.17.
T/Capt., 20.11.15. Capt., 1.6.16.

*McGUIRE, G. P., Sec.-Lieut. Adjt. (August, 1915—February, 1916). Attached 147th Inf. Bde. H.Q., 9.2.16. Returned to duty, 2.8.17. Attached Second Army H.Q., 19.11.17.
T/Lieut., 18.12.15. Lieut., 1.6.16. Capt., 12.9.17.

MEE, E. C., Sec.-Lieut. Joined, 28.12.15. Killed in action N. of Thiepval, 3.9.16.

MELLOR, N., Sec.-Lieut. Joined, 28.5.16. Transferred to R.F.C., 7.12.16.

MILLIGAN, V. A., Capt. Joined, 14.4.16. Returned to England, 24.6.16.

MORRISON, J., Sec.-Lieut. Joined, 30.9.17. To hospital sick, 25.4.18.

*MOWAT, A. L., Capt. O.C. D Coy. (April—June, 1915). Wounded near Fleurbaix, 3.6.15. Rejoined, 28.12.15. O.C. D Coy. (December, 1915—October, 1916). Second in Command (October, 1916—June, 1918). O.C. Bn. (June, 1918—June, 1919). Demobilised with Cadre of Bn., 19.6.19.
A/Major, 13.11.16. A/Lieut.-Col., 18.6.18.

*MOWAT, J. G., Sec.-Lieut. Bn. T.O. (August, 1915—September, 1916). O.C. B Coy. (September, 1916—June,1917). Killed in action near Hulluch, 27.6.17.
Lieut., 14.8.15. Capt., 1.6.16.

NEVILE, A. W., Sec.-Lieut. Joined, 17.9.17. Transferred to 147th T.M.B., 29.10.17.

NEWMAN, H. R., Sec.-Lieut. Joined, 2.11.17. Transferred to 13th Bn. D. of W. Regt., 26.2.19.

NORTON, S. R., Sec.-Lieut. Joined 29.10.17. To hospital sick, 16.6.18.

O'DOWD, M. C., Sec.-Lieut. Joined, 29.1.18. Wounded near Erquinghem, 10.4.18.

OLDFIELD, W., Sec.-Lieut. (M.M.). Joined, 20.9.17. Wounded near Bailleul, 14.4.18.

OLDROYD, W. L., Sec.-Lieut. Joined, 25.9.16. Transferred to 8th Bn. D. of W. Regt., 26.10.16.

PICKERING, E. J., Lieut.-Col. O.C. Bn. (September—October, 1915). Wounded near Ypres, 20.10.15.

POHLMANN, H. E., Sec.-Lieut. Promoted from the ranks; joined as an officer, 26.3.16. Wounded N. of Thiepval, 3.9.16.

POLLARD, H., Sec.-Lieut. Joined, 28.5.16. Wounded in Thiepval Wood, 14.7.16. Rejoined, 14.11.16. Wounded near Hulluch, 27.6.17.

APPENDIX II. 301

PRATT, L. W., Sec.-Lieut. Joined, 9.9.15. Wounded near Thiepval, 25.7.16.

*PRATT, T. D., Sec.-Lieut. O.C. D Coy. (June—August, 1916). Wounded near Thiepval, 18.8.16.
T/Lieut., 10.7.15. T/Capt., 29.12.15.

PURVIS, R. C., Sec.-Lieut. Joined, 6.9.16. Transferred to R.F.C., 30.4.17.

RAWNSLEY, E., Sec.-Lieut. Joined, 3.8.16. Transferred to 2nd Bn. D. of W. Regt., 23.10.16. Rejoined, 9.12.17. Appointed Instructor, XXII. Corps Bombing School, 15.2.18.

RAWNSLEY, G., Sec.-Lieut. Joined, 9.9.16. Killed in action near Berles-au-Bois, 22.1.17.

RHODES, C. N., Sec.-Lieut. Joined, 21.9.16. Bn. Signalling Officer (September—October, 1916). To hospital sick, 20.10.16.

*RILEY, J. T., Lieut. Accidentally wounded, 11.10.15. Rejoined, 29.5.16. Killed in action N. of Thiepval, 3.9.16.

ROBB, A. J., Sec.-Lieut. Joined, 1.3.17. Wounded (gas) near Nieuport, 17.8.17. Rejoined, 14.10.17. O.C. D Coy. (October, 1917—February, 1918). Wounded near Reutel, 19.2.18.
A/Capt., 14.12.17.

ROBERTSHAW, G. F., Sec.-Lieut. Joined, 28.5.16. Wounded N. of Thiepval, 3.9.16.

ROBINS, P. E., Sec.-Lieut. Joined, 2.11.17. Wounded near Ypres, 15.11.17.

ROBINSON, J. H., Sec.-Lieut. Joined, 25.11.18. Left Bn. for demobilisation, 21.4.19.

ROBINSON, O., Sec.-Lieut. Joined, 29.4.18. Wounded near Zillebeke, 5.8.18. Rejoined, 21.11.18. Transferred to 147th T.M.B., 27.1.19.

RODGERS, G., Sec.-Lieut. Joined, 25.9.16. Transferred to 2nd. Bn. D. of W. Regt., 23.10.16.

ROSENDALE, H., Sec.-Lieut. (4th Bn. East Yorks. Regt.). Joined, 18.9.17. Wounded (at duty) in Bailleul, 12.4.18. Killed in action near Roeux, 11.10.18.

SCHOLES, W. T., Sec.-Lieut. Joined, 21.9.16. Left Bn., for demobilisation, 25.1.19.
Lieut., 1.7.17.

SHAW, A., Lieut. Joined, 19.8.18. O.C. C Coy. (October, 1918—January, 1919). Demobilised on leave, February, 1919.
A/Capt., 10.11.18.

SHERLOCK, S. P., Sec.-Lieut. Joined, 21.11.15. To hospital sick, 1.12.15.

SIEMSSEN, G. H., Sec.-Lieut. Joined, 2.11.17. Wounded near Berthen, 17.4.18.

SKELSEY, R. M., Sec.-Lieut. Joined, 25.9.16. Accidentally wounded, 5.11.16.

SMETS, L. J., Lieut. Joined, 9.12.17. Bn. Signalling Officer (February—June, 1918). Certified unfit for service while on a course in England, June, 1918.

SMITH, W., Sec.-Lieut. Joined, 28.5.16. Wounded near Thiepval, 3.9.16.

SOMERVELL, A., Capt. (M.C.) (6th Bn. D. of W. Regt.). Joined, 29.11.18. O.C. C Coy. (January—March, 1919). Left Bn. for demobilisation, 20.3.19.

APPENDIX II.

ST. AUBYN, E. G., Lieut.-Col. Joined, 22.11.15. O.C. Bn. (November, 1915—September, 1916). To hospital sick, 1.9.16.

STANSFIELD, S. P., Sec.-Lieut. Joined, 26.3.17. Killed in action near Richebourg L'Avoue, 30.4.17.

*STANTON, H. A. S., Capt. (Royal Scots Regt.). Adjt. (August, 1914— August, 1915). Appointed Brigade Major, 147th Inf. Bde., 19.8.15.

STARKEY, T. P., Lieut. Joined, 28.11.18. Transferred to 1/7th Bn. D. of W. Regt., 5.12.18.

STEELE, J. A., Sec.-Lieut. Joined, 29.4.18. Demobilised with Cadre of Bn., 19.6.19.

STUBINGTON, R. E., Sec.-Lieut. (6th Bn. Norfolk Regt.). Joined, 20.8.17. Wounded on Belle Vue Spur, 9.10.17.

*SUGDEN, R. E., Major. O.C. A Coy. (April—May, 1915 and September— November, 1915). Second in Command (May—September and November—December, 1915). Wounded near Ypres, 12.12.15. Rejoined, 5.9.16. O.C. Bn. (September, 1916—June, 1918). Appointed G.O.C., 151st Inf. Bde., 7.6.18.
Lieut.-Col., 1.6.16. T/Brig.-Genl., 7.6.18.

SULLIVAN, G. K., Lieut.-Col. Joined, 9.11.15. O.C. Bn. (November, 1915). Wounded near Ypres, 20.11.15.

*SYKES, E. E., Capt. O.C. C Coy. (April—November, 1915 and May— July, 1916). To hospital sick, 26.11.15. Rejoined, 23.5.16. Killed in action at Johnstone's Post, 4.7.16.

SYKES, B., Lieut. Joined, 28.11.18. Left Bn. for demobilisation, 21.3.19.

*TAYLOR, E., Sec.-Lieut. Wounded near Ypres and died of wounds, 16.10.15.

TAYLOR, H. N., Sec.-Lieut. Joined, 11.10.15. O.C. A Coy. (January— June, 1917). Certified medically unfit for service, July, 1917. Rejoined 9.12.17. Bn. L.G.O. (December, 1917—January, 1919). Left Bn. for demobilisation, 22.1.19.
Lieut., 1.6.16. Capt., 29.8.17.

TOMLINSON, C. W., Sec.-Lieut. Joined, 28.5.16. Killed in action N. of Thiepval, 3.9.16.

TURNER, J., Sec.-Lieut. Joined, 29.1.18. To hospital sick, 1.8.18.

TURNER, J., Sec.-Lieut. Joined, October, 1918. Transferred to 13th Bn. D. of W. Regt., 26.2.19.

*WALKER, J., Capt. O.C. B Coy. (April, 1915—April, 1916). Second in Command (April—October, 1916). Appointed Second in Command of 1/5th Bn. D. of W. Regt., January, 1917.
T/Major, 22.1.16. Major, 1.6.16. A/Lieut.-Col. (1/5th Bn.), 26.9.17.

*WALKER, F., Sec.-Lieut. To hospital sick, 6.9.15. Rejoined, 15.2.16; O.C. A Coy. (September—October, 1916). To hospital sick, 19.10.16.
Lieut., 26.1.16. A/Capt., 4.10.16.

WALKER, E., Sec.-Lieut. Joined, 1.3.17. Bn. Signalling Officer (April, 1917—January, 1918). Transferred to R.F.C., 15.1.18.

*WALLER, H. N., Capt. To hospital sick, 7.6.15.

WALTON, P. B., Sec.-Lieut. Joined, 13.3.16. Wounded in Thiepval Wood, 7.7.16.

WALTON, J. C., Lieut. Joined, 29.1.18. Bn. I.O. (February—April, 1918). Killed in action near Kemmel, 29.4.18.

APPENDIX II.

WATSON, J. S., Sec.-Lieut. (4th Bn. East Yorks. Regt.). Joined, 18.9.17. Killed in action near Molenaarelsthoek, 26.11.17.

WENHAM-GOODE, A. F., Sec.-Lieut. (6th Bn. Manchester Regt.). Joined, 15.5.18. Left Bn. for demobilisation, 3.2.19.

WHITTAKER, J. C., Sec.-Lieut. Joined, 29.1.18. Killed in action near Kemmel, 28.5.18.

WILKINSON, H. S., Sec.-Lieut. Joined, 21.9.16. Instructor Third Army S.O.S. School (December, 1916—May, 1917). Rejoined, 16.5.17. Bn. I.O. (September—October, 1917). Wounded on Belle Vue Spur, 9.10.17.
Lieut., 1.7.17.

WILLIAMS, H. E., Sec.-Lieut. Joined, 15.4.16. Transferred to 2nd Bn. D. of W. Regt., 23.10.16.

WILLIAMSON, R. J., Sec.-Lieut. Joined, 19.10.18. Transferred to 13th Bn. D. of W. Regt., 26.2.19.

WIMBUSH, R. M., Lieut. Joined, 29.11.18. Left Bn. for demobilisation, 24.4.19.

*WINTER, D. B., Capt. O.C. C Coy. (April, 1915). To hospital sick, 24.4.15.

WOODWARD, F., Sec.-Lieut. Joined, 25.5.18. Wounded near Zillebeke, 11.6.18.

*YATES, W. B. B., Lieut. To England as Instructor at Cadet School, 16.9.16.

YELLAND, E. J., Sec.-Lieut. Joined, 6.9.16. Transferred to 2nd Bn. D. of W. Regt., 23.10.16.

YOUNG, E. M., Lieut. Joined, 3.11.16. Bn. T.O. (November, 1916—October, 1917). Transferred to A.S.C., 13.10.17.

Medical Officers.

*GRIFFITHS, A. T., April—May, 1915.

GREAVES, S. S., June, 1915—December, 1916.

SCOTT, D. C., December, 1916—July, 1917.

ANDERSON, J. M., July—October, 1917.

FARIE, J. G., October, 1917—January, 1918.

ALLEN, W. B. (V.C., M.C.), January—March, 1918.

HARRISON, F. C., March—October, 1918.

WRIGHT, A., November, 1918—March, 1919.

APPENDIX III.

NOMINAL ROLL OF WARRANT OFFICERS AND COMPANY QUARTER MASTER SERGEANTS.

Regimental Sergeant Majors :—

J. McCormack.	Killed in action, 12.8.15.
E. Bottomley.	Reverted to C.S.M. on return to the Battalion of C.S.M. C. C. MacKay who had been wounded, 18.10.15.
C. C. MacKay.	Killed in action, 19.12.15.
W. Lee.	Reverted to C.S.M. on arrival from England of R.S.M. J. Graham, 30.1.16.
J. Graham.	Evacuated sick, 25.5.16.
F. P. Stirzaker.	Reverted to C.S.M. on arrival from England of R.S.M. T. Glover, 16.11.16.
T. Glover.	Wounded in action, 27.1.17.
F. P. Stirzaker.	Killed in action, 11.4.18.
T. S. Sherwood.	Transferred to 1/7th Bn. Duke of Wellington's (W.R.) Regt., 17.9.18.
W. Lee.	Wounded in action, 18.10.18.
B. Harrison.	Left the Battalion for demobilisation, 14.2.19.
S. Flitcroft.	Demobilised with the Cadre of the Battalion, 19.6.19.

Regimental Quarter Master Sergeants :—

F. J. Cooke.	Returned to England time-expired, 31.3.16.
W. Lee.	Promoted R.S.M., 17.9.18.
B. Harrison.	Promoted R.S.M., 19.10.18.
P. Barker.	Demobilised with the Cadre of the Battalion, 19.6.19.

Company Sergeant Majors (A Company) :—

E. Bottomley.	Promoted R.S.M., 13.8.15.
A. McNulty.	Appointed Sergt. Instructor at the 49th Divisional Technical School, 20.8.15.
E. Walsh.	Wounded in action (Gas), 19.12.15.
A. Stirzaker.	Killed in action, 3.9.16.
A. McNulty.	Appointed Instructor at the 147th Infantry Brigade School, 11.2.17.
A. Day.	Wounded in action (Gas), 20.11.17.
T. S. Sherwood.	Promoted R.S.M., 11.4.18.
F. Gledhill.	Left the Battalion for demobilisation, 8.2.19.

Company Sergeant Majors (B Company) :—

A. Parkin.	Wounded in action, 10.7.15.
W. Lee.	Promoted R.S.M., 20.12.15.
L. Greenwood.	Reverted to Sergeant when C.S.M. W. Lee returned to the Company, 30.1.16.

APPENDIX III.

W. LEE.	Promoted R.Q.M.S., 1.4.16.
W. MEDLEY.	Evacuated sick, 20.7.17.
H. HAIGH.	Demobilised while on leave in England, 22.1.19.
F. BIRTWHISTLE.	Left the Battalion for demobilisation, 3.4.19.

Company Sergeant Majors (C Company):—

E. LUMB.	Evacuated sick, 8.8.15.
V. S. TOLLEY.	Killed in action, 16.10.15.
E. BOTTOMLEY.	Evacuated sick, 12.11.15.
T. H. GREENWOOD.	Killed in action, 17.9.16.
J. PARKINSON.	Reverted to Sergeant on the transfer of C.S.M. A. L. Lord from D Company, 16.11.16.
A. L. LORD.	Proceeded to G.H.Q. Cadet School for a commission, 6.3.17.
J. PARKINSON.	Wounded in action, 27.12.17.
C. NAYLOR.	Reverted to Sergeant on the arrival from England of C.S.M. N. Hobson, 29.1.18.
N. HOBSON.	Wounded in action, 10.4.18.
J. E. YATES.	Proceeded to England for a commission, 1.6.18.
B. HARRISON.	Promoted R.Q.M.S., 17.9.18.
S. FLITCROFT.	Promoted R.S.M., 14.2.19.
J. WIDDOP.	Left the Battalion for demobilisation, 7.3.19.

Company Sergeant Majors (D Company):—

C. C. MACKAY.	Wounded in action, 7.8.15.
T. S. SHERWOOD.	Wounded in action, 30.10.15.
F. P. STIRZAKER.	Promoted R.S.M., 26.5.16.
A. HOWARTH.	Killed in action, 13.7.16.
J. N. FLATHER.	Wounded in action, 27.7.16.
J. C. WALKER.	Killed in action, 3.9.16.
A. L. LORD.	Transferred to C Company, 15.11.16.
F. P. STIRZAKER.	Promoted R.S.M., 27.1.17.
L. GREENWOOD.	Proceeded to England for a commission, 21.5.17.
T. S. SHERWOOD.	Transferred to A Company, 20.11.17.
W. BROOKE.	Wounded in action, 25.2.18.
C. NAYLOR.	Wounded in action, 11.10.18.
F. WOOD.	Left the Battalion for demobilisation, 2.2.19.

Supernumerary Warrant Officers:—

F. SPENCER.	Joined the Battalion in France with the first reinforcement and was posted to A Company. Evacuated sick, 22.9.15.
H. J. WYLDE.	Orderly Room Sergeant. Promoted Warrant Officer, Class II., 22.6.18.

Company Quarter Master Sergeants (A Company):—

C. SOUTHERN.	Returned to England time-expired, 12.3.16.
J. C. WALKER.	Promoted C.S.M. D Company, 28.7.16.
S. MACKENZIE.	Wounded in action (Gas), 14.8.17.
H. HAIGH.	Promoted C.S.M. B Company, 16.9.17.
E. WALSH.	Killed in action, 13.10.18.
P. J. DAVENPORT.	Demobilised while on leave in England, 22.1.19.

APPENDIX III.

Company Quarter Master Sergeants (B Company) :—

D. McKeand.	Proceeded to England for a commission, 10.11.15.
E. Midgley.	Returned to England time-expired, 17.3.16.
C. L. Johnson.	Evacuated sick, 21.1.17.
A. Hodgson.	Wounded in action (Gas), 14.8.17.
B. Little.	Killed in action, 13.10.18.
F. Wood.	Demobilised while on leave in England, 26.1.19.
L. Rodgers.	Transferred to 13th Bn. Duke of Wellington's (W.R.) Regt., 26.2.19.

Company Quarter Master Sergeants (C Company) :—

W. Lee.	Promoted C.S.M. B Company, 11.7.15.
A. L. Lord.	Promoted C.S.M. D Company, 4.9.16.
H. Fitton.	Evacuated (accidental injury), 23.2.17.
E. Midgley.	Reverted to Sergeant on return from England of C.Q.M.S. H. Fitton, 4.7.17.
H. Fitton.	Evacuated sick, 1.8.17.
E. Midgley.	Left the Battalion for demobilisation, 28.1.19.

Company Quarter Master Sergeants (D Company) :—

G. Jackson.	Evacuated sick, 3.7.15.
J. W. Siddall.	Returned to England time-expired, 17.3.16.
G. Edmonson.	Transferred to England, 20.9.16.
P. Barker.	Promoted R.Q.M.S., 19.10.18.
A. Whitaker.	Evacuated sick, 14.11.18.
E. Elsey.	Demobilised with the Cadre of the Battalion, 19.6.19.

APPENDIX IV.

SUMMARY OF CASUALTIES.

Period.	Sector.	Officers. K.	W.	M.	Other Ranks. K.	W.	M.
1915.							
April 18—June 25	Fleurbaix	—	3	—	14	38	—
July 8—Dec. 20	Ypres	7	7	—	116	206	4
1916.							
Feb. 28—Mch. 6	Authuille	—	1	—	—	1	—
Mch. 7—Mch. 29	Mailly-Maillet	—	—	—	1	4	—
June	Aveluy Wood	—	—	—	2	7	—
July 1—Sept. 24	Battle of the Somme	10*	10	—	91	453	155
Sept. 29—Oct. 16	Hannescamps	—	—	—	3	13	—
Oct. 24—Dec. 5	Fonquevillers	—	—	—	10	12	—
1917.							
Jan. 7—Jan. 30	Berles-au-Bois	1	—	—	—	18	—
Feb. 2—Feb. 28	Riviére	—	—	—	6	27	—
Mch. 13—May 16	Ferme du Bois	1	1	—	4	22	—
May 27—June 15	Cordonnerie	—	—	—	1	1	—
June 25—July 3	Hulluch	3	2	—	7	24	1
Aug. 3—Aug. 16	Nieuport	1§	4	—	19	84	1
Oct. 4—Oct. 10	Belle Vue Spur	1	4	—	20	117	2
Nov. 19—Jan. 4 1918	Keerselaarhoek and Molenaarelsthoek	2	3	—	16	75	1
1918.							
Feb. 22—April 3	Reutel	—	3	—	18	60	—
April 9—April 20	Battle of the Lys	2	13	—	47	261	83
April 25—May 3	Battle of Kemmel	2	2	—	32	121	4
June 3—Aug. 20	Ypres	—	4	—	9	77	1
Oct. 11—Oct. 18	Villers-en-Cauchies	7	3	1†	55	377	12
	Totals	37	60	1	471	1998	264‡

K.—Killed.   W.—Wounded (includes Gassed).   M.—Missing.

*Includes several, at first reported " Missing," since " Assumed to be Dead."
†Capt. W. Grantham, since reported " Died of wounds a Prisoner in Enemy Hands."
‡Includes all since reported " Prisoners of War."
§Sec.-Lieut. R. Jury, mortally wounded by an enemy bomb at Dunkerque.

APPENDIX V.

LIST OF HONOURS AND AWARDS.

In compiling this list of Honours and Awards the following rules have been adhered to :—

 1. The Rank and Regimental Number given are those held by the individual at the time the decoration was won. It thus follows that, in several cases, the same name occurs more than once but with a different rank and sometimes with a different regimental number.

 2. Only Honours and Awards conferred on officers, warrant officers, non-commissioned officers and men for services rendered *while actually serving with the Battalion* have been included.

The length of the list might be considerably increased by including such names as Brig.-General R. E. Sugden, who was awarded the C.M.G. while he was G.O.C., 151st Infantry Brigade ; Lieut.-Col. J. Walker, who received the D.S.O. and Bar and the French Legion d'Honneur while he was in command of the 5th Battalion Duke of Wellington's Regt. ; and several other officers. Many N.C.O's and men, such as Sergt. F. E. Lumb, D.C.M., also won decorations whilst attached to such units as the 147th Infantry Brigade H.Q., the 147th Machine Gun Company, and the 147th Light Trench Mortar Battery.

VICTORIA CROSS (1).
24066 Pte. A. Poulter.

DISTINGUISHED SERVICE ORDER (2).
Capt. (A/Lt.-Col.) A. L. Mowat, M.C. Major R. E. Sugden.

BAR TO DISTINGUISHED SERVICE ORDER (1).
Lt.-Col. R. E. Sugden, D.S.O.

MILITARY CROSS (27).

Sec.-Lt. H. H. Aykroyd	Sec.-Lt. T. E. Jessop
Lt. P. G. Bales	Lt. (A/Capt.) A. Kirk
Sec.-Lt. F. V. Blackwell	83 C.S.M. W. Lee
Sec.-Lt. E. V. Blakey	Sec.-Lt. J. W. Lumb
Sec.-Lt. W. N. Everitt	Lt. (A/Capt.) A. M. Luty
Lt. (A/Capt.) N. T. Farrar	Lt. W. G. Mackie
Lt. (A/Capt.) W. C. Fenton	Capt. E. N. Marshall
Capt. N. Geldard	200441 C.S.M. W. Medley, M.M.
Lt. T. T. Gilroy	Capt. A. L. Mowat
Capt. S. S. Greaves (R.A.M.C.)	Lt. (A/Capt.) J. G. Mowat
Sec.-Lt. L. Gumby	Sec.-Lt. H. R. Newman
Sec.-Lt. B. H. Huggard	2353 R.S.M. F. P. Stirzaker
Sec.-Lt. F. A. Innes	Lt. (T/Capt.) E. E. Sykes
Lt. F. Irish	

APPENDIX V.

Bar to Military Cross (2).
Capt. W. C. Fenton, M.C.   Capt. (A/Major) A. L. Mowat, M.C.

Distinguished Conduct Medal (28).

355 Cpl. E. Ashworth
200453 Sgt. J. Bancroft, M.M.
3060 Cpl. W. Bancroft
235519 Sgt. W. H. Binns
235227 Sgt. (A/C.S.M.) W. Brooke
200298 Sgt. F. J. Brown
1597 Pte. W. Brown
2040 Pte. (L/Cpl.) T. H. Clarke
203129 Sgt. F. Constable
200143 Sgt. N. Downes
203340 L/Sgt. F. J. Field
200055 Sgt. S. Flitcroft, M.M.
203252 Sgt. W. D. Foster
200135 C.Q.M.S. H. Haigh
202936 Pte. (A/Cpl.) R. A. Hudson
200352 Cpl. E. Jackson, M.M.
203285 Pte. (L/Cpl.) H. Kane, M.M.
1495 Cpl. C. Landale
15805 Sgt. A. Loosemore, V.C.
203229 Sgt. J. Mann
203351 Pte. (L/Cpl.) A. Moon
6750 Sgt. G. Moscrop
200598 C.S.M. J. Parkinson
242274 Sgt. J. Redpath, M.M.
2353 C.S.M. A. Stirzaker
3406 Pte. H. Sykes
203305 Sgt. R. Wilson
201191 Sgt. F. Wood, M.M.

Military Medal (132).

200471 Pte. C. Andrews
203501 Pte. (L/Cpl.) J. T. N. Atkinson
203414 Pte. J. H. Atkinson
1605 Cpl. G. A. Bailey
1995 Sgt. J. Bancroft
26498 Pte. (L/Cpl.) G. W. Barber
200096 Pte. S. Barker
306365 Sgt. W. Barnes
203178 Pte. J. T. Berridge
200053 Pte. (L/Cpl.) A. Beverley
200331 Pte. H. Bibby
16465 Pte. H. G. Binns
201886 Cpl. G. Birkinshaw
26010 Pte. A. Bishop
203336 Sgt. A. A. Bolt
201893 Pte. (L/Cpl.) C. Bolton
202042 Pte. (L/Cpl.) E. Booth
6596 Pte. (L/Cpl.) J. Bowers
203177 Pte. S. R. Brabben
1775 Pte. E. Braithwaite
202787 Pte. (L/Cpl.) G. Broadbent
202410 Pte. J. W. Brookes
202579 Pte. N. W. Brooksbank
200298 Sgt. F. J. Brown, D.C.M.
242271 Sgt. W. Brown
24960 Pte. S. Brummit
200653 Sgt. R. G. Brunt
203595 Pte. W. Buckley
203217 Cpl. A. Buie
203433 Pte. T. Burfoot
201125 L/Sgt. T. Chilton
5792 Sgt. F. Johnson
33014 Pte. J. E. Johnson
200920 Pte. A. G. Jones
203285 Pte. (L/Cpl.) H. Kane
10737 Sgt. S. Kay
201783 Sgt. T. Knowles
1645 Pte. (L/Cpl.) R. Knox
200139 Pte. J. Lancaster
200488 Pte. O. Lee
200504 Pte. J. Limb
203188 Pte. H. Louth
238181 Pte. W. Lowe
201012 Sgt. P. McHugh
601 Sgt. (A/C.S.M.) A. McNulty
1967 Cpl. W. Medley
201923 Pte. T. Meneghan
200396 Sgt. A. Meskimmon
6520 Pte. W. Metcalfe
201013 Pte. (L/Cpl.) A. R. Mitchell
200681 Cpl. W. H. Mitchell
73 Sgt. P. Moran
200153 Pte. (L/Cpl.) C. Mortimer
1603 Pte. W. H. Murray
201689 Pte. J. H. Naylor
203352 Pte. T. Nicholls
203371 Cpl. G. North
202669 Pte. T. North
203193 Pte. G. Pearson
201336 Pte. F. F. Pettit
306873 Pte. T. Proctor
242274 Pte. J. Redpath

APPENDIX V.

MILITARY MEDAL—continued.

202120 Pte. T. Conroy
26815 Pte. (L/Cpl.) A. Cresswell
30 Sgt. J. W. Crossley
26524 Pte. H. S. Davies
203647 Pte. H. B. Dawson
203650 Pte. A. Denham
200172 Pte. N. Dennis
203649 Pte. J. Dewar
203451 Pte. V. T. Dobson
267198 Pte. (L/Cpl.) H. Driver
201437 Pte. (L/Cpl.) J. A. Ellis
242874 Pte. R. Emmett
200146 Pte. J. Ennis
201535 Pte. C. Firth
242821 Pte. P. Firth
1002 Sgt. (A/C.S.M.) J. N. Flather
200055 Sgt. S. Flitcroft
203513 Pte. G. A. Foster
201879 Pte. J. Galloway
200127 Pte. R. Gledhill
235253 Pte. G. Green
203728 Pte. E. Haggas
200135 C.S.M. H. Haigh, D.C.M.
203517 Pte. T. Hartley
12682 Pte. H. Henderson
203315 Pte. B. Hinchcliffe
1485 Sgt. A. Hodgson
2108 Pte. (L/Cpl.) G. H. Holt
203480 Pte. F. A. Hookham
201687 Pte. F. Howarth
203551 Pte. W. Howker
203072 Pte. W. Inman
1747 Cpl. E. Jackson
202664 Pte. (L/Cpl.) B. Jennings
201219 Cpl. (L/Sgt.) S. Jessop

202746 Pte. (L/Cpl.) F. Rhodes
1889 Pte. S. Royals
242202 Pte. G. Ryder
200134 Pte. (L/Cpl.) J. W. Ryder
32897 Pte. E. Sambrookes
203390 Pte. F. Scales
202888 Pte. W. A. Scruton
2481 Cpl. H. Shackleton
2413 L/Sgt. J. S. Sheard
242567 Sgt. A. Smith
200192 Sgt. H. Smith
2716 Pte. L. Stead
201883 Pte. A. Sutcliffe
6606 Pte. R. Swinburne
202142 Pte. J. W. Taylor
201186 Cpl. (A/Sgt.) V. Taylor
242371 Pte. J. Tebb
13014 Sgt. W. P. Thompson
1455 Cpl. A. L. Thornton
200101 Sgt. E. Turner
238031 Cpl. J. W. Varley
200204 Cpl. H. Wainwright
2164 Sgt. (A/C.S.M.) J. C. Walker
34005 Cpl. A. Wall
200320 Pte. C. Walsh
34007 Pte. M. Webster
200753 Sgt. A. Whitaker
200529 Pte. (L/Cpl.) H. Whiteley
16075 Sgt. J. Widdop
201295 Cpl. B. Wilson
2346 Sgt. J. Wilson
235120 Pte. W. F. Witts
201191 Sgt. F. Wood
235524 Sgt. (A/C.S.M.) J. E. Yates
26271 Pte. J. Young

BAR TO MILITARY MEDAL (5).

200096 Pte. (L/Cpl.) S. Barker, M.M.
200146 Pte. (L/Cpl.) J. Ennis, M.M.
34005 Pte. (L/Cpl.) A. Wall, M.M.
200529 Pte. (L/C.) H. Whiteley, M.M.
203285 Pte. (A/Cpl.) H. Kane, D.C.M., M.M.

MERITORIOUS SERVICE MEDAL (4).

200264 Sgt. H. Deane
200483 Sgt. F. Firth
200688 Sgt. E. Jones
242695 Sgt. F. Smith

ITALIAN BRONZE MEDAL FOR MILITARY VALOUR (1).

1535 Cpl. J. Walker.

APPENDIX V.

MEDAILLE MILITAIRE (1).

200441 C.S.M. W. Medley, M.M.

BELGIAN CROIX DE GUERRE (1).

200064 Sgt. C. Naylor.

MENTIONS IN DESPATCHES (39).

Lt. (T/Capt.) M. P. Andrews
Lt. P. G. Bales
202027 C.Q.M.S. P. Barker
Sec.-Lt. E. V. Blakey
235227 Sgt. W. Brooke
Capt. & Q.M. W. N. Broomhead
2492 Pte. (L/Cpl.) D. Dow
Lt. & Q.M. T. Fielding
Capt. S. S. Greaves (R.A.M.C.)
200036 R.S.M. B. Harrison
2108 Pte. (L/Cpl.) G. H. Holt
Sec.-Lt. F. A. Innes, M.C.
1687 C.S.M. A. L. Lord
Sec.-Lt. (T/Capt.) E. N. Marshall
Lt. G. P. McGuire (twice)
601 C.S.M. A. McNulty
200441 C.S.M. W. Medley, M.M.
204733 C.Q.M.S. E. Midgley
Lt.-Col. A. L. Mowat, D.S.O., M.C.
200598 C.S.M. J. Parkinson
Major (T/Lt.-Col.) C. J. Pickering
Sec.-Lt. T. D. Pratt
2481 Cpl. H. Shackleton
2400 Pte. J. Shelley
2716 Pte. L. Stead
2353 Sgt. (A/C.S.M.) F. P. Stirzaker
Lt.-Col. R. E. Sugden, D.S.O. (5 times)
Lt. (T/Capt.) E. E. Sykes
Major J. Walker (3 times)
2164 Sgt. J. C. Walker
2346 Sgt. J. Wilson
1234 Pte. (L/Cpl.) C. Wood

APPENDIX VI.

THE BATTALION CANTEEN.

A THOUGHTFUL enemy provided the Battalion with most of its excitement, and a deal of its amusement, during the Great War. An equally thoughtful War Office arranged for rations, and a limited supply of such luxuries as tobacco and cigarettes for the men. But it was left to the Battalion to supply itself with a canteen. And it was Sergt. F. Smith who made that institution such a great success.

The Canteen had its beginning in a small affair, started for the benefit of the transport men, in August, 1915. Lieut. J. G. Mowat, who was Transport Officer at the time, provided the necessary capital. Pte. F. Smith, then employed in the Q.M. Stores, managed the Canteen in his spare time. From the very first, the new departure was a great success. Goods were sold out almost as soon as they were displayed, and the small library which was opened was also very popular.

Early in its history, this first Canteen nearly came to an untimely end. One night the roof was found to be in flames, which rapidly spread to the wooden supports of the building. The " proprietor " alone knew that a store of petrol and bombs was lying in the hut. But, largely through the energy of that trained fireman, Cpl. E. Ashworth, the fire was put out before it reached them.

In September, 1915, the transport canteen developed into a battalion institution. Plenty of money was forthcoming to start it, and it soon " set up shop " in a dugout on the Canal Bank. This was not an ideal spot for business, and there is no doubt that it was the first canteen to be set up in that area. When the Battalion went back into rest the Canteen accompanied it, and, before long, it was looked upon as a permanent institution.

In the spring of 1916, the Canteen closed down for a time. Lance-Cpl. F. Smith had been evacuated sick, and no one else was deemed suitable to carry on the business. He returned to the 147th Infantry Brigade late in the Battle of the Somme, but was posted to the 1/5th Battalion Duke of Wellington's Regt. However, shortly after, through the courtesy of that battalion, he returned to his old unit, and the Canteen was immediately restarted.

At Fonquevillers it did excellent service. Stationed in a broken-down building in the village, and frequently annoyed by enemy shelling, it soon became the admiration of all units in the neighbourhood. At first it had only been intended for the use of men of the Battalion, but it was now thrown open to all comers. Within less than a mile of the firing line, it provided such luxuries as fresh fish, eggs, butter, fruit and vegetables. Needless to say, it did a " roaring " trade.

During the rest at Halloy, it was much to the fore, and its activities were greatly extended. In addition to an enormous retail business, it

APPENDIX VI. 313

catered for all the Christmas dinners and for many smaller parties. It also became a buying agency, through which officers and other ranks could obtain goods which they required but which were not ordinarily kept in stock.

When the Battalion went into the line near Berles-au-Bois, the Canteen was set up as usual. There it narrowly escaped a violent death. A shell entered by the roof one day and blew out a side of the shelter, wounding a man who was there, and scattering the cash which was being counted at the time. During the terribly cold weather of that period, hot coffee and rum were supplied free to many a half-frozen man.

Senechal Farm and the Ferme du Bois Sector provided plenty of scope for the Canteen's initiative. Good shopping centres were plentiful in the district, and supplies easily procurable. " Hawking " goods in the front line became quite an institution there, and it was continued in the Cordonnerie Sector. In the line near Hulluch the facilities were not so good. A Canteen was set up near Battalion H.Q., but it was difficult to get goods up to it ; and twice the staff was gassed out.

Little could be done in the Nieuport Sector, though the Canteen still acted as a buying agency. But while the Battalion was training on the coast it was very active. There, whole-day training schemes were not uncommon, and it became customary for a limber to accompany the troops and set up a stall on the ground.

The winter of 1917-18 was a very difficult period. There was never accommodation for a canteen when the Battalion was in the front line ; but it was always at work during rest periods. Its presence in the Westhoek Dugouts was a great success ; beer was never lacking during that rest period.

The sudden order to move from Maida Camp, early in April, 1918, caused much consternation, for the Canteen was particularly well stocked at the time. However, the stock was somehow cleared, and the takings on the last day in that area amounted to 4,500 francs—a Battalion record.

Little business was possible during the Battles of the Lys and Mont Kemmel, but an increase in trade followed the Battalion's return to the neighbourhood of Ypres. Trade again declined when the Battalion went into battle in the autumn ; but the indefatigable Sergt. Smith succeeded in getting a large supply of cigarettes up to the Battalion in Vordon Wood—at a time when there was not a cigarette to be had for miles around.

During the Armistice, trade was good at Auby, in spite of the competition of a number of estaminets and shops which were soon opened in the village. There Sergt. F. Smith laid down his duties and devoted himself to education for the short period before he was demobilised. Yet, right up to the end, the Canteen survived at Douai.

In its long and chequered history the Canteen had many homes. Dugouts and shelters, within easy range of the front line, were occupied on many occasions. Barns, stables, even a pig-sty, did duty in various places when the Battalion was in rest. But, whatever its surroundings might be, it always proved a source of much comfort to the men. There were many rumours of the " row of houses " which was being built in Halifax, for few people were well acquainted with current prices. But actually, the profit was never more than 5 per cent. Out of this profit all expenses had

APPENDIX VI.

to be paid ; the whole of the balance was then spent on the men of the Battalion, who were the chief customers. When the demobilisation of the Battalion was complete, the surplus funds were handed over to the Old Comrades' Association.

The Canteen staff had many duties besides those of buying and selling. The Battalion library, which was run almost continuously for about three and a half years, was in its charge. When billets were available, reading and recreation rooms were organised. Sports material was looked after. Concerts, whist drives, and other social functions were catered for. In all these activities, the efforts of Sergt. Smith were ably seconded by his faithful henchmen, " Jack " Baines and " Johnny " Jackson.

The Battalion was particularly fortunate in having so many good friends at home. Chief among these should be mentioned Mr. W. E. Denison and the *Halifax Courier* Fund. Books, periodicals, whist drive prizes, lamps, and countless other articles, which helped to make life happier for the men at the " Front," were provided by them.

The Battalion had several different Seconds-in-Command and all took great interest in, and spent much time over, the Canteen. But it had only one Sergt. F. Smith. To him was mainly due the reputation of the 4th Battalion Canteen as the most successful institution of its kind in the 49th Division. Everyone was delighted when the Meritorious Service Medal rewarded his great services.

STOTT BROTHERS LIMITED, Printers, Mount Street Works, Halifax.

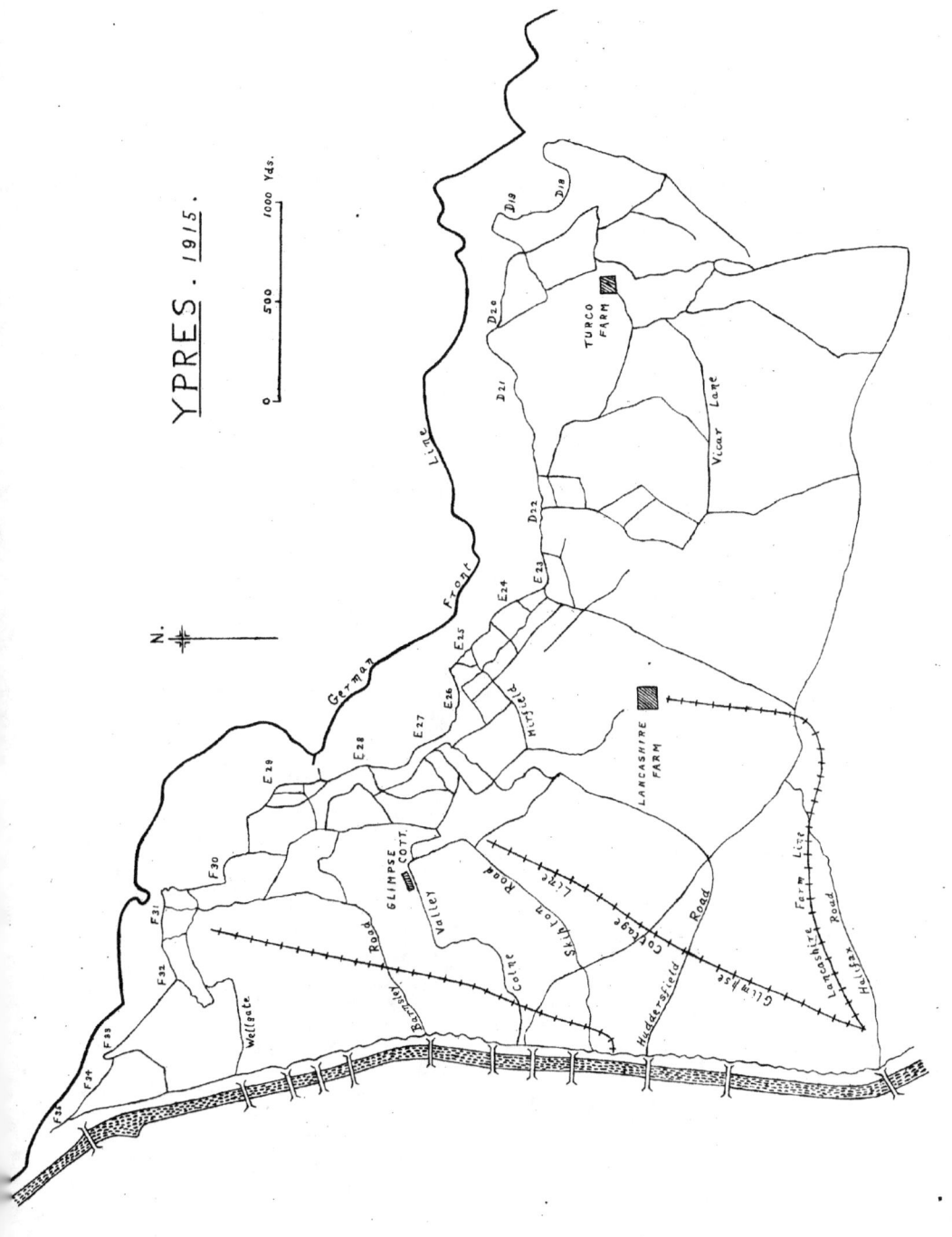

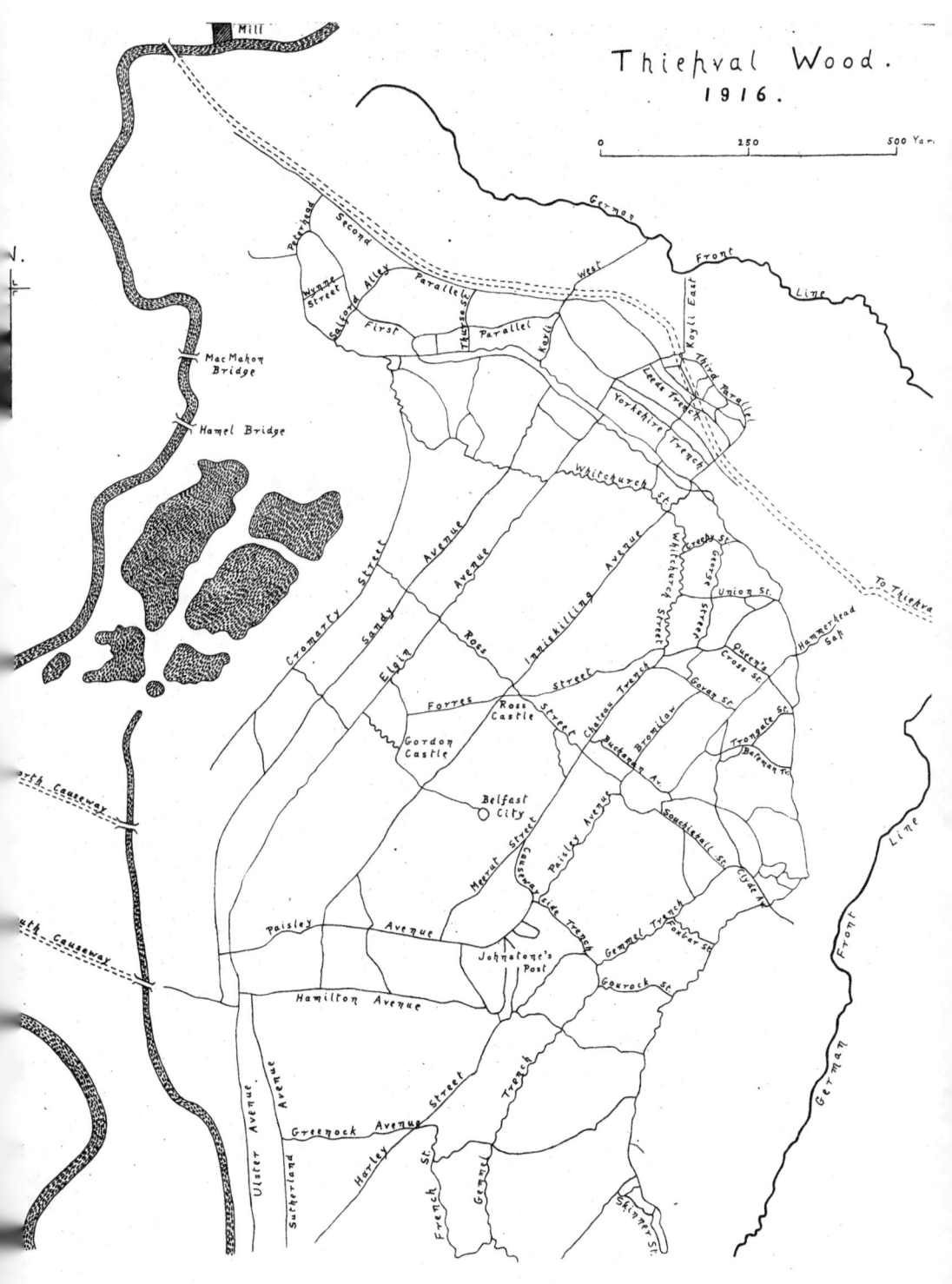

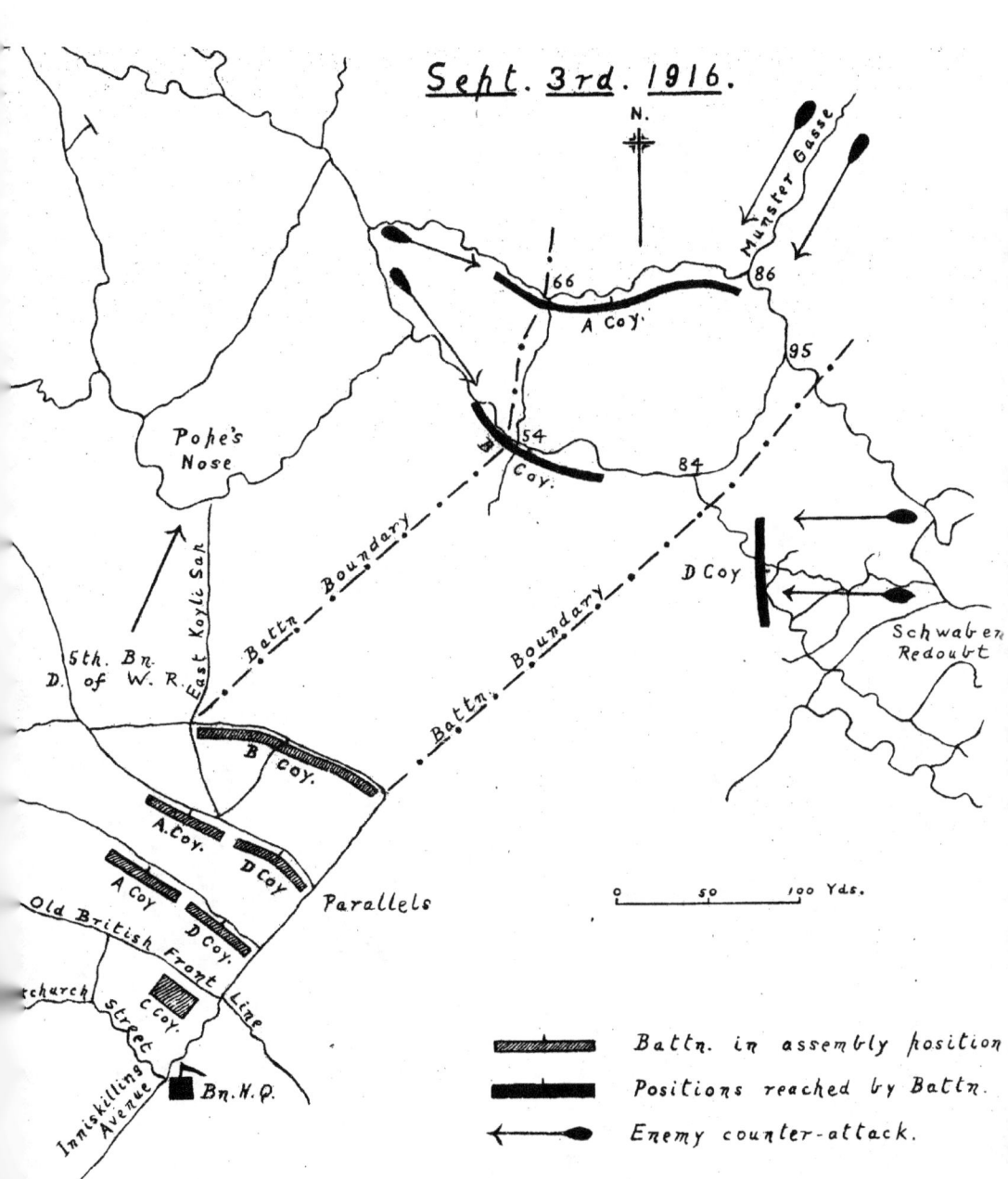

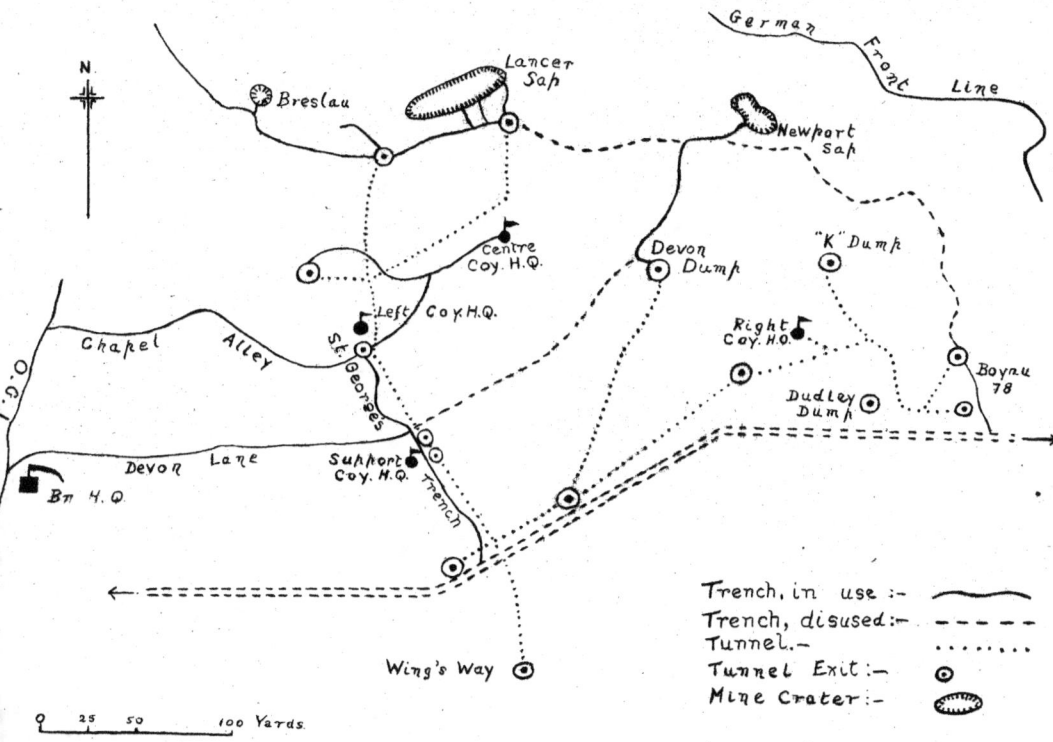

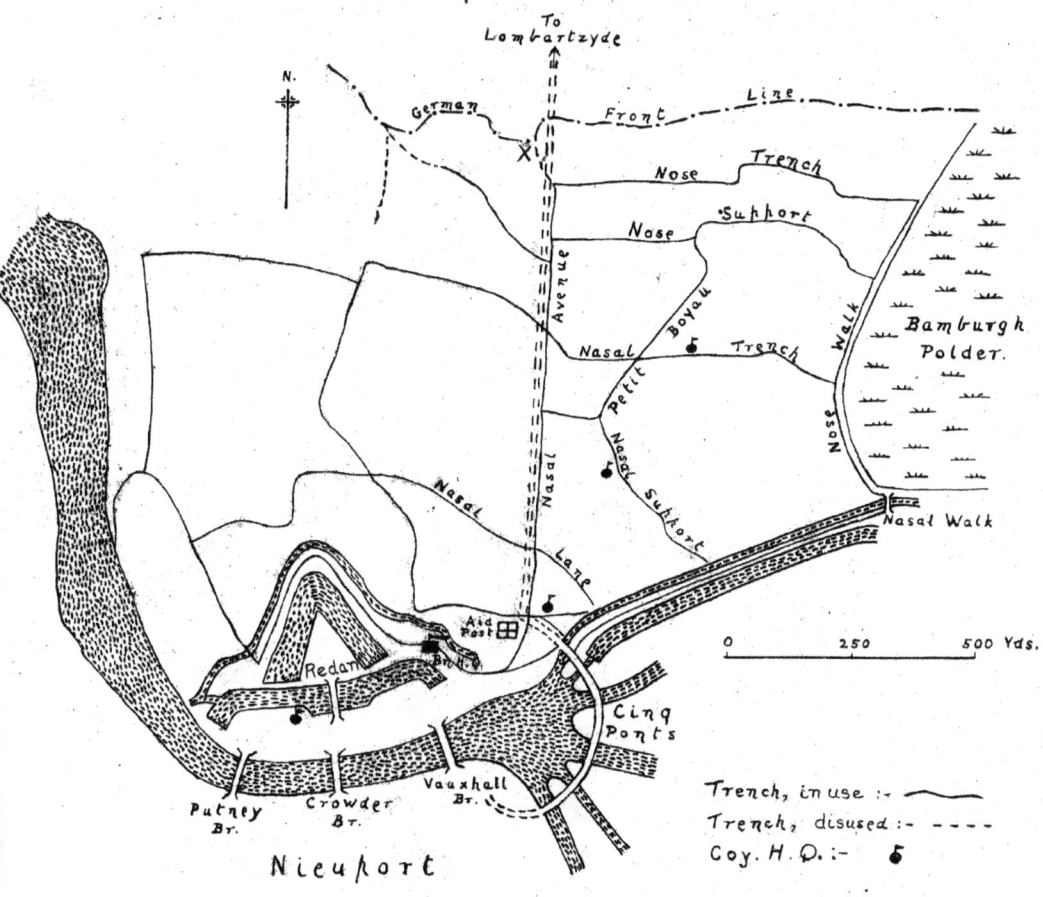

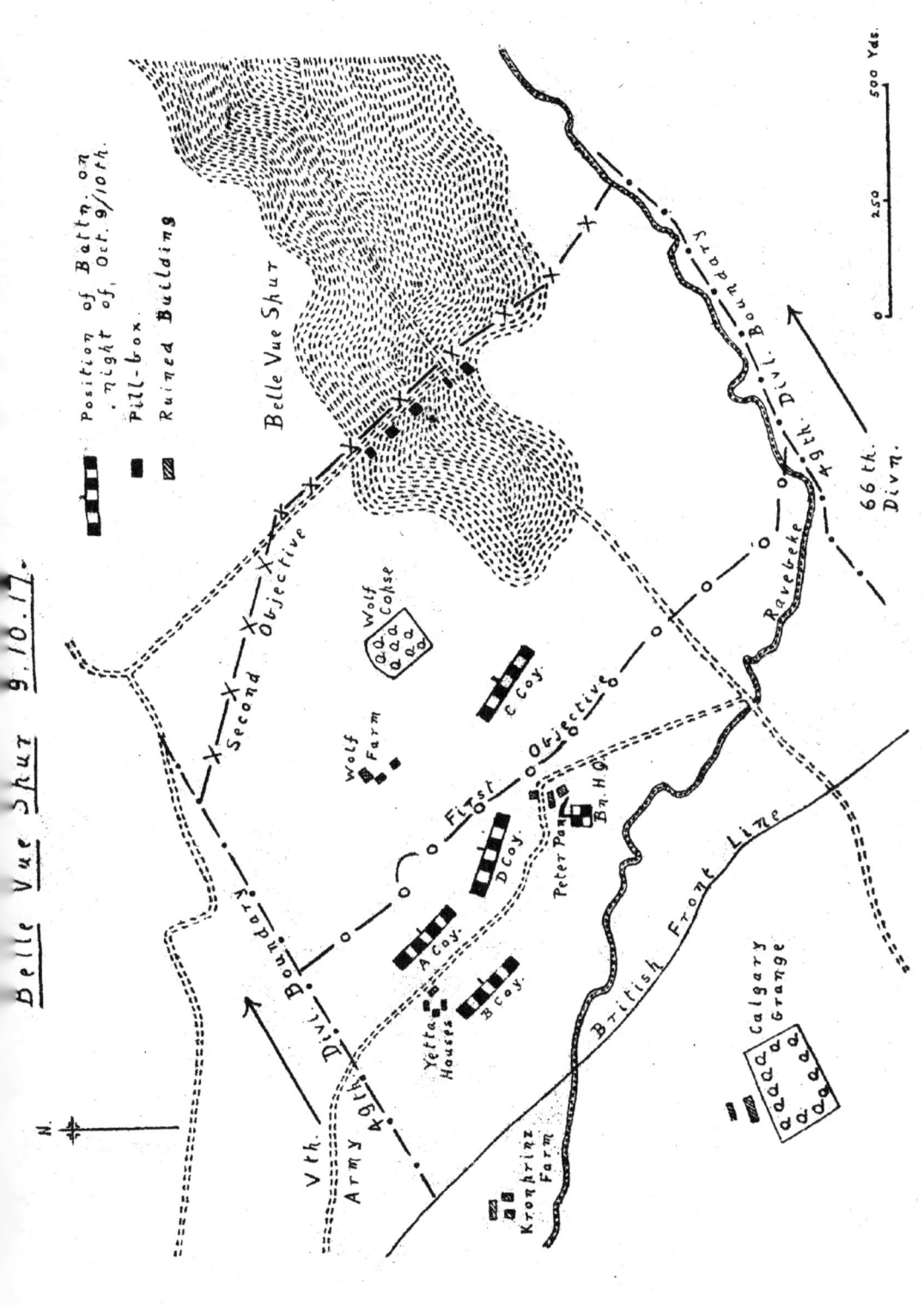

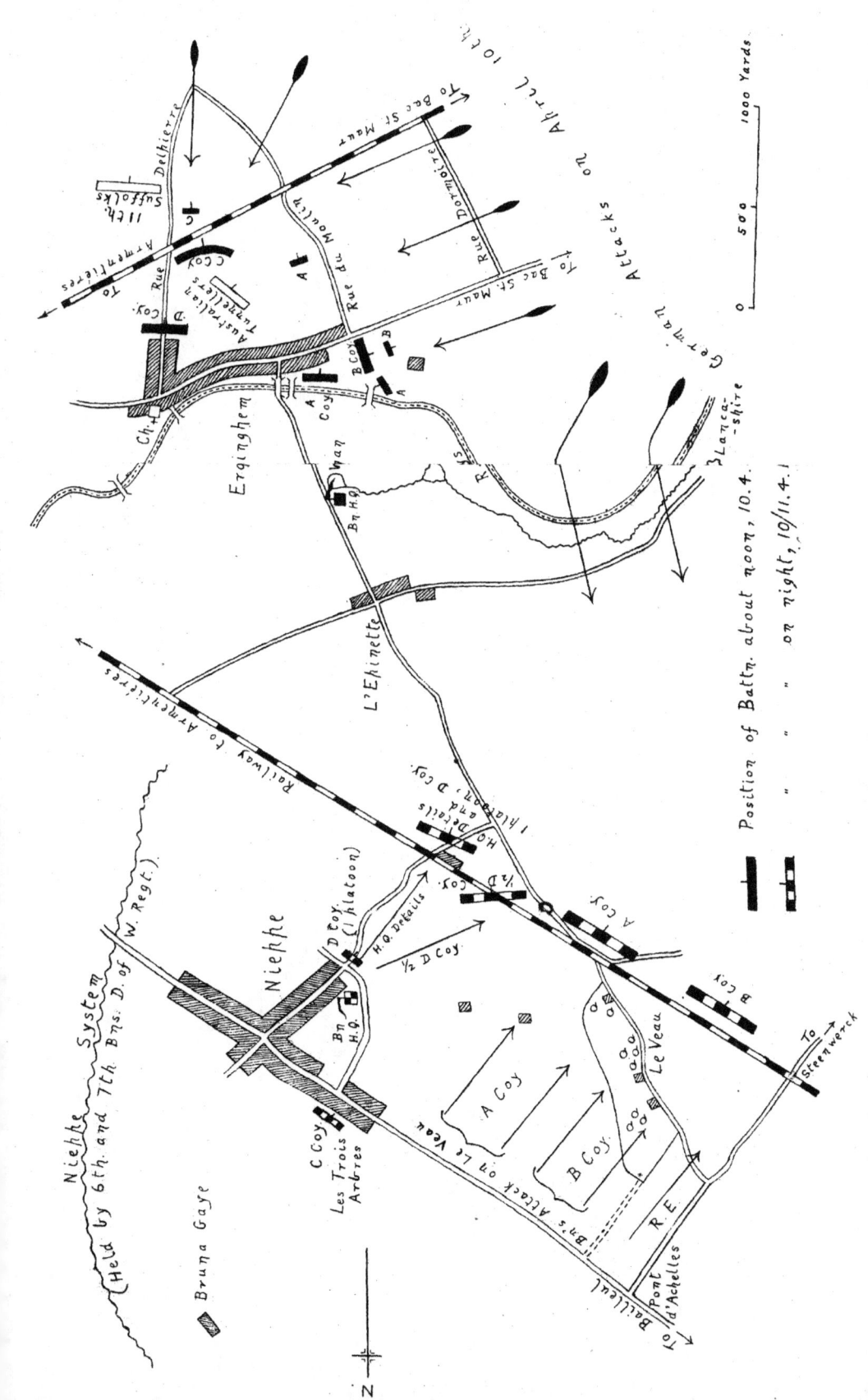

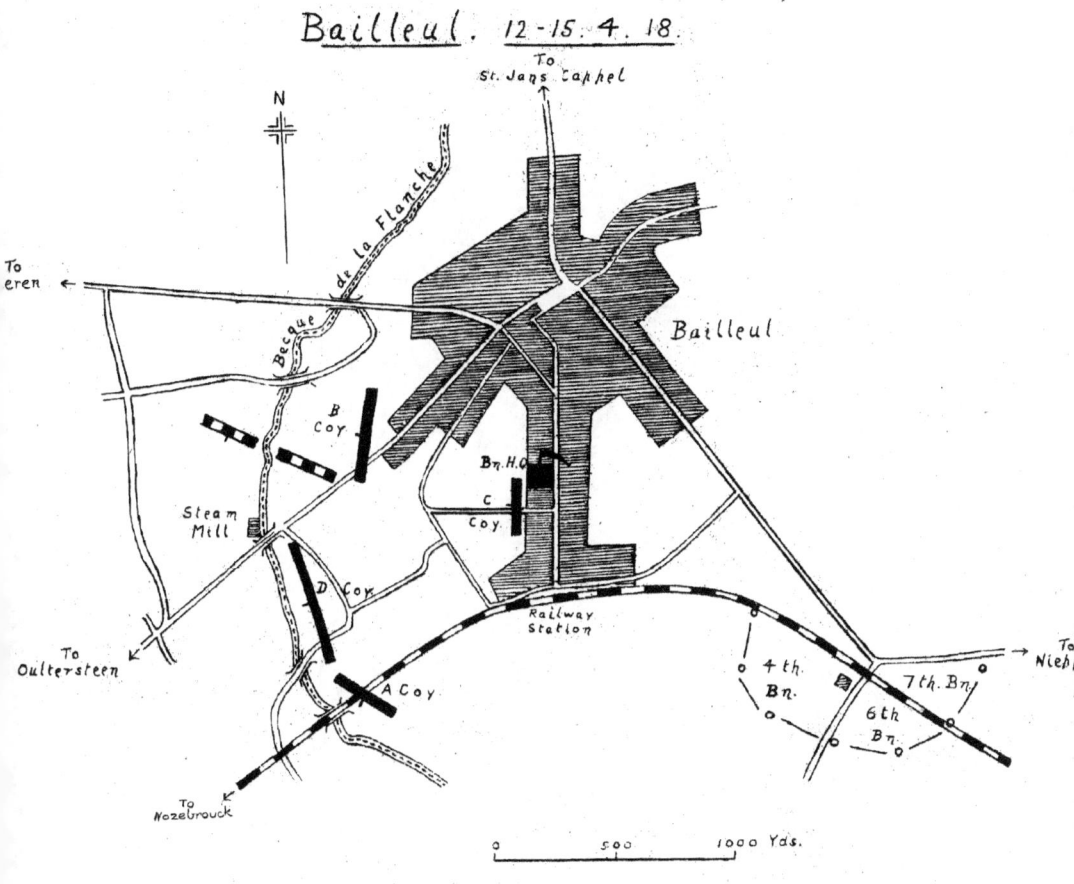

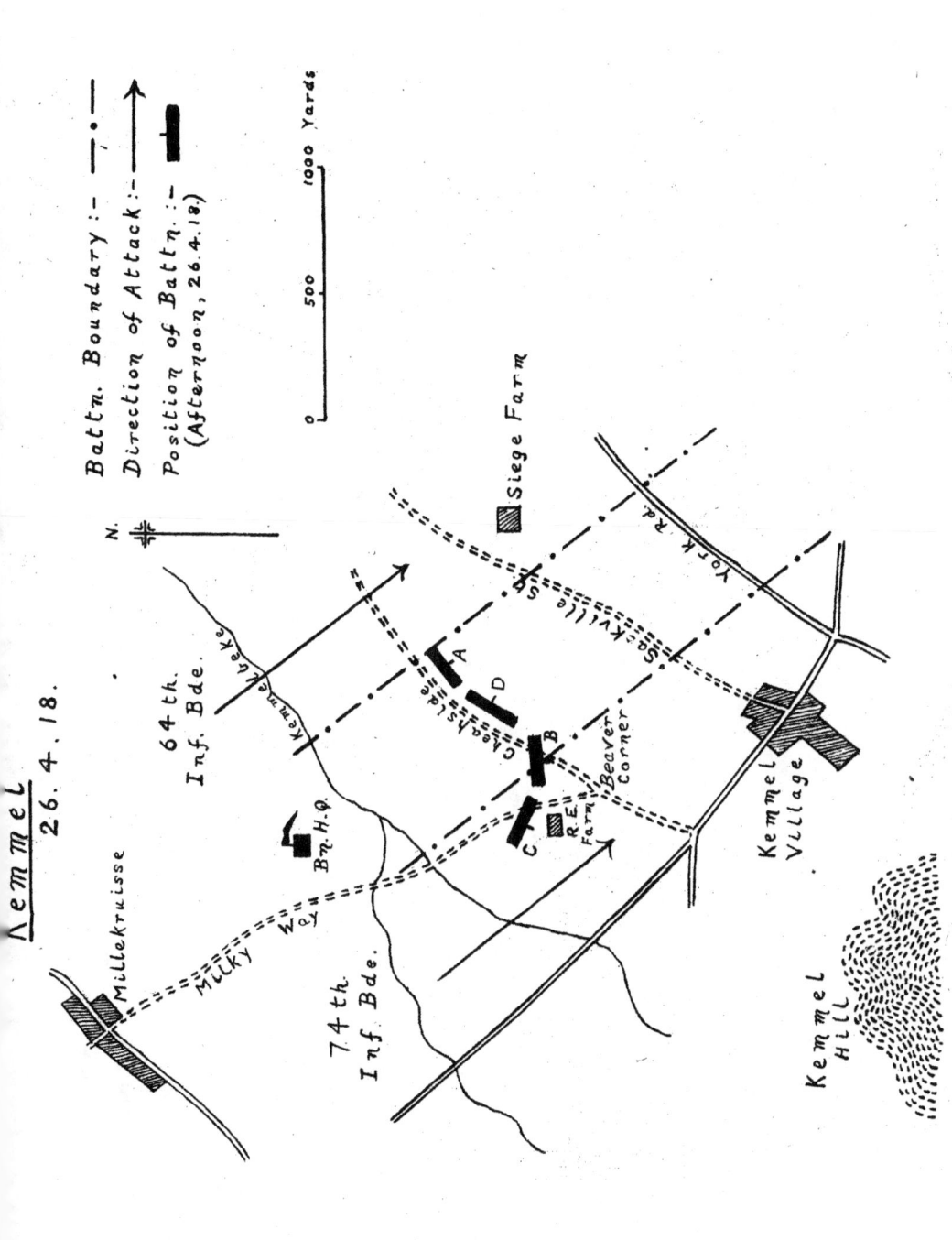

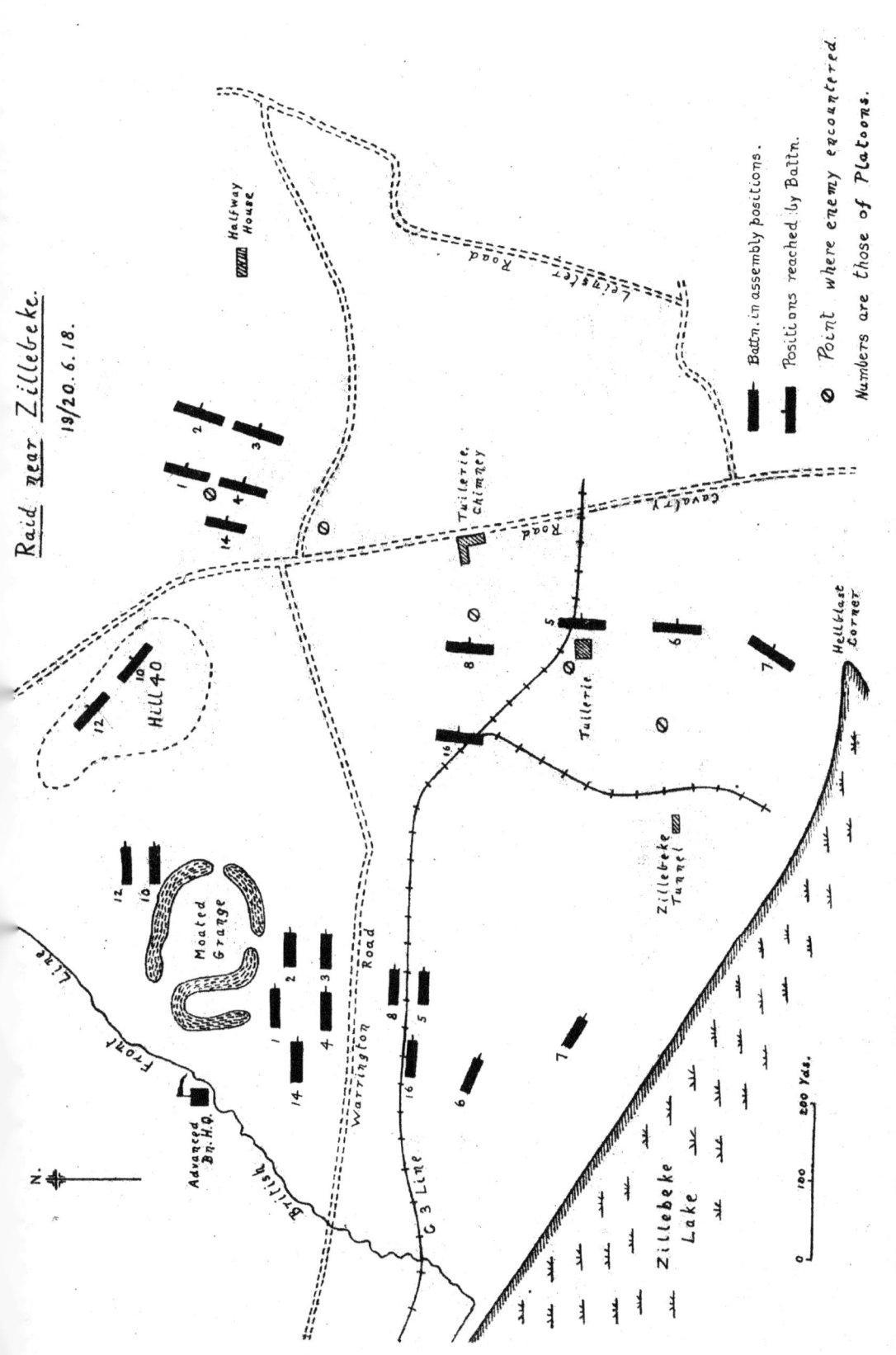

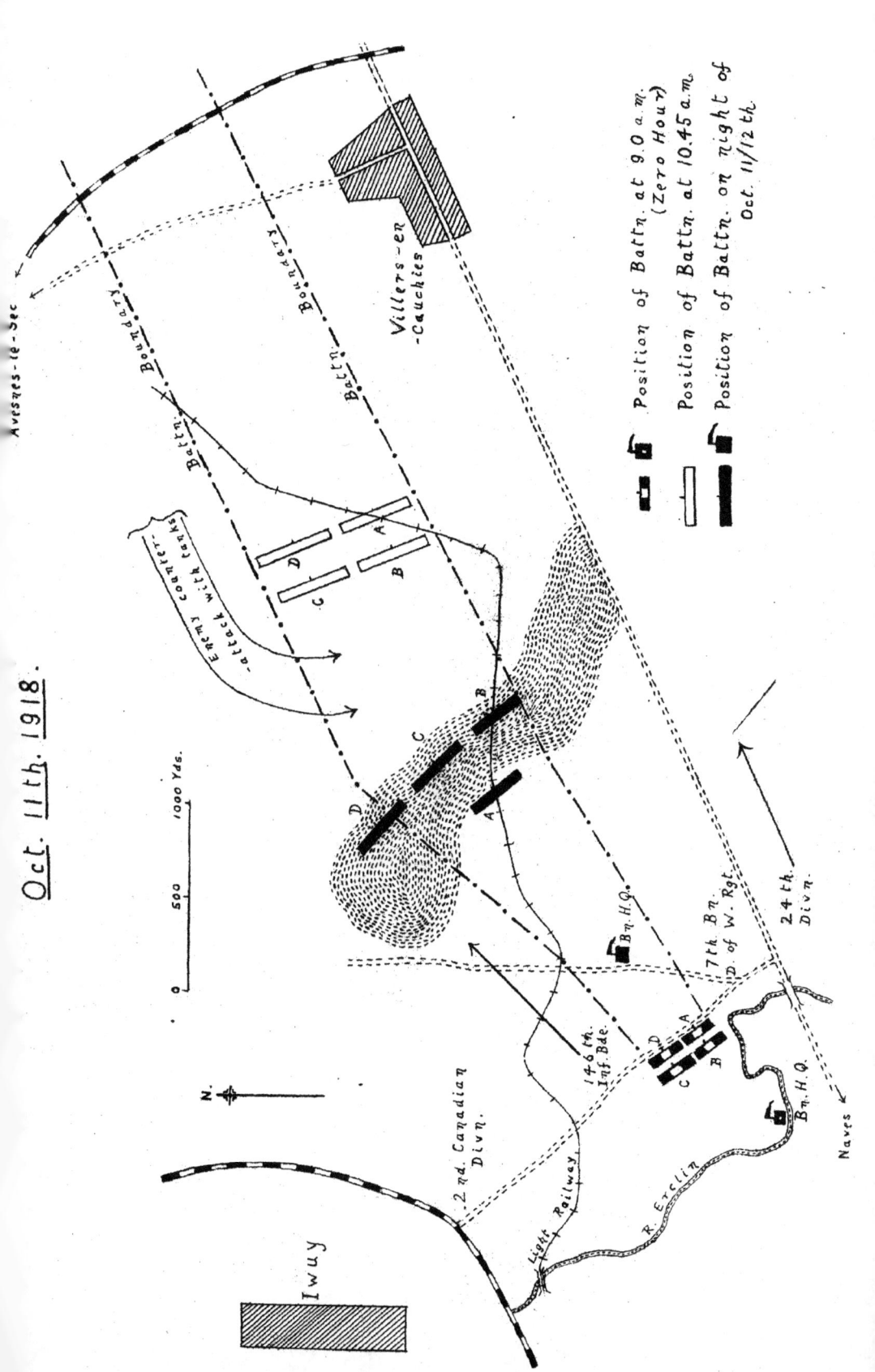

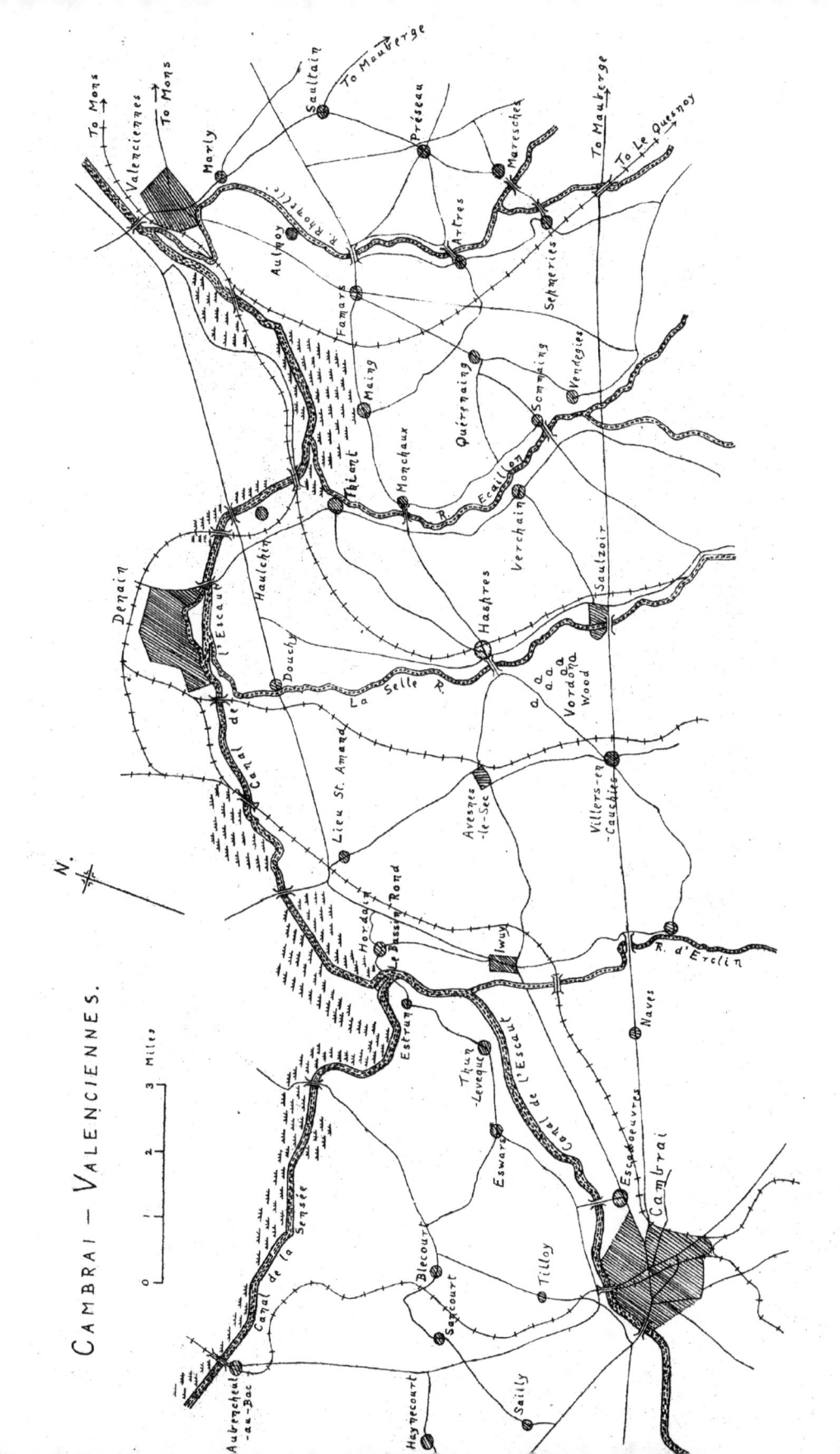

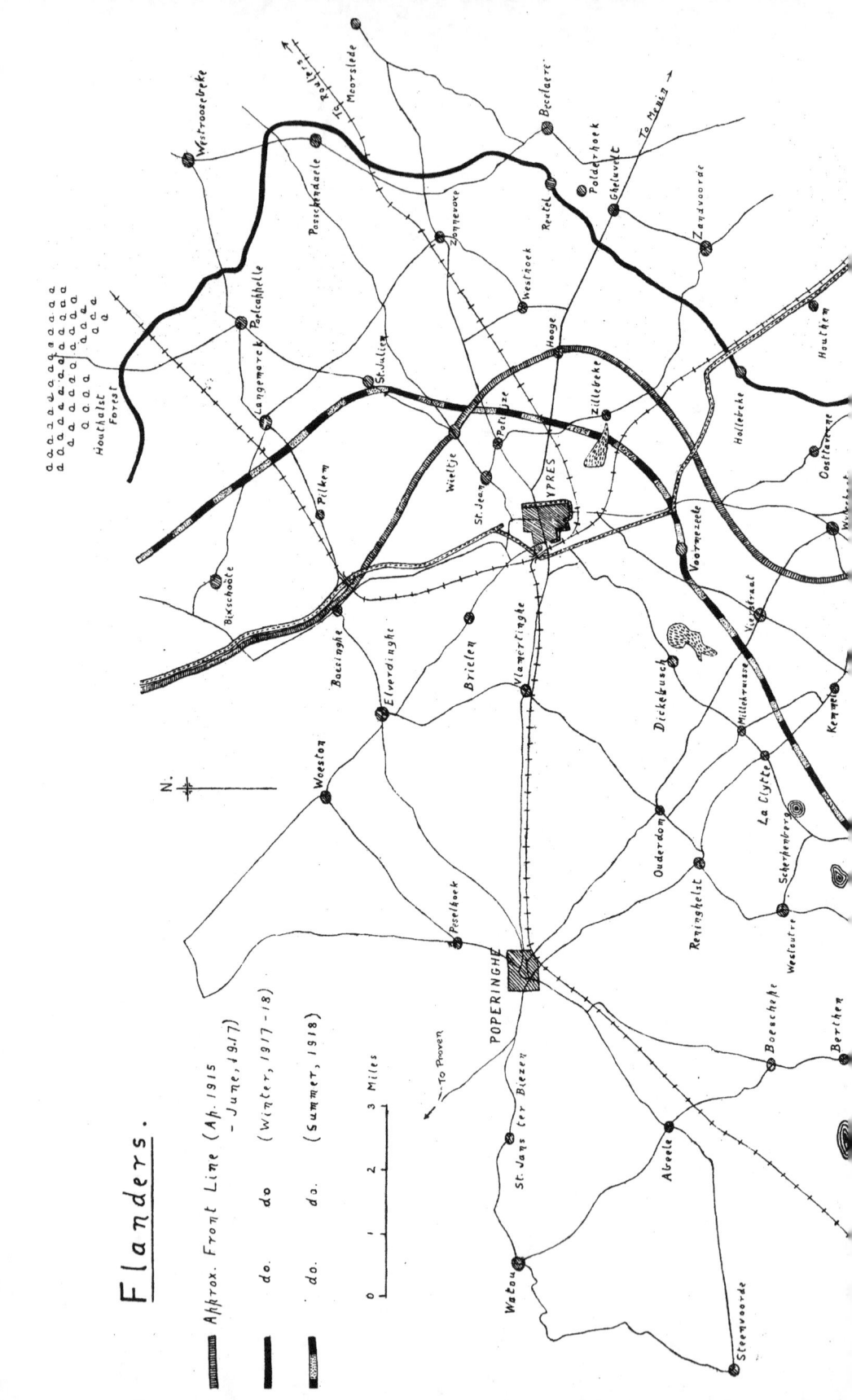

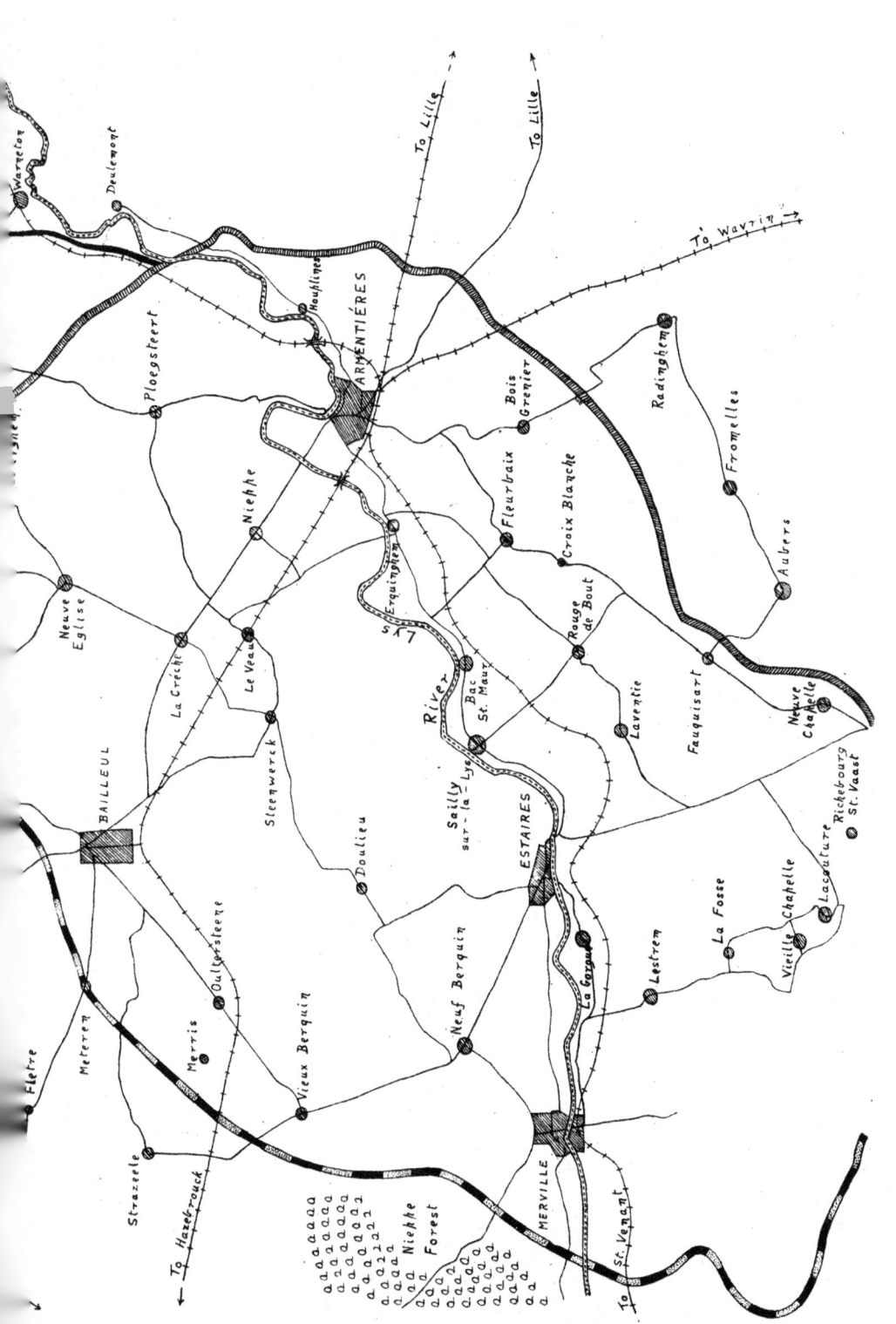

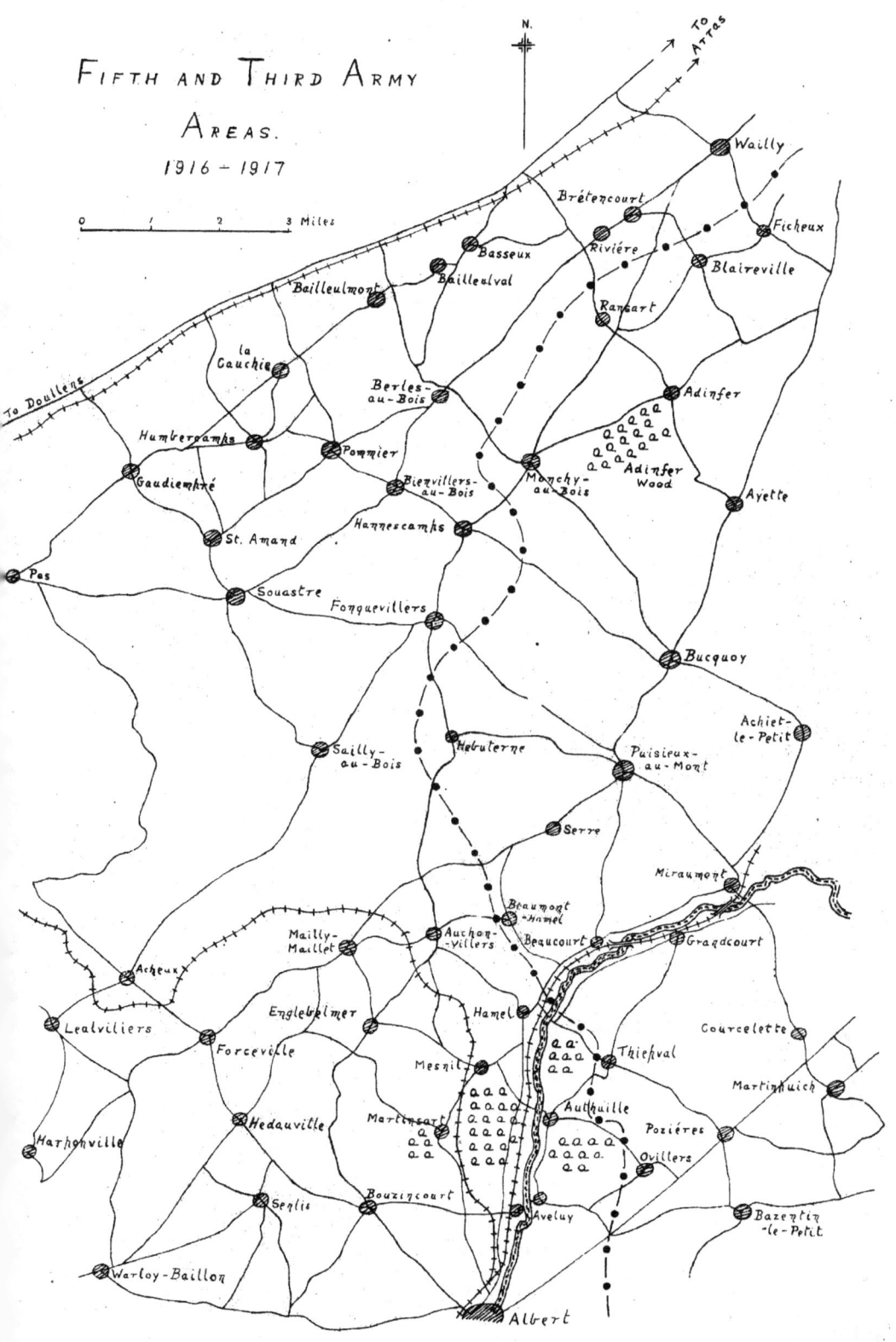